# Commodifying Communism

## Business, Trust, and Politics in a Chinese City

One might expect to find, in the wake of China's remarkable economic growth and the market reforms of the Deng era, a retreat of the state at all levels and the advance of private entrepreneurial autonomy. China's emerging commercial economy, or that of any reforming, emerging socialist economy, should gradually come to resemble the typical ideal of a market economy, with private transactions increasingly free from the influence of position and power stemming from the state hierarchy. David Wank, in this pioneering study of the institutional organization and political consequences of China's unprecedented growth, finds a very different, contrary image of an emerging commercial economy.

Drawing upon almost two years of ethnographic fieldwork in China, Wank reveals a system in which the state continues to play a significant and central, though transformed, role in business. He shows how entrepreneurs running private trading companies in Xiamen (one of China's five special economic zones) in Fujian province must cultivate patron–client networks with local state agents in order to maximize profit and security. The author examines how processes of opportunity, transactions, contracts, and competition are constrained by both statist and popular institutions in commercial clientelism. He considers the implications of this patron–client network system for China's economic dynamism relative to Eastern European, post-communist economies, and looks at the political consequences for state–society and center–local relations. This book offers the most extensive, intimate, and revealing portrait available of how private business is conducted in China's emerging "free" market.

David L. Wank is Associate Professor of Sociology in the Faculty of Comparative Culture at Sophia University, Tokyo.

Structural Analysis in the Social Sciences

Mark Granovetter, editor

Other books in the series:

The series *Structural Analysis in the Social Sciences* presents approaches that explain social behavior and institutions by reference to *relations* among such concrete entities as persons and organizations. This contrasts with at least four other popular strategies: (a) reductionist attempts to explain by a focus on individuals alone; (b) explanations stressing the causal primacy of such abstract concepts as ideas, values, mental harmonies, and cognitive maps (thus, "structuralism" on the Continent should be distinguished from structural analysis in the present sense); (c) technological and material determinism; (d) explanations using "variables" as the main analytic concepts (as in the "structural equation" models that dominated much of the sociology of the 1970s), where structure is that which connects variables rather than actual social entities.

The social network approach is an important example of the strategy of structural analysis: the series also draws on social science theory and research that is not framed explicitly in network terms but stresses the importance of relations rather than the atomization of reductionism or the determinism of ideas, technology, or material conditions. Though the structural perspective has become extremely popular and influential in all the social sciences, it does not have a coherent identity, and no series yet pulls together such work under a single rubric. By bringing the achievements of structurally oriented scholars to a wider public, the *Structural Analysis* series hopes to encourage the use of this very fruitful approach.

# Commodifying Communism

## Business, Trust, and Politics in a Chinese City

DAVID L. WANK

CAMBRIDGE
UNIVERSITY PRESS

PUBLISHED BY THE PRESS SYNDICATE OF THE UNIVERSITY OF CAMBRIDGE
The Pitt Building, Trumpington Street, Cambridge CB2 1RP, United Kingdom

CAMBRIDGE UNIVERSITY PRESS
The Edinburgh Building, Cambridge CB2 2RU, UK   http://www.cup.cam.ac.uk
40 West 20th Street, New York, NY 10011-4211, USA   http://www.cup.org
10 Stamford Road, Oakleigh, Melbourne 3166, Australia

First published 1999
First paperback edition 2001

Printed in the United States of America
Typeset in Sabon 10/12 pt, in Quark X Press [BTS]

*A catalog record for this book is available from
the British Library.*

*Library of Congress Cataloging-in-Publication Data*
Wank, David L. (date)
Commodifying communism : business, trust, and politics in a Chinese
city / David L. Wank.
p.   cm. – (Structural analysis in the social sciences)
Includes bibliographical references and indexes.
ISBN 0-521-62073-2 (hb)
1. Amoy (China) – Economic conditions – 1976–   .  2. China – Economic
policy – 1976–   .   3. Mixed economy – China – Amoy (China).   4. Free
enterprise – Amoy (China).   5. Entrepreneurship – Amoy (China).
6. Industrial policy – Amoy (China).   I. Title.   II. Series.
HC428.A5W36   1998
338.951′245 – dc21                                          98-16537
                                                                CIP

ISBN 0 521 62073 2 hardback
ISBN 0 521 79841 8 paperback

*To my parents and Yoshiko*

Commodities cannot themselves go to market and perform exchanges in their own right. (Marx [1867] 1976: 178)

Marx said that the market economy is social relations (*guanxi*). We used to read him in political study to understand socialism but I find him an inspiration for doing business. (Boss Short Pants, 1989 interview with the author)

# Contents

vii

# Acknowledgments

This book is the result of a long personal and intellectual journey that began when I lived in a North China work unit for two years in the early 1980s. Along the way I have benefited greatly from the advice and support of various persons, institutions, and granting agencies. Because the book draws upon my Ph.D. dissertation, submitted to the Department of Sociology at Harvard University in 1993, it is fitting that I should first thank my dissertation committee members – Ezra Vogel, Andrew Walder, and John Hall. Professor Andrew Walder deserves special mention because he guided me not only in the dissertation stage but also as I was preparing this book.

I would like to acknowledge the numerous persons who helped in reworking the manuscript. I thank Linda Grove, Gary Hamilton, and Susan Young, who read and commented on the entire manuscript. For commenting on parts of the work in one way or another I am grateful to Ole Bruun, John Campbell, Anita Chan, Deborah Davis, Tom Gold, Mark Granovetter, John Hall, Richard Kraus, John Lie, Jean Oi, Susan Shirk, Theda Skocpol, Dorothy Solinger, Jonathan Unger, and Andrew Walder. Wang Ping compiled the Chinese–English glossary. Elizabeth Neal, Mary Child, and Eric Newman at Cambridge University Press guided me through the publication process.

The fieldwork was supported by several institutions and persons in China. Foremost are Mao Disheng and the Foreign Affairs Office staff at Lujiang College, my sponsoring institution in Xiamen. Officials in the Xiamen branches of the Industry and Commerce Bureau, Tax Bureau, and United Front Bureau, and the officers of the Xiamen Chamber of Commerce were helpful in arranging interviews. I am also grateful to Zeng Wei and my two other research assistants. At the beginning of the research I was affiliated with the Contemporary China Research Centre, Chinese University of Hong Kong. Jean Hung of the Universities Service Centre provided guidance to the center's resources.

I have enjoyed several institutional affiliations during various stages of writing. After the fieldwork, Kenichi Tominaga sponsored my affiliation as a foreign research student at Tokyo University, and Linda Grove sponsored my affiliation as a visiting research student at Sophia University. The dissertation was completed while I was a Kukin Fellow at the Harvard Academy for International and Area Studies. I am grateful to the late Akio Kohno, who helped arrange for me to take a leave of absence from Sophia University to be at the Harvard Academy. My colleagues at Sophia University have been supportive companions.

I also wish to acknowledge the generous financial support of several grant-giving bodies. A National Science Foundation Graduate Fellowship supported three years of my graduate study. A fellowship from the Social Science Research Council and American Council of Learned Societies funded my research in Hong Kong; the fieldwork in China was supported by the Committee on Scholarly Communication with the People's Republic of China. The generous support of the Harvard Academy for International and Area Studies helped me finish the dissertation. The findings and conclusions presented in this study are mine alone and do not necessarily reflect the views of these institutions.

The seeds for this study were planted during two years of living and teaching in the Shanxi Agricultural College in Taigu, Shanxi Province, from 1980 to 1982 through a fellowship from the Oberlin Shansi Memorial Association of my undergraduate alma mater, Oberlin College. Living in an out-of-the-way place in China's hardscrabble heartland before the perceptible advent of market reform impressed upon me how the party-state pervaded people's lives, constraining their perceptions of possibilities and the behavior needed to achieve them. This experience led me to graduate school in quest of ideas to better comprehend it. At Harvard, Daniel Bell provided my baptism of fire in social theory, Theda Skocpol introduced me to political sociology, and fellow graduate student John Lie and visiting scholar Richard Swedberg suggested I explore economic sociology. My undergraduate mentors at Oberlin in Chinese studies were Vivian Ling (Hsu) and Dale Johnson in language and literature, Mark Blecher in politics, and Charles Hayford in history.

Closer to home, this book would not have been completed without the support of my families in Japan and the United States. This book is dedicated to them. My parents, Barbara and Solomon Wank, have always encouraged me in my endeavors. Michie and Yuji Ashiwa helped create the necessary conditions for writing this book. My wife and colleague, Yoshiko Ashiwa, has been with me throughout this project. She has generously shared her insights into the conduct of fieldwork, and her comments and suggestions have repeatedly saved me from easy conclusions while suggesting new lines of inquiry and interpretation.

# Tables, Figure, and Maps

## Tables

xi

**Figure**

**Maps**

*Introduction*

# 1

## *Orientation of the Study*

The original purpose of the fieldwork on which this study draws was to discern the political consequences of emerging markets for communist states and societies. Decades of scholarship had developed a view of these societies as highly bureaucratized orders. Power and privilege were defined by bureaucratic rank, and the citizenry were highly dependent on local officialdom. I had tasted this during two years of residence in a North China work unit from 1980 to 1982, experiencing firsthand the pervasive mediation of daily necessities and activities by local state agents. In mid-1988, at the close of the first decade of Chinese market reform, I returned to study the link between emerging markets, social structure, and political change.

I focused on private business, widely viewed as the furthest commercial departure from the classical communist order. My assumption was that private business was creating new resources and careers independent of the state apparatus that were lessening citizens' bureaucratic dependence. The expectation was that interviews with private business operators would illuminate changes in local interactions between state and society, letting me document the increasing autonomy of citizens from the state apparatus.

My expectations were considerably diminished when, upon entering the field, I was unable even to clearly distinguish private businesses from public ones. Some entrepreneurs introduced to me as "private" business operators insisted their firms were "public." Others introduced as the operators of "public" firms claimed they ran "private" ones. Yet others maintained that their firms were "half-public/half-private." A few even claimed different statuses from interview to interview, although the legal registration of their companies had not changed. This situation frustrated my attempts to classify the abundant data flow. I spent much time thinking about classificatory schemes while almost every new interview presented anomalies defying my pigeonholes.

A turning point in my research direction was a conversation in early 1989 with an entrepreneur nicknamed Boss Short Pants (*Duanku

*Laoban*), who ran a business group with a mix of privately owned and public firms. The Boss had previously impressed me with his no-nonsense style, indicated by his trademark casual wearing of short pants in hot weather. I made an appointment to talk to him, hoping to clarify what was "private" about private business. I figured that the Boss must have some scheme for distinguishing it – how else could he manage his commercial empire? During our conversation, I kept turning the topic back to legal property rights whenever Boss Short Pants veered away from what I deemed the crucial issue. He became agitated, finally blurting out, "Read the damn government policy if you want to know about property rights. But if you want to know about the business situation here then listen to what I'm saying!" After my profuse apologies he continued, "Property rights give you only a legal existence. But your market activities depend on the social environment (*yao kao shehui huanjing*). If your connections (*guanxi*) with officialdom are good, then your business can develop, but if they are bad then officialdom squeezes you and you can't get anywhere."

Boss Short Pants insisted that my concern with legal property rights was misplaced. Later I would realize the importance I placed on the issue stemmed from an uncritical, indeed unwitting, acceptance of the ideal-typical market image of standard economic theory. But this realization would not come until later; the immediate upshot of our conversation was that I resolved to stop wasting time trying to square data with the public/private dichotomy of legal property rights and listen to what entrepreneurs were telling me about themselves and their business. During the next year and a half I cast my net wide and deep, meeting many people in Xiamen, entrepreneurs and others, while socializing intensively with some entrepreneurs with whom I developed rapport.

I began to pay closer attention to what people were saying and how they said it. The realization dawned on me that private business operated in networks of personal ties centered on the local government. Personal ties with state agents enhance access to profit opportunities located in the state's bureaucracy and protect subsequent wealth accumulations. Commercial rationality, therefore, also entails the social process of forging and cultivating the personal ties to local government through which business-enhancing resources flow.[1] Business strategies and competition are patterned by the different accumulations of personal ties through social background and skill in the "art of social relations" (*guanxixue*) of

---

[1] My use of the term "local government" corresponds to the *difang zhengfu* of Chinese official terminology, which denotes any level of government below the center (Huang 1996: 20–1); that is, it can refer to governments all the way from the provincial level down to urban subdistrict levels and rural villages and townships. When necessary I distinguish specific levels. The center is referred to as the central state or state elite, while the term "state" refers to the entire complex of central and local government.

specific firm operators. I also realized that the idiomatic ways in which entrepreneurs spoke of their business practices expressed continuities with as well as changes from the clientelist relations of the pre–market reform era.

When I left the field in the summer of 1990, I knew that my observations not only falsified my original hypothesis but raised entirely new concerns. My original question – What are the political consequences of an emerging market economy in a communist order? – had been displaced by a new one – How does a market economy emerge from a communist order? My dissertation, submitted in 1993, described the embeddedness of private business in social networks and political power as I came to understand it in 1988–90 after a decade of market reform. This present study, a more analytically sustained reflection on the field data, pays more attention to explaining the institutional process by which a communist system transforms into a market economy. Why and how does private business operate through clientelist networks? What are the outcomes for economic performance? What are the outcomes for the polity? How does this differ from other post-communist market economies and emerging market economies in general?

In this chapter I do four things. First, I give an overview of the classical communist orders and the commercial departures from them. Second, I summarize this study's central thesis that the revival of private business gives rise to commercialized clientelist networks. Third, I describe the research strategy of the study. Fourth, I give a historical sketch of the fieldsite.

## Communist States and Economic Reform

Observers of communist orders have long pointed out that economic organization and political power are defined by the party-state's bureaucratic control of resources.[2] Central planning places allocation in the hands of communist Party officials, while suppression of household and small-scale private enterprise and retail and wholesale markets creates a monopoly over the production and distribution of goods. This results in a lack of consumer items, the rise of in-kind distribution centered on workplaces, and the rationing of foodstuffs, housing, and other daily necessities. Andrew Walder observes that "all of this further served, for a considerable historical period, to reduce alternatives and reinforce dependence upon superiors for the satisfaction of needs" (Walder 1994a: 301). Access to daily necessities and career opportunities

---

[2] Classic statements of this point are Djilas (1957); Feher, Heller, and Markus (1983); Rizzi ([1939] 1967); and Trotsky ([1937] 1972).

was a function of one's power and influence in bureaucratic allocation procedures.

Much economic allocation and political power came to be embedded in clientelist networks.[3] At the local borders of state and society, officials' discretionary allocation of goods and opportunities created patron–client ties. These ties not only allocated resources but also facilitated local governance as clients took the lead in demonstrating compliance with state initiatives and providing officials with information on societal resistance. Patron–client ties also created cross-cutting cleavages in society that reduced the likelihood of organized popular resistance to the state and local officialdom. Within the bureaucracy, clientelist networks between superiors and subordinates buttressed central authority by enhancing the compliance of lower officials. Promotions depended on the recommendations of one's immediate superiors, inducing the responsiveness of subordinates. The institutionalization of clientelist networks was idiomatically expressed as *guanxi* in China (Walder 1986: 170–85), *protekcio* in Hungary (Róna-tas 1990: 119), *dosjcie* in Poland (Wedel 1986: 79), and *blat* in the Soviet Union (Grossman 1983: 105–8).

For some time social scientists have speculated on the political implications of the introduction and expansion of markets in communist systems. In 1978 the sociologist Ivan Szelenyi wrote that "the interests of the powerless and disprivileged can be best served with increasingly transactive (and consequently *market-like*) relationships in the economic system" (Szelenyi 1978: 63). He speculated that increased market allocation of resources would reduce the party-state monopoly on power and privilege that was maintained by bureaucratic redistribution. Analysts saw commercial departures from bureaucratic redistribution through popular activities like worker moonlighting and state initiatives like private agricultural plots as enhancing individuals' autonomy from the system. However, these activities were deemed incapable of changing the system. Some analysts considered them so petty as to be marginal to the main arenas of political struggle; others saw them as safety valves that helped to maintain the system by channeling popular discontent into individualized strategies of material gain.[4]

In the 1980s communist states shifted to more comprehensive market reform programs to counter stagnating production, obsolescing technology, declining living standards, and labor problems. This stimulated scholarly reassessment of the political implications of emerging markets

---

[3] Key studies in this vein include Baker (1982); Ionescu (1977); Oi (1985, 1989); Tarkowski (1983); Walder (1986); and Willerton (1979).

[4] Key studies include Feher, Heller, and Markus (1983); Kemény (1982); Misztal (1981); and Sampson (1987). For China's second economy see Burns (1982); and Chan and Unger (1982).

in these systems. Such new commercial activities as foreign investment, expanded private business, and leasing of public enterprises were seen as transforming the system itself. In the words of sociologists David Stark and Victor Nee, market "reforms [are] redrawing the boundaries between the state and society and shaping new patterns of transaction, mediation, and bargaining across them" (Stark and Nee 1989: 16). The revival of private business is seen as one of the most consequential economic departures from orthodox central planning. The economist János Kornai concludes that "the rise of the private sector is the most important tendency in the economic sphere during the process of reform. It brings a deep change, since it affects the property relations and it does so in a radical way: private property appears alongside public property" (Kornai 1992: 433). In short, private business is widely considered the most far-reaching departure from the communist order, with profound consequences for economy and polity.

The revival of private business reflects the growing concerns of communist party-states to solve unemployment and provide more consumer goods, concerns that shifted their policies away from constricting private economic activity to a more tolerant stance. The reemergence of private economic activity varied in timing and pace by country. In regard to timing, the Hungarian private sector developed earliest, with policies expanding the scope of private farming and services in the late 1960s; this did not happen in the Soviet Union until the late 1980s. In regard to pace, the reemergence in China has been especially swift. On the eve of market reform in 1978 there were only 80,000 licensed private businesses nationally, mostly peddlers of farm produce and secondhand goods whose activities were an infinitesimal share of the national economy. A decade later there were at least 30 million private businesses of some sort, constituting the fastest-growing sector of the economy.

The revival of private business has followed a similar pattern in diverse communist countries, although there has been considerable variation in pace and timing. Typically, it begins with the state's reduction of restrictions on self-employment in privately owned family businesses (Róna-tas 1994). However, the state restricts their size by limiting the number of employees, permitting only limited shareholding or banning it altogether, and stipulating that private businesses must buy raw materials on retail markets and sell goods and services to individual consumers (Aslund 1985). This keeps private businesses small and prevents public resources and personnel from flowing to the private sector (Gábor 1989: 40). The next step in the revival is state condonement of private endeavors in the collective and state sectors through leasing, work partnerships, and cooperatives. New policies encourage useful aspects of private economic capital in creating jobs and meeting consumer demand while maintaining public ownership of productive resources in accordance with socialist ideology. Again Hungary led in such innovations, while other countries such as China and the Soviet Union adopted similar policies later.[5] The third step is the expansion of the sector of licensed private business as when the myriad policy restrictions against them are reduced to permit incorporated and limited-liability private companies. These firms are the legal equals of public enterprises, can engage in capital-intensive manufacturing and service ventures, and can sell wholesale to public producers.

A similar sequence has occurred in China.[6] Policies from 1978 to 1983 encouraged small privately owned businesses – the so-called *getihu* (individual businesses) – to create jobs and meet consumer demands (Gold 1990a: 158–62).[7] Out of ideological concern to prevent a "capitalist restoration," shops were limited to seven employees,[8] could not issue receipts larger than ¥100, could not use mechanized production or transport, were denied access to bank loans, and could not pool capital.[9] Next, in order to expand the beneficial aspects of private business without challenging socialist ideology, the state permitted private management of collective and state sector firms and assets. Such arrangements spread in the mid-1980s through cooperative, leased, and contracted firms. This created jobs and met demand but caused administrative confusion; for example, it was difficult to distinguish a cooperative from a socialized collective firm in tax matters.[10] To further expand the role of private

[5] For cooperatives in Hungary see Rupp (1983); and Swain (1990). For China see Lockett (1988); and Sabin (1994: 948–54). For the Soviet Union see Jones and Moskoff (1991).

[6] Private business has waxed and waned since the founding of the People's Republic of China. After 1949, the party-state initially encouraged private business in order to revive the economy. The only businesses expropriated in the first years were so-called comprador firms connected to international capital and the state. In fact, many merchants prospered as inflation was checked and kidnappings of businessmen ceased. State tolerance evaporated during the Korean War, when competition between state agencies procuring war resources and private businesses caused inflation. The nationalization of private capitalist firms and the socialization of smaller shops into collectives in the mid-1950s led to the decline of private business. In 1950 private business accounted for 76.1 percent of wholesale trade and 71 percent of industrial output, but by 1955, only 4.4 percent and 18.3 percent respectively (Kuan 1960: 66–7). Private business flourished briefly in the early 1960s, when, because of economic disruption and famine following the Great Leap Forward and the halt of aid from the Soviet Union, the state permitted private stalls and shops.

[7] Urban unemployment had swollen by the late 1970s to between 8.5 percent and 18 percent of the labor force (Gold 1990a: 160).

[8] This figure is widely assumed to be derived from a hypothetical example in Marx's *Capital*.

[9] A 1983 policy revision eased restrictions and permitted joint ventures (*lianying*) with public enterprises, but the seven-employee limit remained.

[10] The actual number of cooperatives is not known, as they are aggregated with socialized collectives in collective sector statistics: a 1988 national figure claimed 50,000 cooperatives, while local statistics suggest a much greater number. For example, according to one

capital while avoiding administrative confusion, the 1988 Private Enterprise Interim Regulation legalized limited-liability privately owned companies. These firms have no restrictions on employee numbers and can issue large receipts.[11] Further policies in 1994 permitted the incorporation of private companies and the issuing of shares on stock markets.[12]

The revival of private business in China has been especially dramatic. By one estimate, private sector share of the gross value of industrial output rose from 0.2 percent in 1980 to 36.5 percent by 1991 (Pei 1994: 92–3) and the private sector share of the retail trade grew from 2.1 percent in 1978 to 33.1 percent in 1993 (State Statistical Bureau 1994: 497).[13] Yet private business also exhibited the generic characteristics of private business in the communist world (Aslund 1985; Grossman 1987; Los 1990). While many restrictions had been removed, others still remained, most notably prohibitions against direct foreign trade and private ownership of real estate. The ideological legacy of hostility toward private business, sudden changes in policies and regulations by the state, and arbitrary regulation by local agencies created uncertainties. Much trade was dubious, consisting of activities that the state did not condemn outright nor explicitly condone. Legal property rights were ambiguous, and despite regulations against party officials conducting business on their own and working in private firms, many of the larger companies used personal ties with officials to gain access to business-enhancing public resources.

## Overview of the Argument

The central thesis of this study is that the revival of private business does not lead to the decline of patron–client ties but rather to the emergence of new commercialized forms of clientelism. Thus rather than talk of the retreat of the state during the market reform era, I describe the

local survey published in 1989, 60 percent of all the collective enterprises in Fujian province are privately run (Lin 1989: 34). Given that there were 510,134 collective enterprises in Fujian province in the late 1980s, consisting of 446,694 village and township enterprises (1988 statistics, Fujian Province Statistical Bureau 1989: 43) and 63,440 trade and service enterprises (1985 statistics, Fujian Province Statistical Bureau 1992: 227), this would mean that the province alone had 306,081 cooperatives, a figure much larger than the national figure of 50,000 firms. According to a survey published in 1989, of 518 collective firms surveyed in Wenzhou municipality, 79.5 percent were cooperatives (Jia and Wang 1989). For problems of statistical measurement see Odgaard (1992: 234–50); Sabin (1994); Young (1995: 4–9).

[11] The companies are single-investor, joint-investor, or limited-liability. By 1994, there were also 374,700 legally private companies nationally (*China Daily* 1994).

[12] The petty private shops, cooperatives and leased firms, and private companies are described in greater detail in Chapter 3. Corporations are discussed in Chapter 9.

[13] Pei's figures include legally private firms and rural village and township enterprises, which are often privately run.

commodification of its local bureaucratic power. Rather than speak of the declining role of *guanxi*, I show how entrepreneurs draw on preexisting ties and create new ones to influence local state agents. And rather than talk of enhanced entrepreneurial autonomy from the state, I describe new patterns of bargaining and alliance across the local boundaries of state and society.

Clientelist ties are a contractual transaction that reflects power asymmetries between exchange partners. Such ties are expressed in terms of personal identity and interpersonal sentiments and obligations; they intermingle potential coercion and exploitation with voluntary relations and mutual obligations, and they involve reciprocal and mutually beneficial exchanges that are labeled as dubious, illegal, and corrupt by the state (Eisenstadt and Roniger 1984: 49; Flap 1990: 237; Foster 1963: 1281; Schmidt 1977). The emergence of patron–client ties is linked to the organization of the state. Such ties are likely to flourish in a state that creates unequal distribution of resources through monopoly practices, has weakly developed standards of impersonal behavior, and has weakly developed class and occupational interest associations (Flap 1990; Scott 1972b: 42). In such a state clientelist ties do the following: they provide weaker parties with steadier access to resources, enabling them to manage their dependence on state agents; they enhance expectations on the likely behavior of others by embedding interactions in social norms and practices; and they provide parties with vertical ties that can be mobilized to meet diffuse challenges.[14]

The embeddedness of Chinese private business in clientelist ties reflects the evolving organization of the communist party-state during market reform.[15] It also reflects new interests and possibilities for profit seeking in the vast resources accumulated by the party-state through the structures of centralized economic planning and redistribution. But clientelist ties also mean that fewer resources reach local levels of the state through central redistribution, inducing local governments to seek profit through the resources they control, thereby lining officials' pockets and filling local government coffers. Clientelist ties also reflect the failure of the state to institutionalize universal standards, as by fully enforcing legal private property rights, in the market economy. Local governments interpret central regulations as they see fit while entrepreneurs cut their own deals with local governments to increase profits and provide security for wealth accumulations. However, the clientelist ties through which pri-

---

[14] For general discussion of networks in economic life see Burt (1992); Granovetter (1973, 1985); Lazonick (1991); Powell (1987); Powell and Smith-Doerr (1994); and White (1992).

[15] For uses of the concept of clientelism in other areas of China's emerging market economy, see Oi (1985) for the rural economy, Pearson (1997) for foreign enterprises, and Paltiel (1989) for a suggestive comparison with Mexico.

vate business operates differ from pre-reform clientelism not only in new
commercial calculations but also in changing dependence: citizens' dependence on officialdom is much reduced as officials and local governments are increasingly dependent on entrepreneurs and their firms for
certain resources. The new ties are therefore symbiotic.

The argument can be sharpened by distinguishing the clientelism I
observed from other manifestations of it in markets. First, it differs from
clientelized ties between buyers and sellers found in many third world
and informal economies that are indicated by such local names as *pratik*
in Haiti, *suki* in the Philippines, *onibara* in Nigeria, *casera* in Peru, and
*sedaqa* in Morocco.[16] These ties diffuse information and produce trust,
processes that I, too, observed in China. But the key difference is that
these other ties are horizontal ones of relative equality, whereas in China
they involve asymmetries between those inside and those outside the state
structure and are therefore more vertical. Furthermore, the entrepreneurs
I observed view relations with officials as supportive and actively cultivate them; in contrast, third world traders see officials as predatory and
seek to minimize contact with them through horizontal strategies.[17] Nor
do the Chinese clientelist ties conform to Southeast Asian "crony capitalism," which is characterized by commercial advantage to an entrepreneur derived by personal association with the head of state, because the
ties I document operate in much lower levels of the government.[18] Also,
the concept of rent-seeking that undergirds crony capitalism is not particularly apt, as it presupposes a functioning market, whereas Communist orders lack markets; thus the analytic task is to explain the
emergence of markets rather than their distortion. Finally, Chinese
clientelist ties do not fit the East Asian model associated with Japan and
Korea.[19] In this model, a strong central state maintains economic guidance of the market economy through particularistic flows of policy
directives and economic capital to commercial firms. The situation I
observed differs: the central Chinese state condemns many market practices and seeks to suppress them. China's emerging market contains
many practices that deviate from central directives and that proceed in
networks of local interests distinct from the center's. These local devia-

---

[16] See Granovetter (1993) for an overview of this kind of horizontal clientelism. Related
terms in the Chinese context, such as *xinyong* (credit), refer to evaluations of honesty
and dependability within the community of businesspersons (Barton 1983; DeGlopper
1972) and therefore also suggest horizontal relations.

[17] See, e.g., MacGaffey's (1991) account of Zaire.

[18] Yoshihara (1988) is the *locus classicus* for the concept of crony capitalism. The members
of the so-called princes' party (*taizi dang*), the offspring of elite central officials, are more
analogous to crony capitalists in the Chinese case. For the concept of rent see Bates
(1981); Krueger (1974).

[19] The East Asian model draws on Gerschenkron's (1962) classic discussions of late
development (Amsden 1989; Johnson 1982; Jones and Sakong 1980).

tions and interests are institutional elements not found in the East Asian model.

The closest parallel for the ties I observed is the industrial districts of Western Europe, such as Emilia-Romagna in Italy, where market economies are constituted by cooperation between private business and local government, and private firms have extensive subcontracting not only with each other but also with state enterprises. These myriad links among local governments, state enterprises, and private firms are embedded in particularistic identities of person and region.[20]

## Character of the Research

Debate surges back and forth on the performance of post-communist market economies and their political consequences. At stake are not simply academic theories but also perceptions of emerging markets in political policy debates and popular media images that help constitute the reshaping of the post-communist world in the late twentieth century.[21] This study considers the operation of private business, a quintessential market institution and potentially far-reaching departure from communist orders. The goal is to explain an institutional organization of commercial behavior significantly different from the conventional ideal-typical market economy and to suggest the outcomes of this for economic performance and political change.[22] The argument developed is an alternative to extant market transition, political economy, and traditional culture accounts of the causes and consequences of the emergence of private business in communist orders. I call my argument the institutional commodification account.

The analysis embodies the core premise of economic sociology on the contingent nature of economic organization and behavior with respect to historical, cultural, and political factors, in contrast to the standard economistic view of the market as a universal, ideal-typical form. I view the operating processes of the emerging market economy as the outcomes rather than the starting point of historical patterns of state and society.[23] It follows that there are numerous possible transacting configurations for markets: the actual transacting modes prevalent in an

[20] For Emilia-Romagna, see Lazerson (1988, 1993).
[21] Chapter 2 reviews the academic debate in regard to private business. For an example of how this debate appears in media and policy circles see Blustein and Smith (1996).
[22] For a discussion of a sociological analysis of the economy as contrasted with standard economic analysis, see Hirsch, Michaels, and Friedman (1990).
[23] For other classic statements of the economic sociology perspective, see Polanyi ([1944] 1957); and Weber ([1904–5] 1958, [1922] 1978, [1922] 1961). For recent formulations see Etzioni (1988); Friedland and Robertson (1990); Granovetter (1985); Smelser and Swedbord (1994); and Zukin and DiMaggio (1990).

economy or in the exchange portfolio of a firm are best determined by empirical investigation.

The methodology is primarily ethnographic and rooted in a single locale.[24] Ethnography gives the researcher insight into enduring relations and their manner of institutionalization.[25] I employed such standard fieldwork methods as formal and open-ended interviewing, socializing and conversations, and limited participant observation, as well as surveys of relevant published documents and brief visits to other locales to gain broader perspective. The data emphasize multiple points of observation in the locale to uncover the institutional pattern of relationships in the emerging market economy.[26] I pay close attention to the idioms used by people to express their actions and goals, as this sheds light on the institutional construction of values, firms, contracts, and bargaining, which constitutes markets.[27]

The fieldsite is Xiamen, an old port city in Fujian province on China's southeastern coast, and one of the most economically dynamic locales in the reform era. It has a history of extensive overseas Chinese emigration and, since 1980, has been one of China's five special economic zones designed to take the lead in establishing a market economy and attracting foreign investment.[28] I resided in this dynamic commercial city for eighteen months between June 1988 and June 1990; subsequent data were obtained by ongoing contact with a research assistant and several infor-

---

[24] Recently sociologists and anthropologists who study late and post-communist societies, noting how poorly these emerging market economies approximate an ideal-typical market image, have stressed the need for enthnographically informed accounts of Communist market reform. See Parish and Michelson (1996: 1046); and Verdery (1996: 210–16).

[25] Institutions are cognitive categories and behavioral norms, whether expressed in legal codes or customary ways, that define entities and legitimate action in social relations. Institutionalized social relations are routinized in practice and have a "taken for granted" character. Institutions therefore shape the rationality of social action, defining ends and the means to obtain them (Meyer, Boli, and Thomas 1987; DiMaggio and Powell 1991; Hamilton and Biggart 1988; and Jepperson 1991).

[26] The fieldwork strategy is captured in Clifford Geertz's concept of divergent data, defined as "descriptions, measures, observations, what you will, which are at once diverse, even rather miscellaneous, both as to type and degree of precision and generality, unstandardised facts, opportunistically collected and for the simple reasons that the individuals they are descriptions, measures or observations of are directly involved in one another's lives" (Geertz 1983: 156).

[27] Idioms reveal the cognitive and normative constraints on practical action (Bourdieu 1979; Wuthnow 1987: 145–6). Theda Skocpol writes that "it [does] make a difference which idiom or mixture of idioms is available to be drawn upon by given groups. Indeed, the very definition of groups, their interests, and their relations to one another will be influenced by cultural idioms" (Skocpol 1985b: 91).

[28] I use such terms as "overseas Chinese" and "Chinese overseas" to refer to all Chinese who are not residing in the People's Republic of China, including Chinese who reside in Hong Kong (British territory at time of fieldwork), Taiwan, and Macao as well as ethnic Chinese in other countries.

Map 1.1. Southeastern China.

mants and by two weeks of follow-up research in mid-1995. Xiamen's liberal economic policies and cosmopolitan history were very conducive to ethnographic fieldwork by a foreign researcher. My sponsoring institution was Lujiang College, a new college for training administrative and office personnel for the special economic zone. I lived in a teachers' apartment dormitory and could come and go as I pleased. I had a private telephone with a direct outside line and could call businesspeople and others to make appointments or to chat. Foreign tourists and businesspeople often visit Xiamen, so it was not unusual for a foreigner to be roving about discussing economic matters with people. Consequently, my comings and goings were not visibly restricted and my interaction with members of the community was relatively uninhibited.

The core data are a sample of one hundred private companies and the entrepreneurs who run them. All of the entrepreneurs were interviewed at least twice by me, while numerous follow-up contacts with some were maintained by me or research assistants. In addition I socialized intensively with several entrepreneurs with whom I established rapport. Because of the importance of these data for the study, this aspect of the fieldwork is discussed at length in an appendix. I broadened my perspective by interviewing various other members of Xiamen's business world. These included other businesspeople – petty private shopkeepers, overseas Chinese businesspeople, Western businesspeople, and managers of state enterprises, foreign trade corporations, and collective trading firms. They also included administrative officials at the city, district, and sub-district levels of such relevant government agencies as the Industry and Commerce Bureau and Tax Bureau, and at state and cooperative banks. Finally, I interviewed officials and citizen-officers of state-sponsored business associations, such as the Self-Employed Laborers Association and the Artists and Entrepreneurs Association, and of some government-sponsored social organizations (*shehui tuanti*) under the authority of the Communist Party's United Front Department, such as the Xiamen Chamber of Commerce, the Xiamen Civic Association of Private Industry and Commerce, and the Young Factory Director and Manager Association. These wide-ranging contacts helped me place private business in broader contexts.

The fieldwork centered on Xiamen city's old downtown districts of Siming and Kaiyuan on Egret Island. About 70 percent of the city's wholesale companies and retail shops are located here as well as major hotels and department stores. Some interviews also took place on Gulangyu, a tiny island district five minutes by ferry from Xiamen Island. I also did fieldwork in Xiamen's suburban Jimei and Xinglin districts on the mainland. In addition to Xiamen-based fieldwork, I visited towns and villages in nearby Tongan, Longhai, Huian, and Jinjiang counties and other southern Fujian cities, such as Quanzhou, Shishi, Zhangzhou, and Chongwu. Finally, I talked with entrepreneurs in Fuzhou, Fujian's provincial capital, in Guangzhou and Fuoshan cities in Guangdong, and in Taiyuan city and Taigu county in North China's Shanxi province.

Further insight was gained by documentary research. This included a thorough reading of the *Xiamen Daily* newspaper from 1978 through 1990 and selective reading of earlier periods, as well as local, provincial, and national publications obtained from city and university libraries. I also read local official documents on such matters as economic crimes, regulatory matters, and the floating population, and publications of the aforementioned associations. This was invaluable for grasping the central state's intentions in market reform and its implementation strategies through policies and programs. Reading about new policies and events in the daily newspaper and then discussing them with those affected provided many insights.

Although the observations are mostly gleaned from one locale, the study is comparative. The data do not represent China's market economy as a whole but rather a variation linked to liberal economic policies and access to transnational trade and capital through kin networks.[29] Focusing on processes in the locale and evaluating my hypotheses with my data provide insight into the organizational principles of the local market economy. Then, by comparing my findings with studies from other locales in China to note the differences and similarities, I can hypothesize on the sources of regional variation in the national market economy. Finally, I sharpen my interpretations with comparisons of the process of market emergence in other communist countries.

Fieldwork is also shaped by the historical context in which it is conducted. During my fieldwork, two events occurred that entrepreneurs viewed as the most severe crises for private business since its revival in 1978: the economic rectification campaign, launched in September 1988, three months after I entered the field; and the 1989 student movement, which occurred at the fieldwork's midpoint. The campaign was a massive bureaucratic action to combat the blurred boundaries of legally defined public and private property rights in the market economy. It merged with the crackdown that followed the student movement and did not end until the early 1990s. The student movement erupted in the spring of 1989,

---

[29] Regional heterogeneity is often noted in studies on market reform (Falkenheim 1988; Shirk 1989; Xie and Hannum 1996). In terms of William Skinner's (1977) division of late imperial China into seven macroregions based on the administrative and economic communication hierarchies and resource flows, Xiamen is in the "Southeast Coast" region, which includes the coastal regions of Fujian province and neighboring Zhejiang province to the north. However, in terms of its history of outmigration, and favorable concessions from the central state and inflows of foreign investment capital, Fujian province has more in common with neighboring Guangdong province to the south (Vogel 1989: 80–7).

reaching its bloody climax in Tiananmen Square on June 4. The severe political repression that ensued included a campaign against corruption and tax evasion in private business. The heightened political tension from 1988 to 1990 cast certain orientations and actions into sharper relief than would have been the case in less troubled times.

## The Fieldsite

Xiamen has a long history as a commercial entrepot because of its natural harbor, one of the few along the southern coast capable of handling deepwater ships. Culturally, Xiamen is in the Minnan dialect region, which stretches 160 kilometers north of the city to Huian county, 300 kilometers south to the Chaozhou region in Guangdong province, and west into Fujian's mountainous interior. Minnan dialect is also spoken by 80 percent of the inhabitants on Taiwan, which lies about 150 kilometers to the east across the Taiwan Strait, and whose people's ancestors came from southern Fujian beginning in the seventeenth century. Approximately one-fifth of the world's overseas Chinese population have ancestral roots in southern Fujian, and Minnan dialect is widely spoken in overseas Chinese communities in the Philippines, Singapore, Malaysia, Indonesia, and Thailand.[30]

Administratively, Xiamen is a city (*shi*), a term with several meanings. First and most broadly, it refers to Xiamen as an administrative region encompassing the 128 square kilometers of Egret Island and 1,385 square kilometers on the adjacent mainland, including rural Tongan county, with a total population in 1988 of 1,076,834. Second, it refers to Xiamen as a municipality of urban and suburban districts encompassing Egret Island and the districts of Jimei and Xinglin on the mainland, which are not part of Tongan county. Xiamen municipality has a total land area of 554 square kilometers and a population (1988) of 579,510. Third, it refers to the urban districts of Xiamen municipality, which encompass half of Egret Island and the tiny island of Gulangyu for a total of 66 square kilometers. This area's population (1988) is 371,000, with an average population density of 4,250 per square kilometer and a density of over 20,000 people per square kilometer in the old business section.

The history of transnational trade in southern Fujian province dates to

[30] For a general history of overseas Chinese, see Pan (1990). For the history of Chinese in Southeast Asia, see Fitzgerald (1972). For the economic activity of overseas Chinese in Southeast Asia, see Lim and Gosling (1983). For overseas Chinese entrepreneurs in the twentieth century with ancestral roots in southern Fujian, see Chan and Chiang (1994); and Yong (1989). For the economic sophistication of overseas Chinese from Fujian province, see Freedman (1959).

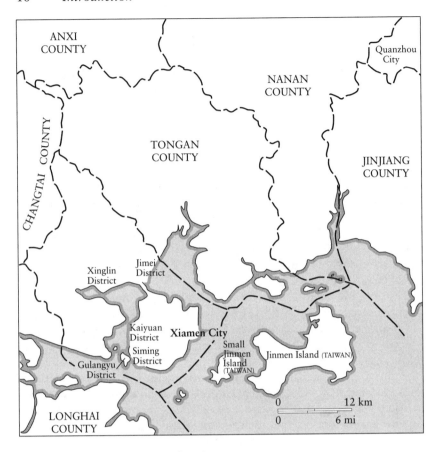

Map 1.2. Xiamen and environs.

the Song dynasty (A.D. 960–1127). At that time, Quanzhou, the Zaytun of Marco Polo's accounts, was the regional port for trade between China and Southeast and South Asia and the Middle East. The silting of its harbor shifted trade fifty kilometers south to Xiamen Island, where a natural deepwater harbor was favored by the oceangoing ships of Spanish, Portuguese, and Dutch traders in the sixteenth and seventeenth centuries. Following the defeat of the Ming dynasty by Manchu invaders in the mid-seventeenth century, Xiamen became a military base for Ming dynasty loyalists. The loyalists were forced to retreat to Taiwan in 1662, where they were defeated by the Manchu forces of the newly established Qing dynasty. The Qing set up a customs house in Xiamen in 1683 to control trade with Taiwan and prevent smuggling. By 1838, on the eve of the Opium War (1840–2), 140,000 people lived in Xiamen. Following China's defeat in this war it became a British treaty port, with the tiny Gulangyu district eventually becoming an International Settlement outside of China's jurisdiction. The collapse of the region's rural handicraft industry from foreign competition and a land squeeze from overpopulation pushed thousands of peasants to emigrate to Southeast Asia and the Americas as coolie labor. In the nineteenth century, Xiamen was the second largest exporter of coolie labor, after Guangzhou.[31]

The golden era of business in Xiamen, as elsewhere in China, began during World War I, when the war effort intensified demand for raw materials while reducing European and American business competition. Many southern Fujianese emigrants in Southeast Asia had prospered and their investment capital flowed back to Xiamen. Real estate and public utilities were developed with this capital from overseas Chinese (Lu et al. 1989: 119). The economy depended mostly on trade and services, including 5,000 shops and 1,000 restaurants, banks, and casinos, as well as about two dozen factories manufacturing opium, ships, and other products. By 1936 the population exceeded 200,000 and Xiamen accounted for 72 percent of provincial foreign trade and 5 percent of the national total. The golden era was brought to a close primarily by renewed foreign business competition after World War I and the world depression of the 1930s. The outbreak of World War II disrupted the sea trade routes essential to Xiamen's economic vitality. During the war Xiamen was a major Japanese supply base because of its excellent harbor and was bombed by American airplanes.[32]

---

[31] For the economic history of southern Fujian province from the third to the thirteenth century, see Clark (1991). For southern Fujian overseas traders from the thirteenth to eighteenth centuries see Ng (1973–4); and Wang (1991). For the economic rise of Xiamen in the late seventeenth century see Ng (1983).

[32] I am unaware of English-language scholarly accounts of Xiamen during this period. However, an idea of it can be gained by reading the extensive literature on Shanghai in

After World War II, Xiamen was a Nationalist Party stronghold that was spared the ravages of the civil war. The economy boomed, as thousands of overseas Chinese streamed through its port to visit their ancestral homelands in Fujian. By the founding of the People's Republic of China in 1949, Xiamen was a site of very intense commercial activity. Contemporary census figures show a population of 263,406 in 56,805 households (State Statistical Bureau 1989: 26) and an economy with 21,875 shops and 3,837 registered street peddlers (Lu et al. 1989: 117). This means that roughly one of every three families or at least one in ten people could have been a business proprietor of some sort, a high proportion even for South China.[33]

Xiamen was the Nationalist Party's last toehold on the mainland before its forces retreated to Taiwan in 1949; since then the city has been the front line of the cold war between Communists and Nationalists. From time to time, this cold war has heated up. In 1958 Communist forces shelled the Nationalist force occupying the Greater and Lesser Jinmen (Quemoy) islands, several kilometers off the coast of Xiamen, and artillery duels sputtered on for years. Even as late as 1990 huge loudspeakers on Lesser Quemoy blared Nationalist propaganda that was audible in Xiamen. Nevertheless, some development took place in Xiamen over the decades. A causeway built in 1955 linked Xiamen to the mainland and a link to the national railroad network was completed in 1957. Industrial growth through state investment took place in food processing, tobacco, textiles, ship-building, and light electrical equipment. To avoid Nationalist shelling, these factories were located in the new Xinglin Industrial District on the mainland.

The socialist transformation of industry, commerce, handicrafts, and stalls in Xiamen in the 1950s conformed to the national pattern.[34] Larger businesses were first nationalized in the early 1950s. According to city housing records, there were 950 families locally with "capitalist" labels (*Annals of Xiamen City Real Estate* 1989: 105). The nationalization of larger businesses was followed by the collectivization of private shops and peddlers in 1956–7. By the beginning of the Great Leap Forward in 1958, private business had ceased to exist. During the economic re-

the interwar period. See Bergère ([1986] 1989) for the situation of the Shanghai bourgeoisie; for relations between the Shanghai capitalists and the Nationalist party-state see Coble (1980). See Lin (1947) for a fictional chronicle of two families and their business ventures in Fujian during this era. Lin's account is sociological: he describes the rise and fall of the families in terms of the management of *guanxi*.

[33] According to a 1955 aggregate survey, one out of every 28.4 people in the major cities of Beijing, Shanghai, Tianjin, Canton, Wuhan, Shenyang, Chongqing, and Xian was in commerce. In Canton, where the historical situation most approximates Xiamen's, the figure was one out of every 13 people (Kuan 1960: 27).

[34] See Vogel (1969: 156–73) for the process in Guangzhou; for the expropriation of capitalist enterprises see Lieberthal's (1980) account of Tianjin.

Table 1.1. *Xiamen's population and economy since 1949*

|  | 1950 | 1978 | 1980 | 1983 | 1985 | 1987 | 1992 | 1994 |
|---|---|---|---|---|---|---|---|---|
| *Population* (1,000) | | | | | | | | |
| Administrative region | 454 | 908 | 934 | 988 | 1,027 | 1,061 | 1,154 | 1,194 |
| Municipality | 263 | 474 | 492 | 521 | 546 | 570 | 627 | 655 |
| Island | 169 | 237 | 251 | 271 | 349 | n.a. | 403 | 426 |
| *Economy* | | | | | | | | |
| Combined agricultural and industrial output (million ¥) | 62 | 913 | 1,134 | 1,408 | 2,247 | 3,246 | 15,089 | 25,369 |
| Gross industrial output (million ¥) | 25 | 701 | 911 | 1,177 | 2,585 | 3,129 | 13,298 | 24,925 |
| light industry (%) | 94.2 | 70.8 | 69.0 | 68.7 | 68.3 | 64.4 | 70.1 | 68.2 |
| heavy industry (%) | 5.8 | 29.2 | 31.0 | 31.3 | 31.7 | 35.2 | 29.9 | 31.9 |
| GNP (million ¥) | n.a. | n.a. | 436 | 599 | 1,032 | 1,595 | 7,369 | 13,851 |
| Per capita GNP (¥) | n.a. | n.a. | 1,234 | 1,420 | 2,529 | 2,401 | 6,257 | 11,082 |

*Source*: Figures for 1950–87: Li and Zhao (1992: 229). For 1992: China Statistical Publishers (1993: 10, 22, 23, 32). For 1994: China Statistical Publishers (1995: 14, 21, 28, 183).

trenchment of the early 1960s, peddlers and artisans, who had been the last to enter the collectives, were allowed to leave. Some did so, using what remained of their original economic capital to set up shop once again. However, during the Cultural Revolution many were resocialized, while the few who remained in private business were harassed as "tails of capitalism" and conducted trade furtively. By 1978, on the eve of market reform, there were only 395 legally registered private businesses, mostly fruit vendors or peddlers of secondhand goods.[35]

In 1980 a turning point occurred in Xiamen's economic development with its designation as one of China's five special economic zones, created to attract foreign investment and lead the way in forming a market economy. The Xiamen Special Economic Zone, originally confined to a small district, was expanded in 1984 to the entire island. Many infrastructural improvements were made, including the 1983 construction of the Xiamen International Airport and the construction of four deepwater berths for 10,000 ton container ships. Also, the Xiamen city government was given special economic zone privileges, such as lower import duties and the authority to approve direct foreign investments not exceeding U.S. $30 million.[36] The result has been the rapid growth of

[35] For Xiamen during the Cultural Revolution from the perspective of a Red Guard, see Ling (1972).

[36] For the special economic zone policy with reference to Xiamen, see Howell (1993). For Taiwanese investment in Xiamen, see Luo and Howe (1995).

Xiamen's economy. From 1980 to 1987 gross industrial output rose from ¥911 million to ¥3,129 million, a 3.4-fold increase. The growth of services and commerce has been even more rapid; Xiamen's GNP, which includes nonindustrial activity, increased by 3.7 fold during this same period (Li and Zhao 1992).[37]

Obviously Xiamen is not a typical Chinese city. Rather, it provides a window on some of the furthest departures from the classical Communist order in the reform era. I have woven my multiple observations from Xiamen into a tapestry depicting the institutionalized organization of business and its political and economic consequences as I came to understand them in this commercially dynamic locale on the South China coast in the late 1980s and early 1990s. This tapestry portrays the commingling of sentimental expressions of personhood and loyalty with instrumental concerns for profit and control. The story that unfolds is about the evolutionary transformation of Communist social structure and state power during market reform.

---

[37] For an ethnographic account of a suburban village on Xiamen Island from the revolution to the mid-1980s as narrated by its Communist Party secretary, see Huang (1989).

# 2

## Institutional Commodification:
## Concepts and Categories of the Analysis

The emergence of China's market economy in the late twentieth century challenges fundamental Western beliefs on the link between markets and politics. It is a basic tenet that markets – economic activity driven by capital interests in competition with each other – and democracy – political freedom and popular participation in government – go hand in hand.[1] Markets are said to create values of freedom and a middle class, giving rise to democracy.[2] Democracy is said to restrain the state from arbitrary interference in the economy, stabilizing private property rights to stimulate market growth.[3] Yet the emergence of China's market economy since 1978 belies these tenets. For despite having the most dynamic market economy in the communist world, only the Chinese party-state survived the popular upheavals of 1989: this confounds the axiom that markets promote democracy. Events since 1989 are equally paradoxical. Despite the shift to democratically elected regimes in post-Communist Eastern Europe, China's market economy is still much more dynamic: this confounds the notion that democracy is more conducive to markets. How can China's emerging market economy be explained?

[1] The literature on this topic is voluminous. For recent surveys see Rueschemeyer, Stephens, and Stephens (1992); and Lipset (1993).

[2] For classic statements on the link between the rising middle class and democracy see Schumpeter ([1943] 1987); Moore (1966); Skocpol (1979). For application to China in the economic reform era, see Glassman (1991); Prybyla (1990). As for the idea that market freedom promotes political democracy, consider the following statement in regard to China by Jan Prybyla: "Once a market system is in place, protected and encouraged by even a nondemocratic political system, it will tend to permeate the political realm with its ideas of freedom and its 'democratic' assumptions, eventually weaning away that realm from authoritarianism" (Prybyla 1990: 38).

[3] See, for example, North (1981, 1990a); Olson (1982). Jan Winiecki uses North's and Olson's ideas to explain the inefficiency of emerging market economies in communist economic reform. He writes: "In Soviet-type economies the rulers agree to maintain a property rights structure favorable to [apparatchiks and economic bureaucrats], regardless of the effect upon efficiency. In fact, modes of wealth distribution resulting from the Soviet-type economy structure of property rights differ so much from those in other pre-representative government states (i.e., traditional and "modern" autocracies), that institutional change leading to lower transaction costs and increased wealth is much more difficult to achieve" (Winiecki [1990] 1996: 66).

23

This is an ethnographic study of the institutional organization of China's emerging market economy and its economic and political outcomes. It draws on almost two years of fieldwork in a city on the southern coast, site of 70 percent of China's private businesses and the most dynamic region of the world capitalist economy. Private firms here hire hundreds of employees, are diversifying from commerce into manufacture and services, and pursue interregional and international trade. Yet this is occurring in a commercial context quite different from the ideal-typical market economy that undergirds the aforementioned Western beliefs: legal rights to private property are haphazardly enforced and clientelist networks between private business operators and local state agents are pervasive. Examining the operation of this private business highlights the organization of the emerging market economy, and the institutional basis of its performance and political consequences.

## Contending Accounts of Private Business in Communist Orders

There are three accounts of the operation of private business in the social science literature on economic reform in communist orders.[4] Each contains a distinct image of the market and suggests certain political and economic consequences. The market transition account sees private firms as moving toward an ideal-typical market economy: this account most embodies the aforementioned Western tenets. The political economy account sees the operation of private business as embedded in the shifting power distribution wrought by economic reform. The traditional culture account sees the operation of private business as largely constituted by relatively enduring popular norms and values. This study develops an alternative account that emphasizes the operation of private business through social networks that constitute markets, trust, and politics: I term it the "institutional commodification account."

### Market Transition Account

This account views market emergence as a transition from a planned to a market economy in which the two economies are defined in ideal-

---

[4] This study does not engage the Chinese literature on private business. The Chinese complement to Western concerns with markets and democracy is the link between markets and socialism (cf. selected articles in Rosen 1987–8). Some sociological studies survey the characteristics of private entrepreneurs and consider their class character and social status (e.g., Jia and Wang 1989; Zhang 1994).

typical terms as logical opposites (Blanchard, Froot, and Sachs 1994; Bunce and Csanadi 1993; Hankiss 1988; Kornai 1992; Nee 1989a). The market economy is characterized by private property, legal equality, horizontal transactions, voluntary exchange, and price calculations, all of which cohere around the principle of supply and demand. The planned economy involves public property, bureaucratic hierarchy, vertical transactions, and exchange by central fiat, which cohere around the principle of redistribution in the state structure. In keeping with the definition of a market economy as the antithesis of state control, private business springs up "naturally" when the party-state releases its grip on the economy and society by removing administrative barriers to it.[5] Therefore, private business is a new organizational form that marks a break with the communist era.[6] Politically, the market transition corresponds to a shift in the polity from party-state domination to a more autonomous society as the power of bureaucratic redistributors declines (Hankiss 1988; Glassman 1991; Gold 1990b; Pei 1994; Szelenyi 1989; Tong 1994).[7]

However, the market transition image fits poorly with findings that the structures of central planning and bureaucratic control continue to pervade the emerging market well after the onset of formal market reform policies. These findings belie the view of the market economy as emerging *ex nihilo* in society, creating autonomous resources that circulate in horizontal transactions outside the purview of the state's bureaucratic redistributors. The market transition perspective attributes these anomalies to a "partial" and "incomplete" transition but maintains that they will disappear when the transition to a market economy is complete. Some view this partial transition as a liminal stage of disorder, while

---

[5] According to the economist Janos Kornai, "large numbers of people voluntarily undertake economic activity on a private property basis. Not even constructive support is needed. It just means dismantling the bureaucratic barriers. . . . [P]eople move spontaneously into the private sector, and the various forms of private enterprise sprout like mushrooms" (Kornai 1992: 434–5).

[6] As Simon Johnson and Gary Loveman point out, "private sector firms . . . are set up from scratch and the founding entrepreneurs choose all aspects of the firms' operation anew, without directly inheriting the constraints of the old organization" (Johnson and Loveman 1995: 105).

[7] Victor Nee claims that "the growth of markets expands the range of opportunities outside the boundaries of the redistributive economy changing the structures of opportunity and incentives and stimulating entrepreneurship and economic performance. . . . The shift from hierarchies to markets causes a decline in the significance of positional power in the redistributive sector" (Nee 1991: 267). The declining power of officialdom is coterminous with the erosion of patron–client ties (Nee 1991: 279). In a compatible vein, Jan Prybyla maintains that "market relations are rendered objective by the cash nexus, rather than being subjective – that is, based on loyalty to one's hierarchical superiors, personal-political duties and obligations, backdoor connections, *guanxi*, *blat*, and other nonprice links (Prybyla 1990: 24–5).

others view it as a hybridized order that mingles the institutions of plan and market.[8] Whichever, both views see the partial transition as lacking an indigenous institutional base and therefore its characteristic elements, such as patron–client ties, are a corruption of more pure economic orders. While commercial activity does occur in a partial transition, this is deemed less efficient and equitable than what would occur in a more complete market economy.

If one believes in the value of studying existing economic activity as deviations from ideal types, then the market transition view is undoubtedly compelling; if not, then it raises questions that it cannot answer.[9] The assertion that private business arises *ex nihilo* through the dismantling of the communist era state is ahistorical, raising questions about how economies change. If political power pervades the market economy during the transition, then would not this power also shape whatever market and polity emerge when the transition is completed? How, therefore, is it possible to speak of the economy and polity of commercializing communist orders as necessarily moving toward an ideal-typical market and democracy? Also, almost two decades have passed since the state first launched market reform, and China's economic organization is still far from an ideal-typical market. How long does it make sense to speak of a "partial" transition? And if a partial transition contains conflicting exchange principles and unstable economic arrangements, then how can the dynamism of China's market economy as marked by conventional measures be explained?

### Political Economy Account

The political economy account differs from market transition imagery by seeing power as an institutional element of the emerging market economy. Market reform policies devolve control over public resources to the lower bureaucracy; therefore the expansion of markets is linked to the decentralization of power within the state structure. Even as central economic coordination wanes, local governments still control vast resources and the state bureaucracy remains the dominant integrative

---

[8] This image of a chaotic transitional stage is evoked by János Kornai: "The reform destroys the coherence of the classical system and proves incapable of establishing a new order in its place. The old regularities apply only partially, and new permanent regularities fail to coalesce. Everything is fluid, or rather gelatinous. Society is full of elements that have no affinity; they repel rather than attract each other" (Kornai 1992: 571). The image of a hybrid order is described by Victor Nee: "Under partial reform, the institutional foundations of a market economy are only partially in place and the state-run redistributive economy remains the dominant integrative mechanism of the economy" (Nee 1991: 268).

[9] For relevant critiques of the ideal-typical concept of the market, see Hirsch, Michaels, and Friedman (1990); and Swedberg, Himmelstrand, and Brulin (1990: 76–9).

institution in the realm. Consequently, the *nomenklatura* are well sited to profit in the emerging market economy by turning power over goods in short supply and with a certain market value into personal profit (Glinksi 1992; Nee 1992; Róna-tas 1994; Staniszkis 1991).[10] Even private entrepreneurs without any prior government position need to cultivate access to officially brokered resources to improve business (Bruun 1993; Liu 1992; Solinger 1992; Young 1989, 1995; Wank 1993, 1995b).[11] This results in new forms of commercialized dependency of the rising private business class on local officialdom.

The political economy perspective raises two issues for further inquiry. One concerns the function of exchanges between entrepreneurs and officials. The political economy account attributes the involvement of officials in the market economy to the existence of arbitrage opportunities stemming from the state's residual redistributive control over resources. This argument is close to the partial transition of the market transition account. And similarly, it implies that as arbitrage opportunities decline, exchanges between entrepreneurs and officials will wane accordingly, as presumably a truer market economy takes hold. However, my own findings indicate that clientelist ties survive the decline of arbitrage opportunities, suggesting that they are a more enduring feature of the emerging market economy than political economism maintains. Further inquiry is needed into how business operates through these networks.

The second issue is the institutional underpinnings of the market. In the political economy account the market appears as the sum of spot transactions by utility-maximizing actors within decentralizing hierarchies. This study maintains that an interest convergence is a necessary but insufficient condition for a market transaction to occur. A market also consists of expectations of future gains from investments and future deliveries based on contracts. Yet emerging market economies lack the expectation-enhancing institutions of "mature" market economies, such as universal laws and impartial courts. And even if such institutions did exist, many contracts would be unenforceable in courts of law because

---

[10] Jadwiga Staniszkis has termed this "political capitalism." She writes: "Its basic features are: first, the power in industry and the state administration is linked with activities on one's own account in a private company. Second, the main customer of these companies is not the consumer market but state industry. . . . Third, profits are derived from the exclusive access to attractive markets, information, and supply (made possible by the dual status of the nomenklatura owners)" (Staniszkis 1991: 136–7).

[11] As the political scientist Dorothy Solinger writes, "for the Chinese urban entrepreneur who operates on a scale of some size, the state and its institutions remain the principal source of start-up capital; in addition, entrée to the state's means of production and guidance through its regulatory and informational labyrinth has been the sine qua non for business activity" (Solinger 1992: 123).

they entail activities deemed illegal or dubious by the state. The trenchant issue is the institutional basis of patron–client exchange in the market economy. How are commercial expectations forged and enhanced in the context of marked asymmetries of political power?

## Traditional Culture Account

The traditional culture account sees markets as embedded in traditional culture, variously defined as norms of sharing (Weitzman and Xu 1994), kin-based networks (Lin 1995), and civilizational cosmologies, such as Confucianism (Bruun 1993). It differs from market transition imagery by seeing society as patterning the market rather than vice versa. This patterning also addresses the issue in the political economy account on the market's institutional underpinning. Cultural institutions shape local commercial activity by imparting regularity to interactions: traditional values and norms of sharing coordinate claims over residual income (Weitzman and Xu 1994); social networks add "stability and persistence" to the local authority structure (Lin 1995: 311); traditional conceptions of authority and status routinize interactions between private businesspeople and street-level officials (Bruun 1993). The cultural embeddedness of commercial behavior solidifies a distinct "local" sphere of values and practices that blunt initiatives by the central state to penetrate and organize society in accordance with its own projects (Bruun 1993: 140; Lin 1995: 342).[12]

This account's portrayal of culture raises two questions. One concerns institutional change. Culture is depicted as an enduring or purely local phenomenon.[13] Whichever, this depiction begs the question of how institutions change and ignores the interaction of the central state with the local society in processes that could drive change.

The second issue concerns the constitution of markets. The portrayal of culture in generalized terms as social norms of loyalty and sharing and mutual identities of kinship and friendship explains cooperation *among* actors but not competition *between* them. This generalized emphasis

---

[12] For example, Bruun posits that the Confucian cosmology of personalized authority between local officials and private shopkeepers is "highly contradictory to any legal construction in which individuals are equally positioned. Thus local authority builds its existence on principles that obstruct all attempts by central government to enforce the rule of law" (Bruun 1993: 140).

[13] Bruun suggests an enduring and unchanging culture when he writes that "modernization and development seem to have taken place alongside a strong continuity in fundamental ideologies, values and orientations among the social groups within the locality (1995: 185). The entirely local character of culture is suggested by Lin, who sees the kin network as an "indigenous institution . . . based on the traditional Chinese family-village elements, decidedly unassociated or dictated by the principles of state socialism or market mechanisms" (Lin 1995: 310).

needs to be balanced by a more particularistic account of the individuated manner by which loyalties and identities constrain the support a specific actor can claim from certain others. In other words, culture is simultaneously generalized morality and norms, and particularistic identities and claims. The generalized aspects help explain how cooperation is possible, and the particularistic aspects explain patterns of competition. Social networks reflect both aspects, and therefore both cooperation and competition proceed through them.

### Institutional Commodification Account

In this study I develop an alternative account of private business that explains its operation in an emerging market economy pervaded by bureaucratic power and popular values. I label this account "institutional commodification." A commodity is something that can be bought and sold in markets for a value gauged by a constant quantitative measure, such as money. Commodification is the process by which such value comes to be attached to things that are then transacted in markets.[14] The vast range of public resources accumulated by the state and administered by the bureaucracy have become commodified, as they are now the object of price calculations and profit seeking in commercial transactions. Commodities cannot, of course, go to market by themselves; it follows that commodification is the transformation of institutionalized social relations of control over these vast resources, either through cadres' position of office or through clientelist ties by citizens to office holders.[15] This

---

[14] My inspiration for the concept comes from anthropological studies that examine the meetings of pre-capitalist traditional societies with modern capitalism as the commodification of values, personhood, and social relations (e.g., Appadurai 1986; Bohannan 1959; Parry and Bloch 1989; Taussig 1980). They see commodification as a process of changing conceptions of personhood and social relations as market value displaces values of kinship, religion, and community. Several anthropologists and sociologists have expressed comparable concerns in regard to market reforms in Communist countries. Some examine how the principle of market value introduced by party-state reforms interacts with the principle of redistribution in the planned economy and reciprocity in the gift economy (Humphrey 1991; Stark 1989; Yang 1994) while others describe new values and statuses, conceptions of personhood, and strategies of gain and exchange in the market reform era (Stark 1996; Szelenyi 1988; Wank 1996; Wilson 1997; Yang 1994).

[15] The term "planned commodity economy" was also widely used in official Chinese state documents in the mid-1980s to describe the emerging economic order. Documents indicate central state concern that commodification could spill over from the economic sphere into the social and political sphere. This is seen in the following statement from an article titled "Profit and Morality" in the state-funded English-language *Beijing Review*: "The change from allocation in kind . . . to exchange in cash will increase the importance of money. Emphasis on the principle of exchange of commodities at equal value may lead to bargaining in human relationships where the exchange of commodities is not involved. The influence of the decadent bourgeois idea of putting profit-making first may encourage egoism, neglect of public interests and even corruption, theft and

transformation is apparent in the evolving idioms of *guanxi*: private entrepreneurs use *guanxi* idioms to talk about their business activities, although embellished with new terms that reflect the commodified values of the market reform era.[16]

Economic reform policies commodify the state monopoly by enabling the previously unpriced assets "owned" by the state (in the name of the people) and administered by the bureaucratic staff to be the objects of price calculations. The introduction of money and prices transforms patterns of control and influence regarding bureaucratically mediated public resources. Commercial operators draw on preexisting affiliations with state agents to secure access to these resources. Commercial competition centers on particularistic access through personal ties to resources brokered by the administrative, policing, distributive, and manufacturing organs of the party-state. Private business operators are among the various contenders created by market reform that seek to control some of these assets to further their own ends. They mobilize diffuse social resources to influence the allocation of these resources so as to enhance the capital accumulations of their firms.

Institutional commodification, therefore, is the reconfiguration of communist networks toward commercially competitive ends in the reform era.[17] To explain competition in the market economy it is necessary to recognize a social structure that creates patterns of differences and similarity in trade.[18] Patterns of similarity stimulate competition, whereas differences encourage cooperation. This requires viewing institutions not only as constraints on generalized social behavior but also as differential attachments to entities that variably constrain their particular interactions. In other words, social action reflects the evolutionary systemic (macro) constraints as well as the individuated (micro) constraints of personal history and status. Traders inherit different ties and other resources from the old system. These particularistic legacies constrain

racketeering. . . . The principle of exchange of equal value, so important in the commodity economy, is not applicable to non-commodity fields, such as politics, ideology and culture" (Geng [1986] 1989: 32–3).

[16] The prominence of *guanxi* as an idiom of social relations appears to be a product of the communist era. In the 1930s and 1940s ethnographers noted the role of agnatic and affinal ties in social life through such practices as nepotism. Instrumental practices toward non-kin were expressed in the idioms of *renqing* (human sentiment), less blatantly calculating than *guanxi* (Yang 1994: 148–9). For a sweeping discussion of clientelist networks in different periods of China's modern history, see Yang (1994: 114, 146–72). For *guanxi* idioms and practices in the market reform era, see Bian (1994); Kipnis (1997); Smart (1993); Wank (1996); Wilson (1997); Yan (1996); and Yang (1994).

[17] Institutional commodification is therefore an evolutionary view of a market economy. See Campbell and Lindberg (1990); Nelson and Winter (1982); and White (1993a).

[18] For more general discussion related to this point, see Burt (1992); Geertz (1963); Lie (1992); and Sahlins (1972: 313).

their advantages and strategies, driving processes of cooperation and competition in the emerging market economy.[19]

The focus of analysis is the clientelist network. I consider these networks to be an integral element of the emerging market economy. In this I differ from the market transition account, which sees them as inherently unstable and inefficient structures doomed to disappear as the market more closely approximates its ideal-typical form. Instead clientelist ties have an institutional base – social trust.[20] They cannot be characterized as unstable forms located along a continuum between institutionally pure planned and market economies, but rather are commercial processes and decisions in their own right (Róna-tas 1994; Stark 1989, 1996; Xie and Hannum 1996: 984). Furthermore, a market has no essential consequences for political order: its rise can just as likely lead to an authoritarian as to as a pluralist polity (Walder 1996: 1061).

In its emphasis on strategic social action, the institutional commodification approach shares with the political economy approach a concern for interests and power but broadens these concepts considerably. Patron–client ties reflect not only the profit-maximizing interests of the exchange partners but also the institutional obligations and identities that inhere in personalized patron–client ties. Thus links with officialdom reflect not only utility-maximizing interest calculations but also the rationality of social trust. Entrepreneurs are also interested in forging and maintaining personal ties, enhancing and discharging obligations, and manipulating mutual recognition of relative identities to enhance expectations. Power is embodied not only in the monetary gains derived from trade but also in position in networks. Diffuse forms of social, symbolic, and cultural capital shape relative resources and outcomes in interpersonal bargaining.[21]

[19] Although there are points of overlap between the institutional analysis of this study and David Stark's (1996) study, there are key differences. First, Stark sees the reconfiguration of communist era networks as "recombinant property rights," but never specifies why property rights are important. The argument presented in this study is that the reconfigurations are not driven by property rights but rather the search by entrepreneurs for profit and security in competition with others (see also Fligstein 1996: 1078–9). Second, Stark sees new commercial actors as bricoleurs who select from among the institutional resources at hand, including prior affiliations, to build their enterprises. However, there is little account of social structure in Stark's analysis that can explain the varying constraints the specific actors face in their capacity for such institutional improvisation. Without an account of social structure, it is difficult to explain how competition and cooperation is constrained by the prior communist era as well. This study fills this gap by introducing such variables as position vis-à-vis the state hierarchy and social background.

[20] The possibility for multiple legitimating principles is linked to economic sociology's concern with the framing of economic activity. See Block (1989, 1990); DiMaggio (1990); and Friedland and Robertson (1990).

[21] For these more diffuse forms of capital see Bourdieu (1986).

Table 2.1. *Contrasting accounts of emerging private business in Communist orders*

|  | Market transition account | Political economy account | Traditional culture account | Institutional commodification account |
|---|---|---|---|---|
| Concept of market | Exchanges between legally equal private firms | Resources exchanged in dyads | Embedded in traditional culture | Socially embedded exchange networks |
| Key process of emerging market | Shift from planned to market economy | Decentralization of control to lower state | Reemergence of traditional culture | Reconfiguration of clientelist ties for commercial ends |
| Economic rationality | Efficiency | Reflects power distribution | Morality and social values | Social trust |
| Patron–client ties in private business | Market corruption | Mutually beneficial exchanges | Traditional forms of deference and local solidarity | Market contract embodying future expectations |

In its emphasis on social trust, the institutional commodification account shares the traditional culture account's view of the importance of norms of obligation and sharing and identities rooted in kin and community; however, it differs in several key respects. First, the traditional culture account conflates these institutions with the behavior of persons. By contrast, the institutional commodification account sees them as social knowledge diffused in the population that helps people form expectations about the likely behavior of others, constraining rationality and choices but not necessarily determining behavior. Second, these institutions are not only traditions that predate the communist era but also organizations and practices from the communist era "that can become assets, resources, and the basis for credible commitments and coordinated actions in the postsocialist period" (Stark 1996: 995). Third, the institutions are not reified but are evolving. Change is the evolutionary recombination of legitimating principles through innovations in practical action, resulting in new organizational forms. Institutional evolution is driven by the interaction of short-run innovations in practical activity with long-term shifts in legitimacy: an institution constrains practical activity even as it is altered by innovations in this activity (e.g., Fligstein 1990).[22]

---

[22] Stark writes: "actors in the postsocialist context are rebuilding organizations and institutions not *on the ruins* but *with the ruins* of communism as they redeploy available

## Commodification of the State Monopoly

The monopoly characteristics of communist party-states that gave rise to clientelist ties in the prior "high" communist era have evolved in the economic reform era. Some aspects of the prior direct monopoly over resources have declined, while new regulatory monopolies have emerged. The intertwining of communist legacies and new market activities have created a distinct configuration of state power in China's emerging market economy that constrains commercial trade networks.

One set of transformations concerns profit opportunities in the state's direct monopoly over resources. First, there is the large monopoly over material resources, a legacy of central planning in which all productive assets were publicly owned and managed by the bureaucracy. In the reform era, much commercial wealth is created by the shift of these public resources to markets. Many of the resulting transactions are labeled "corruption" and "economic crimes" by the state and are therefore more likely to occur between individuals who know and trust one another.[23] Second, there is the legacy of the valorization of public property and status in socialist ideology. This creates some hostility toward private business in the social environment, as well as in policy biases, while simultaneously conferring certain advantages on firms that are legally "public." Even private entrepreneurs seek legal registration as public firms as a cover for their trade, a practice called "red-hatting" (*dai hong maozi*) or "hanging on" (*guakao*).

---

resources in response to their immediate practical dilemmas. Such a conception of path dependence does not condemn actors to repetition or retrogression, for it is through adjusting to new uncertainties by improvising on practiced routines that new organizational forms emerge" (Stark 1996: 995).

[23] The case of a former official in the Fujian Province Highway Bureau nicknamed "the God of Fortune" illustrates the ambiguity surrounding what is permissible (Meyers 1987). This official resigned his position to engage in partnerships with several local governments in Fujian province. He was subsequently charged with economic crimes that carried the death sentence. However, one analyst who studied reports of the case in the Chinese media concludes that it is unclear what crimes were, in fact, committed. He writes: "If we look at the particulars of the canned mushroom business, the case which appears to involve the most serious charges against Tu Kuo-chen, it is not easy to discern exactly where the aspect of 'speculation and fraud' was involved. It certainly does not appear that Tu defrauded the authorities of Ningte Prefecture with whom he was involved. On the contrary, it seems just as plausible to suggest that they may have looked to the God of Fortune as someone who could help them with their mushroom business. . . . Most of the efforts of Tu Kuo-chen and his co-conspirators appear to have been directed toward getting the mushrooms shipped and sold, and though the mushrooms are described as 'smuggled goods,' Tu and the others are nowhere said to have stolen, embezzled, or otherwise illegally obtained them. How the mushrooms were turned into 'smuggled' goods is not clear" (Meyers 1987: 37).

Another set of transformations occurs with the emergence of new monopolies over distribution through increasing regulatory and administrative controls in the market economy, even as direct state monopoly over goods and services declines. An example is in foreign trade, where liberalization of import-export authority has been accompanied by the rising number of goods subject to import-export licensing. Also, the role of some state agencies has been enhanced, thereby creating new forms of control. For example, state banks previously had only an accounting function, but now make loans and are a source of financial capital. Other kinds of new administrative controls are the proliferation of administrative agencies, regulations, and licenses to administer the market economy and private business. For example, entrepreneurs need permission from the Industry and Commerce Bureau to trade in a specific type of item; this is listed in the business scope (*jingying fanwei*) of their business license. In an effort to control the local economy, local bureaus set quotas for the number of firms dealing in any given good or service, creating further scarcities in the number of licenses and in information on their availability. These various kinds of monopolies over material resources and administrative and regulatory mechanisms are widely perceived by traders as "strategic passes" (*guanka*) to be traversed by ties with officials.

Another institutional element is central policy instability. In part this stems from the diverse interests of the state. There is tension between its drive for growth in market activity and its drive to maintain social order and political control. Goals such as increasing employment opportunities, enhancing living standards, stimulating public enterprise productivity, and reducing the state's welfare burden have to be balanced with goals to maintain the support of public workers, prevent significant wealth imbalances, and control local governments. Instability also stems from conflicts among the elite that are largely opaque to the general population. Questions as to the extent and pace of reform are matters of intra-elite contestation. These elite conflicts can suddenly generate shifts in central state policies. Expansive policies that legalize new market activities are followed by drives to target offenders and punish them in bureaucratic mobilization techniques reminiscent of the political campaigns of the Maoist era. The following ditty chanted to me by several entrepreneurs reflects concern with these uncertainties:

> The Communist Party is like the sun (*Gongchandang xiang taiyang*);
> wherever it shines all is bright (*zhaodao nali nali liang*).
> The party's policy is like the moon (*Dang de zhengce xiang yueliang*);
> it waxes and wanes every month (*chuyi shiwu buyiyang*).

Local government regulation and administration constitute yet another distinct institutional element, called "homegrown policy making" (*gao tu zhengce*). First, the state tolerates much variation in local implementation. Central policies often seem little more than statements of general ideological slant, while local branches of government called Policy Research Institutes (*Zhengce Yanjiu Suo*) create guidelines for local agencies that then further interpret these guidelines to suit their interests. Second, agencies implement policy locally by established particularistic techniques to reward the compliant while punishing the uncooperative. Commercial operators who show compliance are favored with streamlined administrative procedures, looser applications of regulations, and special dispensations from national and local restrictions. The uncooperative are burdened with special levies and fees and administrative red tape, and are targeted as offenders in bureaucratic campaigns. This process has helped build local government support for market reform by letting them interpret and implement policies in accordance with their own interests and needs (Shirk 1993). The upshot is that some variation in local market dynamism stems from differences in the homegrown policy making of local governments. Locales in which the local government is less strict in conforming to central policies can have livelier market activity.

## The Rise of Commercial Clientelism

In commercial activity, clientelist ties are multifaceted, being simultaneously market transactions, social trust, and political contestation (Eisenstadt and Roniger 1984: 49; Unger 1987: 135–44). First, they are market transactions: although couched in sentiments of loyalty and trust, goods and services are voluntarily exchanged at commercial prices (Ensminger 1992: 109–22; Geertz 1978). Second, they embody social trust, defined as the expectations that others will behave in socially legitimate ways. This enhances predictability in interactions and facilitates long-term calculations in market activity (Dore 1983; Granovetter 1993: 20–38). Third, patron–client ties embody political contestation to define the institutions of the emerging market economy (Leff 1964; Levine 1989).

### Markets

In reforming communist economies, clientelization enhances the circulation and exchange of goods and services by creating new information flows. A legacy of the planned economy is its vertical channels for information flows on supply and demand between the center and locales within the state structure. Consequently, linkages between market sectors are weak, particularly early in the reform era (Kornai 1992: 127–30). Information on supply and demand between market segments moves in clientelist ties, enhancing the circulation of goods (Róna-tas 1994: 216–17).[24] Clientelization allocates other scarce, bureaucratically mediated resources, such as real estate, licenses, administratively priced goods, exemptions from restrictions, and subcontracting opportunities.[25]

Clientelist allocation can serve to enhance efficiency in an emerging market economy. A major criterion for receiving assets via clientelism is payment of money as bribes, capital investments, and firm shares to state agents, so the capacity to muster revenue is put at a premium. Many of these resources require periodic renewal, enabling adjustments in costs, ensuring that only the most profitable companies can afford them in the long run.[26] Also, clientelization reduces uncertainties stemming from the laws and their implementation process. Formal rules specifying what is permissible are often vague, incomplete, or nonexistent, while those that do exist can suddenly be changed by the central state or particularistically enforced by local agencies. The popular normative base of clientelism permits long-term calculation, encouraging the shift from speculative to long-term investments. Therefore clientelist allocation could actually stimulate more investment than would otherwise be likely to occur in its absence.

Clientelization also enhances enforcement. This can occur in several ways. In first-party enforcement, self-sanctioning is produced by feelings of shame for nonobservance of such ethical imperatives as reciprocity and respect, which are internalized by prior socialization. In second-party enforcement, failure by a person to honor an agreement induces sanctions by the other in the form of the reduction or withdrawal of future cooperation. Third-party enforcement can occur in closed social networks, which are dyads linked to a mutually known third individual.[27] Sanctioning occurs because malfeasance in a dyad will be known to the third person, and possibly the wider community as well,

---

[24] Eric Wolf comments that clientelist ties "are especially functional in situations where the formal institutional structure of society is weak and unable to deliver a sufficiently steady supply of goods and services. . . ." (Wolf 1966: 17).

[25] In a similar vein Yanjie Bian argues that *guanxi* performs an allocatory function in labor markets in China. *Guanxi* is used to "collect internally circulated information on jobs, to obtain influence from powerful cadres, to initiate an assignment or grant a labor quota, to press favorable decisions from leaders of hiring organizations on jobs, to locate a work unit to which one wanted to be transferred, and to influence the current employer to allow one to leave the work unit or job. . . . [T]his study suggests that job allocation and job mobility in China are not purely bureaucratic processes, but are mixed with and largely affected by social relations among individuals and social groups" (Bian 1994: 999).

[26] This point is derived from Leff (1964).

[27] For the concept of closed social networks see Coleman (1988).

reducing the likelihood of future cooperation. Another third-party arrangement is linked to state agencies and associations. Commercial actors lobby official entities to help enforce contractual expectations. Some organizations are appendages of the Communist Party representing societal and occupational groups, while others are distributive, manufacturing, and administrative units that are business partners or direct sponsors of commercial firms.

Finally, clientelist ties constitute competition. Personal ties are used for access to bureaucratic resources, and therefore the character of one's ties and the level of the bureaucracy they reach affect the profitability of enterprises. Paradoxically, the ties can also function to limit competition, as entrepreneurs forge them not only to seek access to a particular bureaucratic resource but to ward off other entrepreneurs. Personalistic ties create a greater commitment of the exchange parties as the identities of the exchange partners enter into the use value of the good or service being transacted. This precludes patrons from readily switching clients in response to price signals (as in spot-market transactions). Thus by both enhancing access and warding off challengers, patron–client ties pattern competition.[28]

### Trust

In economic life clientelist ties enhance expectations that others will honor contractual obligations and not be malfeasant or take undue advantage of one. It follows that social trust is embedded in the relative identities of persons in exchange dyads as well as institutionalized behavioral norms and cognitive categories that define identities and relational obligations.

In commercial clientelism, contractual expectations are sensitive to the personal relationship in which they are embedded (Granovetter 1993: 34–38; Sahlins 1972: 313). Because of the extralegal character of much market activity in reforming communist economies, the character of the tie is a crucial factor in determining whether sufficient trust exists to make a contract in the first place. The character of the relationship subsequently affects the price of the public resources, with entrepreneurs often paying little or no money for a resource directly controlled by a kin. The character of the personal tie also constrains the delivery of other services as well; the greater the sentiment the more diffuse the expectations and the more likely that reciprocity can be deferred.

As the institutional identities and obligations of social trust change

---

[28] For a discussion of particularistic ties as competitive strategies in Chinese contexts see Wong (1988: 109–31).

more slowly than state policies, predictability is enhanced, even in the face of more volatile formal policies and particularized implementation (North 1990a: 6). State power as expressed in its policies comes to be redefined in terms of personal ties to the local state agents who implement them, and who are more accessible to entrepreneurial influence. In other words, personalization lets entrepreneurs define ends in regard to state power and the means to achieve them in terms of institutions that are more accessible to them, a process that often subverts state goals as expressed in policies. Capitalist business strategies are the ongoing quest for and cultivation of ties with strategically placed individuals inside, as well as outside, the state structure. Entrepreneurs mobilize obligation and reputation through widespread social practices to elicit support from others.

Thus "doing business" (*zuo shengyi*) is perceived not solely as utility-maximizing in market transactions but as cultivating the social relations, mostly with the bureaucracy through which flow a broad range of business-enhancing benefits. This is seen in the widespread usage in the local business world of idioms that intermingle personal, bureaucratic, and commercial considerations; for example, a bureaucratic supporter is called a "power family" (*quanli hu*), a license obtained through an official's discretion is referred to as a "sentiment license" (*renqing zhizhao*), and dealing with an employee in a personalized relation is called "affect management" (*ganqing guanli*). This underscores two points. One is that such commercial variables as the price and availability of resources, the likelihood that contracts can be renegotiated to deal with future contingencies, and the rates of return on investments are linked to the character of the human sentiment between the contracting individuals. The other is that market rationality as utility-maximizing cannot be considered separately from the normative and cognitive rationality of personal ties.

### Politics

The institutionalization of a market economy – the process by which certain entities and actions come to be routinized in social practice – is simultaneously political contestation. This is because institutions are not neutral: cultural rules bias action by framing certain actors, behaviors, and interactions as legitimate and others as less so, thereby channeling certain resource distributions. In other words, specific institutions are often more in the interests of certain actors than others, leading to contestation between different actors to generalize their institutional preferences (Appadurai 1986: 57; Knight 1992). Entrepreneurs' redefinition of state power and commercial activity in terms of popular institutions of social relations is resisted by the central state.

Contestation centers on asserting the values that "explain and justify intention, agency, and actions" (White 1993a: 63). Market practitioners seek to convert actions into the buying and selling of commodities in which value is measured as monetary price. The state attempts to convert diverse human situations and activities into routine bureaucratic decisions that can be dealt with by regulations and in which value is expressed as statistical indicators of compliance in attaining goals. Kin and communities attempt to convert social relations into unconditional obligations that enhance their reproduction and in which value is measured by loyalty. Different actors orient their behavior and purposes in various ways toward these values.

As different actors have different interests, they may emphasize dissimilar values in their social action. To enhance its monitoring and revenue extraction, the state seeks to embed market transactions in bureaucratic processes by, for example, requiring payments to public units to be by bank transfers and encouraging the use of notarized contracts. These instruments create transparency in economic activity, facilitating central monitoring and revenue extraction, and the statistical measurement of economic value. Entrepreneurs emphasize kinship values of loyalty and obligation in market transactions to facilitate the concealment of allocation in personal ties and the provision of enforcement mechanisms separate from the state's legal system. Situated between the state and society, local state agents face the often conflicting principles of the state's emphasis on professional ethics and bureaucratic procedure, and society's legitimation of loyalty to kin and community.[29] In a situation of multiple possibilities political contestation is embodied in the diffusion of practices that embody specific values and exclude others.

Although patron–client ties are ultimately dyadic phenomena, they are consequential for the systemic polity. As H. D. Flap writes: "Since similar clientelist network structures impose largely similar restrictions on the behavioral alternatives of the actors, the outcomes will be more or less similar across a diversity of social contexts" (Flap 1990: 230). The aggregation of a multitude of similar localized behavior that deviates from central goals and policies confronts the state with a form of mass action achieved through the homogenization of interests rather than their organization (Kelliher 1992: 31; Zhou 1993). This action compels the state to respond while constraining the kinds of responses that are possible. A key constraint is that, as the ties reflect the broader organization of the state, they are unlikely to disappear if the state response fails to address the organizational context that gives rise to them in the first place.

---

[29] For the importance of seeing local officials as a distinct group positioned between state and society, see Ding (1994).

## Synopsis of the Analysis

The following study is divided into two parts. Part I explains the organization of the market economy as seen in the operation of private business as I came to understand it in my fieldsite from 1988 to 1990. Each of the four chapters in Part I examines a specific institutional process. Chapter 3 describes how the opportunity structure and commercial competition is constrained by the state's hierarchical power, and the trade networks that emerge. Chapter 4 focuses on one such network, the mutually beneficial patron–client exchange between private firms and public units. Chapter 5 considers how private firm operators develop stable expectations through popular norms of obligation and reciprocity, and such social identities as family, friend, and acquaintance and how these expectations interact with state-promulgated institutions of bureaucratic legality. Chapter 6 looks at how commercial advantage in private business is constrained by the family background and life experiences of particular entrepreneurs.

Part II extends the analysis of Part I to consider the thematic questions posed at this chapter's beginning regarding the economic performance and consequences for the polity. Chapter 7 offers an interpretation of the superior performance of the Chinese economy relative to the market economies of post-communist Eastern Europe. Chapter 8 elaborates on the political consequences of clientelist markets in China. Chapter 9 updates the analysis by considering the evolution of market and polity in the first half of the 1990s. The processes I observed in the late 1980s and described in Part I are updated by data from fieldwork in 1995. The conclusion reflects on the process of commodification.

# Part I

*Instituted Processes of
Commercial Clientelism*

# 3

## The Structure of Commercial
## Opportunity in Xiamen

To the naked eye, Xiamen has changed much in the first decade of market reform. A visitor in 1979 would have found a small city of narrow streets lined with drab, decaying buildings and few pedestrians. Ten years later, the visitor would have noticed great changes. The old buildings have been repaired, painted in pastel colors, and festooned with vertical signs of companies and shops announcing a wide array of goods and services. The rice paddies that once surrounded the city have been covered by broad tree-lined boulevards flanked by office towers. Customers from all over China now come to compare, bargain, and buy. What is not apparent to the naked eye is how the power of the party-state permeates this bustling commercial world, constraining the organization of firms and patterns of competition.

This chapter describes the organization of Xiamen's commercial world as I came to understand it in the late 1980s, after a decade of market reform. I describe how the manner in which traders engage in Xiamen's burgeoning commercial life is constrained by their position vis-à-vis the state's hierarchy. The firms they operate are organized as trading networks and different types of firms are linked to different levels of the state hierarchy, embodying a distinct connection to its power and monopoly privileges. Commercial competition within market sectors is constrained by patterns of similarity and difference among firms in their connections to the state hierarchy. In other words the formation of trade networks is not a purely voluntary phenomenon but depends on the existence of an opportunity structure (Lie 1992: 510; see also Tilly 1978); in Xiamen this structure reflects the prior positioning of traders vis-à-vis the state hierarchy.

### The Reemergence of Trade

Numerous commercial activities have arisen since 1979 in Xiamen (see Table 3.1). The growth of foreign trade is linked to Xiamen's status as a

43

Table 3.1. *Selected items traded wholesale in Xiamen*

*Imported*
Vehicles (passenger cars, motorcycles, trucks, buses), vehicle parts, clothing (shoes, designer fashions, cloth), home electrical appliances (VCRs, color television sets, refrigerators, hot water heaters, air conditioners, sound systems), Western medicines, high-tech equipment (medical equipment, computers), liquors, cigarettes, gift foods, hand-held electrical machinery (drills, sanders, paint compressors), heavy machinery (printing presses, textile equipment).

*Exported*
Seafood, textiles (jeans, sports jackets, sneakers, slippers, handbags, luggage), food items (mushrooms, teas, preserved fruits, canned food), hand tools, religious items (stone carvings, wood statues of gods, incense), porcelain and pottery, minerals, chemicals, traditional medicines, lighting fixtures, cement, steel, tiles, granite blocks.

*Domestically procured and sold*
Construction materials (concrete, pipes, tiles, timber, plastic tubes, glass, lighting fixtures, wire and cable), jewelry (jade, gold), beer and wines, clothes (jeans, sneakers, suit jackets), grain, seafood, food products (soda, snack foods), sundries.

special economic zone. Exports rose by 15.2 percent a year during the first half of the 1980s, and by 1988 the total value of foreign trade was U.S. $874 million, of which $576 million was export and $298 million was import (Lu et al. 1989: 84). Common export products are canned foods, fresh seafood, chinaware, traditional handicrafts, tea, textiles, leather, religious paraphernalia, minerals, bicycles, televisions, hardware, light industrial products, instruments, and meters and telecommunication equipment. Many labor-intensive handicrafts and light consumer goods are made by private and collective enterprises in the rural hinterland, while capital-intensive goods are often manufactured by state enterprises in Xiamen or the inland industrial cities of Zhangzhou and Sanming. Imports include light industrial products, automobiles and automobile parts, Western medicine, construction materials, computers, and home appliances. Public purchasing agents and private entrepreneurs come from all over China to obtain goods in Xiamen.

A second source of demand concerns real estate. On the eve of the revolution, Xiamen's developed urban area was 7.5 square kilometers. From 1949 to 1979 only 41,720 square meters of new construction took place. In 1979 there were 2,556,720 square meters of building and housing and the per capita living space was 4.1 square meters. From 1980 to 1987, the city's developed area mushroomed to 41 square kilometers, 7,464,000 square meters of construction was completed, and per capita living space increased to 7.17 square meters. By the late 1980s, another 5,785,412 square meters was being developed (Lu et al. 1989: 115–16). This construction boom has created robust demand for subcontractors ranging from construction teams to interior decorators and for specialized suppliers of cement, tiles, bricks, and tubing. It has also stimulated the establishment of over 400 firms in the hardware business. Demand for furniture is high, and many local craftsmen directly market their products. Demand for construction goods and services is also fueled by the extensive restoration of the buildings in the old urban center, which have been gradually returned to their former owners in great disrepair after having been confiscated decades earlier.

A third source of market demand is manufacturing firms established by overseas Chinese capital. By the end of 1988, U.S. $1.6 billion of foreign capital was invested in 485 ventures. During the early 1980s this capital came mostly from Hong Kong and Singapore, but in 1988 Taiwan became the most important source of outside capital. By 1988, Taiwanese had invested in more than ninety concerns, with about 80 percent of these investments made in 1988. Taiwanese investment was growing so rapidly in the late 1980s that it spilled out of the special economic zone into the adjacent Xinglin Industrial District on the mainland, where much of Xiamen's state industry is located. These manufacturers also stimulate trade. As they can legally sell a portion of their products domestically, they are a source of inexpensive "foreign" goods for wholesalers and retailers alike. Also, the manufacturers demand services such as packaging and trucking.

A fourth commercial activity is tourism. In 1979 there were 300,000 domestic and 5,836 nondomestic tourists, whereas in 1988 there were 2.2 million and 152,169, respectively (Lu et al. 1989: 166–9). This growth has created opportunities in the service industry. During the 1980s, fifteen luxury hotels were built for nondomestic tourists, while those for domestic tourists increased to 258. By 1988 the number of restaurants had grown to 1,774, ranging from privately owned eateries with a single table to large luxury restaurants that are joint ventures between the Xiamen city government and Hong Kong restaurateurs. In 1988 there were also 1,500 taxis, many privately owned or contracted to drivers by public units. There were 3,706 buses run by public and private transportation firms plying local and long distance routes. Tourists also stimulate trade by buying clothes, makeup, home appliances, handicrafts, traditional medicine, pottery, and tea. Dozens of shopping centers of various sizes were built in the 1980s that cater to tourists and local consumers, while many small shops depend entirely on tourists.

A fifth area is trade in such consumer items as air conditioners, color televisions, video recorders, and motorcycles. One source of demand is the local populace, which has much disposable income through both employment in private and foreign businesses and remittances from overseas kin. Demand is also from northern traders who come to Xiamen to buy goods for resale elsewhere. These imports are cheaper in Xiamen, as import duties on consumer goods are 50 percent lower in the special economic zone. Also, Xiamen's position as the northernmost special economic zone is attractive to northern traders because it offers some cost advantage in transportation fees over other zones.

Finally, it is necessary to mention smuggling, which interacts with the other forms of trade. One form is evasion of import duties. As just noted, imports into the special economic zone are subject to only half of the duties imposed elsewhere. When goods are transported outside the zone, the remaining duty should be paid. This regulation is widely flouted by traders, and local government enforcement appears lax. Indeed, one of the main reasons buyers flock to Xiamen is the low price of imports in the special economic zone, an advantage that would be negated by stricter enforcement. Goods are also smuggled across the Taiwan Straits in fishing boats. Boats from Taiwan carry consumer goods, such as motor-cycles, home appliances, outboard engines, and power tools, to be exchanged with mainland fishing boats for Hong Kong and U.S. dollars and freshly caught fish. These goods are unloaded on the coast near Xiamen, providing tax-free stock for traders.

## Idioms of Opportunity

The various commercial activities just described are embedded to varying degrees in access to bureaucratically mediated assets. Therefore participation in them requires different kinds of networks and practices of varying degrees of legality. A general principle is that the more profitable activities require more ongoing and highly placed bureaucratic access and are often of dubious legal status. For example, it is extremely lucrative to sell raw materials on foreign markets; participation in this trade requires solid bureaucratic connections at every step, from procuring the commodities from state enterprises to receiving the payment in a restricted foreign exchange bank account. By contrast, the sale of tourist items requires much less official brokerage and is more easily entered by traders.

Local perception of the commercial opportunity structure among wholesale traders reflects this matrix of commercial calculations and bureaucratic connections. It is expressed in the maxim "favorable climate, advantageous position, and harmonious relations" (*qi hou, di li, ren he*). This maxim was repeated mantra-like during numerous interviews in response to my question on the requisites for business success.

Favorable "climate" refers to the ideology of the central state toward the market economy and private business. Businesspeople are constantly looking at the rhetoric of state proclamations on the economy to determine "which way the wind is blowing" in order to foresee possible policy changes. They voraciously read newspapers, often subscribing to half a dozen, and intensely query visitors coming from such political centers as Beijing and Fuzhou. Rhetoric that condemns commerce as "parasitic" and private business as "bourgeois" signals the possibility of broad and highly restrictive measures. Rhetoric that emphasizes the need for social order and market ethics signals a rectification effort targeted at specific problems, while rhetoric glorifying the market economy and praising private entrepreneurs as new heroes indicates the state's favorable stance and the likelihood of further policies of opening (*fang*) and liberalization. Since 1979 state rhetoric has oscillated between calls for order and opening up, although the harsh condemnation of private entrepreneurs in the aftermath of the 1989 student movement led many to believe that the state would once again prohibit private business.

Central state rhetoric provides the ideological parameters for the willingness of local governments to support trade and private business activities. The scope of activities explicitly permitted by central policies, initially quite small, has been gradually expanding. Many of the more profitable activities "skirt the edge of the policy" (*zou zai zhengce de bianshang*) and are politically risky. Therefore a crucial question for business operators is not what or when to trade but whether to trade at all. The risks are gauged by the local climate, namely the willingness of local governments to tolerate often dubious activities and for public distribution and manufacturing units to participate in them. A "liberal" (*kaifang*) local officialdom authorizes activities not explicitly proscribed by central policy; a "conservative" (*baoshou*) officialdom permits only those explicitly condoned. Locals reckon the Xiamen city government to be more liberal than administrations in northern locales but less so than those in Guangdong province to the south. The Xiamen government has tolerated the hiring of more than seven employees in private firms (before this was legalized in 1988) and the resale by state trading companies of unused import-export quotas, and licenses privately owned general wholesale trading companies.[1]

"Advantageous position" refers to location regarding hierarchical state power. How one skirts the policy depends on one's connections to local officialdom. For firm operators, who, as officials or public

---

[1] Other local governments tend to prohibit such companies in order to keep control over prices in their jurisdictions. Therefore private trading firms elsewhere appear under different legal guises, such as the sales departments of private manufacturing firms or as research institutes. By contrast the Xiamen government has encouraged privately owned general trading companies in an effort to hasten the circulation of goods through the special economic zone, but does not permit foreign direct investment or control of general trading companies.

managers, are state agents, position is synonymous with bureaucratic rank. Higher-ranking agents control more significant public resources through direct positional power and links with other high-ranking agents. For operators who are citizens without bureaucratic posts, advantage inheres in their influence ties with the bureaucracy. Status therefore refers to two aspects of bureaucratic positioning. One is the level of control in terms of bureaucratic hierarchy; higher status is linked to potentially greater assets. The other is how control is exerted in the bureaucracy, either directly through power of office (*quanli*) or indirectly through influence connections (*guanxi*) with those in office.

"Harmonious relations" is the character of personal ties. Ideally, ties are embedded in the sentiments of kin and friendship, rendering them more long-term and oriented to mutual benefit. Trust in such ties can encourage transactions that would otherwise be less likely by enhancing expectations that other parties will uphold their end of the exchange. Such trust is particularistic and attaches to the identities of the exchange parties. In firms operated by state agents, trust is relational contracting among state agents who know each other (Solinger 1991).[2] For entrepreneurial operators who are not state agents, warm human relations with officials occur through an exchange mode I term "clientelist contracting." Clientelist contracting differs from relational contracting in that it involves power asymmetries between those inside and outside the state structure and has its own characteristic idioms, as discussed in Chapter 4.

## State Hierarchy and Trade Networks

Traders distinguished among four types of firms in Xiamen's wholesale trade in the late 1980s and early 1990s. Each type reflects the location of its operator in the aforementioned opportunity structure; each is constituted by networks of a certain position toward state hierarchy that constrains transactions. Two types are referred to as "public" (*gongjiade*) firms, as their operators are officials enjoying privileged access to state monopoly resources through office. They vary by degree of privilege that reflects their bureaucratic rank; state companies enjoy highest-level privileges, such as import-export authority, while local government companies have fewer privileges. Two types are viewed as private firms; their operators are not officials and do not enjoy privileged access to public resources by virtue of office. They are distinguished by whether or not their operators can influence officialdom. Private com-

[2] For similar relational contracting in Poland, see Kawalec (1992).

pany operators possess significant social ties to influence officialdom and pursue growth through clientelist contracting with a range of public administrative, manufacturing, distribution, and commercial units. Private shopkeepers have little or no influence and do business through horizontal contracting with equally positioned private firms.

### The State Foreign Trade Company

State foreign trade companies are an expansive organization of wholesale trade, driven by access to the most lucrative state monopoly – import-export authority. They are referred to in Xiamen as "nationally run" (*guojia ban de*), "centrally run" (*zhongyang ban de*), or "foreign trade" (*wai mao*) companies. Only they are legally authorized to obtain the import-export licenses for transnational trade and set up foreign exchange bank accounts to handle international transactions. In 1979 all of China's foreign trade was handled by a dozen foreign trade companies under the Ministry of Foreign Economic Relations and Trade; a decade later there were over 5,000 state foreign trade companies (Lardy 1992: 39). These companies are attached to city, provincial, and national levels of the administration, central ministries, large state enterprises, and the military. The number of such firms in Xiamen has grown rapidly, numbering 253 by 1988. State foreign trade companies can profit by exploiting the large differentials between international and domestic prices in some goods, especially for energy and mineral products (see Table 3.2).

Much trade is facilitated by the firms' high-level bureaucratic connections. Many export items are obtained via transregional networks with public producers. For example, steel, which is in demand in the booming construction industries of Southeast Asian countries, is obtained from state enterprises in North China. State companies also import products, such as vehicles and medical equipment, for public buyers located in other parts of China. The creation of such trade networks is enhanced by belonging to conglomerates attached to central ministries and provincial governments at the highest level or, more locally, to major city governments, improving information flows between market segments. The company managers also have personal ties at high levels. For example, the manager of one company set up by the Henan provincial government was the son of a deputy provincial governor, which gave him privileged access to information on the availability in Henan of scarce minerals for export. Also, the high bureaucratic rank of the companies gives them prestige that buffers them from actions by more local regulatory agencies, while the personal ties of the managers enable them to invoke high-ranking support if harassed. State companies also enjoy much prestige, which can induce cooperation from administrative agencies. For these reasons, they are also

Table 3.2. *Relative Chinese and world prices for selected products, 1984*

|  | State-fixed price as % of international price (international price = 100) |
| --- | --- |
| Agricultural products | 74.6 |
| Light and textile industry products | 79.0 |
| Energy | 24.5 |
| Building materials | 33.2 |
| Metallurgical products | 53.4 |

*Source*: Lardy (1992: 92–3).

attractive as partners for foreign and overseas Chinese businesspeople. Many groups run joint ventures with overseas Chinese, such as department stores, luxury hotels, and manufacturing concerns.

An example of a national conglomerate is the China Xinxing Corporation, run by the Logistical Department of the People's Liberation Army. By the early 1990s, it had a commercial empire of over 20,000 companies and trade offices in major coastal cities such as Xiamen, Tianjin, Shanghai, and Guangzhou and abroad in Dubai, Hong Kong, Japan, Russia, North America, and Singapore. The group's total import and export value in 1992 was U.S. $60 million (Li, Ma, and Ma 1993: 6–7). A local conglomerate is the Xinda Corporation, operated by the Xiamen city government. It has two trade firms, one specializing in vehicles and one in general trade, a computer development company, manufacturing firms for plastics, cement, and textiles, and an investment branch in Hong Kong.

### The Local Government Company

Local government trading companies are attached to government and enterprise units in the lower reaches of the state bureaucracy. Ones from rural locales are attached to rural regional, county, and township levels, while those from urban areas are affiliated with city, district, and even subdistrict organs. They are referred to as "locally run" (*difang bande*), "government-run" (*zhengfu bande*), and "bureau-run" (*bumen ban de*) companies. In the late 1980s there were several hundred such companies in Xiamen. Their rank is too low for foreign trade authority, and they seek advantage through the more circumscribed state power available to them. Much profit is derived from profiteering (*guandao*), with some companies serving exclusively as conduits for shifting the administratively priced goods controlled by the parent unit to the market economy. Others have diversified into services. Because of their lack of high-level state power and far-flung bureaucratic connections, government companies are less expansive than state companies.

There are several types of government companies that differ in operation and performance by the constraints they face in state policies and their operators' relations with their legal public owners. One type has evolved from May 7th firms, so named after the date of a speech by Mao Zedong exhorting citizens to combine productive labor with other activities. These were founded in the late 1970s and early 1980s to employ dependents of state workers (Tang and Ma, 1985: 633–49).[3] They have close links with parent units, which constrains the operators in various ways. One constraint is parent unit intervention in business decisions. For example, a leading official in one parent unit pressured one firm into taking a Hong Kong businessman who was his relative as a partner in a joint venture even though the firm's operator preferred a different partner. Another constraint is parent unit intervention in personnel decisions. At one company set up by a high school, officials from the school and the city Education Bureau sent underemployed teachers to work in the company. Two former teachers of Russian who lost their work when English replaced Russian in the school curriculum were assigned as assistant managers even though the company operator considered them unsuitable. Another constraint involves use of company assets. The cars and conference rooms of companies can be commandeered by parent unit cadres for official and personal matters. Other operators told of struggles for control of decision-making authority that ensued when the children of officials from the parent unit came to work in their firms. These offspring were often portrayed as loose canons who usurped decision-making power in the firm and used the name of the firm to conduct business for their own accounts.

Also, some operators of these firms that I interviewed complained of a lack of personal incentives. They are pressured to keep their salaries low to prevent employees in the parent unit from becoming jealous. To monitor the company finances, the accountant is often also dispatched by the parent unit. Parent units tap company profits to provide perks for officials and bonuses for employees, depleting reinvestment capital for the firm. Given these constraints, it is not surprising that many of the May 7th companies did not appear very profitable. Several managers I interviewed openly expressed their dissatisfaction and talked of quitting for private business.

[3] For an example of a subsidiary collective firm in Beijing, see Yang (1989a).

In 1984, a new state policy permitted the leasing of such unprofitable collective sector firms as May 7th companies to private operators.[4] The lessees obtained exclusive legal income and user rights to the firm for the leases' duration, usually three to five years. The policy intention was to create more entrepreneurial incentives to run the firm by giving private income rights to operators while enabling the parent units to receive income, either as a percentage of profits or as a fixed monthly leasing fee. To ensure that the leasing fee reflected the market value of company assets, regulations stipulated that leases were to be allocated through bidding.[5] My findings suggest that the bidding was almost always rigged to favor the former managers. Of twenty-three leased companies for which I have data, eighteen were leased to their former managers and five to parent unit officials or their offspring.[6] However, bid rigging is considered functional, as the former managers have the most complete information about the companies' activities and the personal ties with parent unit leaders to get low interest bank loans and other resources necessary to make the firms viable (Wank, 1999).

Leasing a company is extremely profitable; monthly leasing fees in Xiamen in 1987 and 1988 ranged from ¥1,000 to ¥3,000, typically a fraction of the company's profit potential. The operators use the public status and affiliation of the leased companies to amass as much personal gain as possible during the leasing period. Through personal ties with parent unit officials, they obtain bank loans in the name of the public company. In trade they represent themselves as a public company, enhancing legitimacy and perceptions of trustworthiness. While the lessees reap profits, the liability for debts is vague; some operators have simply declared bankruptcy after borrowing money from banks, leaving the parent public unit to pick up the debt. Other operators negotiated leases that eliminated all their business risk. For example, one lease contained three clauses voiding it if the operator became sick and unable to work, if the administrative bureau that owned the firm stopped supplying the scarce commodity it regulated, or if state policy support for leasing changed. Such clauses were broad enough to let the operator abandon the company at any moment, leaving the parent unit to shoulder out-

---

[4] The practice of leasing first began in 1982 and began to spread in 1984. See Kraus (1991: 107–14); Young (1995: 98–102); Yue [1986] 1989. In theory the operator has greater control in leasing than in contracting. My own research suggests that there is little practical difference in degree of control. The difference in Xiamen is that the subletting of commercial firms is called "leasing," while the term "contracting" refers to the subletting of manufacturing and service enterprises.

[5] Interview, Xiamen Industry and Commerce Bureau, spring 1989.

[6] Bidding appears more open for smaller retail shops and service concerns, such as restaurants, that accumulate capital less rapidly than trading firms. Although networks with the officials are still required, it is possible for individuals not employed in the parent units to obtain leases.

standing liabilities. Other lessees subcontract out less profitable assets of the leased firms to focus on the most profitable activities. One operator who leased a company for ¥3,000 contracted its three retail counters to private individuals for ¥1,000 a month each, an amount that covered the monthly leasing fee.

Another variant of the government company is the branch or representative enterprise (*neilian qiye*). These are trading companies set up in a special economic zone by a parent unit located elsewhere in order to establish a beachhead in the special economic zone. They were established beginning in the early 1980s; by the end of the decade there were approximately 500 such companies in Xiamen. Although their operators enjoy no legal private property rights, geographic distance from the parent public unit gives them leeway in business operations. They are more or less able to hire their own accountants, fill managerial positions with family members, and reinvest profits as they choose. When officials from the parent units visit Xiamen, operators entertain them lavishly, treating them to fancy restaurants, nightclubs, and high-class hotels, to ensure their cooperation in continuing lax monitoring of companies.

At branch companies I visited, operators were shifting the public resources they managed to their personal control in dubious and illegal ways. One such shifting practice is called "pocket-swapping" (*huan koudai*) and refers to dubious shifts in legal control of assets. Pocket swapping often concerns real estate as illustrated in the case of a branch company specializing in seafood. The company was founded with startup capital from a township government in a rural coastal region. Of its net profit, 30 percent goes to the township government, 7 percent to the county government, with the remaining 63 percent for reinvestment. The company has spent much of this reinvestment income on Xiamen real estate, including four condominiums costing HK$300,000 each in a luxury complex built by a Hong Kong construction company. The condominiums are registered in the name of family members. Ownership of a house or apartment in Xiamen confers a highly prized urban residency permit on the legal owner, and the operator's family now resides in Xiamen. His daughter studied accounting at a local night school and is now the company's cashier; his two sons are buyers for the company. When I asked who actually owns the condominiums, the operator laughed and said they were "public accumulation" (*gonggong jilei jin*). Yet the apartments legally belong to his family, not to the company.

Another strategy is to shift the public resources of the branch company to private operations run by the operator's societal accomplices. One practice is called "pulling over connections" (*ba guanxi laguolai*) and consists of the transfer of a branch company's trading networks to a private firm. For example, an operator lent his son money from his branch firm's public accumulation fund to set up a private company dealing in the same goods as the branch firm. The operator then began transferring branch firm clients to the son's private company. The strategy was to wait for an opportune moment to declare the branch firm bankrupt and continue to do business through the private company. A variant of this practice is to establish a specialty department within the private firm, lease it to an accomplice, and then favor the department with sweetheart deals. The advantage of this arrangement is the ease of setting it up, as the leased department can continue to use the firm's bank account for receiving payments. For example, the son of one operator subleased three trucks belonging to his father's branch company. The operator paid his son more than market price for transporting goods, thereby diverting profits that should have accrued to the branch firm into the private coffers of his son's operations in the form of the legal income accruing to the lessee.

### The Entrepreneurial Private Company

The private company is an expansive organization of commercial activity, driven in good measure by the personal ties their operators have with state agents.[7] The operators are endowed with such ties by family background or acquire them through prior life experiences in school, the army, and political campaigns, as will be discussed in Chapter 6. Many are quite well educated and have resigned from secure public jobs in state and large collective units, experiences that have also created personal ties with officials. Those who lack endowed ties when they embark on business subsequently cultivate them through proficiency in the "art of social relations" (*guanxixue*) to build influence ties into the bureaucracy. Many also have kinship ties with overseas Chinese.

By the end of the first decade of reform, there were 621 private trading companies in Xiamen. Of these, 441 were cooperatives, called "popularly run collectives" (*minban jiti*) to distinguish them from socialized collectives, which are called "officially run collectives" (*guanban jiti*).[8] These are collective sector firms started with private capital, are run by persons who are not officials, are responsible for their own profits and losses, enjoy operational autonomy from their nominal public sponsors, and have shares that are freely traded among the original

---

[7] This chapter describes these companies in broad strokes. They are more fully portrayed in Chapters 4–6.

[8] For a discussion of cooperatives nationally, see Kraus (1991: 118–21). For discussion of the collective sector that includes cooperatives, see Lockett (1988); and Tang and Ma (1985). For cooperatives in Hungary, see Rupp (1983); for the Soviet Union see Jones and Moskoff (1991).

partners.[9] The largest ones are sponsored by district-level labor service companies, established in the early 1980s to help unemployed youths find jobs; a minimum of four people with unemployment certificates were needed to establish such a firm.[10] Other cooperatives are sponsored by certain organs in the city government, most notably the Science and Technology Committee, which sponsors scientific research institutes that also trade in the goods they are ostensibly developing, such as computers, medical equipment, and plastics. Lower-level cooperatives are affiliated with street and neighborhood committees. Sponsoring units generally receive a monthly management fee, which was about ¥1,000 in the late 1980s. The growth of cooperatives was spurred by new central policies in 1984 and 1985 that permitted the establishment of urban cooperative banks, giving private businesses new sources of capital.

Although ownership is legally collective, many cooperatives that I visited were controlled by one of the original investors who had bought out the other partners. This process of capital concentration in the hands of a single partner is seen in a cooperative company that deals in construction materials. It was founded in 1984 by four partners who had been friends since childhood. Each had provided a certain form of startup capital: one, the business site, a house confiscated from his family during the Cultural Revolution and recently returned; another, several hundred yuan; another, human capital acquired by a prior career in a public construction enterprise; and another, social capital as the son of a city government official in the City Planning Commission, which develops long-range blueprints for Xiamen's infrastructure development. As profits soared, conflicts developed over the principle for allocating profit: the partner who contributed the house felt his share should be revalued to reflect skyrocketing real estate prices; the official's son felt his share should be revalued to reflect the importance of the bureaucratic connection; the partner who provided the human capital proved to have the most business acumen and sought more managerial power. The latter also wanted to reinvest profits, while the others wanted to enjoy larger dividends for personal use. Harmony among the partners deteriorated and eventually the latter partner bought out the others' shares for ¥150,000, giving him full control. Despite the partnership's breakup, the firm still red-hats as a collective.

The remaining 180 private companies are legally licensed as private

---

[9] Although regulations require that after-tax profits be divided among a public accumulation fund, a welfare fund, wages, and dividends, the partners decide on the proportions, the only stipulation being that share dividends not exceed 15% of the shares' value.

[10] They are often distinguishable by the characters for "service" (*fuwu*) in the company name, as for example in "Number 1 Car Parts Service Company" (*Diyi qiche peijian fuwu gongsi*).

firms under the 1988 Private Enterprise Interim Regulation.[11] Some were previously private petty shops that had outgrown the strictures of the Individual Business Household policy. A few were cooperatives that switched registration. Yet others were firms that started up in the late 1980s as licensed private companies. The larger firms are limited-liability firms, while the smaller ones are single (*duzi*) or joint (*hezi*) ownership. The city government initially required only ¥50,000 in registered capital to obtain a private company license. However, owing to the large number of applicants, this was raised so that those with ¥50,000 would be licensed by district-level branches of the Industry and Commerce Bureau, while those with ¥500,000 would receive licenses from the city level. City-level registration carries the advantage of authorization to use the words "company" (*gongsi*) and "Xiamen city" in the firm's name, creating an impression of public affiliation and large scale. In 1989 there were 104 such companies. The remaining 76 firms are licensed with district-level bureaus and are creatively called "business department" (*jingying bu*) by their owners to give the impression of attachment to a public enterprise, as well as "commercial emporium" (*shanghang*), the traditional term for wholesale businesses.

Much of the business strategy of private companies is to expand through bureaucratically mediated profit and protection opportunities forthcoming through personal ties with state agents. One entrepreneur said, "Your skill and ability as an entrepreneur are less important than having suitable support from the local authorities. With suitable support you can get whatever you need. If you don't have capital, then you can get capital. If you need scarce goods, then you can get scarce goods" (informant no. 27). Another entrepreneur said, "Everything depends on personal ties. If you have good ties with officialdom, everything is easy to deal with. If you do something wrong, your friends in the relevant bureau will see that the matter is forgotten. But if your ties are bad then officialdom will make trouble for you . . ." (informant no. 17).

Transnational kin networks to Taiwan, Hong Kong, and Southeast Asia also provide resources. One is substantial financial capital. Many entrepreneurs received their startup capital from overseas relatives. Another is real estate. Many overseas Chinese had their houses confiscated in the 1950s and the Cultural Revolution. As a gesture of goodwill since then, the party-state has been returning them to overseas Chinese who then often turn them over to kin still living in Xiamen. Such housing is often centrally located in the old commercial district, and entrepreneurs use it for business sites or sell it to raise financial capital. A third resource is foreign trade connections. Some entrepreneurs with relatives in busi-

---

[11] For a succinct overview of this policy see Young (1995: 102–16).

Table 3.3. *Business lines of private companies in Xiamen*

| Commerce | Manufacture | Service |
|---|---|---|
| Car parts | Food items | Restaurant |
| Clothes | Boats | Transportation |
| Seafood | Textiles | Hotel |
| Foodstuffs | Printing | Night club |
| Daily use items | Construction | Car repair |
| Electrical appliances | Lighting fixtures | Research institute |
| High-tech items | Fish processing | Game center |
| Hardware | Religious items | Interior |
| Stones | Furniture | decorating |
| Chemicals | Handicrafts | |
| Porcelain | Computer parts | |
| Stationery | Medical | |
| Building supplies | equipment | |
| Jewelry | | |
| Minerals | | |
| Electronic games | | |
| Grain | | |
| Medicine | | |
| Religious items | | |
| Handicrafts | | |
| Lights | | |

*Source*: Interviews with private entrepreneurs.

ness abroad pursue foreign trade, using their kin to help with international purchasing and sales.

Larger private companies belong to diversified business groups (*qiye jituan*). Each component firm is headed by a manager who is a kin or friend of the entrepreneur. The component firms are, in turn, overseen by a board of directors. The board director is the founding entrepreneur and members are officials, family, individuals from families with overseas business empires, and individuals with specialized knowledge such as professors of economics and finance from local universities. In my sample of 100 companies, 46 have diversified out of trade, with 20 into manufacturing, 19 into services, and 7 into both (see Table 3.3). Some diversification is vertical, called a "single dragon" (*yitiao long*), and involves central coordination by the entrepreneur. For example, a company selling cement will invest in factories to produce it and a trucking company to transport it. Diversification can also be horizontal into apparently unrelated activities. Although there is little coordination among the firms, their activities tend to be complementary. For example, trading companies run luxury restaurants so as to discreetly and inexpensively entertain officials and customers, and run hotels to provide housing to employees and out-of-town customers. Other groups have research institutions on the theory that when there is an economic slump other firms will hire the research institute to develop new products.

Another form of diversification in business groups is political: it seeks to reduce uncertainties stemming from shifts in state policies and ideology and in local government regulatory actions. It consists of various business affiliations of private companies with public enterprises and agencies. Affiliations are less under the entrepreneur's control, and profit is often divided in proportion to the original investment. Affiliations are more geographically dispersed than other firms in the business group.[12] Many entrepreneurs also profit through the public status that inheres in business affiliations by reselling the status to other private businesspeople through subcontracting and subleasing arrangements. For example, many transportation firms that are cooperatives or joint ventures with public units sponsor private taxi drivers who need a public affiliation to get a license. Some companies sponsor over a dozen drivers, collecting a monthly management fee of ¥1,000 from each. So pervasive is this practice in the larger business groups that their operators often have no idea of the actual scale of business conducted by their firm. They have little way of knowing how many contracting arrangements the managers of each component firm engage in or how many of these lessees in turn subcontract out assets.

The 100 private companies I visited ranged from small single firms to medium-sized business groups. Average annual business turnover ranged from under ¥1 million to ¥120 million; their number of employees ranged from less than a dozen to 240. Some companies had national sales networks, and 17 engaged in direct foreign trade in such products as leather, hardware, minerals, and seafood through connections with state companies. One company had even opened representative offices in San Francisco and Manila. However, these indicators of size and scale are limited to firms in the business groups that are under the direct control of the entrepreneurs. If the assets of the more diffuse affiliations and subcontracting arrangements are included, then firm size would appear much larger.

---

[12] This view of business groups in Chinese societal contexts as interfirm networks embedded in particularistic ties is widespread in the literature. See Greenhalgh (1988); Hamilton and Biggart (1988); Hamilton and Kao (1990); Numazaki (1991); and Wong (1985, 1991). In terms of economic activities this literature tends to emphasize diversification of the firms across production lines and internal diversification of the management structure (e.g., Hamilton and Kao 1990: 143–4) as ways to reduce risk and enhance smooth operations. However, the process of political diversification across the legally defined property sectors of the economy has not been documented in this literature and no doubt reflects the peculiar status of private business in a communist party-state.

### The Petty Private Shop

At the bottom of the wholesale trade are petty private firms licensed under the Individual Business Household Policy.[13] They are referred to as "shops" (*shangdian*) and "stalls" (*tanzi*). By the late 1980s, there were about 1,500 of these shops in Xiamen doing modest wholesale trade.[14] Most were owned by a single individual, although some were joint share (*hehuo*), owned by two or more families (usually relatives), and their small staff consisted almost entirely of family members. Many proprietors of shops have stigmatized social backgrounds, such as unemployed youth, black marketeer, and ex-criminal. They lack significant ties with state agents and consequently have little or no access to bureaucratically mediated profit and protection opportunities. Instead, to be profitable, these operators take advantage of geographic price differences.

The trade networks of private shops reflect their lack of influence connections with state agents: they are mostly intraregional and involve widely available consumer commodities. Such products as jeans and toys come from the private factories of Jinjiang county, about 100 kilometers away. Consumer goods such as cigarettes, cameras, and video cassette recorders are purchased from smugglers. In addition, factories in Xiamen owned by Taiwan, Hong Kong, and overseas Chinese sell consumer items such as down jackets and cosmetics to local traders. Some shop operators venture farther afield to the private factories in Zhejiang province's Wenzhou municipality, to the village and township enterprises of southern Jiangsu, and to the export-processing factories of Guangdong's Pearl River delta. These wares are then sold wholesale to Xiamen retail stores or North China wholesalers who come to Xiamen; many shops also have retail counters for sales to domestic and Taiwanese tourists.

The interactions of petty shopkeepers with officials are primarily exploitative and fleeting. Ole Bruun writes:

> alliances between entrepreneurs [petty shopkeepers] and
> officials tend to be unstable and shifting. . . . Relations tend to

---

[13] For the businesses under this policy, see Bannan (1992); Bruun (1993); Gold (1990a); Hershkovitz (1985); Shi (1993); and Yudkin (1986).

[14] In Xiamen City, as in other urban settings, household enterprise is heavily involved in trading activities. In 1988 there were 13,714 single-ownership and 1,670 joint-share household shops in Xiamen. Of these, 61 percent ($n = 8,372$) of the single-ownership and 44 percent ($n = 725$) of the joint-share shops were in trading activities. While most single-ownership establishments are small stands and petty retail stores, a number have moved into wholesale trade. The Xiamen Industry and Commerce Bureau estimated that approximately 10 percent of the single-ownership firms or 837 were involved in the wholesale trade, while most of the joint-share shops were in wholesale trade. In other words, of the 9,097 trading enterprises licensed under the Individual Business Household policy trade, about 1,572 had moved into wholesale.

> be focused on cash payments or goods given to officials, who either show an openness to such offerings or explicitly demand them in exchange for a friendly handling of the business owner's affairs. Since cooperation among different departments of the local administration tends to be minimal, a business owner can rarely count on a friendly official in one bureau to smooth relations with other bureaus. (Bruun 1995: 201)

They tend to see themselves as victims or passive (*beidong*) in interactions with officials. The character of relations between private shopkeepers and street-level officials contrasts quite sharply with those between private company operators and officials. Company operators develop relatively stable and institutionalized bureaucratic connections that enhance cooperation, while their ties with higher-level officials can reduce the problem of multiple demands from local agencies. Also, as company operators obtain goods and services from officials, the relationship is more mutually beneficial as compared with petty shopkeepers, who experience more extortive encounters.

The business strategy of the private petty shopkeepers is driven by their distrust of officialdom and fear of exposing their assets; like ethnic middlemen minorities they emphasize quick profits and concealment of wealth (Bonacich 1973). To lessen administrative harassment, they seek to reduce contact with officialdom by forging horizontal market networks with private manufacturers in rural areas and private retailers in urban areas. As Tom Gold notes, "*getihu* prefer to deal with other private enterprises ... [because] they feel less exploited" (Gold 1989: 187). The resulting loops of commodity circulation are colloquially called "societal circles" (*shehui quanzi*) and "societal circulation" (*shehui liutong*) because they seek to avoid state power.[15] To reduce officialdom's demands, shopkeepers minimize the apparent scale of their business, a strategy called "wearing a small hat" (*dai xiao maozi*). A logical extension of this strategy is a practice called "closed-door business" (*wumen jingying*), in which the proprietor shutters the storefront to appear out of business or on vacation and carries goods directly between producers and consumers. This practice is especially widespread

---

[15] There is an intriguing parallel with the period of economic liberalization in the Soviet Union during the 1920s known as the New Economic Policy (NEP). Increasing state regulations and taxes drove out the larger private firms and induced the remaining private businesses to emphasize concealment from the state by forming "closed circles" (*zamknutye krugi*). "These were networks of private manufacturers and traders that shunned any contact with state agencies or officials. More specifically, private craftsmen obtained raw materials from peasants, either directly or via private middlemen. They sold their finished products to private traders, who then retailed them to private customers" (Ball, 1987: 140).

during times of heightened political uncertainty, as in the months following the suppression of the student movement in 1989. However, a strategy that avoids officialdom precludes shopkeepers from obtaining bureaucratically mediated resources to fuel business growth, resulting in smaller capital accumulations. Not surprisingly, private shops are the least expansive type of firm in Xiamen's wholesale trade.

This strategy reflects the shopkeepers' experiences and attitudes. Those who went into business earliest, in the late 1970s and early 1980s, were often from petty business families whose assets had been socialized in the 1950s. They tended to worry that the policy might once more swing against private business, inducing them not to reinvest profits. They failed to invest in fixed assets such as real estate in the early 1980s when it was relatively cheap and now lack the economic resources to diversify and expand business. Their attitude is expressed in their oft-voiced desire to "be the boss" (*dang laoban*). In their desire for autonomy, they place a premium on exclusive private property rights over business assets. The similar "petty capitalist" mentality in nearby Taiwan, as described by Hill Gates, "holds private property sacred" and emphasizes being "absolutely free to run her business in her own way" (Gates 1996: 239). Such an orientation is inimical to the private company operators' willingness to court risk by "walking on the edge of the policy," a strategy that emphasizes ambiguous legal property rights to keep officials off guard and easier to manipulate. Thus, whereas petty private businessmen seek a clearly defined sphere of autonomy from the state, entrepreneurial company operators seek to penetrate the bureaucracy and obtain support from officials. What to the petty businessmen appears as a promise of autonomy is viewed by company operators as a commercial dead end. In the eyes of company operators, petty shopkeepers are doomed to "fall by the wayside in the face of competition" (*taotai*) because of their failure to develop supportive relations with officialdom.

The following three sketches reveal the range of private shops and their business orientations. The first concerns an operator in his early fifties from a peddler family who exemplifies the traditional petty capitalist mentality of the private shopkeepers and traditional *getihu*. During the 1950s his family operated a stall that bought produce from peasants to sell to urban residents. He spent the next two decades living on the margins of society as a trader of secondhand goods, such as bottles and pots. In 1979, he obtained one of the first Individual Business Household licenses in Xiamen and opened a small restaurant in a rented room, buying produce from the villages his family had patronized decades before. This first private restaurant in the downtown district received extensive publicity in the domestic and overseas Chinese-language media. Business boomed. He rented another room in the same building and opened the first private banquet facility in Xiamen. Every night the two tables in the banquet room were booked by Hong Kong and Taiwanese businessmen to entertain local officials. However, by the late 1980s business had declined, as the restaurant was shabby in comparison with newer ones. The operator wanted to expand his restaurant but could not afford to. He had not bought real estate in the early 1980s when it was cheap because he feared that it would be confiscated if the policy changed.

Other shopkeepers have resigned from public jobs because they see the state sector in decline and private business as better able to generate the income for an acceptable standard of living. The situation of a forty-two-year-old former assembly-line worker in a state food-processing factory is a case in point. He is descended from a family that hawked incense and hell money at temple festivals. In 1986 he came into ownership of a building on the old downtown's main street that had been returned to a Singapore relative. He said he resigned from the factory because he was bored with the job and because of his luck in receiving ownership of a prime commercial site. He now runs a private store that sells film, cameras, and computer games to tourists who stroll along the avenue. His profits exceed ¥5,000 a month. His wife, on extended sick leave from her public unit, works in the store. By maintaining her public position she assures the family of such public welfare benefits as medical insurance and a subsidized apartment. His oldest son is the purchaser because the shopkeeper is illiterate and cannot read contracts. Several Taiwanese businessmen have proposed partnerships because of the store's excellent location but he did not trust them and the discussions have led nowhere. His wife considers him naïve (*laoshi*) and lacking in social skills, the result of twenty years of interacting with machines on a factory production line. He is satisfied and his plans for the future are to "maintain the present situation" (*weichi xianzhuang*).

But some shop operators who resigned from public jobs seek to maximize profits rather than maintain an acceptable level of comfort. This is particularly true of those who have entered business in the latter part of the 1980s and are better educated. An example is a forty-year-old former purchasing agent. After graduating from junior middle school in 1967, he was sent down to the countryside as part of the "Up to the Mountains and down to the Villages" state program to rusticate urban youth.[16] Returning to Xiamen in 1978, he was assigned to be a purchasing agent in a state food factory. In 1987 he resigned when his brother in Hong Kong gave him ¥80,000 in startup capital to open a shop specializing in teapots, antique replicas, and other items sought by Taiwan tourists. The

[16] This program ran from the early 1960s until the late 1970s. See Bernstein (1977) for an overview of the program. For the experiences of the sent-down youth in the villages, see Chan, Madsen, and Unger (1992).

brother runs a Hong Kong travel agency that arranges mainland tours for Taiwanese and brings them to the store to buy souvenirs. The shop sells goods on commission from a public enterprise in Guangzhou. Recently, the operator traveled to Guangxi and Zhejiang provinces to buy directly from factories, halving procurement costs. His low prices have attracted northern entrepreneurs and he has tendered bids for concession stands in hotels catering to overseas Chinese. His stance is clearly entrepreneurial, emphasizing economic capital accumulation, network cultivation, and reinvestment of profits. He appears on the road to developing a private company.

## Patterns of Competition

Differing orientations to state power also pattern the relative competitive positions of the different firm types. The key variable is degree of access to state monopoly resources. This gives rise to several configurations of competition in market sectors. Each configuration embodies a certain institutionalized presence of state power in commercial competition in market sectors. I call these configurations *dualism, symbiosis,* and *conflict.*

In *dualism,* a market sector becomes partitioned along the lines of state monopoly. Public firms react to competition from private companies by concentrating on activities sheltered by their privileged access to state monopoly assets and licenses. The automotive trade is illustrative. Before market reform most vehicle repairs were done in-house by public units and there was only one public garage, a state sector unit under the Transportation Bureau. Until the early 1980s most repair involved mechanical work on cars made in China, Eastern Europe, and the Soviet Union. Little body work was done because there were few accidents in the light traffic and thick metal outer shells protected the vehicles. The influx of imported cars in 1984 turned this situation upside down. Imported cars, mostly Japanese sedans, vans, and trucks, required less mechanical repair but more body work because of the lighter construction of the outer shell and the rising number of accidents occasioned by increasingly crowded roads.[17] A dozen private garages emerged to meet demand. Private garages work fast, completing in a day jobs that would take weeks in the public garage.

The new private garages attracted much business by their flexible

---

[17] This also upset the status and gender order within the garage. Before market reform, mechanics, who were all men, had the highest-status jobs and the most work, while the body repairs and repainting were done by women. With the influx of Japanese cars, this order was reversed, as these imported cars had fewer mechanical problems but required more body work and repainting.

approach to customer needs. Their willingness to work round the clock drew business from moonlighting public unit drivers who, in the event of an accident, needed repairs done immediately, before their public unit superiors found out. The need for skilled body repair people who could work long hours quickly attracted men from two townships in Zhejiang province with long traditions of metalworking. These Zhejiang workers were more hardworking than the local Xiamen workers and lived in the garages, so that they were always available. The old state and the newer local government garages were unable to hire the Zhejiang workers because of resistance from their public employees, so the Zhejiang workers labored only in private garages. The local government garages were soon leased to private operators, while the state garage disengaged from the repair business and obtained import-export privilege to become a dealer of Japanese cars.[18] This increased the number of foreign cars locally, driving up demand for car parts. A number of garages expanded by setting up trading firms that dealt in imported car parts to meet this demand.

In the second configuration of competition, *symbiosis*, public and private firms control different assets in a market sector and cooperate in mutually beneficial exchanges. This can be seen in the trucking industry. Lying near the main coastal highway, Xiamen is ideally located for long-distance trucking on the north–south axis. Also, the Shantou Special Economic Zone to the south in Guangdong province lacks a railway or deepwater harbor; goods destined for Shantou are often shipped to Xiamen and then trucked to Shantou. Demand for short-haul trucking comes from the private factories in nearby Jinjiang county to haul their light manufactures to Xiamen's railroad and port for shipment. The rise of private trucking has led to earnings differentials between public and private drivers. In the late 1980s a driver for a public unit earned about ¥200 a month, while those in private firms earned over ¥1,000 a month.[19] Public enterprises found their drivers increasingly uncooperative; deliveries were late and drivers refused to move

[18] Most of the state garage's mechanics have taken leaves of absence to work for the private garages. Those unable or unwilling to retrain – older mechanics and female body repair personnel who have taken internal retirement (*neitui*) – simply stop coming to work and receive no salary, although they continue to accumulate seniority toward their retirement benefits. Most of them are now running petty shops in trade and restaurants, while some of the women have reportedly become full-time housewives.

[19] Private long-distance trucks ply the north–south commercial routes, whereas public unit drivers usually traverse east–west routes between Xiamen and the "third front" industries that were built inland in the 1950s to prevent their capture by the Nationalist Party in the event of a military invasion (Naughton 1988). Therefore, private company drivers have more opportunities for lucrative sideline smuggling. A few television sets or video cassette recorders, imported at the half-duty rate permitted in the Special Economic Zones and stashed in the corner of the truck on the northern route to the cities of Fuzhou or Wenzhou, could bring profits of several hundred yuan in the late 1980s.

their trucks to unloading docks if the dock was inconveniently located or the ground was muddy. By the late 1980s, some public units were bypassing their trucking departments altogether to contract private hauling companies.

However, public units have found ways to profit from trucking industry expansion even as their involvement in actual hauling declines. First, public unit drivers have been given unpaid leaves of absence (*tingxin liuzhi*) to work for private companies. They pay a monthly management fee to preserve their public seniority and benefits for a specified period. This gives public units some stake in the development of private business. Second, public units purchase imported heavy-duty trucks with funds allocated by the state budget or obtained in bank loans, which they then lease to private companies.[20] This further reinforces the rationale for private companies to hire public drivers: the drivers' personal ties to state enterprise trucking departments can provide entrepreneurs with useful information on the availability of trucks and help arrange favorable leasing terms.

The trucking industry illustrates how exchanges between public units and private companies create mutual benefit from the commodification of public resources. Although public units are no longer in the trucking business, they reap profits from it by "subletting" skilled drivers and imported trucks to private companies. Public units are advantaged in "producing" such resources because of state subsidies; it is the state that bears the drivers' training costs and the trucks' depreciation costs. This also shows how specific public units can profit from a public asset while the state loses out as it bears the overhead costs of training drivers, provides bank loans to import the trucks, and pays drivers' medical costs after accidents.

The third configuration of competition, *conflict*, centers on the bureaucracy's administrative procedures. Conflict occurs when a public unit is unable to find a secure monopoly niche in the face of private competition and resorts to administrative methods to quash the competition.[21] The printing business is a case in point. The influx into Xiamen of foreign manufacturers producing goods for export in the late 1980s spurred demand for high-quality color packaging that Xiamen's state printing factory could not meet. Two dozen private and foreign joint-venture color printing firms were established to meet demand. Some of the private companies were partnerships that included former employees

---

[20] Kraus (1991: 133) also reports profiteering in trucks. A truck bought at the administrative price of ¥28,300 can be resold for a ¥10,000 profit.

[21] See Young (1992: 80) for examples of this reported in the Chinese press. In one case a county marketing and supply cooperative persuaded local authorities to revoke the licenses of 900 private businesses that it blamed for its falling sales. See also Kraus (1991: 177).

of the state factory and obtained large cash infusions from overseas relatives to purchase modern printing presses. To operate this equipment they lured skilled employees from the state factory with promises of higher wages. On top of monthly wages of ¥1,000, production heads with thirty years of work experience received one-time bonuses of ¥20,000, huge sums that offset the loss of pension and retirement benefits they would have received had they stayed in public employment till the end of their careers.

The leaders of the state factory were reputedly shocked and furious because of the rapid drain of their most experienced and talented personnel, but they lacked the financial resources to match wages in the private factories. Instead they sought bureaucratic intervention to shut down the private printing companies. First, they appealed to the Industry and Commerce Bureau to revoke the licenses of the private printing factories that hired the employees of the state factories. The bureau refused to do this on the grounds that central state policies now permitted such competition.[22] The public factory leaders had a second chance to seek administrative intervention when, following the 1989 student movement, they participated in a city-government-sponsored effort to root out pornography as part of a larger national campaign against pornography and other illegal publications. The state factory leaders accused their private competitors of printing pornography and got an investigation team to search their companies. However, the charges were dropped for lack of incriminating evidence.

The above patterns of competition also illustrate the tendency for cooperation between private companies and public units along a broad front. Some cooperation is passive, as in the case of dualism, where public and private actors concentrate on different aspects of the market sector. Yet the dualism is complementary: private firms would not have a market for car parts if state firms did not import automobiles, while the concentration of private firms on car parts lets state firms focus on the more lucrative trade in foreign cars. Symbiosis consists of active cooperation in sharing overhead costs and spreading risks. Even conflictual interaction stimulates some cooperation. Private printing companies rode out the administrative attempt to crush them by invoking the support of other bureaus. It is hardly surprising that the Industry and Commerce Bureau refused to crack down on highly profitable private firms, which pay it special fees to get printing licenses. The competition in the printing

---

[22] A high-ranking cadre in the Xiamen Industry and Commerce Bureau told me he had advised the state printing factory leaders to solve their problem by raising their workers' salaries. This indicates the degree to which commercial competition is a legitimate part of economic life in Xiamen, even when private firms outcompete public ones in the competition for scarce resources.

industry also underscores the importance of bureaucratic support to protect economic capital accumulations.

The preceding discussion also indicates that the focus of the competition is access to a wide range of bureaucratically mediated resources. In a highly commercialized locale such as Xiamen, wealthy private firms can readily afford to buy privileges comparable to lower-level government firms. For this reason local government firms are losing out in the intense competition and many are simply leased or contracted to private entrepreneurs. It is the state enterprises, which enjoy certain monopoly privileges as well as interregional bureaucratic connections that are not yet readily attainable by private operators, that thrive in this commercial environment. Among entrepreneurial private businesses, there is competition to develop patrons in the bureaucracy to provide privileged access to assets, information, and legitimacy. As petty private shops are unable to develop these ties, they are largely outside this competition and trade primarily with each other. The next chapter focuses on the clientelist trade networks forged by entrepreneurial private companies.

# 4

## Symbiotic Transactions
## Between Private Firms and Public Units

Much exchange conducted by private companies is embedded in clientelist ties with various administrative, policing, distributive, and manufacturing organs of the local state. These ties are symbiotic transactions of commercial wealth for political power. On the one hand, they let private firms manage their bureaucratic dependence by obtaining access to state power that they can use to enhance profit and security. On the other hand, they enable local officialdom, as agencies and individuals, to maintain an income stream in the face of declining central budgets and economic inflation. However, the ties reflect not only the utility-maximizing interests of the exchange parties but also the patterning of the commercial environment by the state hierarchy, as described in the previous chapter. For entrepreneurs the specific resources sought depend on what type of public unit is being engaged and the stage of company growth. Furthermore, there appear to be significant regional variations in the extent of clientelist transactions that reflect differences in the overall degree of commercial activity in locales.

## The Preference for Clientelist Contracting

For entrepreneurs keen to promote their business, a patron is highly valued, while for public units, exchanges with private companies are also sought for certain reasons. To understand their desirability relative to other possible transactions, I begin with Peter Blau's classic discussion (1964: 21–2) of a situation in which a person wants something controlled by another. In such a situation there are four possible alternatives to patron–client ties: immediate reciprocity, coercion, securing the benefits elsewhere, and forgoing the benefits (see also Flap 1990: 234; Scott 1972a). The first alternative, immediate reciprocity, precludes the development of patron–client ties by restoring the balance of exchange. Such an alternative is less desirable because it weakens the open-ended obligations that inhere in patron–client ties, reducing expectations of future benefits. Also, as many of the benefits are transacted in dubious and illegal exchange relations, willingness to engage in them is heightened when the parties trust each other. Toward this end, time lags in reciprocity stimulate trust and durability in the tie by enhancing future expectations of cooperation (Mauss [1925] 1969; Sahlins 1972). Clientelist contracting expresses this desire for delayed reciprocity to heighten expectations of future cooperation.

The second alternative is coercion. A private company acting by itself cannot coerce a public unit because the relative power advantage lies with the public unit as an organ of the state. Therefore the only possibility for coercion lies in collective action by a number of private companies against potential patrons. This possibility will be explored in Chapter 8. For now suffice it to note that it is not likely to occur, and the more prosperous a private company, the less preferable this alternative becomes. For public units, coercion in which they extract resources from private companies without payment is a possibility because public units are more powerful. However, coercion is not a viable long-term strategy. It would impel private companies to conceal resources, hinder the reinvestment of economic capital, and cause the stagnation of private business. Therefore, the benefits public units gain by coercion would be reduced in the long run as private business stagnates. This is undesirable because a goal of public units is not so much maximizing short-term gain as ensuring predictable income flows over time.

The third alternative is for an entrepreneur to secure benefits elsewhere. As the benefit is controlled by a more powerful public unit and is forthcoming only in the context of a patron–client relation, securing it elsewhere necessarily entails clients' seeking other patrons. Patrons, in turn, would have to seek new clients. For both parties, this is not desirable because the benefits are particular to the relationship. The trust that accrues in a relationship cannot be transferred to another one. Therefore entrepreneurs prefer to secure benefits in an existing relation rather than seek them elsewhere.

The fourth alternative is to forgo the benefits of clientelist contracting. As the benefits are derived in exchanges between asymmetrical parties, forgoing them would likely entail contracts between parties of similar status. For a private company this would mean exchanges with other private businesses that are its legal equals. Such an alternative is the strategy of the petty private shops described in Chapter 3. But for a private company this alternative is not desirable because the benefit flow is poorer than that in a patron–client tie and cannot sustain expansion. For public units this alternative necessarily involves exchanges with other public units. Such exchanges do occur in relational contracting (Solinger 1991) that involves barter of the resources each public unit controls.

However, this often does not generate the cash that public units increasingly need in the market economy to meet such diverse needs as servicing debt, subsidizing wages, and entertaining officials in other units. Therefore public units also desire cash-producing links with private companies.

In sum, patron–client ties are more desirable than other realistically possible contracting arrangements. Exchanges between private companies and public units generate benefits for each that are unobtainable in other possible exchange relations. For entrepreneurs they provide access to crucial assets in the state structure, while for state agents and their public units they generate a cash income to cope with such reform era pressures as inflation and declines in state-allocated resources. And for both, exchange provides local-level stability in a turbulent political and economic context.

## Idioms of Patron–Client Ties

Entrepreneurs refer to state agents who provide benefits over time as "backstage bosses" (*houtai laoban*) and "backers" (*kaoshan*). Ties that provide greater backing are deemed more "efficacious" (*ling*). Efficaciousness is expressed in distinct sets of idioms, each signifying an aspect of the clientelist tie. Each set is an evaluative criterion that, by reifying an aspect of the social relations of state power, enables entrepreneurs to "hold in place" the pervasive state presence in the market economy as they forge commercial strategies.

One set of idioms signifies the benefits an entrepreneur expects to derive through a tie. "Creating opportunities" (*chuangzao jihui*) refers to profit-enhancing decisions and actions by backers. There are several kinds of such backer-created opportunities. "Supplying news" (*tigong xinxi*) refers to information on supply and demand from public units. "Writing official instructions" (*piwen*) and "affixing an official seal" (*gaizhang*) refer to privileged access to regulated and therefore scarce commodities or to administratively priced commodities at below-market cost. "Obtaining support" (*dedao zhichi*) refers to discretion in such administrative matters as licensing and taxation.

Another benefit is backers' protection and security-enhancing acts, also indicated by the idiom "gaining support." There are several kinds of such protection. "Paving a route of retreat" (*pu houlu*), "sheltering from the (political) wind" (*bifeng*), and providing a "protective parachute" (*baohusan*) all refer to information and actions forthcoming from backers that enable entrepreneurs to ride out changes in state policies and major regulatory actions such as economic rectification campaigns (*jingji yundong*).[1] "Speaking on your behalf" (*ti ni jianghua*) occurs when a backer intercedes on the side of an entrepreneur in a jurisdictional conflict or against predatory actions by local government agencies.

"Hardness" (*ying*) is an idiom of efficacy that classifies the kind of advantages linked to a backer's bureaucratic position (*quan*). Greater advantages are linked to loftier bureaucratic position and so higher-ranked patrons are said to be "harder" than lower ones. Hardness enhances a tie's efficacy in several ways. First, higher cadres provide more benefits than lower ones because they have greater discretionary control over a wider range of resources. Second, a single tie with a higher cadre confers benefits that require multiple ties with lower cadres, dramatically reducing the time and energy an entrepreneur spends in face-to-face cultivation of the social relations to obtain them. Also, whereas lower cadres can usually provide only profit or security, but rarely both, higher cadres can provide both as need be.

Closely linked to hardness is the idiom of "promoting connectivity" (*bangzhu lianluo*), which refers to the access a patron provides to other persons in the bureaucracy. "Vertical access" (*zhixiang lianxi*) refers to the connections to the superiors of a patron. In this sense higher-ranking patrons provide access to other even higher-ranking officials. "Lateral access" (*hengxiang lianxi*) refers to links to bureaucratic actors and resources that cut across formal bureaucratic hierarchies and jurisdictions. Higher-ranking patrons provide more of this resource as well. Horizontal and vertical access are efficacious because a tie with one cadre gives an entrepreneur access to the cadre's ties with other persons, reducing the probable cost to the entrepreneur of cultivating each tie from scratch.

Another set of idioms refers to the "durability" (*naiyong*) of a patron's backing. One aspect of durability is its open-endedness – the likelihood that claims for reciprocity can be deferred to deal with future uncertainties. In time of urgent need an entrepreneur may need bureaucratic support without being able to offer immediate compensation to the relevant cadre. In this regard durability can be enhanced by not seeking immediate reciprocity and the claim is "put aside" (*fangzai yibian*) or "reserved" (*liuzhe*) for future use. Another aspect is the nonspecificity of the content of future backing. This is crucial because, while entrepreneurs can anticipate the range of problems they will face, such as sudden policy changes and administrative harassment, they do not know which problem will occur when. Therefore, entrepreneurs prefer more vague commitments from backers rather than specific agreements to provide

---

[1] These campaigns are discussed at length in Chapter 8.

certain services. Yet a third aspect of durability is the spontaneity of support. As backers have privileged access to information on state policies and regulatory actions, they can know of potential problems facing an entrepreneur before he or she is aware of it. Therefore, entrepreneurs seek to encourage backers who will "think matters out for you" (*ti ni xiang banfa*) and "actively" (*zhudong*) intercede on their behalf.

## Patterns of Clientelist Transactions

### Transactions with Local Government Agencies

Relations between private companies and administrative agencies are transactions of commercial wealth for administrative services. Entrepreneurs view these exchanges not as extortion but as a kind of market transaction for security. They are up-front payments to ensure future cooperation from agencies. Extortion, entrepreneurs say, mostly characterizes the interactions between petty store proprietors and street-level officials. Petty proprietors pay to prevent these officials from harming them in the event of nonpayment, while private company operators see themselves as getting services in return for payments. Services are discretionary decisions that benefit a client in such routine administrative matters as licenses, taxation, and registration and in such regulatory matters as sanctions, campaigns, and policy restrictions.

The following examples indicate the kinds of charges that specific administrative agencies levy and the discretionary services they perform. The Tax Bureau levies various surtaxes and administrative fees and assesses fines for tax evasion and regulatory violations. These charges are numerous; of the dozens of charges assessed for private shops, only two – the income tax and the industrial and commercial tax – are imposed by the central state (Odgaard 1992). An investigation in one city found forty-three different charges levied on private shops (Kraus 1991: 157–8).[2] Officials have discretion in whether or not to levy them on specific entrepreneurs as well as in the amount. They can also arrange for

[2] The range of levies on private businesses is seen in Bruun's (1993: 260, n. 6) list of the twenty charges levied on one private restaurant in Chengdu city: industrial and commercial tax (*gong shang shui*), income tax (*suode shui*), city reconstruction charge (*cheng jian fei*), education charge (*jiaoyu fei*), city grain fund (*liangshi jijin*), provincial grain fund (*liangshi jijin*), meat fund (*roushi jijin*), management charge (*guano fei*), business administration charge (*yingye fei*), revenue stamp (*yin hua*), public order charge (*zhi an fei*), sanitation charge (*qing jie fei*), "putting in order charge" (*paiwu fei*), energy source fund (*nengyuan jijin*), "front-door-three-guarantees" (*menqian san bao*), "self-evaluation-make-up-for-evasion" tax (*zicha bubao*), clean transportation charge (*qingjie yunshu fei*), association membership fee (*hui fei*), employees' contract charge (*chengbao fei*), and excessive signpost charge (*chao biao fei*).

discretion in assessing the tax bills of specific entrepreneurs. Tax officials assume that all entrepreneurs are evading taxes and that account books have been doctored.[3] Entrepreneurs therefore need to ensure the cooperation of Tax Bureau officials in accepting their books.[4] Indeed, tax evasion is so institutionalized as standard practice that charges of this crime against an entrepreneur are viewed by other businesspeople not as an indicator of the entrepreneur's wrongdoing but as lack of influence with the Tax Bureau to forestall the charge. The Tax Bureau can also warn entrepreneurs of impending actions against them, enabling them to forge a route of retreat. For example, the operator of a well-known private company was tipped off of his impending arrest for tax evasion, giving him time to flee to Bolivia. In another case, an entrepreneur was alerted that his stock would be impounded in lieu of back taxes, giving him time to hide valuable merchandise.

Public Security Bureau substations (*gongan paichusuo*) charge public order fees (*zhi an fei*) and solicit contributions for their retirement pension funds and other activities. In return, substations provide profit-enhancing discretionary services. One service concerns the temporary residency permits (*linshi hukou*) instituted in the early 1980s, which permitted rural migrants to work in urban areas. According to regulations, a private entrepreneur should obtain a permit for each nonlocal worker hired. However, in order to minimize the apparent scale of their business for tax purposes and to avoid the cumbersome paperwork of hiring and firing, some entrepreneurs prefer not to register nonlocal workers. Other entrepreneurs seek to overregister their workers in order to launder money; funds are withdrawn from the bank as wages for ghost workers and then used for other purposes.

The Customs Bureau provides both security and profit-enhancing services. Security is provided through discretionary information on policy changes. For example, one entrepreneur purchased a large quantity of beer in another province where, because of lower taxes, it was cheaper than in Fujian province. After he loaded it on a boat to Xiamen, the Fujian provincial government, in an effort to protect its "domestic" brewers, issued an edict prohibiting the shipment into the province of beer produced in other provinces. A backer in the bureau warned the entrepreneur that his shipment would be impounded when unloaded in Xiamen's harbor. So forewarned, the entrepreneur unloaded the beer secretly in a nearby fishing village. The Customs Bureau also provides profit opportunities by reselling at low prices goods it has confiscated

---

[3] Interview, Tax Bureau, spring 1989.
[4] One book is for tax purposes and one book for the entrepreneur's personal use, the latter being accurate. In the case of partnerships and business affiliations, a third book, also inaccurate, is kept to show partners.

from smugglers. As part of the practice called "insider discounting" (*neibu chuli*), invitations to buy are extended to entrepreneurs known to the bureau. Favored entrepreneurs can obtain brand-new home appliances and high-quality clothing at up to 40 percent below market prices.

The Industry and Commerce Bureau charges sundry fees, such as licensing fees, annual renewal fees, and management fees. In exchange it provides significant profit- and security-enhancing opportunities. Its officials are the ones who determine a firm's business scope – the categories of goods that it can legally trade as specified on its private business license. Bureau officials can also grandfather the licenses of companies trading in a good that central policies suddenly ban for private trade. For example, in 1988 the state precipitously forbade private trade in sheet glass because of rapid price increases in this commodity and directed local Industry and Commerce Bureau offices to strike it from the licenses of private companies authorized to trade it. However, several entrepreneurs, through the intervention of local bureau officials, kept their legal authorization to trade glass. The Industry and Commerce Bureau can also grant exemptions from restrictions. For example, prior to the 1988 policy legalizing private companies, private businesses could not issue receipts with a value over ¥100, effectively limiting the capacity of private firms to do business with public units. When this restriction threatened to be a bottleneck in the development of local market sectors, a limited number of exemptions were granted to entrepreneurs. Cement is a case in point. Although much demanded by public construction firms, cement could not be sold to them by private shops, which had many sources of supply. The shortage of cement was a drag on the local construction boom. So the Industry and Commerce Bureau, in cooperation with the Tax Bureau, authorized a limited number of private shops to issue large invoices for cement sales. My interviews suggest that the handful of entrepreneurs who received this lucrative dispensation were individuals who had "warm human relations" with bureau officials.

Interactions with residents' (*jumin*) and street (*jiedao*) committees are largely nonspecific exchanges. Although these committees wield no direct regulatory authority in the market economy, entrepreneurs told me that, as the most local urban organ of the state, relations with them are important. As one entrepreneur explained, "the old ladies on the street committee are really fierce. You cannot take them lightly. They are all tongues and lips when it comes to gossip. They are therefore very important for how people think of me" (informant no. 19). During administrative campaigns, the implementing agencies seek local information from committee officers on the private businesses in their jurisdictions. Entrepreneurs strive to ensure that committee officers put in a good word for them. Toward this end they actively "donate" goods and cash to committees. One entrepreneur gives small sums of money to his street committee toward refreshments at their meetings. Another donated glass to his committee after its office windows were shattered in a storm. Entrepreneurs also buy up the quotas of national bonds that street committees are required to sell, relieving their officers of the onerous task of pressuring neighbors to buy them.

Finally, relations with public banks are also crucial. Banks can be considered administrative agencies, because they are charged with disbursing subsidies to state enterprises under the guise of loans. In general, it is difficult for private companies to obtain bank loans, but with the proper public sponsor and the cooperation of bank officials, this can be arranged. Also, banks administer some state policies to control the money supply. One is a measure to check inflation that involves sudden restrictions on the amount of money that can be removed from bank accounts in order to limit the volume of money in circulation. These measures are announced suddenly, but "warm human relations" with bank officials enable entrepreneurs to get wind of these measures before they are instituted and, in some cases, to bypass them after they are in force.

### Domestic Trade

For various reasons private companies and public units that control economic resources seek to trade with each other. For private companies the reasons are so compelling that entrepreneurs have little motivation to trade with other private companies. As one entrepreneur said, "If you do business only within the private sector you will never be more than the proprietor of a small shop" (informant no. 69). One reason is that public units tend to place the largest orders for the most lucrative commodities. This is partly due to the large purchasing power of public units because of their easy access to bank loans and their large size, and partly due to their demand for goods with higher profit margins. Public units demand construction materials, chemicals, and other producer goods with higher profit margins than consumer items, which are relatively unrestricted and therefore less profitable. Also, joint-venture deluxe hotels formed by state public units and foreign capital demand luxury goods, such as high-priced fresh fish and expensive porcelain handicrafts, for their foreign and overseas Chinese customers.

Clientelist contracting also generates trust, which lowers the costs of business transactions. For private companies, trade with public units is more likely to emphasize a long-term relationship than trade with private companies because private companies, driven by hard budget constraints, seek spot contracts for the lowest price at a given moment. By contrast, public units have softer budget constraints and are less sensitive to minor price variations. Therefore, public units can be steady customers. One private company became a supplier of a variety of home appliances to a newly constructed oil exploration enterprise under the direct control of a central ministry. This was a very profitable contract, as the enterprise was willing to pay premium prices in return for quick delivery. Also, after the establishment of trust in the relationship, some public units give goods to private companies to sell on consignment (*dai xiao*), relieving the burden for private companies of tying up financial capital in unsold stocks of merchandise.

Clientelist contracting is also desirable because it deepens cooperation between private company and public units to more diverse areas. One form of cooperation is that a private company can become a steady conduit for shifting the administratively priced goods of a public unit to the market economy. For example, a private company sold imported car parts to a large state industrial enterprise in the northern city of Shenyang. In return, the public enterprise sold the private company scarce products that it manufactured, such as cable, much in demand in South China's booming construction industry. Another private company began by selling hardware to a local forestry bureau in western Fujian province, leading to cooperation in the marketing of lumber, a scarce and highly restricted product. The forestry bureau classified almost new lumber as secondhand lumber, thereby evading restrictions on marketing lumber to sell to the private company.

Another form of cooperation occurs when a public unit shelters a private company from a regulatory action. In the wake of the 1989 student movement, the operator of a private cement trading company was concerned that new state regulations would prohibit private trade in cement. A rural township cement factory with which he had an exclusive marketing agreement for Xiamen allowed the entrepreneur to contract out the factory's trucking fleet to deliver the cement and offered the factory's bank account to receive payments. This tactic, by masking the private trade as public, shielded the private company from new possible restrictions on private business. Local state agents also provide valuable insider information on upcoming regulatory campaigns that they learn of in classified documents and bureau meetings.

For public units too, exchange is beneficial. Private companies are eager customers for the administratively priced resources that public units control, creating a cash return on the state authority vested in them. Also, trade enables public units to enhance earnings through tax evasion. According to regulations, all market transactions involving a public unit should take place through state banks in the form of direct account transfers or bank drafts. This legal arrangement is intended to facilitate central state monitoring and taxation of market transactions. While intra–public unit trade can circumvent this regulation by barter exchanges, this exchange does not generate cash, as noted earlier. Trade with private companies can more easily evade monitoring, shifting the transaction outside of the banking system and generating off-the-book income for the public unit. Such income forms a slush fund called the "small treasury" (*xiao jinku*), used to provide officials with office perks and employees with bonuses, as well as to bribe officials in other units to ensure cooperation in obtaining bank loans and other matters.

Trade also enables public units to cope with insecurities in procurement since administrative allocation of materials to fulfill plan quotas is only a fraction of necessary requirements. For example, in the mid-1980s, the allocation of the coal, wood, steel, and cement to fulfill planned production reached only 50 percent, 30.7 percent, 56.9 percent, and 19.4 percent, respectively, of the needed amounts (Kraus 1991: 132). Such reduction in allocation reflects the efforts of the central state to subject state enterprises to hard budget constraints by encouraging them to seek productive inputs in the market economy (Naughton 1995). Private companies help to procure these resources for the public units in the market economy.

### Foreign Trade

Foreign trade can be very profitable. However, only state companies have legal import and export authority. Yet private companies do participate in foreign trade, and state foreign trade companies encourage them to do so. One type of participation is a less profitable indirect trade in which private companies serve as domestic subcontractors for state companies. A state company receives an order (*dingdan*) from a foreign company and contracts with a private company to procure the ordered good. In this trade configuration, it is the state company that profits from the large differences between international and domestic prices, while the private company profits from smaller domestic differences. The export goods are usually labor-intensive products of rural private and collective manufacturers, such as dried mushrooms, tea, handicrafts, religious paraphernalia, seafood, and textiles.

For several reasons, private companies find openings in indirect foreign trade. One is that rural manufacturers find it cumbersome to sell to state companies because of requirements that transactions with state units must be via bank transfers. Many rural manufacturers do not have bank accounts, either because they are too small to have them or because they prefer cash transactions in order to evade taxes. This creates a middle-man niche for private companies. A second reason is that entrepreneurs have better personal networks in rural areas than do many state company buyers. Many buyers I met were younger men from urban backgrounds, often with college degrees in enterprise management, international finance, and economics. Many are not from southern Fujian province and do not speak Minnan dialect. By contrast, entrepreneurs have close ties with the southern Fujian hinterland and are native dialect speakers. Those from the lower social strata are only a generation or two removed from villages, while many from urban backgrounds lived in rural areas during the campaign that sent urban high school graduates to live in rural areas in the 1960s and 1970s. Therefore, entrepreneurs often have better information about rural product sources than state company buyers.

In another type of participation, private companies trade directly with foreign businesses. This is more profitable than indirect trade as the private company captures the profit generated by larger differences between domestic and foreign prices. Some exports are administratively restricted raw materials, such as coal, chemicals, and manufactures such as steel and glass. Other trade is in producer goods for which there is great demand abroad, such as hardware and light machinery. Many of these goods are sold by private companies through transnational ties with kin who operate trading companies in Hong Kong and elsewhere. Imports are manufactured products, such as car parts, home appliances, computers, medical equipment, boat engines, and power tools.

For state foreign trade companies the key benefit in sponsoring private companies' direct trade is reduced exposure to fluctuations in supply and demand, creating a more stable income flow. State companies are authorized by the Foreign Trade Bureau to import or to export specific goods. In exchange they hand over quotas of foreign currency earnings to the bureau. The risk is that a quota reflects the market value of goods when the authorization was issued rather than future earnings when the goods are actually sold. While the foreign currency quota is fixed, actual earnings fluctuate according to supply and demand. As a hedge against lower earnings, state companies obtain foreign currency in commissions generated by sponsoring private company trade with foreign businesses. Commissions are based on the value of the transaction, ranging from about 1 percent in the highly competitive seafood trade to higher rates for exports of highly restricted raw materials. This sale of foreign trade authorization buffers state companies from supply-and-demand fluctuations. Profitability of an export item can rapidly decline as competition by state companies to fill international demand pushes up domestic price while the resulting international supply glut simultaneously depresses the international price. For example, in the early 1980s the price difference between local and international prices of some seafood was about 1 : 10, but by the late 1980s some fish were actually more expensive locally because of domestic shortages created by the massive export of seafood to Hong Kong, Japan, and elsewhere. A similar process occurs with imports: rising domestic demand generates a flood of imports that pushes the domestic price down. In other words, by treating foreign trade authorization as a commodity, state foreign trade companies can spread their risk by selling authorization to private companies.

The personnel situation in state foreign trade companies also encourages the direct participation of entrepreneurs in foreign trade. Through interviews with the staff of the business departments of these companies, I found that the companies' quotas of foreign exchange are divided among individual staff members as personal quotas. They can contract to obtain specific amounts of foreign exchange and receive bonuses for going over the quota. Thus there is competition among the personnel to obtain foreign exchange, and reliance on private entrepreneurs is one recourse.

### Business Affiliations

Cooperation between private companies and local bureaucracies can lead to business affiliations. These are legally constituted firms created through partnerships between private companies and specific public units or agencies. Such partnerships are viewed favorably by entrepreneurs; the colloquial term for them, "wearing a red hat" (*dai hong maozi*), reflects their favorable status in a communist social order. Private companies gain from affiliations as they are legally licensed as public enterprises, conferring such public sector advantages as tax holidays, easier access to bank loans, less bureaucratic harassment, and fewer restrictions on trade. Business affiliations serve public units well too. They generate income in the form of the flat fees or percentage of profit that entrepreneurs pay to use the often underutilized or idle assets of the public units such as real estate and machinery. Affiliations provide employment opportunities for public unit members. They also institutionalize the market connections of specific entrepreneurs in the public unit. This helps public units, particularly the lowest-level ones, compensate for their relative lack of connections, a lack due to the fact that officials with connections often resign to go into private business rather than use their connections on behalf of their public units.

There are several types of affiliated firms. One is the cooperative. The urban variant of this type, discussed in Chapter 3, can be sponsored by a range of public units. Larger cooperatives are sponsored by urban district governments and smaller ones by lower levels. They are usually in trade rather manufacture, receive few benefits from sponsoring public units other than public status, and operate independently. The rural variant of the cooperative is the township and village enterprise (*xiangzhen qiye*). These are usually manufacturing firms set up in a partnership with rural village and township governments. The rural government provides the business site, while the entrepreneur provides the startup capital and sales outlets. Such affiliations can be a boon for rural officials: by giving them managerial positions, the officials obtain prestige in the market economy as well as an income and new sources of patronage in the local allocation of jobs and profits. Workers are initially recruited locally, but increasingly come from more distant rural areas as village living standards rise and the work becomes less desirable to locals.[5] In the Xiamen suburbs some lucrative affiliated businesses are small shopping centers on the land controlled by villages and towns along major highways. Entrepreneurs provide the money, while the villages provide the land. Shops are constructed and then rented out as restaurants, inns, and stores. Many firms in the textile trade establish village and township factories in the adjacent counties to produce clothing items.

Another type of affiliation business is the jointly managed (*lianying*) firm. Entrepreneurs provide a share of startup capital, management expertise, and market connections, while the public unit provides the business site and public status. Profits are shared according to the amount of economic capital provided. An urban joint venture entails close cooperation between the entrepreneur and the public unit. They use sites controlled by the public unit, actively draw on the public units' bureaucratic connections, and hire public employees. Such cooperation can be seen in the aforementioned clothing boutique, a joint venture between a state department store in Shanghai and a Xiamen entrepreneur. The department store provided floor space in the store, while the entrepreneur provided the clothes, many of which were produced in his private textile factories. Close cooperation can also be seen in the protection provided by a public unit in a joint-venture automobile parts store established by a Xiamen-based entrepreneur and a state enterprise in Shenyang city, Liaoning province. Initially, the Tax Bureau wanted to tax the firm as a private company, but the state enterprise "spoke on behalf" of the joint-venture store to prevent this.

Leasing is a third form of affiliation. In Xiamen, it usually concerns commercial and service businesses such as hotels and restaurants. A number of public units in Xiamen established large restaurants and hotels in the mid-1980s that proved unprofitable. They were leased to entrepreneurs who turned them into successful enterprises. An example is a small luxury hotel built by the Harbor Management Bureau and Real Estate Corporation in 1987. It was a financial failure, largely because its

---

[5] In southern Fujian province many workers in rural industries are from Siquan province and, to a lesser extent, from poorer areas in Fujian such as Huian county and the western mountain region.

employees were the children of officials in the two bureaus and did little work. The public units leased it to an entrepreneur who fired those employees unwilling to accept his new work discipline and created a profitable hotel catering to Taiwanese and Hong Kong businessmen on long-term stays.

## Measuring Gains from Transactions

Data on annual sales turnover at the time of the fieldwork for private companies indicate how beneficial the kinds of exchanges described above are for private companies. Companies that are more prosperous – as suggested by higher sales turnover – engage in clientelist contracting to a greater extent than less prosperous companies. This can be seen in Tables 4.1–4.3, in each of which I divide the companies into three categories in terms of relative prosperity. One category consists of the twenty-four most prosperous companies, with annual sales turnovers of over ¥6,000,000 at the time of the fieldwork. The second category contains twenty-three moderately prosperous companies, with sales turnovers of from ¥2,040,000 to ¥6,000,000. A third category comprises the least prosperous twenty-two companies, with the smallest sales turnovers of less than ¥2,040,000. The tables clearly demonstrate a positive correlation between prosperity on the one hand and propensity for clientelist contracting in the areas of domestic trade, foreign trade, and business affiliations on the other hand. The sample for this purpose consists of sixty-nine firms for which my data on sales volume are accurate, drawn from the larger sample of one hundred firms. A discussion of the accuracy of these data can be found in Appendix B.

The positive correlation between prosperity and clientelist contracting can be seen in the trade relations of private companies (see Table 4.1). During interviews I asked entrepreneurs what type of units and enterprises constituted the bulk of their domestic sales. I further pressed them on the issue of whether these enterprises were formally public or private. Some entrepreneurs answered with specific percentages, while others responded with more vague statements such as "mostly public" or "a mixture of both." Even though the answers were of varying precision, when considered together they indicate the link between prosperity and clientelist contracting. More of the most prosperous companies conduct the bulk of their trade with public units: 71 percent ($n = 17$) of the most prosperous companies trade mostly with public units, compared with 39 percent ($n = 9$) and 18 percent ($n = 4$) of the moderately and least prosperous companies, respectively. Furthermore, the most prosperous companies are more heavily involved in trading such bureaucratically

Table 4.1. *Predominant trading partners of private companies, by sales turnover of companies*

| Sales turnover (1988 or 1989) | No. of firms | Predominant trading partners | | |
| --- | --- | --- | --- | --- |
| | | Mostly private units | Private & public units | Mostly public units |
| Over ¥6,000,000 | 24 | 0 | 7 | 17 |
| ¥2,040,000–¥6,000,000 | 23 | 6 | 8 | 9 |
| Under ¥2,040,000 | 22 | 12 | 6 | 4 |
| Total | 69 | 18 | 21 | 30 |

brokered producer goods as chemicals and construction materials, whereas the least prosperous firms trade in more readily available consumer goods, such as home appliances and foodstuffs.

Private company prosperity also positively corresponds to propensity to form business affiliations with public agencies and enterprises (see Table 4.2). All of the most prosperous firms have affiliations, as compared with 78 percent ($n = 18$) and 46 percent ($n = 10$) of the moderately and least prosperous companies. This trend is slightly more pronounced in regard to multiple affiliations. Fully 83 percent ($n = 20$) of the most prosperous companies have multiple affiliations, as compared with 44 percent ($n = 10$) of the moderately prosperous firms and 23 percent ($n = 5$) of the least prosperous firms. There are further variations not indicated in the data. One is that the affiliations of the most prosperous companies are with higher-ranking state sector enterprises and department stores, city governments, and army units, while the other companies affiliate with lower-ranking collective enterprises and district and subdistrict agencies in urban areas, and village and township governments in rural areas. Another variation is that the affiliations of the most prosperous companies tend to be interregional, with some located in such key urban areas as Shanghai and Beijing. By contrast the other companies tend toward intraregional affiliations limited to southern Fujian province or even to Xiamen itself.

Participation in direct foreign trade is also positively linked to prosperity (see Table 4.3). A greater proportion of the most prosperous companies participate in it than is the case for the other companies: 42 percent ($n = 10$) of the most prosperous companies have direct foreign trade sales as compared with 31 percent ($n = 7$) of the moderately prosperous companies and 5 percent ($n = 1$) of the least prosperous companies. Furthermore, the more prosperous companies handle administratively

Table 4.2. *Private companies' affiliations with public units, by sales turnover of companies*

| Sales turnover (1988 or 1989) | No. of firms | Companies without affiliations | Companies with one affiliation | Companies with multiple affiliations |
|---|---|---|---|---|
| Over ¥6,000,000 | 24 | 0 | 4 | 20 |
| ¥2,040,000–¥6,000,000 | 23 | 5 | 8 | 10 |
| Under ¥2,040,000 | 22 | 12 | 5 | 5 |
| Total | 69 | 17 | 17 | 35 |

Table 4.3. *Participation in direct foreign trade, by sales turnover of companies*

| Sales turnover (1988 or 1989) | No. of companies | Companies in direct foreign trade |
|---|---|---|
| Over ¥6,000,000 | 24 | 10 |
| ¥2,040,000–¥6,000,000 | 23 | 7 |
| Under ¥2,040,000 | 22 | 1 |
| Total | 69 | 18 |

restricted and therefore more profitable export commodities such as minerals, raw materials, and chemicals and more sophisticated import goods, such as computers, technologically advanced medical equipment, and power tools. In contrast, less prosperous firms export less lucrative seafood, native products, hardware, and textiles and import home appliances and textiles.

# Evolutionary and Regional Variations

## Evolutionary Variations

Clientelist transacting arrangements change with the growth of private firms. A private company can develop up to a point with a certain portfolio of exchange relations, but further expansion is more forthcoming in a new portfolio mix. The process is an evolutionary steplike sequence; the attainment of a certain threshold of economic capital accumulation generates a shift in a private company's emphasis on patron–client ties to facilitate further growth.

An examination of the development histories of the private companies in my sample suggests three stages in the evolution of clientelist contracting arrangements.[6] The first, seen in the least prosperous companies, occurs when a company shifts away from the extortive interaction of petty shops to forging networks that provide some profit opportunities as well. This is a crucial shift; resources are no longer expended only to prevent state agents from inflicting harm but also to ensure that they provide profit opportunities. Support also becomes more active and officials will also protect an entrepreneur from harassment by other officials. Furthermore, contracts no longer involve administrative cadres exclusively; they increasingly include state agents in lower-level public distributive and manufacturing organs.

In this first stage private companies still maintain many horizontal links with other private companies in regard to sourcing of commodities. Entrepreneurs in these firms have little economic capital; if they receive a large order, they count on being able to borrow some stock from other companies in their line of business to fill it. Such cooperation is encouraged by the trade structure of specific commodities. The commodities dealt in by these companies are generally not administratively restricted and are therefore widely available. An entrepreneur who fails to lend his stock to another businessperson is unlikely to gain a new customer, but will definitely be spurned by the other businessperson when he himself needs stock, and risks soiling his reputation in the local business community at large. One entrepreneur in the car parts trade commented that he moved into this line without any stock in parts. He said that "the other companies in Xiamen were all my warehouse" (informant no. 4). He would find a buyer, go around to visit different firms until he had borrowed enough parts to fill the order, and pay back the friends from the sale's proceeds.

A second stage is reflected in the sample's moderately prosperous companies. It consists of forging networks with higher-level state agents. This enhances wealth accumulation by solving the efficacy problem of the previous stage. In the previous stage each network is relatively monobeneficial by the criterion of hardness. Lower-level officials control only limited resources under their immediate authority. They rarely provide multiple profit opportunities and cannot provide both profit and security. Significant bureaucratic support can be acquired only by amassing numerous patronage links, each providing one or two benefits. Yet as the cultivation of a network requires investments of time and money, the danger is that the drive to amass support expends more capital than derived. The likelihood of depleting means before attaining ends can be

---

[6] See the Tysons' (1995: 39–62) account of the Guoxi Group for a case study that illustrates the process of firm development that I describe.

lessened by ties with higher-level agents. As higher-level cadres control more resources, a single network provides more benefits, reducing the relative means that an entrepreneur must expend to get them.

In this second stage, the private business shifts to trade in more restricted producer commodities and often has a limited range of public sources and customers. At this stage some private companies become so thoroughly embedded in clientelist contracting arrangements that they practically lose their organizational discreteness. An example is the afore-mentioned private company trading in cement whose operator got protection from a new state restriction on private cement trade by contracting out the public factory's trucking department, making deliver-ies in its trucks and receiving payments through the factory's bank account. This "wind shelter" (*bifeng chu*) from the upcoming campaign obscured the trade's private character by concealing profit and protection within the organization of the public unit. The private company became, in effect, a division of the public unit.

The third stage, seen in the sample's most prosperous private compa-nies, is acquiring support from even higher-level officials, enhancing not only hardness but also connectivity across bureaucratic jurisdictions and geographic regions. This shift overcomes the limits on wealth accumula-tion in intraregional orientation and the most prosperous firms trade interregionally. The trade in construction materials illustrates this. The cement firm just mentioned acquired its goods in Xiamen's hinterland for sale in Xiamen, creating a moderate profit. However, the most prosper-ous companies engage in interregional trade in construction materials. Cement acquired domestically is exported to Hong Kong and Southeast Asia, while steel obtained from northern factories is sold in South China.

The most prosperous companies expand along clientelist networks as well as other contracting arrangements, especially with overseas Chinese and foreign businesses. One the one hand, profits accumulated by clientelist networks may be invested in activities that require little bureaucratic brokerage. For example, the aforementioned entrepreneur who obtained the lease on a luxury hotel and a bank loan to refurbish it through officials' support used the resulting profits to venture into the catering and interior decorating businesses, areas that require much less backing. On the other hand, accumulation in horizontal networks may stimulate investment in officially brokered activities. For example, I found that many private companies used infusions of financial capital from overseas sources for bureaucratically brokered activities. Some of these activities were merely the amplification of existing clientelist con-tracting efforts. For example, one entrepreneur in the computer business solicited financial capital from abroad to intensify his sales efforts among the state's educational and research organizations. In other cases the infusion stimulated new efforts to forge clientelist contracts. An instance of this is seen in the activities of an entrepreneur who ran a trucking firm that initially transported the goods produced by rural private factories in the Minnan region to urban markets. After he received cash from an overseas relative, the entrepreneur persuaded a cousin who was working as a reporter for a chemical industry publication to resign and take a job in the trucking firm. Thereupon the entrepreneur expanded his truck fleet to transport chemicals obtained from state enterprises and distribution agencies through his cousin's bureaucratic connections to the state enterprises and foreign-owned export-processing factories that bought them.

The exchange portfolios of the most prosperous companies have several additional tendencies. First, they have few mutual aid links with other private companies of the sort often found in the first stage and least prosperous companies. This is because they tend to trade administratively restricted producer commodities and, as supplies are scarcer, they are unwilling to share them with competitors while customers are relatively easier to find; this is quite the opposite from the first-stage firms. Second, their complex contracting arrangements are embodied in sprawling business groups with different firms embedded in different networks. For example, an entrepreneur began his business career by leasing out two collective sector restaurants in the mid-1980s and investing the profits in two private ones. He then leased a hotel from city government bureaus and developed several private companies to support this operation, such as a private taxi company and an interior decorating company, and has entered into partnerships with Taiwanese companies to develop new hotels. In this enterprise the variety of contracting arrangements consists of networks with various kinds of officialdom, Taiwanese businessmen, and private subcontractors.

The sequence of these stages is visible in the development of the largest private company operating in Xiamen in the late 1980s. It began in 1979 as a private grocery stall owned by Chen Youfu, a former unemployed youth who worked sporadically as a stevedore on the Xiamen docks. Chen assumed a leadership position in the Self-Employed Laborers Association (*Geti Laodongzhe Xiehui*), in which membership is compulsory for petty shop owners. In this position he developed ties with the subdistrict-level officials of the Xiamen Industry and Commerce Bureau who managed the association. In 1984 these street-level officials recommended him to district officials for authorization to operate a cooperative trading company that quickly came to specialize in car parts. Chen's district-level supporters then arranged large loans from state banks so that he could buy the controlling share in a new savings and loan cooperative founded in 1985. Using a large loan from this cooperative, he held a national sales convention in Xiamen. He created goodwill by hosting public unit purchasing agents in local hotels and landed orders from all over China by liberal use of kickbacks. His firm's explosive growth caught the eye of city-level officials, who helped engineer his election as a national model youth entrepreneur. During the subsequent awards ceremony in Beijing he met state factory chiefs from China's industrial Northeast, who sold him steel cable and other scarce products that he resold for large profits in Fujian and Guangdong. This brief history of Chen's firm shows how the benefits derived from the activities at one stage of growth can generate the wealth necessary to acquire more efficacious support of state agents that drives further business expansion.

*The Variable Demand for State Power.*    Some evolutionary aspects of patron–client ties in the emerging market economy can be gleaned from the preceding discussion. First, private entrepreneurs demand different kinds of goods and services from different organs in the state bureaucracy. From administrative and policing agencies, entrepreneurs largely seek security-enhancing services in the form of information on impending policy changes and regulatory actions. Administrative agencies can also provide profit-enhancing opportunities by granting particularistic privileges that are largely dispensations from existing regulations. From manufacturing and distributive organs, entrepreneurs largely seek profit enhancement opportunities in the form of access to scarce goods and sales outlets. However, such organs can also provide protection to private companies that they do business with by forging partnerships and creating "wind shelters" to disguise trade with private firms during more severe campaigns.

Second, the demand for bureaucratic backing in regard to profit opportunities is of different intensity than for security services. In regard to profit opportunities, the utility of patron–client ties is for a limited duration. One reason is the shrinking of direct state monopoly over goods as the number of administratively priced goods in the two-tier pricing structure declines. Thus the range of scarce goods that officials can provide access to declines accordingly. Another reason is that patrons can help entrepreneurs to get their foot in the door by providing introductions or initial purchase orders, but subsequent trade depends on the quality of goods and services provided by the entrepreneur. Except in the case of businesspeople with access to the highest patrons – the 4,000 or so entrepreneurial offspring of the state elite, the so-called princes' party (*taizi dang*)[7] – one cannot continue to rely solely on bureaucratic connections for commercial profit. In other words, for more local entrepreneurs such as in Xiamen, a patron can provide an initial commercial advantage, but having bureaucratic backers does not in itself guarantee profitability over time. To ensure continuous growth, entrepreneurs must

---

[7] See Pin and Xin (1992) for this group.

also provide good-quality goods and services at reasonable prices. This is illustrated by the development of a firm that started in 1984 as a car body repair shop. At the time there were few privately owned vehicles in Xiamen, and the low status of private business hindered the shop from getting business from public units. To surmount this, one of the company's partners asked his father, who was the second-ranking official in a city bureau, to send bureau vehicles to the shop for repair and to persuade colleagues in other bureaus to do likewise. The bureaus were very satisfied with the service on their first orders, because the private shop worked around the clock to complete jobs in two or three days that took the state garage a month to finish, and the bureaus gave further business to the firm. While bureaucratic backing generated the initial business, subsequent orders depended on the quality of service.

The provision of protection and security services over time remains crucial to the development of a private company. Policy changes, regulatory actions, and bureaucratic harassment are ongoing. A backer at a certain bureaucratic level can provide ongoing support in these matters. Furthermore, even as the scope of bureaucratically mediated profit-seeking activity declines as a proportion of a private company's activities, the need for bureaucratic backing in protecting the expanding scale of capital accumulation increases. Indeed, in such a commercially dynamic locale as Xiamen, the quest for bureaucratic backing increasingly shifts from profit-seeking to security-enhancing services. In Xiamen there are numerous profit opportunities involving foreign and overseas Chinese and the thriving domestic nonstate sector that increasingly do not need bureaucratic backing for access. However, the economic capital accumulated by nonofficially brokered opportunities needs officials' security just as much as capital obtained in patron–client ties. This results in a somewhat paradoxical situation. It is the operators of Xiamen's largest private firms who most vociferously insist that business acumen and not political connections is the key to business success, while those running lesser firms are more likely to claim that everything depends on officials' backing. Yet these larger-firm operators are busy packing their boards of directors with bureau heads and politically connected individuals and hiring Communist Party members for visible managerial positions, while the lesser firms are likely to number only friends and kin among the partners and managers. This difference illustrates the shifting character of bureaucratic backing sought at different levels of capital accumulation in private companies.

## Variations in the National Economy

The clientelist market transactions described in this chapter are proliferating in a locale widely seen as the forefront of the emerging market economy. This is puzzling in light of claims within the market transition and the political economy accounts that patron–client ties are furthest eroded in southeastern coastal regions. Considering their respective arguments locates the Xiamen situation in the national economy, highlighting principles of regional variation.

The market transition account sees the utility of patron–client ties in private business as corresponding inversely to the degree of "marketization" of the economy. This is because marketization generates autonomous resources, obviating the need for such ties.[8] This chapter's findings do not support this claim. Keeping in mind the distinction made in this chapter between officialdom's sale of profit opportunities and security, it appears more accurate to say that the kind of services sought by entrepreneurs from patrons shifts. In marketized coastal regions it may well be that officials are less involved in mediating profit-enhancing transactions but in such regions their security-enhancing services are increasingly crucial. In more commercialized areas, the greater economic accumulations of private companies spur their demand for security services, driving up their price and enhancing gains to officials who sell them. By contrast, in less commercialized areas, with smaller economic concentrations in private enterprises, the demand for officials' services may simply decline or disappear.

Within the political economy account, an argument is made that the dense transnational networks of overseas kin in the southern coastal regions create more autonomous resource flows that reduce entrepreneurial dependency on the state.[9] This chapter's observations suggest a different process. Entrepreneurs who use financial capital from overseas kin do not necessarily achieve autonomy from the state economy, because they use these investments to expand into more lucrative commercial activities that involve greater clientelist contracting. Thus, a businessperson who received money from an overseas relative would be less dependent on patrons for financial capital but could nevertheless become more embedded in clientelist contracting as the outside capital infusion drives diversification into more lucrative and officially brokered undertakings. Also, as this chapter has clarified, even if an entrepreneur reduces reliance on patrons for access to profit opportunities, these

---

[8] Victor Nee writes, "as both general and specialized markets develop in volume and size, at some point most transactions will be free of cadre involvement. . . . The erosion of redistributive power corresponds to the increased reliance on market coordination" (Nee 1991: 279). Such a process is said to be most advanced in the coastal provinces as measured by more rapid increases in the income of entrepreneurs there relative to officials (Nee 1996).

[9] Dorothy Solinger writes that "it is those living in the southeastern coastal provinces who have relatives abroad or who have managed to underwrite their new economic ventures with investments from those places and so have become released from the hegemonic dominion of the state economy" (Solinger 1992: 137).

patrons still remain crucial for access to protection. Increased capital flows from overseas relatives could therefore hasten economic capital accumulation and drive entrepreneurs to forge ties with higher levels of the state bureaucracy to enhance security.

The points I have just advanced can be sharpened by comparisons of local officialdom in the commercial activity in other regions studied by fieldworkers. At one possible extreme lies Xiajia village in North China, as described by the anthropologist Yunxiang Yan (1995). The village is distant from market centers and is dominated by petty agricultural commodity production. Yan writes:

> the reforms have eroded cadres' previous power and privilege by breaking their monopoly over resources and by creating new income opportunities that make the accumulation of personal wealth more attractive than the political rewards offered by the party state. . . . For villagers, the reforms have ended their dependence on the collectives and the cadres who ran them, and have thereby to a great extent freed them from cadre domination. (Yan 1995: 238–9)

This egalitarianism stems from the character of household commodity agriculture. The human capital skills necessary for such business ventures are widely distributed in peasant communities, and local officials control fewer excludable resources. Therefore, market reform, by redistributing land to households and legalizing production for sale in markets, has given villagers the means to compete with village cadres on a more equal footing, eroding their monopoly of power in the village (see also Róna-tas 1994). In an especially telling symbol of this erosion, villagers have stopped giving presents to cadres on important ritual occasions, such as weddings and funerals in the cadres' families, and in some cases have even beaten cadres in heated arguments.

At another extreme is Chen village, bordering Hong Kong in Guangdong, as described by a trio of sociologists. Like Xiajia village, Chen village had an agricultural economy before the market reforms. However, its proximity to international markets via Hong Kong and its extensive kin networks with overseas Chinese have stimulated the local proliferation of private export-oriented factories in the 1980s. The sociologists note that even though the overall scope of activities of the government has declined, what remains has been concentrated into the hands of the village's Communist Party secretary and supplemented with new sources of power. This power not only includes the mediation of family quarrels and disputes as before, but now includes new forms of power such as the issuing of permits to build new homes and the mediation of property rights disputes. They write that "both formally and informally, Baodai [the village party secretary] plays the role of mayor, prosecutor, and judge, and through a myriad of discretionary acts has it within his power to favor some families and obstruct others. He does not do so blatantly: he appears to maintain a relatively even hand. But it is little wonder that to keep on his good side, just in case, almost all families ply him with small gifts" (Chan, Madsen, and Unger [1984] 1992: 319–20).

The more far-reaching transformation wrought in Chen village as compared to Xiajia, evident in the industrialization and transnationalization of the former's economy, results in a somewhat contrary finding regarding the position of local government in the market economy. In Xiajia, with a lower level of marketization, the position of officials is more eroded. The local Communist Party secretary has endeavored to convert what remains of his declining political position into economic capital in order to support his sons in their successful private businesses (Yan 1995: 226). One reputed example of this support is permitting his son to lend as usury state funds allocated to the village (Yan 1995: 231). Such practices have enabled him to advance his family from one of the poorest to among the richest in the village. In sharp contrast, the party secretary in Chen village plays a vital and apparently expanded administrative role. He is able to garner much economic gain from office without actively striving to convert political into economic capital. "Baodai does not have to go out of his way or resort to literally corrupt activities to generously supplement his salary" (Chan, Madsen, and Unger [1984] 1992: 320). So thoroughly has state power become commodified in Chen village that bribes to officials are simply seen as part of doing business and reflections of market value for brokering state power.

Lying between these two situations, both geographically and metaphorically, are the rural villages of the lower Yangzi River region in east-central China. In this region village and township officials appear to have transformed their control over public resources to the role of commercial managers, while the rural populace does not have the dense transnational kinship ties that exist along the southern coast, and therefore has fewer outside routes of investment capital. Jean Oi observes that in the villages of southern Jiangsu province, market reform has decentralized farming but not the management and assets of rural industry, giving the local government much power in running the local economy. "Village leaders, township heads, and heads of economic commissions decided questions ranging from spending, investments, and loans to hiring, and also make provisions to assist their enterprises in acquiring credit and needed inputs" (Oi 1990: 34). In these villages private nonagricultural firms are largely subcontractors for state and collective enterprises (Oi 1994: 68–9).

The difference between the industrialized villages of southern Jiangsu and the villages of Guangdong province can be explained partly by variation in local social structure and partly by the prior existence of rural industry. Southern Jiangsu villages have few overseas networks and so it is the local government that makes the various economic decisions, and private enterprises are merely subcontractors. By contrast, in Guangdong province's Chen village, economic decisions as to what to invest, what to produce, and where to sell are made by private entrepreneurs and their overseas kin. Yet this access to foreign capital and shift of economic decision making from officials to entrepreneurs, especially marked in the southern coastal regions, has not released entrepreneurs from the hegemony of local party-state officials, as has been claimed in the political economy view. Even though Chen village officials play little direct economic role, they wield significant administrative power that can facilitate or hinder the enterprises of those who fail to proffer the necessary gifts.

In sum, a comparison across regions that are marketizing in different ways suggests that the further emergence of markets may encourage rather than undermine the presence of local government in the market economy. Chen village has undergone much more rapid marketization and a clear shift from agriculture to industry as compared to Xiajia village. The Chen village party secretary has been able to exert new commercialized forms of patronage. Indeed, so munificent is the stream of gifts that he does not have to engage in the kinds of actions that might outrage villagers. Instead, the gift-giving practices that reaffirm his power locally are generally viewed as payment for his brokerage of state power. The key variable appears not to be degree of commercialization in terms of the extent of the market principle, but rather substantive factors such as scale of capital concentration in private businesses and presence or absence of overseas Chinese kin networks.

# 5

## Enhancing Expectations:
## The Social Organization of Contracts

Distinguish between insiders and outsiders (*neiwai you bie*). (Chinese proverb)

The transactions of private firms take place through the personal ties of their operators with others in the social environment. Contractual expectations are informed by social trust – the assumptions that others will most likely behave in socially legitimate and therefore somewhat predictable ways. The terms of contracts in regard to degree and kind of reciprocity are therefore embedded in the relative identities and norms of the exchange parties. However, this does not mean that expectations are forged without reference to state-promulgated legal statuses and norms. Although entrepreneurs are wont to talk about their activities in popular idioms, much contracting is forged by interplay between popular and statist mechanisms. State attempts to institutionalize legal statuses and practices interact with popular identities and norms to create innovations in contracting arrangements. In this chapter I first describe the popular idioms of social trust used by entrepreneurs to characterize their activities. Then I examine how interactions between entrepreneurs and others are coordinated in more or less predictable ways by reference to these idioms. Next, I describe ways in which stable expectations are produced by the interplay of popular and statist institutions.

## Idioms of Social Trust

Entrepreneurs refer to their social relations of business by several sets of idioms. One set expresses popularly legitimate expectations of behavior. A second set delimits the identities around which expectations cohere. A third set refers to the utility of various mixes of expectation

93

and identities for business purposes and the strategies of manipulation and enhancement.[1]

First, in regard to expectations of behavior, a common idiom is *zuoren*, which means "upright conduct." I heard it in response to my inquiries on how entrepreneurs cope with such problems as popular envy, the so-called "red-eye disease" (*hong yan bing*), demands of officialdom, and enforcement of contracts. The most common response was, "if you know how to conduct yourself, then matters are easier to solve" (*Ni dongde zemma zuoren, shiqing jiu hao chuli*). The word *zuoren* is composed of the character *zuo*, meaning "to contract a relation," and the character *ren*, meaning "person." Entrepreneurs proffered various definitions of *zuoren*. One said, "to know how to conduct yourself means to recognize that you live in society. Anything you achieve is because society lets you. Therefore you must always show a concern (*guanxin*) for others and exhibit a spirit of helping. Otherwise, society will resist you, nobody will help you, and you will find it hard to get things done" (informant no. 35). Another said, "You are not an independent unit. In everything you depend on others. *Zuoren* is behavior that recognizes this reality" (informant no. 25). Another put it simply: "It means that you are not selfish" (informant no. 15). The popular definition of upright conduct expressed in *zuoren* attaches higher value to the relational ethics of personal ties than the professional ethics of occupations and the legal ethics of the state.[2]

Reciprocity and face embody expectations of upright conduct. Reciprocity (*bao*) in social interactions is the basic principle of upright conduct. It acknowledges that one always depends on others. A person reciprocates both as moral imperative and in pursuit of interests. At one end is reciprocity through moral obligation to repay a debt of gratitude for kindness (*baoen*); the relative identities of individuals define expectations of behavior. At the other remove is reciprocity in material incentive as payment for services rendered (*baochou*); the terms of exchange reflect monetary calculations of the exchange value of the goods and services. Much private business is conducted through ties that lie between these two extremes. This is expressed in such characteristic idioms as "gift giving" (*songli*) and "doing favors" (*renqing*).

Face heightens expectations of reciprocity through sanctioning. Face is an evaluation of social honor in terms of an individual's capacity to live up to legitimate social expectations. Failure to establish sufficient social

---

[1] The literature on this is growing rapidly. For recent accounts see: Kipnis (1997); Yan (1996); M. M. Yang (1994). Earlier writers who have stimulated my thinking on these issues are Fried (1953: 99–135); Jacobs (1979); Hwang (1987); Hu (1944); Wong (1988); and L. Yang (1957).

[2] This valuation can be seen in a conversation I had with a Chinese acquaintance in Japan. She criticized her Japanese co-workers for taking work too much to heart (*gongzuo shang tai renzhen*) because they "wouldn't even take time off from work to help a friend in need."

honor as called for by a situation draws sanctions. There are two distinct aspects of face, each linked to a different sanctioning process. One aspect is *lian*, which refers to face as self-worth. Here loss of face (*diu lian*) refers to the shame felt by somebody for failing to live up to expectations. This is first-party sanctioning as it is invoked by the transgressor on him or herself, although it is possible only through prior socialization and internalization of social norms. The other aspect is *mianzi*, which refers to public evaluations of worth by such visible criteria as occupation, education, and wealth. To say that one has "no face" (*meiyou mianzi*) means that one has not comported oneself in a manner befitting public expectations of status. It is also possible to "give face" (*gei mianzi*) through actions ranging from showing respect to presenting gifts. Having no face or failing to give face where due attenuates social trust and can invite sanctions. Second-party sanctioning is reduction or withdrawal of support in further endeavors by the offended party. Third-party sanctioning can occur when knowledge of the improper behavior spreads beyond the dyad into the social environment, resulting in declining cooperation by third parties as well.

The effectiveness of reciprocity and face in invoking sanctions is suggested by a discussion I had with a young official in a Tax Bureau substation. It seems that when people he did not know wanted special consideration in a tax matter, they made the request through a mutual friend. As the request came from a mutual friend, he felt that he had to grant it. I asked him why he felt this way. He said:

> If you don't give special consideration then your friend loses face (*mianzi*). Others will come to see you as someone who does not behave properly (*zuoren*). [But isn't special consideration illegal?] It may not be legal (*hefa*) by the center but it accords with local sentiment and practice. . . . You also have to think realistically. Xiamen is a small place and everybody knows each other. You must realize you will live here for your entire life. You must pay attention to your reputation. If you do not show sufficient spirit to help others, you will find it difficult to live here. Nobody will support you when you need it.

The second set of idioms expresses the personal identities around which expectations cohere. These expectations can be expressed as a continuum. At one end are identities that embody the consanguinity ties of family (*jia*) and contain the greatest expectations. Family ties contain high expectations of reciprocity through strong moral imperatives to cooperate that inhere in these identities. Such relations are said to be "thick" (*hou*), a reference to the significant blood and expectations that inhere in them. Thickest expectations lie in the male descent group (*fang*), which refers to the father–son relation. The *fang* perpetuates the lineage (*jiazu*) name; therefore the strongest obligations inhere in father–son relations, and then in relations between brothers.[3] Fairly thick expectations inhere in relations with paternal (*tang*) uncles and cousins. Few expectations inhere in sisters, as they marry out (*wai jia*) of the family and do not pass the family name to their children. Similarly, almost no expectations inhere in maternal (*biao*) uncles and cousins.

Expectations outside the family cohere in *guanxi* or personal connections. *Guanxi* embodies the principle of social closeness. Close relations contain strong expectations of cooperation as the moral obligations of affect: such ties are called affective or emotive (*ganqing*) *guanxi*. Relations of thickest affect merge into family ties, as a very good friend is called "one of the family" (*zijiaren*) or "one of us" (*zijiren*). Strong affect is produced in shared formative experiences, such as those of playmates and classmates in childhood, students and their teachers, and army comrades-in-arms in early adulthood. Affect diminishes with lesser experiences such as those among work colleagues in adulthood. Thinnest ties have no history of interaction; reciprocity reflects material calculations and is quid pro quo. Such ties are called "money connections" (*jinqian guanxi*) and "utilitarian connections" (*liyong guanxi*).

There are various idioms to express closeness in *guanxi* relations. One is *tong* or sameness, which refers to a characteristic possessed by two individuals. One can speak of compatriots – individuals from the same native place (*tongxiang*), as well of colleagues (*tongshi*), schoolmates (*tongxue*), and classmates (*tongban*).[4] The importance of *tong* as a basis for cooperation can be seen in the fact that the character *tong* together with the character for heart (*xin*) mean "unity of purpose" (*tongxin*). Another is the idiom of familiarity, expressed in the dichotomy of cooked (*shu*) and raw (*sheng*). A high-affect relationship is considered "cooked," as in the phrase "He and I are very well-cooked (familiar)" (*wo gen ta shudehen*); in contrast, a low-affect relationship is viewed as "raw."[5] Finally, the terms "inside" (*nei*) and "outside" (*wai*) indicate such distinctions as those between native (*neidiren*) and outlander (*waidiren*) and between organization members (*neibu*) and nonmembers (*waibu*).

*Jia* and *guanxi* are highly flexible idioms in which boundaries are context-specific. This is reflected in the fluid and slightly inconsistent usage of these idioms in Xiamen's business class. Some entrepreneurs

---

[3] For a brief discussion of the *fang* and *jiazu* in Chinese family enterprises, see Tu (1991). The classic discussion of these social categories is by Chen Chi-nan. For references see bibliography in Tu (1991). For a related discussion see Watson (1982).

[4] The word for "comrade" in the Chinese Communist lexicon is *tongzhi*, which translates literally as "same ideals" or "same purpose."

[5] See Yang (1994: 193–4) for a similar discussion of this idiom.

apply the idiom of *guanxi* to relations outside the *jia*, while for others the *jia* is a subcategory of *guanxi*, as in the term *jiating guanxi* (family *guanxi*). Some maintain that *guanxi* is inherently instrumental, whereas others view it as the aforementioned continuum bounded by emotion and instrumentalism. This terminological inconsistency is not evidence of entrepreneurs' confusion or institutional disorder but is rather evidence of flexibility and innovation in social networks. Andrew Kipnis notes a similar phenomenon in a village in Shandong province. He writes that "as new entrepreneurs adapt their social tactics to emergent opportunities and risks, they worried little about consistency in their terminology. They invented new ways of creating, manipulating, and talking about *guanxi*, and perhaps even new forms of social relations" (Kipnis 1997: 184).

The third set of idioms has to do with holding and forging efficacious networks and refers to optimal mixes of social identity, expectations, and interests and optimizing strategies to achieve such mixes. The optimal mix is a tie that balances moral obligation and material incentives because excessive emphasis on only one has efficacy problems. A tie that stresses moral obligation lacks sufficient material incentive to ensure ongoing cooperation. As one entrepreneur said, "No matter how close a relative or friend is, they will want some money. If you don't give it to them, they will not run around for you the second time. You can't get by on the basis of *ganqing* alone" (informant no. 51).[6] A tie that emphasizes material incentives is problematic because quid pro quo reciprocity, by restoring balance of exchange, reduces expectations of future cooperation. Therefore, entrepreneurs seek to balance obligation and incentive to create durable contracts in the market economy.

Such a balance is achieved through a variety of strategic practices. In one collection of practices, material reciprocity is muted and revolves around displays of human sentiment or human kindness (*renqingwei*) that stimulate warm feelings of goodwill and gratitude by the recipient. This involves expressions of concern for another's welfare and well-being through shows of "solicitude" (*guanxin*) and making "special allowances" (*zhaogu*) for others. Another collection of practices involves monetary incentives such as giving company shares and salaries to strategically placed individuals. In between lie practices of gift giving (*songli*) in which material rewards are presented in a manner that infuses them with shades of human kindness. One common form of gift giving is

---

[6] Yanjie Bian also notes the increased need for material reward even when approaching kin for help. "During my trip to Beijing, Shanghai and Tianjin from March to May of 1992, I was most impressed by the increased use of *guanxi* for exchanging resources among friends and acquaintances. Material rewards were necessary even for relatives who were asked for help" (Bian 1994: 986, n. 30).

banqueting, which in Chinese contexts is a highly obligated action, reflecting the long history of a fine line between subsistence and starvation in a densely populated peasant society.

There are several idioms that express this optimal balance of moral obligations and material incentives. One is "mutual understanding" (*huxiang liaojie*). Because I heard this term so often I asked entrepreneurs to define it. According to one, it means that "you not only know another's objective needs but also their subjective desires. Therefore you can anticipate how they will behave in a situation" (informant no. 7). Another said, "It means that you understand what the other is thinking. He will not say one thing but in his heart of hearts be thinking another" (informant no. 63). Yet another said that mutual understanding means "the person will not seek advantage at your expense" (informant no. 18). In other words, both parties acknowledge their self-interest but also value the relationship, precluding overtly opportunistic behavior. In business this functions to lower the costs of evaluating contractual commitments and ensures ongoing cooperation. Another idiom is "heart-felt collusion" (*xinli goutong*), which emphasizes the intertwining of social norms and self-interested behavior in a personal tie. Heart-felt collusion occurs when there is both some element of obligation as well as material reward to ensure unity of purpose.

## Popular Identities and Norms in Interactions

The operation of private companies involves ties not only between entrepreneurs and state agents but also between entrepreneurs and persons from such other social groups as managers, employees, neighbors, and former colleagues. While many of these individuals are not state agents, ties with them are crucial to maneuvering within state power because they live in the community and can be located in the networks between entrepreneurs and state agents. Their actions affect relations between entrepreneurs and state agents and they are encompassed in entrepreneurial strategies and the operation of private business.

### Interactions with State Agents

Entrepreneurs enhance the likelihood of cooperative interaction with state agents through payoffs, employment, and partnership. Payoffs are offerings of material reward to agents who are not formally integrated into the company as employees and partners. They go mainly to street-level administrative officials and buyers from public distributive and manufacturing enterprises. For example, entrepreneurs give kickbacks (*huikou*) to public purchasing agents who order commodities from them and cash bribes (*huilu*) to other officials. However, payoffs are too instrumental to ensure ongoing support and are usually supplanted by gift giving.

In gift giving, the material reward is represented as a favor (*renqing*) stemming from concern for the receiver as a human being rather than as a calculated means of obtaining an advantage from an official. This heightens the goodwill of an official toward an entrepreneur as well as feelings of gratitude and obligation. One entrepreneur said, "You give them gift certificates from the East Wind Department Store, saying, 'I have some extra ones for friends so why don't you take these'" (informant no. 3). One entrepreneur visits officials at their homes during Spring Festival, when it is customary to give small gifts of money in red envelopes (*hong bao*) to children. He gives envelopes of several hundred yuan to officials, saying that it is for their children's education. During festival and ritual occasions such as Spring Festival in late winter and the Ghost Feeding (*Pudu*) festival in the summer, entrepreneurs treat officials to banquets. Banqueting is so ubiquitous that larger firms include restaurants in their business groups, letting entrepreneurs be discreet in entertainment and reducing its costs.[7] Other entrepreneurs give officials money in exchange for their signatures artfully painted with a calligraphy brush (*rongbi*), as an expression of admiration for their technique.

Entrepreneurs also create obligations from officials by calculated shows of concern. For example, one businessman counseled a young official on bride selection, an act that favorably disposed the official to the entrepreneur. Another entrepreneur paid social visits to officials in their offices to enhance affect. As he describes it, "I often drop by (*chuan men*) to shoot the breeze and smoke some cigarettes. Sometimes I will just sit for several hours chatting about this and that. Sometimes they [officials] will talk about their families or some problem that I can help them with.... If you sit with somebody long enough you develop *ganqing*" (informant no. 4). Such dropping by allows the entrepreneur to assess the needs of the officials so that appropriate gifts can be selected to proffer on opportune occasions. However, gift giving is a time-consuming strategy, demanding much face-to-face interaction as well as time spent thinking about appropriate gifts and planning opportune moments to present them. In an era when "time is money," one can ill afford to do this.

---

[7] This is similar to the tendency of public units to have guest houses and banqueting facilities to take care of their networking needs. Wilson (1994) documents how a village government in suburban Shanghai developed orchards to produce fruit for gift giving by village factories and started a mushroom factory to provide delicacies for factory banquets.

By employing local state agents in their businesses, entrepreneurs routinize the ties in their firms and reduce the time spent maintaining them. Payoffs to officials are regularized as salaries and bonuses disbursed by the cashier, and their loyalty is augmented by their greater participation in the social activities for the firm's employees, as discussed below. Some officials are partially integrated as advisors (*guwen*). One entrepreneur explained the work of an advisor as follows: "If there is a problem he invites the relevant officials out for dinner. This is all he does" (informant no. 25). Many entrepreneurs also establish "brain trusts" consisting of professors of economics, accounting, and international business from Xiamen-based colleges and universities whose former students work in such strategic agencies as the Customs Bureau, Policy Research Institute,[8] Tax Bureau, and various banks. While visiting former students, these professors also obtain insider information and lobby officials on behalf of entrepreneurs they "advise."

To integrate supportive state agents more securely into a firm, entrepreneurs may employ them as full-time managers. These managers receive social welfare benefits reserved for core employees, such as health insurance and pension plans, which are often comparable with similar benefits in the public units.[9] The practice of administrative officials moonlighting for private companies was the target of state rectification policies in the late 1980s, which led some to resign from public units for full-time work in private firms. These officials were given bonuses of tens of thousands of yuan as a reward for taking the job and to allay their concerns over the loss of their social welfare benefits in their public job.

This integration of officials into private firms through employment may also proceed by family ties. A recently retired official who is the mother of a businessperson might be "hired" to work in her son's company; she then uses her personal ties in the bureaucracy on behalf of the company. In some cases, the children are fronts and the parents are the de facto entrepreneurs. Designating offspring as legal owners deflects criticism that the parents are cashing in on their bureaucratic connections. For example, the managers of a firm ostensibly run by a woman in her mid-twenties are her parents, who recently retired from government bureaus that allocated textiles and chemicals, respectively. Not surprisingly, the company deals exclusively in these two items. I found similar cases in the construction business, food companies, and firms that trade raw materials.

Finally, officials can be made into partners. However, only the leading

---

[8] These local agencies study central policies and advise their local governments on adapting them to suit local conditions.

[9] For the practice of private companies offering social welfare benefits comparable to public units, see Francis (1996).

officials in district and city government agencies and public units, those who have a great deal of authority and therefore much discretionary control over public resources, achieve these positions. They are given paid positions on boards of directors as well as nontransferable company shares. These shares are colloquially called "power shares" (*quanli fen*) because officials invest bureaucratic power rather than money in the business. These officials are not involved in the firm's daily matters. They make appearances at such ceremonial occasions as Spring Festival parties, visibly signifying a company's high-level backing. They give support by providing timely insider information on state policies, making introductions to other officials, and intervening, when needed, to fend off harassment from other agencies.

Family ties, too, can undergird partnerships. For example, an entrepreneur established a fish farm producing shrimp and eels for export in his ancestral village along the coast. The farm is a village enterprise managed by his cousin, the local Communist Party secretary. This cousin arranged for the village ponds to be contracted to the firm for a long period at a low rate. In the case of high-ranking officials who are kin, their high position and prominence precludes such close integration into the firm. Nevertheless they provide crucial support when needed. This is well illustrated by the cooperative car repair firm mentioned in Chapter 4. Early on it obtained a large order from the city government, arranged by a partner whose father was deputy director of a bureau. This was the firm's big break, and it went on, without further direct reliance on the father, to become one of the most prosperous in its line in Xiamen.

### Interactions with Managers

Family ties are prominent in management. Potential conflicts are rife in relations with managers. Entrepreneurs fear they might collude with employees, withhold information, or simply not be responsive. Entrepreneurs prefer not to seek legal solutions to conflict because this invites scrutiny by authorities and expends resources to influence the court's decision. Reliance on family in management is said to reduce conflicts by augmenting the loyalty of managers.

In smaller, less prosperous companies, nuclear family members fill managerial positions. The father is the head manager and chief buyer. Wives and daughters are cashiers. Some sons are buyers, while those less skilled in the art of *guanxi* are stockroom supervisors. When management needs expand, the first individuals outside the nuclear family to whom entrepreneurs turn are siblings. However, married sisters are not utilized because, as noted above, women marry out of the lineage and are seen as obligated to their husbands' families. Entrepreneurs voiced concern that a married sister would even embezzle the firm's money to meet financial difficulties in the husband's family. Also, the use of nieces, nephews, and cousins should be avoided if possible. One entrepreneur explained:

> These relatives will feel they can rely on your company but won't exert themselves. No matter how many times you tell them to do something a certain way, they won't do it. They are not afraid of you because you are a relative. But they also feel that because you are the boss, you have a lot of money and they see the money as a large sum from which they can steal. Sons . . . are not like this. They think that the money is the father's and belongs to the family. (Informant no. 20)

However, as the management capacity of a nuclear family is limited to about 50 employees, further expansion makes it necessary for entrepreneurs of larger, more prosperous companies to increasingly seek managers and trust personnel beyond this core.[10] In doing so they expand on the principles of *fang*, which emphasizes male descent in the lineage. They rely on nieces and nephews of brothers and even male members of the wife's immediate family, on the principle that, as the wife married into the entrepreneur's lineage, her male siblings and their children have a special relation with the lineage. However, the aforementioned distrust of married sisters carries over, as entrepreneurs are unwilling to employ their sisters' offspring. Entrepreneurs will also hire a person seen as "one of us" because of strong bonds of affective *guanxi*. Finally, when entrepreneurs are forced to seek managers outside their families and direct personal ties, they turn to individuals introduced by close friends and family members, indirectly extending the social trust of consanguinity and affect to these new employees. This is a critical juncture for firm growth. Many entrepreneurs are unable or unwilling to transcend familism in management recruitment; therefore the extent of their nuclear family's management capacity defines the possibilities for the growth of their business.

### Interactions with Full-time Employees

Entrepreneurs are keen to avoid dissatisfaction among employees. Firing lazy employees or those who steal can backfire if disgruntled employees go to local authorities and accuse entrepreneurs of exploitation or tax evasion. China is, after all, a state-socialist country with a longer history since 1949 of protecting the interests of workers than those of businesspeople. Older entrepreneurs recall how the Communist Party

---

[10] This accords with Greenhalgh's (1988: 237–38) finding that Taiwanese firms of up to fifty employees are in the management capacity of one family.

mobilized workers during the economic socialization campaigns of the 1950s to publicly accuse capitalist businessmen of exploitation. Similar fears were ignited during the economic rectification campaign launched in late 1988, when the city government set up public hot lines for the populace to anonymously report on tax evasion and other irregularities of businesspeople. In fact, one entrepreneur I interviewed had been investigated for tax evasion and bribery because of charges made by a recently fired employee.

When entrepreneur–employee interactions are embedded in family-like expectations, the possibility of such conflicts is reduced by greater loyalty. The interactions induce in employees feelings of obligation, duty, and selflessness toward the entrepreneur, attitudes that entrepreneurs heighten by representing the firm as a family. One businesswoman said:

> We celebrate employee birthdays together. When an employee has a child, we send something over for the recovery period. Many of the employees eat here as their homes are far away, and so I have put in a kitchen and bathroom. On the second and the sixteenth of every month, all of the employees worship the God of Wealth to maintain the good fortune of the firm. Each time we worship it costs about ¥100 to ¥200.[11] Sometimes guests come and we invite the employees to eat. This way the employees feel like this is their family. They feel the affairs of the company are also their affairs and this lessens embezzlement and theft. (Informant no. 12)

Another entrepreneur, who owned, among other things, a restaurant, said:

> My feeling is that I am not their boss but their older brother. During work I will treat them according to the work requirements but afterwards we are like a family. We tease and scold each other in a joking way. This makes for a feeling of closeness. . . . If one of the customers wants to go out with a waitress, I will check out the customer and see if he is faithful or simply looking for fun. These are simple country girls and if a guy mistreats them, they are likely to commit suicide. . . . So our hearts become united. This is very good for business. They will think that the boss is not bad and will be moved so that when I am not here they will still work hard. If business is bad they will think it is because of their poor service or bad cooking and will cry. (Informant no. 26)

---

[11] Offerings of food and wines are laid in front of a figurine of the God of Wealth and then eaten as part of the ceremony.

Potential conflict is also reduced by nativism. Entrepreneurs distinguish between natives and nonnatives in assigning jobs. The functional definition of nativism varies by type of business. This reflects the different needs for trust in different undertakings and underscores the highly manipulative aspect of these social categories as control strategies. In trade activities, the definition of "native" (*bendiren*) is narrow – including, for example, only individuals from Xiamen's urban districts. This is because in trading companies, goods and money are more likely to pass through employees' hands than in manufacturing firms. A narrow definition of nativism augments cooperation, since Xiamen, by Chinese standards, is a relatively small city where people either know each other or are likely to be connected through a mutual acquaintance. Expectations and obligations are heightened because defections from them can be subject to third-party sanctioning in the community. Furthermore, should an employee steal, the problem can be resolved through a go-between known to both parties.

In manufacturing, the definition of "native" is broader than in commerce, including anyone from southern Fujian who speaks Minnan dialect. In many instances, Minnan-speaking people are placed as supervisors over production workers who come from the inland provinces of Guangxi, Hunan, and Siquan. Nativism helps ensure the loyalty of the foreman to the entrepreneur rather than to the workers. Entrepreneurs can forestall loyalty between supervisors and workers by having the former assess the latter's productivity and distribute bonuses. This puts relations between foreman and workers on a more instrumental basis, driving a wedge between possible collusion in shirking work and pilfering. Nonnatives are also given the most strenuous work; entrepreneurs are less worried about unrest among them. Because nonnatives come to Xiamen simply to make money, they are unlikely to cause trouble. Should a nonnative worker become upset, she or he will simply quit to seek work elsewhere. In the unlikely event that a nonnative worker turns to the authorities, officials would likely side with the entrepreneur as a fellow Xiamen native.

Cooperation with employees can also be enhanced by various *guanxi* practices. Some entrepreneurs consciously attempt to augment emotion in relations with workers, much as they do with the officials. One way is by showing solicitude (*guanxin*).

> My view is that the workers are capital. You have to take care of them. Several days ago, five workers got food poisoning. I thought it was heatstroke. So I helped them by rubbing their throats. You have to use a lot of energy to do this. When I realized it was not heatstroke I sent them to the hospital. They

have to pay the hospital fee themselves but I express my concern for them. I tell them that their bodies are their capital and that as long as they are healthy, they will earn money. I provide them with living accommodations such as beds, mosquito nets, fans, and some coal for cooking. But they are responsible for their own food. They all live in the factory. I show my concern for them. Now when it comes time to pay wages, they bring me cigarettes. But it didn't used to be this way. I used to have to go down to order them to work harder. But now I don't have to. (Informant no. 4)

When done publicly, such shows of concern by the boss also give face (*gei mianzi*) to the recipient, heightening this individual's sense of gratitude and obligation to the entrepreneur.

### Interactions with the Part-time Labor Force

Interactions with people from an entrepreneur's prior reference groups – neighbors and former public unit colleagues – can be problematic. The rapidly acquired wealth of the entrepreneurs can stimulate the smoldering envy of "red-eye disease" in these people. Goaded by envy, they can seek to harm the entrepreneur by negative gossip and by reporting business irregularities to the authorities. To avoid this, entrepreneurs integrate some of these people into their firms, enhancing their cooperation by heightened normative obligations.

Neighbors' envy has several sources. They may be jealous because they feel unable to benefit from the market economy. As one entrepreneur said, "There is no problem with neighbors when we are all poor. But then I go into business and soon have a full set – a washing machine, refrigerator, color television, and motorcycle. My wealth does not make them feel society is getting better but rather that they are falling behind" (informant no. 51). The wealth of the entrepreneurs also violates the egalitarian values of Chinese peasant tradition and socialist ideology. Another businesswoman commented, "If you don't earn that much money, then people will help you and cheer you on. If you earn a lot of money people will think, 'You are a person and I am a person so why should you earn more money than me?'" (informant no. 17).

Envious neighbors can cause manifold problems for entrepreneurs. A key concern of entrepreneurs is neighbors spreading negative rumors about an entrepreneur through gossip or reports (*xiao baogao*) to the authorities. For companies located in an entrepreneur's neighborhood of residence it is relatively easy for someone to obtain information about the firm through casual conversations with an entrepreneur's family and friends. It is also easy to observe the comings and goings of visitors to the company, as well as the employees' working and living conditions. For instance, the visit of a particular official or the long working hours of the workers might be noted. Such information can cause trouble for an entrepreneur if it reaches the ears of the officers of neighborhood and residents' committees and local authorities in police substations and tax bureaus. The trouble may not be immediate but can arise later – for example, during a bureaucratic campaign against economic crimes when local agencies are under pressure to fill quotas of transgressors and can reinterpret this information as evidence of corruption and mistreatment of workers.[12]

Another problem is property destruction. One entrepreneur's store was vandalized by a neighbor incensed when the construction materials for the entrepreneur's new four-story mansion were unloaded in the public lane, blocking passage for several days. Another businessman found his car tires slashed after he refused a neighbor's request for a loan. In such matters, local authorities can be loath to intervene for fear of alienating themselves from the community by siding with a "new capitalist." For example, the entrepreneur whose store had been ransacked told me that when he reported this to the public security substation, the policemen simply laughed and said that he was lucky because in rural areas businesspeople had been murdered over such matters.

To ensure cooperation from neighbors, entrepreneurs employ them in part-time work. In the urban districts many of these part-time employees are women who resigned from public jobs in return for cash compensation or internal retirement. They do labor-intensive work on a piece-rate basis for the private firm in their neighborhood. This lets them work flexible hours that fit in with their home-making schedules of shopping, food preparation, and child rearing. Private companies in Xiamen employ neighborhood women to assemble picture frames and small toys for export, baste clothes on an out-work basis, and collate and fold printed materials. In Xiamen the number of women so employed by a single firm rarely exceeds several dozen, but in nearby rural areas the number is much larger. One entrepreneur with a private textile factory in Jinjiang county has farmed out work to 800 families at a time. Such arrangements also benefit private firms by providing a flexible workforce that can be expanded or contracted to meet changing demand.

Families in Xiamen who depend on public employment and have no overseas relatives are financially strapped and therefore grateful for this chance to supplement their income. Entrepreneurs represent the work as a favor (*renqing*) bestowed on neighbors, enhancing cooperation through

---

[12] Such campaigns are discussed in Chapter 8.

obligations of affect and human sentiment. Additionally, entrepreneurs enhance personal ties in the neighborhood. They pay neighborhood employees by a different wage scale that appears to give them greater returns on their labor than full-time employees who are not natives.[13] This also creates a native–nonnative distinction between the part-time and full-time employees, in which entrepreneurs represent themselves as standing on the side of the natives. This is also advantageous to entrepreneurs because local officials see them as filling a social welfare function by creating employment opportunities for cash-strapped members of the neighborhood. Indeed, the officers of street and residents' committees might have family members among the part-time employees.

The case of one company illustrates the preceding discussion. I lived one week with a family that operated a wholesale business in office supplies and a printing factory that produced stationery and document forms for public units and agencies. The printing factory had twelve full-time employees from rural villages in southern Fujian who lived in lofts above the presses. It also employed part-time two dozen neighborhood women. The neighborhood women collated and folded printed materials, a different work from that of the full-time employees, who operated and cleaned the presses and made deliveries. Local part-time employees appeared to make more money per hour than nonlocal workers. In addition, locals worked in an air-conditioned room in the entrepreneur's house and tea was readily available; in contrast, the full-time workers rarely entered the entrepreneur's house. In their language, the entrepreneur and his family carefully distinguished between part-time and full-time employees. The latter were referred to as "neighbors" (*linju*) and their work as "help" (*bangmang*), while the former were called "workers" (*gongren*) and their work referred to as "labor" (*zuo gong*). Such linguistic distinctions emphasized the close, neighborly ties between entrepreneur and part-time employees. Indeed, whenever a neighbor woman came to the entrepreneur's house, I could not tell at first if she was coming to work or to pay a social visit. Some even played in the wife's mahjong games.

Relations with former colleagues are sensitive for entrepreneurs who resigned from public units. One entrepreneur explained this as follows:

> Under the socialist system no one was jealous if you were more capable because we all ate from the same pot. But now the most capable people are leaving the public units and the people who remain behind are worried. If you take your

---

[13] Neighbors tend to be a paid only on a piece-rate basis, while full-time workers are paid a combination of base wage, piece rates, and bonuses. The point is that the piece rates of neighborhood employees are higher, although, because their work is only part-time and they lack the other types of pay, their overall income from the firm is lower.

> ability and go out to do private business, they think you are
> taking away their rice bowl. They feel unhappy and want to
> pull the rug out from under you. They want so badly to see
> you fall flat on your face that they will even find some way to
> harm you. (Informant no. 25)

Another entrepreneur said, "They don't think I am successful because of my ability but because I use many tricks . . . bribing, tax evasion, pulling *guanxi*. . . . It is difficult to know what [former colleagues] are thinking when you meet them. With their mouths, they all say, 'Aaahhh . . . you are doing quite well.' But I do not know what they are really thinking in their hearts" (informant no. 12).

Former colleagues can cause problems as well, such as spreading sensitive information. There is a twist to this problem for entrepreneurs who use commercial connections accumulated during their public employment. These connections sometimes overlap with those of former co-workers still in public employment. This is particularly true of public unit purchasing agents who became entrepreneurs. When they resign from public employment, another purchasing agent takes over their routes. Therefore, these entrepreneurs often buy from the same public units as former colleagues, giving the latter potentially sensitive information about the private company. For example, one entrepreneur who formerly procured chemicals for a public unit now uses the connections made during his public tenure for private business. On several occasions he has run across purchasing agents from his former unit seeking to acquire the same chemicals from the same state enterprise. In this situation, should the public chemical manufacturer not have any chemicals to sell to the purchasing agent, it might be apparent to the purchasing agent that the chemicals were sold to the entrepreneur. The purchasing agent would therefore have sensitive information about the businessman.

Entrepreneurs who are Communist Party members face another problem. Although there were only two party members in my sample, both expressed a similar worry. Each year members are evaluated by the other members in their public unit. The entrepreneurs are concerned that former colleagues will give them low marks because of their private business activities. As one entrepreneur who had taken a leave of absence from his unit explained:

> Each year party members are evaluated to see if they are
> qualified to be members . . . to see if they embezzled or re-
> ceived bribes. . . . the party members judge and the people
> judge. The final judgment on me was that I was basically
> qualified *(jiben hege)*. Basically qualified means that you are
> barely qualified to be in the party but just manage to make it.

You will not be kicked out. But if I was still working in the unit, I would have been judged definitely qualified *(juedui hege)*. But when you are a private boss, people's impressions are different. You are earning money for yourself and this kind of behavior will develop capitalism. It is definitely not in the spirit of struggling for communism that party members are supposed to have. So people look at you and wonder what kind of party member are you, and judge you differently. So I have to be more careful than other private bosses in how I do things. If they are discovered doing illegal things like mistreating workers, cheating on taxes or violating regulations, at the most they will be fined. But I will be expelled from the party. This black mark would affect my children. (Informant no. 51)

To reduce jealousy among former colleagues who are still publicly employed, entrepreneurs give them employment opportunities. Again, this is especially common for entrepreneurs who were once purchasing agents and whose co-workers are still employed as such. The purchasing agents work for entrepreneurs on a sporadic commission basis as middlemen, arranging deals between private companies and public units. One entrepreneur said: "My friends [who are still purchasing agents] often come around and say 'I can get some of this at such and such a price.' So I work quickly and if I can line up a buyer who will put up the money, I tell my friend to go ahead. We split the profit" (informant no. 43). This arrangement is obviously of mutual benefit. It enables former co-workers to supplement eroding public salaries by sideline private business while giving entrepreneurs a supplementary sales force that is bureaucratically well connected and travels at public expense. The sporadic employment relationship also injects self-interest into what was previously an affective tie, enhancing durability.

## The Interplay of Popular and Statist Institutions

In this section I examine how stable expectations are produced by the interplay of popular and statist institutions in the networks by which entrepreneurs operate. The point is that there is no necessary inverse correspondence between reliance on statist and popular mechanisms, as is often maintained. This section will show that the function of popular institutions will not erode with the promulgation of statist institutions in a mechanistic fashion because the interplay of these two kinds of institutions helps constitute emerging markets. This accords with my more general argument in this study that clientelist ties are a durable contracting mode in a market economy and can operate in an institutionally plural context.

### Differential Recourse to Popular and Statist Institutions

Entrepreneurs view statist and popular institutions as discrete strategies, to be variably invoked in different circumstances. This can be seen in how entrepreneurs settle breaches of contractual understandings. It is possible for entrepreneurs to pursue breaches of contracts in courts, but few appear inclined to do so. During my interviews they made it clear that solving disputes through personal ties was preferable to the court system. One reason is that filing a legal suit saddles an entrepreneur with the reputation of being prone to carping over trifles (*jijiao*) and unable to solve problems through personal ties. Such a person does not understand upright conduct, and others will not want to deal with him. If the case is against a public unit, local regulatory agencies will view the entrepreneur as a troublemaker who is bypassing them to appeal to higher authorities. The offended administrative officials might harass the entrepreneur to withdraw the suit and warn other entrepreneurs not to bypass them. The public unit that is being taken to court may also lean on administrative agencies to pursue a strategy of harassment. In my entire sample of one hundred entrepreneurs only one had taken a public unit to the local court; in this case the public unit was not from Xiamen but from a distant rural county.

Entrepreneurs expressed a greater willingness to turn to the courts to settle conflicts in business conducted outside their home base of Xiamen; nevertheless few indicated that they had done so. This is because they assumed that judges outside their home turf would be biased against them as nonnatives and because they lacked influence in the court. The only instances I heard of where entrepreneurs saw any real benefit in taking legal action against a public unit occurred during the business slump that followed the 1989 student movement when the central state froze public unit expenditures and public units could not pay their bills. When political tension eased the following year, several entrepreneurs told me that they had filed suit against public units to pressure the state to unfreeze the public units' assets so that the entrepreneurs could be paid. In each instance, entrepreneurs had discussed the matter beforehand with officials from the public units in question and received their acquiescence in this.

There are several situations in which entrepreneurs are more likely to resort to the courts to settle breach of contract. One is when there is no possibility of achieving resolution through personal ties, as for example in problems occurring far from an entrepreneur's native turf (*lao xiang*).

Resorting to the legal system here stems from the failure to achieve a solution via popular norms because of a perceived lack of sufficient *guanxi* or "native" identity. In another situation, entrepreneurs resort to courts as a form of local public/private collusion to prod the central state to bail out the public unit. Taken together, these contexts suggest that the embeddedness in popular institutions is not merely a negative indicator of the degree of legal noninstitutionalization. Instead, popular norms and state laws represent a range of available and discrete alternatives. Furthermore, the institutional preference reflects not just which is more likely to solve the immediate problem at hand but also more diffuse concerns. The fact that legal solutions are rarely sought reflects not just entrepreneurs' low evaluation of the effectiveness of courts but also their acute concern for their maintaining their reputation in the community.

### Using Statist Institutions to Enhance Expectations in Popular Institutions

The intermingling of popular and legal institutions can also be mutually and simultaneously reinforcing. The use of legal contracts in employment practices shows how entrepreneurs' adoption of state-promulgated legal instruments can reinforce the normative and cognitive content of popular practices. It also shows how an institution can be manipulated to simultaneously signify different things to different actors, enhancing cooperation simultaneously along diverse fronts.

Many prosperous private companies use legal employment contracts that stipulate salary and benefits. The legal intention of such contracts is to protect the rights of both parties by clarifying expectations and subjecting them to state administrative sanctions. However, entrepreneurs use employment contracts in ways that have little to do with this purpose. Employment contracts are used to enhance the obligational norms by integrating employees more fully into the company as "family." The contracts are selectively bestowed, representing them more as a particularistic favor (*renqing*) rather than a universal right of employment, enhancing the obligation of the favored employees. Also, contracts contain clauses such as a fruit allowance in hot weather that heighten the paternalistic aspects of employee–entrepreneur relations.

From an entrepreneur's perspective, legal contracts bolster the loyalty of certain key personnel. For core staff – nuclear family members, agnatic kin, and individuals considered "one of us" – contracts are not deemed necessary because of the strong expectations of morally obligated cooperation that inhere in family ties. Nor are contracts given to the outer ring of employees, consisting of sales-counter personnel and laborers. Instead, contracts are used among such inner-ring staff as key sales personnel, skilled foremen and technicians, and non-kin managers. Since not all company members have contracts, those who do gain face (*mianzi*), enhancing loyalty to the entrepreneur. Also, as nonnatives tend to be in the outer ring and natives in the inner ring, contracts enhance the in-group/out-group dichotomy of nativism (*tongxiang*). This ensures that native employees take the entrepreneur's side in disciplining nonnatives in the outer ring.[14]

In addition, use of contracts bolsters the standing of entrepreneurs in the eyes of administrative agencies. In the late 1980s, in keeping with central state directives, the Industry and Commerce Bureau encouraged private companies to use employment contracts. Entrepreneurs who adopted them were also demonstrating compliance with the bureau in implementing this policy, a pattern reminiscent of the political activists (*jijifenzi*) of the earlier Maoist era.[15] Bureau officials reciprocated by holding these entrepreneurs in high regard. In my interviews with bureau officials on this subject, they praised companies that adopted contracts by calling them "modern" and "civilized" (*wenming jingying*) and their operators as "obedient" (*tinghua*) and unlikely to abuse workers. By using employment contracts, these entrepreneurs increased their standing in the bureau officials' eyes, enhancing likelihood of favorable consideration in other administrative matters.

### Invoking Statist and Popular Institutions in a Single Practice

Some practices enhance expectations of support simultaneously through statist and popular institutions. This can be seen in the practice of gift giving. Thus far, I have described such practices in terms of popular *guanxi* practices: they enhance expectations of cooperation by deepening the personal obligation in a tie through the addition of sentiment to an instrumental exchange. However, gift giving can also enhance expectations of cooperation and loyalty by another completely different logic that proceeds with reference to the state's legal and administrative sanctioning organs. Paradoxically, expectations are enhanced not by seeking to activate legal and regulatory sanctions but rather from fear that they might be activated.

This somewhat contrary invoking of statist institutions operates quite simply. An official who accepts an entrepreneur's gift or invitation to a banquet is party to exchanges that are routinely condemned by the state as corruption. Acceptance therefore inherently involves the official in the

---

[14] Anita Chan, Richard Madsen, and Jonathan Unger ([1984] 1992: 299–308) describe a similar pattern of the division of the labor force and social control in a village in Guangdong province.

[15] For political activism see Walder (1986: 147–53, 166–70).

entrepreneur's activities in ways deemed illegitimate by the state; the official could be implicated (*lianlei*) in any wrongdoing by the company. It follows that such officials are more inclined to keep silent about the dubious activities of the firm, to actively seek to deflect regulatory investigations of the firm, and to attest to the entrepreneur's honesty and the soundness of his or her activities to other officials.

A particularly vivid example of this concerns the operator of a branch company in the seafood business described in Chapter 3. I socialized with him a number of times at his apartment, at my apartment, and in various eating establishments, and gradually came to understand his strategy. As previously described, he had purchased a number of apartments with company profits from the firm's public accumulation fund. Therefore the apartments should have belonged to the rural township government that legally owned the firm as a form of public accumulation. However, the operator registered the apartments in the names of his family members and therefore it was his family that legally owned the apartments. He kept their purchase secret from township officials, with the intent to sell them and personally pocket the profit. However, in case township officials discovered this, he wanted to avoid conflicting claims to the apartments. Therefore, whenever township officials visited Xiamen he feted them at sumptuous banquets. An official's acceptance of his largesse gave him a "handle" (*babing*) to ensure both the official's silence in the event that he or she should discover the apartments and the official's intervention to prevent closer supervision of the company by the township government.

One of the ironic results of ongoing state efforts to classify economic crimes and ethical behavior by its agents is that the proliferation of these classifications can increase the "handle" held by entrepreneurs to induce officials to cooperate or tolerate activities that violate state definitions of standard operating procedures. For example, a 1989 ethics code for Industry and Commerce Bureau officials called the "Eight Imperatives and Eight Prohibitions" (*Ba yao ba buzhun*) listed such taboos as showing favoritism, accepting gifts, and practicing extortion.[16] Yet it is unclear what behavior may constitute such crimes in interactions between officials and entrepreneurs. Furthermore, the state's definitions of deviations

---

[16] The code proclaims: "It is not permitted to be lax to colleagues and strict to noncolleagues, to indulge superiors and discipline subordinates, to be lenient with intimates and harsh with strangers, to show laxity toward natives and severity toward nonnatives; it is not permitted to issue sentiment (*renqing*) licenses, receive sentiment fees, handle sentiment cases; it is not permitted to do business, hold a part-time job, or hold company shares; it is not permitted to buy at low prices on credit or to eat and take things for free in the market place; it is not permitted to sell confiscated goods at low prices or appropriate money received through fines; it is not permitted to take advantage of the authority of office to accept dinner invitations, to receive gifts, to demand money and other goods; it is especially not permitted to demand and receive bribes, and engage in racketeering and extortion" (*Xiamen Daily* 1989e).

in terms of personal self-interest overlook the fact that exchanges are impelled by a broad range of institutional constraints and opportunities, of which personal gain is only one consideration. As these institutional structures do not diminish, the behavior is inevitable and the result is the further criminalization of behavior. Company operators utilize these ambiguities for advantage. They are keenly aware that an official who accepts an entrepreneur's largesse is likely to provide more durable support both through the pull of *guanxi* obligations as well as to avoid the perception of having abetted the entrepreneur's wrongdoing.

There is an interesting variation in entrepreneurs' perceptions of these dual strategies that reflects the scale of the firms' operations. Entrepreneurs running the smallest and least prosperous firms in my sample were most likely to characterize relations with officials by *guanxi* idioms and to view the purpose of these ties as providing benefits through personal obligation. Those running moderately prosperous companies tended to view their bureaucratic networks in dual terms as inducing officials to provide benefits through personal inducements and fear of being implicated. The entrepreneurs who operated the largest and most successful firms were least likely to view relations with officials in terms of *guanxi*. They often held lavish year-end parties and sumptuous banquets to celebrate new business ventures to which they invited dozens of higher-ranking officials. It is highly unlikely that these entrepreneurs expected discretionary decisions as personal favors from officials who might attend their year-end party. The number of officials was simply too large to develop any personal relationship. Instead, they sought, in part, to link a large number of high-ranking officials with their firms, however tenuously, in order to increase the likelihood that these officials would spontaneously make supportive decisions to avoid any unpleasantness that this link might bring them. These lavish affairs also augmented an entrepreneur's reputation among the invited officials, who, by seeing each other, could be impressed by the extent of the entrepreneur's influence.

### Conclusion

Expectations in private business are socially organized. By "socially organized" I mean "putting together . . . diverse elements into a common relation" ([1951] 1964: 35–6); in economic activity, this refers to how multiple institutions constitute markets for goods and services (Zukin and DiMaggio 1990: 2–3). The interplay of statist and popular mechanisms produces and enhances expectations in social interactions. Each mechanism has relative advantages and shortcomings that help stimulate their interplay. Statist mechanisms are considered arbitrary, as they are linked to state power, which is driven by decisions and struggles within the bureaucracy that can be opaque to nonofficials and people in outlying locales. Statist mechanisms are also unpredictable because the central state can suddenly promulgate new laws and abrogate old ones, while local agencies enforce them according to their own interests and interpretations. By contrast, popular identities and obligations are seen as more accessible, because knowledge of them is widely diffused in society and people can manipulate them, within the constraints of legitimate practice, in dealings with others. They are also more predictable, because they change relatively slowly. Although contractual expectations in popularly based relations are often not as clear-cut as in statist ones, this ambiguity can facilitate contractual adjustments in a volatile political and economic environment.

The relationship of legal and popular mechanisms for producing contractual expectations is not zero-sum: the institutionalization of legality does not necessarily drive out reliance on popular institutions. I have described three kinds of nonexclusive interplay. The case of going to court suggests that legal and popular mechanisms can coexist as distinct choices with selection depending on the interest at stake. The example of employment contracts shows how one mechanism can be used to enhance expectations produced in the other. Entrepreneurs use the preferential granting of legal employment contracts to solidify particularistic bonds based on popular in-group/out-group distinctions. They also institutionalize them in firms in order to demonstrate compliance and loyalty to the government agency that is seeking to institute them. Finally, these mechanisms can operate simultaneously in a single practice to enhance expectations: I have shown how gift giving heightens expectations in regard to officials through popular norms of reciprocity and obligation as well through fears of legal sanctions from the state regulatory apparatus. In sum, commercial practice evolves through the interplay of multiple contracting institutions rather than tending to cohere in any single one.

# 6

## Entrepreneurial Paths and Capital: Personal Attributes as Competitive Advantage

The social backgrounds of entrepreneurs constrain the kinds of clientelist ties they operate through. This is because norms and identities attach themselves to individuals in idiosyncratic ways that reflect personal family background and life experiences. Therefore the strategies by which entrepreneurs forge links with the bureaucracy vary, as does the utility of these ties in profit and protection enhancement. These differences advantage some entrepreneurs over others, serving a competitive function.

As successive state policy waves have expanded the scope of private business, successive groups of entrepreneurs have entered the private business field, each having more efficacious capital to forge links with local state agents than the previous one.[1] Each group follows a distinct path with its own characteristic social backgrounds and motivations and strategies, creating patterns of competitive advantage among private firm operators.

### Entrepreneurial Paths

Three paths to entrepreneurship are apparent among Xiamen's private company operators (see Table 6.1). I label the earliest path the "speculator" path. This category includes 18 persons (from my sample of one hundred entrepreneurs) who did not have a job in the state or collective sectors, and were classified as unemployed. They supported themselves by illicit trade that, prior to the reforms, was largely unlicensed and labeled "speculation" (*toujidaoba*) by the state. I label the next path to emerge the "worker" path. This category comprises 38 people who were blue-collar workers in public units before becoming entrepreneurs. Their

---

[1] The tendency documented in this chapter of the positive correspondence between successive policies expanding private business and the successive entrance of persons better positioned in regard to the state structure has been noted in other studies (e.g., Róna-tas 1994; Gold 1990a: 172). Data on general social characteristics of private entrepreneurs are contained in *Research Report on Private Entrepreneurs*, compiled by the All-China Society of Private Economy and published in 1994; see Tao and Ho (1997) for discussion and results of the survey.

Table 6.1. *Prior occupation of entrepreneurs before obtaining business license*

| Speculators (N = 18) (Previously in unlicensed commercial activities) | Workers (N = 38) (Previously in manual public job) | Functionaries (N = 44) (Previously in nonmanual public job) |
| --- | --- | --- |
| *Smuggler (n = 1)* | *Factory worker (n = 5)* | *Petty personnel (n = 8)* teacher, guard, tour guide, receptionist |
| *Peddler (n = 14)* traders of produce, fish, ration coupons, sundries | *Manual laborer (n = 7)* cart-hauler, stevedore, construction worker, pedicab driver | *Professional (n = 7)* doctor, artist, reporter, college teacher |
| *Artisan (n = 2)* appliance repair, carpenter | *Craftsman (n = 19)* blacksmith, carpenter, driver, tool maker, welder | *Purchasing agent (n = 21)* six were in supervisory positions |
| *Scavenger (n = 1)* Seller of waste products (coal dust, cracked buttons, bottles) | *Technician (n = 7)* mechanic, machine repairman, electrician, printer | *Manager (n = 8)* army officer, factory manager, workshop leader, department chief |

occupations ranged from unskilled manual laborers and semiskilled assembly line workers to skilled craftsmen and technicians. The "functionary" path is the last entrepreneurial wave to emerge in the first market reform decade. This category includes 44 persons previously employed in public units in white-collar positions. Of these, 30 were in nonsupervisory positions, while the remaining 14 were lower-level managers.

The onset of entrepreneurship varies by prior occupation category (see Figure 6.1) and appears stimulated by specific state policies that successively expanded the scope of private business. Among former speculators, 61 percent (n = 11) began licensed business in 1979 and 1980, the period in which the Individual Business Household policy was first implemented. Of the former workers, 61 percent (n = 23) entered private business between 1984 and 1986, the high tide of the policy for privately run cooperative companies. Among former functionaries, 55 percent (n = 24) obtained business licenses in 1988, the first year of the Private Enterprise Interim Regulations that legalized private companies.[2]

A brief description of each path is in order. Seven people in the prior

---

[2] The trend of higher-status persons entering private business later in the reform era is suggested by various survey studies. For example, Sabin cites one unpublished finding that 25% of the operators of larger private companies have more than a high school education, 43% previously worked in the state sector, and at least one-third have overseas Chinese connections (Sabin 1994: 963, n. 30). See also Jia and Wang (1989).

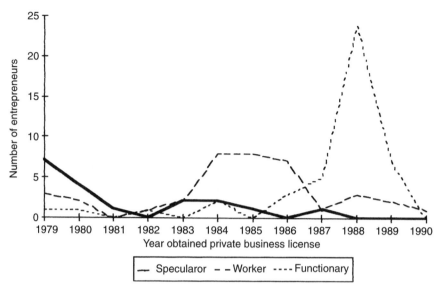

Figure 6.1. Onset of entrepreneurship, by prior occupation category.

occupation category of speculator are in their late forties and fifties. Some ran private shops after the revolution until forced into collective enterprises managed by the Number Two Light Industry Bureau in 1956 and 1957, where they languished, waiting for government procurement orders that never materialized. Taking advantage of a policy shift in the early 1960s that once again permitted petty private shops, they left these collectives for private business, taking what remained of their original assets. With the onset of the Cultural Revolution in 1966 private business was once again suppressed; they survived as best as they could in trade again deemed illicit. Others had worked in public units in the 1950s and 1960s before being forced out for political problems. They had been labeled as rightists in the 1957 Anti-Rightist Campaign or were persecuted for their capitalist family background during the Cultural Revolution. They too survived as best as they could in the underground economy.

The other 11 members of the former speculator category are former unemployed youths in their late twenties and thirties. Their education had been derailed by the closing of the schools in the Cultural Revolution: they never completed primary school and were therefore ineligible for public job assignments. Their meager education also precluded participation in political study sessions. They lived on the streets, joining gangs for companionship and protection. These gangs survived by illicit trade in ration coupons and smuggled Taiwan-made watches and shoes. For all entrepreneurs in this category, the acquisition of a business license in 1979 and the early 1980s amounted to legalization of what they were already doing.

The former worker category has the largest number of younger entrepreneurs. Fully 76 percent ($n = 29$) are in their twenties or thirties. They are mostly skilled workers (*jishu gong*) who left their jobs in the mid-1980s. Many had already been moonlighting in the market economy, especially in construction activities; they quickly realized they could earn more money in the market economy in a few years than in a lifetime in public employment. Also, by the mid-1980s there was increased confidence that the market reforms were permanent, reducing their concern about "throwing away their iron rice bowl" – a tenured public job with desirable social welfare benefits. However, since they were among the most talented young workers, their superiors sought to persuade them to stay in the factories. Many took unpaid leaves of absence, paying the equivalent of a third to a half of their public wages for a period of three to five years to maintain their seniority and benefits in their public units. This was also a risk-averse strategy that created a route of retreat by letting them return to public employment should their private business fail or state policy become hostile to private business.

There are two other types who took the worker path to entrepreneurship. One is the entrepreneur in his fifties from a pre-revolutionary capitalist business family who became a manual laborer in the Cultural Revolution because of political problems. These were the first of the worker category to undertake business, establishing private shops in 1979 and 1980. The other type is the former unskilled assembly line worker in his forties. These were the last of this category to leave public units. Their startup capital came from overseas kin rather than from their moonlighting activities and they were the least entrepreneurial in the entire sample, viewing business as an alternative to public employment and a route to a more comfortable lifestyle.

Of the three prior occupation categories, the functionary one has the widest age distribution. The oldest entrepreneurs, in their fifties and sixties, are descended from capitalist business families. Some began private business careers after retirement; they now enjoy both public pensions and private incomes. Others, who had promising careers that were derailed when they were labeled rightists in 1957, see entrepreneurship as a way to achieve the success that has thus far eluded them.

The second-oldest former functionaries belong to the "lost generation" that entered adulthood during the Cultural Revolution. They are in their thirties and forties and also descended from capitalist business families.

Stigmatized by "capitalist class" labels, they were denied admission to college and were subsequently posted to villages as "sent-down" youth during the rural rustification launched in the 1960s. They suffered further discrimination by being posted to villages in the distant mountains of western Fujian. In the 1970s some returned to Xiamen without authorization. As illegal residents (*hei hukou*), they could not get allocations of food ration coupons; they relied on odd jobs and their families to survive. In the early 1980s they got public jobs by filling vacancies created by their fathers' retirement, a practice permitted by state policy. However, in their public jobs they experienced feelings of inadequacy, particularly those whose fathers had been highly educated professionals, such as doctors and engineers. After a few years they resigned for private business. Their prior experience of scavenging for a living in Xiamen gave them confidence that they could make it in private business.

A third group in the former functionary category are people in their thirties who previously were purchasing agents in public units. Unlike their age counterparts in the worker category, they met little resistance from their superiors and resigned outright rather then take unpaid leaves of absence. This reflected both their confidence in private business and changing perceptions of leaves of absence; by the late 1980s leaves were viewed less as a risk-averse escape route (*houlu*) than as a complicating factor that let the authorities in former work units continue to make demands on them. By the late 1980s, the large profits from business were common knowledge. Public unit officials were demanding more money to approve leaves of absence, and even unilaterally raising fees. A clean break with public employment is even more pronounced in the fourth kind of entrepreneur in the former functionary category. These are persons in their twenties or early thirties who are also descended from capitalist business families. They either resigned very early in public careers or went directly into private business after completing school, bypassing public employment altogether. In this they have been encouraged by overseas kin who gave startup capital and business training.

Finally, it is notable that the one hundred entrepreneurs in my sample are mostly males. Only six are women. Four women are former functionaries, one a former worker, and one previously a speculator. Five women are descended from capitalist families, giving them overseas financial capital and trade links. The older women, those in their early fifties, have stigmatized social statuses: two are widows, one is a divorcee, and one had been severely persecuted for her bad class label. These women said they entered private business largely to provide more support for their families. Of the younger women, one became an entrepreneur by default after her husband, who had operated the company, was arrested for economic crimes, while the other resigned a good state-sector job for private business after receiving a large sum of money from overseas kin.

My data suggest that company entrepreneurship is primarily a male undertaking. This is consistent with other findings that show business-women to be much more numerous in the petty private sector than as operators of private companies (Entwisle et al. 1995). However, women do participate to a greater extent in private business than my figures indicate; the wives of some entrepreneurs are especially active in company operations, particularly in the former worker category, as will be discussed below. In fact, these wives should be considered the entrepreneurs and the husbands merely the legal license holders. My conversations with businesswomen also suggest that gender could be a variable in patterning societal capital accumulations and business strategies. For example, several of these female entrepreneurs mentioned that being a woman elicited greater trust in business dealings.[3]

## Idioms of Societal Capital

The kind of support that an entrepreneur can muster from the social environment stems from his or her personal capacity to elicit it. Such a capacity is colloquially called one's "societal capital" (*shehui ziben*).[4] One set of idioms refers to the forms of this capital, while another set refers to their modes of accumulation. Varying forms of capital are acquired in different modes of accumulation, differences that in turn reflect the social backgrounds of the entrepreneurs. These forms of capital can in turn be converted into economic capital in the form of land and money, either directly or through first converting the capital into political capital in the form of officials' discretionary favor to enhance profit and security.

---

[3] For a brief description of how these women entrepreneurs use perceptions of femininity as part of their business strategy, see Wank (2000). However, due to the small number of women in my sample, my data do not address the issue of gender and entrepreneurship. The only ethnographic work on private businesswomen during economic reform that I am aware of is by the anthropologist Hill Gates, who focuses on female proprietors of small shops (Gates 1991, 1993).

[4] The indigenous concept of "societal capital" is broader than the concept of social capital found in American sociology. The latter generally refers to personal ties and obligated norms (e.g., Bourdieu 1986; Burt 1992), whereas in the indigenous usage such ties and norms are only one form of societal capital. The various forms of societal capital and the manner of conversion closely approximate Bourdieu's (1986) discussion. The use of capital idioms by Xiamen's entrepreneurs no doubt partly reflects their familiarity with the same writing of Marx that inspired Bourdieu's typology of the forms of capital.

The forms of societal capital are indicated by several idioms. *Guanxi* capital is the degree of obligation that an entrepreneur can expect in a personal tie. It consists of norms of reciprocity stemming from moral obligations and material incentives linked to the identities of individuals in dyads. This type of societal capital entails much face-to-face interaction and communication to ensure mutual recognition of relational identities. *Guanxi* capital, as suggested in Chapter 4, is transferable through the principle of connectivity: when two persons are introduced by a third mutually known individual, the social trust is enhanced between the two persons by the shared link to the third individual.

A second form of societal capital is reputation, and is indicated by several idioms. "Renown" (*mingsheng*) refers to reputation stemming from one's family name. "Fame" (*mingqi*) is favorable image created by widespread knowledge of one's deeds and exploits, either by informal networks of gossip or by publicity in the state-run media. "Repute" (*mingyu*) refers to the perception by others that one has behaved in accordance with rather well-defined expectations held by these others, be they members of the business community or officials in specific agencies.[5] These forms of reputation consist of the attribution to a person of certain characteristics valued by society. Cooperation from others is forthcoming on the basis of goodwill if the reputation emphasizes contributions to the community. Cooperation can also be induced through awe and fear, as it is assumed that someone with a significant reputation is well connected to officialdom, and can initiate reprisals for noncooperation. Reputation is also somewhat transferable. For example, a high official's offspring can derive fame from the parent's name if awareness of the parent–offspring relationship is diffused in the population in which the entrepreneur is active.

A third form of societal capital is the "impression" (*yinxiang*) that one conveys in social intercourse. This is a person's possession of the sorts of comportment and behavior that encourage a favorable reaction from others. It inheres in an individual's style. Certain mannerisms and clothing are more likely to convey authority and generate perceptions of trustworthiness in social interactions. Therefore it also inheres in the skills for social etiquette. One skill is a person's ability in the "art of social relations," which refers to enhancing obligation by the calculated manipulation of the cultural rules of reciprocity. Impression is transfer-

---

[5] Repute with the business community is similar to the idiom of credit (*xinyong*) documented in studies of business in Hong Kong, Taiwan, and overseas Chinese business communities. Credit is one's reputation for meeting dyadic obligations in repeated transactions. As knowledge of breach of expectations can circulate in the wider community, credit is also general evaluations of trustworthiness by the business community. For discussion of *xinyong* see Barton (1983); DeGlopper (1972, 1995); Kao (1991); Silin (1972); Wong (1991).

able in that a person can learn these rules, although much impression is acquired in early childhood socialization and is somewhat ascriptive.

While idiomatically discrete, the various forms of capital are mutually constitutive. Knowledge of how to convey certain impressions can enhance reputation and obligation. Reputation is more useful if one knows how to project authority. This interconnectedness of forms creates numerous possibilities in social interactions. It enables individuals who possess an abundance of one form of capital to use it to produce other forms. As will be shown below, the distribution of the forms of capital among Xiamen's private company operators is patterned by variations in social backgrounds, which constrains business strategies.

The routes of societal capital accumulation are indicated by another set of idioms. These idioms reveal how these routes vary by the timing of accumulation. One idiom of accumulation is "endowment" (*tianzi*). Endowment consists of the obligations, reputations, and impressions that one acquires by virtue of birth or "congenitally" (*tianshengde*) into a family of a particular economic class or bureaucratic rank. It can be the most advantageous, as obligations are formed well before entrepreneurship with no intent to profit, impression is acquired through early socialization, and reputation is ascriptive. Another accumulation mode is signified by the idiom of "savings" (*jilei*). Savings is societal capital acquired through life experiences that predate the entrepreneurial career in childhood, education, work, and political experiences. It is acquired without any initial intent to profit commercially and is considered to be durable, and, therefore, relatively desirable. Another mode is "investment" (*touzi*). This is societal capital acquired after the onset of the business career. It can be personal ties that develop during the course of business, reputation that stems from business success, or new skills of social interaction gained through doing business. Such capital is acquired and manipulated with an eye to enhance business and contains less affect or obligation. It is the least advantageous and is most heavily used by those lacking societal capital endowments or savings.

## The Distribution of Advantageous Societal Capital

Societal capital accumulation in entrepreneurship varies broadly in the three entrepreneurial paths. Certain paths facilitate certain kinds of capital accumulations and preclude others. In other words, an entrepreneur's social background prior to embarking on entrepreneurship in the reform era constrains the societal capital endowments and savings available at the onset of business and shapes subsequent investment strategies to augment it. Those who are on the functionary path have the most advantaged societal capital. They were born into cadre families or prerevolutionary *grande bourgeoisie* families and possess significant capital endowments and savings that produce hard and durable connections. Former workers and then former speculators are from lesser social backgrounds and rely more heavily on investment strategies after embarking on business to enhance societal capital. This section describes the distribution of advantageous societal capital among the three entrepreneurial paths; the next section considers strategies of investment in societal capital.

### The Functionary Path

Former functionaries are endowed with the most advantageous societal capital when they began business. As the offspring of local government officials or descendants of capitalist business families they have the most supportive ties with officialdom and thick transnational networks. Such advantages attach to individuals by birth and are amplified through subsequent life experiences of schooling and employment.

*Societal Capital Endowments.*    Family background endows some entrepreneurs with strong obligated ties to officials in the city government. To have a father who served in the Thirty-first People's Liberation Army, which wrested Xiamen from Nationalist troops in 1949, confers great advantages in local business. The Thirty-first Army numbered many peasants from Shandong and northern Jiangsu provinces in its ranks, who, upon demobilization after 1949, were appointed to city government positions in such bureaus as Transportation, Harbor Management, and Public Security. Their sons grew up in Xiamen, speak fluent local dialect, and consider themselves "locals" even though their fathers do not speak dialect and are considered "outsiders." When the sons began business, they enjoyed their fathers' support and access to their fathers' networks of army comrades-in-arms throughout the city government.

Another advantageous background is descent from a prerevolutionary capitalist business family. Some fathers, those who operated trading firms, became salaried public employees after their firms were appropriated by the state in the early and mid-1950s. They were appointed to positions that, given the anti-capitalist ideology of the time, were relatively undesirable: accountant and payroll supervisors in such distributive units as the Grain Bureau, such commercial units as the Foreign Trade Bureau, and such commercial administrative agencies as the Tax

Bureau.[6] Although these fathers were not party members and were persecuted during the Cultural Revolution, many had risen to important positions in these bureaus by the 1980s and could provide support to their entrepreneurial offspring by their networks among officialdom. Other fathers, those who once owned manufacturing firms, were retained as managers in the firms after expropriation, as they had the technical skills necessary for the firms' operations. While occupying less strategic positions than those in nonmanufacturing public units and agencies, these fathers have helped their offspring through introductions to officials and knowledge of the bureaucracy. These family backgrounds also advantage entrepreneurs in obtaining startup capital and transnational commercial connections through overseas kin.

The functionary path clearly possesses more of these advantageous obligated networks than the other paths (see Tables 6.2 and 6.3). Former functionaries have the largest percentage of fathers who are Thirty-first Army veterans – 16 percent ($n = 7$) as compared with 13 percent ($n = 5$) of the former workers and none of the former speculators. This category also contains the largest percentage of entrepreneurs descended from capitalist business families, through either the father's or the grandfather's occupation:[7] 46 percent ($n = 20$) of former functionaries are so descended as compared with 29 percent ($n = 11$) of former workers and 22 percent ($n = 4$) of former speculators.

Several important qualitative variations are not apparent from the statistics. One concerns fathers who are Thirty-first Army veterans. While the percentage of former functionaries and workers from such an advantaged background is almost the same, the fathers of the former occupy higher bureaucratic positions than those of the latter. Several fathers of former functionaries hold leading positions in city-level bureaus, whereas fathers of former workers are in district and subdistrict positions. This difference is also linked to long-term intergenerational processes. Although all the grandfathers are from rural villages, there are differences between the two paths. The grandfathers of the five former workers with veteran fathers were poor peasants. In contrast, the grandfathers of former functionaries include wealthier peasants and even landlords: this enabled the fathers of the functionaries to get a better

[6] They were given shares in the firm based on the state's valuation of the business and received incomes often several times higher than workers. Many of them were forced out of their positions during the Cultural Revolution. Their positions and back pay were restored after the Cultural Revolution.

[7] In some old business families, the grandfathers had been in business, while the fathers became professionals. Because their fathers were not in business, they were given class labels such as "independent professional," which carried less stigma than the capitalist class label.

Table 6.2. *Entrepreneurs' fathers' occupations, by prior occupation category*

| Father's occupation (1949) | Prior occupation category | | | |
|---|---|---|---|---|
| | Speculator | Worker | Functionary | Total |
| *Manual* | | | | 27 |
| Peasant | 0 | 3 | 0 | 3 |
| Laborer | 3 | 3 | 0 | 6 |
| Factory worker | 3 | 5 | 4 | 12 |
| Craftsman | 1 | 4 | 1 | 6 |
| *Commerce* | | | | 38 |
| Smuggler | 0 | 1 | 0 | 1 |
| Peddler | 2 | 2 | 0 | 4 |
| Shopkeeper | 3 | 1 | 1 | 5 |
| Merchant | 4 | 9 | 13 | 26 |
| Rural landlord[a] | 0 | 1 | 1 | 2 |
| *Cadre* | | | | 35 |
| Functionary[b] | 1 | 3 | 12 | 16 |
| Soldier (PLA) | 0 | 5 | 7 | 12 |
| Official (KMT) | 1 | 1 | 2 | 4 |
| Enterprise manager | 0 | 0 | 3 | 3 |
| Total | 18 | 38 | 44 | 100 |

[a] These were absentee landlords who lived in Xiamen.
[b] Many entrepreneurs whose fathers were professionals are from merchant families because their grandfathers were merchants (see Table 6.3).
*Source*: Interviews, 1988–90.

education and achieve higher positions in the army before 1949 and in the urban government afterward.

A second qualitative variation is that the advantages of a capitalist family background in providing connections with officialdom are greater in the functionary path. A number of its entrepreneurs come from *grande bourgeoisie* families that were locally prominent before the revolution. Such families once owned diversified enterprise groups of factories, traditional banks, trading firms, and inns. This contrasts with the former workers and speculators whose business fathers mostly operated single firms not much larger than shops. Furthermore, *grande bourgeoisie* families have resided in Xiamen for generations – six in the case of one family – and have more extensive local networks. Such backgrounds have amplified the aforementioned advantages. The parents are well educated and rose to relatively high positions in public employment. *Grande bourgeoisie* families are most likely to have overseas kin in business who can provide transnational resources.

Table 6.3. *Entrepreneurs' grandfathers'*
*occupations (when the grandfathers were in*
*commerce and the fathers were not), by prior*
*occupation category*

| Grandfather's occupation (pre-1949) | Speculator | Worker | Functionary | Total |
|---|---|---|---|---|
| Peddler | 0 | 0 | 1 | 1 |
| Shopkeeper | 1 | 1 | 0 | 2 |
| Merchant | 0 | 2 | 7 | 9 |
| Total | 1 | 3 | 8 | 12 |

Family background also endows former functionaries with significant business-enhancing fame via family name. This is highly efficacious if a parent is a high official. Knowledge that the entrepreneur is related to this official induces others to cooperate out of awe as well as fear of possible reprisals for noncooperation. The use of fame for commercial gain is most apparent among the entrepreneurial offspring of the central state elite, the so-called princes' party. A comparable instance of such fame in my sample concerns an entrepreneur related by marriage to a leading official family in Guangdong province. She said, "I use their name in doing business and so people know that I belong to this lineage. I don't actually have to use their power in business as people trust me because of the family connection" (informant no. 12). This tie lets her, among other things, buy at low prices smuggled goods confiscated by the Guangdong Provincial Customs Bureau.

In my sample such fame most often stems from a father who is highly placed in the city bureaucracy. The father of one businessman was previously posted in Sanming, an industrial city built after the revolution in central Fujian province, as part of the party-state strategy in the 1950s and 1960s to relocate heavy industry away from the militarily vulnerable coastal regions.[8] The father is now a vice bureau chief in the Xiamen government, but the son has invoked the family name to obtain chemicals and raw materials in Sanming for export. Fame can also augment protection, as seen in the case of an entrepreneur who is the son of a city government official. After his company moved to a new location, local officials from regulatory agencies visited his company to seek payment of sundry charges. He graciously received each official, casually dropping his father's name and title in conversation. "I said I'd be happy to pay

[8] This was part of the so-called "Third Front" industrialization program (Naughton 1988).

charges but that I would first consult with my father. Each official soon left after sitting a while and there was no more mention of fees" (informant no. 73).

For descendants of the most illustrious of Xiamen's prerevolution *grande bourgeoisie*, family name alone can produce reputation. An example is an entrepreneur whose father was one of the wealthiest businesspeople in Xiamen before the revolution. Although publicly vilified as a "capitalist prince" in the Cultural Revolution, the father is now nostalgically remembered for contributions to the community; he operated Xiamen's first movie house and paved the road to his ancestral village. This reputation generates a measure of goodwill toward the son as well. The reputation value of a *grande bourgeoisie* name is boosted by the special economic zone policy to attract overseas Chinese investment. The names of *grande bourgeoisie* families are known among overseas Chinese communities. Favorable treatment of their descendants in Xiamen by officialdom is a sign to the overseas Chinese community of local government openness and commitment to a market economy.

Family backgrounds can also generate impression-enhancing endowments of cosmopolitan style and knowledge. Officials' offspring have special opportunities to go abroad on study tours to gain business expertise. One entrepreneur spent three months working in a corporation in Japan. This corporation, which had local investments, agreed to send the entrepreneur, the son of a high city government official, to participate in a three-month training course at the parent plant in Japan. As for descendants of capitalist business families, they are sponsored by overseas kin to go abroad for work, study, or family visits. When they return to Xiamen, they impress others by their cosmopolitan talk and wearing of fashionable business suits.

These advantaged family backgrounds also provide crucial forms of knowledge in social interactions. The children of officials know how to project authority. They are more able to keep their emotions in check and use calculated displays of approval or displeasure to create desired reactions in others. They command more authority by speaking in measured tones and gesturing in deliberate, forceful motions. The importance of this self-control is suggested by the disparaging way that officials talked in interviews and conversations with me about the peddlers in the daily produce markets. They were described condescendingly as "haggling in loud voices," "waving their hands wildly," and "rolling their eyes." One official shrewdly noted that exaggerated body language is a way for people who lack social standing to draw attention to themselves; it is the mark of an "insignificant person" (*xiao ren*). Finally, officials' children are not hesitant to project their authority to challenge those in power. They are less likely to comply unquestioningly with street-level officials, threatening to check with higher authorities on the "legality" of the various fees and taxes imposed by the officials.[9]

The greater capacity of the former functionaries to project authority can be seen in the issue of dress. Entrepreneurs from the former worker and former speculator categories are more likely to wear such simple garb as blue or gray trousers, thin white shirts, and even plastic sandals when interacting with officialdom to prevent any impression that they are attempting to "one-up" the officials. This contrasts with entrepreneurs from the former functionary group, who dress more or less as they please. They are confident enough to display their wealth without worrying about jealous officials and convey an aura of prosperity, power, and cosmopolitanism in their dress. An example is the thirty-year-old son of a high city government official. He had done graduate study in the United States, and his trade in lucrative raw materials and reputed impending receipt of foreign trade authority, among the first private companies in China to receive it, testified to his excellent bureaucratic connections. He dressed as he pleased. I once saw him dining with officials in a restaurant while wearing jeans and sneakers; on another occasion at a government bureau he wore an expensive business suit.

*Societal Capital Savings.*    The various forms of advantageous capital acquired as savings are created in the contexts of schooling and prior employment. A high level of education can enhance cooperation from others. The former functionary category has the greatest accumulation of this capital (see Table 6.4). Fully 80 percent ($n = 35$) have at least a middle school education as compared with 37 percent ($n = 14$) and 11 percent ($n = 2$) of the entrepreneurs in the former worker and former speculator categories, respectively. Furthermore, 27 percent ($n = 12$) have some tertiary education as compared with 8 percent ($n = 3$) of former workers and no former speculators. Among the former functionaries were two graduates of elite national universities and one with an M.A. from a North American university. Tertiary education is in the fields of engineering, science, mathematics, finance, and business management.

There is a positive correspondence between higher levels of education and the hardness of bureaucratic support. Because all high school graduates were assigned public positions, usually in state sector public units, former functionaries have more classmates in state sector employment. Furthermore, more former functionaries have networks with higher-level

---

[9] In regard to private shopkeepers, Ole Bruun notes that they "rarely . . . venture to check with higher authorities when met with commands from local officials. Either requests are silently complied with or attempts are made to manipulate them within a *guanxi*-type of relationship" (Bruun 1993: 120).

Table 6.4. *Entrepreneurs' educational attainment, by prior occupation category*

| Educational level | Speculator No. | Worker No. | Functionary No. | Total No. |
|---|---|---|---|---|
| Did not complete primary school[a] | 9[a] | 10 | 4 | 23 |
| Primary school graduate | 4 | 6 | 0 | 10 |
| Junior middle school graduate | 3 | 8 | 5 | 16 |
| Middle school graduate | 2 | 11 | 23 | 36 |
| Received college education | 0 | 3 | 12[b] | 15 |

[a] This includes one illiterate person.
[b] This includes eight people in evening colleges or with at least one year of college, three holders of the B.A., and one of the M.A. degree. The B. A. degrees are from Qinghua, Fujian Normal, and Xiamen universities. The M. A. degree is from Ohio State University in the United States.
*Source*: Interviews, 1988–90.

officials than the other entrepreneurs. This is because they were educated at more elite schools, such as Xiamen's Number One Middle School, whose graduates are assigned to higher-ranking public units. Also, those who graduated from elite universities have valuable networks via alumni connections and associations. An entrepreneur who graduated from an elite technical university in the 1950s now operates a trading company that sells computers. He obtained startup money through the local branch of the university's alumni association. Further capital came from its international branches in Hong Kong, Taiwan, and America. He sells through his personal network of alumni, which, comprising graduates of such an elite university, contains university presidents, faculty deans, department heads, and leaders of scientific research institutes.

Higher education also enhances impression by inculcating greater facility with language in face-to-face social interactions. By speaking in complete sentences and using elegant phrases and classical quotations, one projects an aura of refinement and credibility. One businessman noted perceptively that "doing business is closely related to use of language" (informant no. 25). He elaborated:

> To do business you have to speak with others. You need poise (*fengdu*). . . . This is very closely connected with your level of education. If your level is high then you can speak with much wit. You use more appropriate words and express yourself with greater clarity. Each sentence comes out of your mouth

effortlessly and follows the other in a definite order. This makes others feel comfortable and you make a very good impression. People will like to speak to you. You will find it much easier to get things done.

The importance of education was underscored by the comments of poorly educated entrepreneurs. They viewed their meager education as a handicap not because of lesser human capital skills but because of reduced capacity to create a good impression. Those with a good education, they commented, could find an apt classical phrase to convey a complex idea or subtle meaning while they struggled in coarser vernacular. Some recounted tensing up in social interactions, especially with officials, stuttering and gesticulating as they sought to express themselves. They worried that they lost face by "making fools of themselves" (*chuchou*) in their speech and projecting "unstable" (*buwending*) and "unreliable" (*bukekao*) impressions.

My interviews and conversations with administrative officials suggest these concerns were justified. Entrepreneurs with more formal education were considered more trustworthy and cooperative. Officials at the Industry and Commerce Bureau during my interviews there referred to problematic entrepreneurs as "illiterates," prone to "stuttering," and having a low "cultural level" (*wenhua shuiping*). An official at a district tax substation said that entrepreneurs with low cultural levels commit more economic crimes because they do not understand laws nor realize that businesspeople have a social responsibility beyond self-enrichment. The frequency with which officials link impressions that are virtually synonymous with formal education to trustworthiness and cooperativeness suggests that entrepreneurs exhibiting such behavior command respect from officials, making them less subject than more gauche entrepreneurs to bureaucratic harassment and targeting during campaigns.

Another key context for creating societal capital is prior employment. Entrepreneurs who worked in higher-status state units are more likely to have former colleagues in higher public positions than those who worked in lower collective units. And, as shown in Chapter 4, higher rank confers the advantages of hardness and connectivity. Also, many state units belong to nationally affiliated bureaucratic organs (*xitong*) that are useful avenues along which to expand business networks. For instance, a Xiamen entrepreneur who had been an army officer stationed in Siquan province heard through army connections that a trading firm in Xiamen run by a Siquan-based military unit was to be leased. He thereupon arranged to get the lease.

Of the three paths, the functionary path provided the most valuable

Table 6.5. *Status of entrepreneurs' prior work unit, by prior occupation category*

| Status of prior work Unit | Speculator No. | Worker No. | Functionary No. | Total No. |
|---|---|---|---|---|
| Unlicensed | 18 | 0 | 0 | 18 |
| Collective | 0 | 28 | 12 | 40 |
| State | 0 | 9 | 29 | 38 |
| Private | 0 | 1 | 3 | 4 |
| Total | 18 | 38 | 44 | 100 |

*Source*: Interviews, 1988–90.

prior work experience: 66 percent ($n = 29$) of former functionaries worked in state sector units, while only 24 percent ($n = 9$) of the former workers and none of the former speculators worked in them (see Table 6.5). Although 27 percent ($n = 12$) of the former functionaries worked in collective sector units, these were all higher-level collectives with none below the district level. By contrast, 74 percent ($n = 28$) of the former workers were previously in collectives, many of which were below the district level. Of the former workers, 29% ($n = 11$) were previously in street-level collectives and 45% ($n = 17$) in district-level ones. None of the former functionaries were in street-level collectives and only 27% ($n = 12$) in district-level ones.

Also, several former functionaries had previously worked as managers of private foreign enterprises in the Xiamen, Shenzhen, and Hainan special economic zones. This work gave them advantageous obligated networks in these key commercial centers as well as human capital experience in operating a commercial enterprise. They obtained these positions via the mix of bureaucratic and overseas ties that characterizes the functionary path. For example, one entrepreneur was formerly an administrative secretary in a southern Fujian county famous for its tea. He used this position to help a Singapore relative get high-grade tea for export. He then resigned his offical post to help another relative establish manufacturing enterprises in Hainan and Xiamen. In 1988 he set up a private company specializing in tea.

### The Worker Path

Former workers have smaller accumulation of advantageous societal capital than former functionaries. Some former workers have family members who are officials or are descended from prerevolutionary capitalist business families. However, as earlier noted, these family backgrounds create less benefit-rich networks than in the functionary path. Former workers' fathers who are officials occupy lower bureaucratic positions at subdistrict and street levels. Some of the former workers' fathers work in administrative posts in street committees, while others are managers in small collectives (*xiao jiti*) at the subdistrict level. These networks provide access to public assets controlled at the lowest levels of the bureaucracy. For example, a father working in the street committee arranged for his entrepreneurial son to rent a shop owned by the street committee. Another entrepreneur whose father managed a district transportation unit leased trucks from the unit at a low price. Parents-in-law can also amplify the networks with officialdom: a number of entrepreneurs had spouses whose parents are also local officials.

Several former workers were descendants of prerevolutionary business families that were too petty to have created obligated endowments to officialdom from the parents but have provided support via siblings. This is illustrated by an older entrepreneur who once worked in a state bank in the 1950s. During the Hundred Flowers Campaign he criticized the bank's leaders and was subsequently labeled a rightist. He left the job and wound up as a coal cart hauler for his street committee. In 1979, he opened a small private clothing shop. He has been supported by his sister, who had earlier renounced her family ties to overcome her stigmatized capitalist class background. By the 1980s she had become a ranking official in the local Commercial Bureau and was reconciled with her brother. She gave him letters of introduction to the managers of state textile factories in Shanghai that manufactured export-quality clothes, enabling him to be the first to sell them locally.

Entrepreneurs from prerevolutionary business families who are only two or three generations removed from ancestral villages use these ties for access to resources in the hinterland controlled by strategically positioned kin in rural governments. I have already mentioned the example of the seafood farm in Chapter 5. Other instances of this are entrepreneurs in the textile trade who set up clothing factories in their ancestral villages and entrepreneurs who helped establish trucking companies in their ancestral villages.

Some former workers have acquired the advantages of *grande bourgeoisie* family background through marriage to women born into such families. In the 1960s and 1970s these women wed men from worker backgrounds; at the time this was considered a good match for the women, given their stigmatized capitalist class labels. Since 1979 some of their families' former properties have been returned and they have received money from overseas kin that they invested in business. One entrepreneur, for example, was married to the eldest daughter of an artist from a prominent business family. In 1949 her parents sent her to the family's ancestral village in Fujian province and took the sons to Taiwan, where the father became a prominent cultural figure. The daughter grew up in the village and married a mechanic in a nearby army unit. In 1980 she reestablished contact with her family in Taiwan, who gave her money that she and her husband used to start a transportation company.

Several married couples in the worker path run the business together, increasing societal capital through teamwork. The husbands have artisan and technical skills but are naïve (*laoshi*) and not versed in manipulating social interactions for self-gain, while their wives are more capable. Such husband–wife business teams involve the aforementioned instances of workers married to women from prerevolutionary business family backgrounds. These women are better educated than their husbands and more adept in manipulative social interaction as a result of coping with stigmatized social backgrounds. The firms are run by a division of labor: the husbands oversee production while the wives handle external relations with officials and customers.

Former workers also draw on friendships with people who are the offspring of high officials. Fully half the former workers attended junior middle school where the offspring of officials numbered among their classmates. In other cases such friendships developed during the rural rustification program when they resided in the same village. Because of their good class labels of worker or poor and lower-middle peasant, they were sent to nearby suburban villages rather then to poor and distant villages. Here they met the offspring of urban officials, who also had received favorable postings because of their parents' status. These friendships later enabled entrepreneurs who lacked connections with officials to obtain them indirectly through business partnerships with these friends. This tendency can be seen in the partnerships of cooperative companies, which are mostly run by entrepreneurs in the former worker category.[10] Partnerships are formed by three or more friends from lower-status backgrounds and one friend who is the offspring of a well-placed official. The latter represents the company in administrative dealings and public functions to heighten perceptions of the company's official backing. As one entrepreneur said of his well-connected partner, "we have him 'show his face' (*chumian*) at public occasions. Although he is not representing his father, everyone knows who he is" (informant no. 4).[11]

---

[10] Cooperatives are formed by at least four partners. The former worker category had fifteen individuals running cooperatives while the former functionary and speculator categories contained nine and one respectively.

[11] Such partnerships had mostly broken up in all but name at the time of my fieldwork. However, bureaucratic support derived from such partnerships was crucial to the early growth of firms.

In short, such friendships enabled entrepreneurs from low social statuses to obtain bureaucratic support.

To set up business affiliations in village and township enterprises, many former workers use ties developed during their rustification in the Cultural Revolution, as the villages they resided in were suburban and often conveniently located in adjacent Longhai and Tongan counties. One entrepreneur who remained for seven years in a village adjacent to the coastal highway has built a roadside shopping mall there. In another case, an entrepreneur's brother put down roots in a suburban village where, because of his good education, he rose through the management ranks of township enterprises, eventually becoming director of a conglomerate of township factories. The brother has arranged for the entrepreneur to lease factory workshops to produce disposable chopsticks and umbrellas for export and colored light bulbs for domestic sale to discotheques and nightclubs.

### The Speculator Path

Former speculators have the least societal capital endowments and savings. While four in the sample are from capitalist business families, the scale of these family firms was very small, leaving no societal capital endowments. Also, their subsequent life experiences created few opportunities to cultivate personal ties with those in power. Their only endowed societal capital comes from prior black market activities.

Entrepreneurs in their fifties and sixties could come to know some officials during their involvement in illicit trade before 1979. One entrepreneur who was highly skilled in glass etching came to know several high-ranking officials when, during the 1960s and 1970s, he was occasionally commissioned by them to etch mirrors given to newlyweds. In this way he came to know personally some ranking officials. More common is for entrepreneurs to have developed mutual understandings with the officers in street and residents' committees and cadres in police substations during the 1960s and 1970s through run-ins with authorities. Although in some cases these officers and cadres had persecuted the entrepreneurs, it was not malicious, never exceeding the minimum required to demonstrate compliance with central policies. Some of these officers were still occupying local positions and, after years, and in some cases decades, of interaction, mutual accommodation of the "live and let live" sort had been reached. One businessman during the 1960s and 1970s ran a succession of private underground black factories (*dixia hei gongchang*) that hired neighbors. The local residents' committee turned a blind eye to this activity until pressured to expose it in a "wipe out the tails of capitalism" campaign during the early 1970s. In the market reform era the local residents' committee has supported the entrepreneur's efforts to reclaim confiscated family real estate.

Younger entrepreneurs who had previously been unemployed formed similar ties with local officials. They tended to be the eldest sons of poor families with physically handicapped members or a deceased father. Local officials sympathized with their plights and tolerated their desperate attempts to provide for their families. This is illustrated in the case of a thirty-year-old entrepreneur whose schooling was disrupted by the Cultural Revolution. When his father died of illness in the early 1970s, he turned to illegal street trade in grain ration coupons and smuggled watches to support his illiterate mother and four younger siblings. Local authorities tolerated this trade as long as it was small-scale because it was the family's sole income. Tolerance turned to active support when he was caught in 1980 during an anti-smuggling sweep. He avoided severe punishment through the intervention of the local residents' committee and the police substation. Sympathetic officials urged him to get a business license and guided him through the administrative process. His business grew and he became a neighborhood success story. Local authorities have continued to provide him with inside information on impending crackdowns and are lax in regulatory matters.

## Enhancing Societal Capital

All entrepreneurs pursue investment strategies to extend the range of their societal capital, even those possessing many advantageous endowments and savings. They do so for two reasons. One reason is what Mark Granovetter (1973) calls the "strength of weak ties." Beyond the initial startup stage, new opportunities are much more likely to be found in more socially distant acquaintances rather than closer friendships or family ties. This is because an entrepreneur is embedded in pretty much the same networks as friend and family, so they are all privy to the same information; in the words of Ronald Burt, the networks are "redundant," providing similar benefits (Burt 1992: 18–20). By contrast, an acquaintance is embedded in networks that do not overlap with those of the entrepreneur and is so more likely to have different information. The other reason has to do with the shift by entrepreneurs into interregional trade as business expands. Xiamen is a small city with a hinterland far smaller than that of Guangzhou or Shanghai, so it presents limited trade opportunities. As they expanded into new regions, even the advantageous societal capital base of former functionaries could no longer support these more far-flung activities, and so they invested in new societal capital. As one entrepreneur put it, "even if your father has power and influence (*shili*) in Xiamen, he won't be able to pull connections for you in Fuzhou, let along in Guangzhou or Shanghai" (informant no. 59).

### Participation in Associations

Participation in certain business associations can dramatically increase interaction with officialdom, personalizing relationships with them and increasing support. For example, some entrepreneurs without prior ties to officials developed them in the Self-Employed Laborers Association, which is supervised in each locale by the Industry and Commerce Bureau. Membership is mandatory for private shops licensed under the Individual Business Household policy. Although the Association is a regulatory tool of the bureau, some entrepreneurs have turned membership to advantage by assuming leadership positions in local branches. This let them work closely with the supervising officials in a broad range of matters, generating some affect in the relationship. The hardness of these ties can be used to obtain regulatory advantages, while their connectivity can provide stepping stones to higher officials.[12] For example, several entrepreneurs sought the support of subdistrict association officials to be included in the first groups of district-level cooperatives in the early 1980s. This generated many new resources, including more economic capital as well as enhanced renown and obligated ties, enabling the entrepreneurs to join even more significant business associations.

The Young Factory Director and Manager Association (*Qingnian Changzhang Jingli Xiehui*) is one such higher-level association that creates ties to officials at the city government level and beyond.[13] It was founded in 1985 for the purpose of helping promising public enterprise

---

[12] See Young (1995: 129–30) for a similar discussion of the utility of the Self-Employed Laborers Association.

[13] This association was founded in 1985 by the Young Worker and Peasant Department (*Gongnong Qingnian Bu*) of the Youth Association (*Qingnian Lianhehui*) and the Communist Youth League (*Gong Qing Tuan*), all of which are branches of the Communist Party's United Front Department (*Tong Yi Zhan Xian Bu*), which manages social groups. Members must be under thirty-five years of age and their company's legal representative. Members who turn forty years old or who leave enterprise management posts for other administrative posts in the government can be honorary members, of which there were fifty in 1989. The association organizes classes on enterprise management, commercial law, and computers. It has sister relations with a Hong Kong professional business association and has sent sixteen entrepreneurs there for two-week sessions and one to a Japanese factory to learn Japanese management methods. Also, members can ask the association to speak out on their behalf when they face various bureaucratic problems. Young managers in larger state enterprises often institute changes that upset older leaders and the association can smooth things over. The association also commends several dozen talented managers each year to the city government based on their cultural and political level, work accomplishments, and evaluations by subordinates. Commendations are put in their work file (*dangan*) and are useful in promotions.

directors and managers under the age of thirty-five to develop bureau-cratic connections. In mid-1989 about one-third of its 130 members were the operators of cooperative firms. According to its handbook, the association's purpose is to help young managers "create connections" (*lianluo*), "make friends" (*jiaoyou*), and "exchange information" (*hutong xinxi*). The association regularly arranges meetings with city government officials in lectures and parties, which businesspeople find useful for cultivating personal ties. It also holds provincial and national conventions where entrepreneurs can meet even higher officials.

A number of other associations provide useful venues for encountering foreign trade officials and meeting overseas Chinese businessmen. Some of the large private companies have joined the Xiamen Chamber of Commerce (*Xiamen Shi Shanghui*), the local branch of the All-China Federation of Industry and Commerce (*Gong Shang Lian*), which amal-gamated the prerevolutionary Chamber of Commerce under the control of the Communist Party in 1953.[14] Although the Federation ceased functioning during the Cultural Revolution, it has actively promoted business since its revival in 1979. One of its activities is arranging meetings between the heads of local private and public firms and potential foreign investors. Other entrepreneurs have joined one of the alternative political parties, such as the China Democratic National Construction Party (*Min Jian Dang*), whose members come largely from the prerevolutionary business class. They have also joined such civic associations as the Indonesia Overseas Chinese Union and the Philippine Overseas Chinese Union. These associations give access to transna-tional business connections and assets, and can also sponsor business affiliations.

Some entrepreneurs enhance renown by assuming political positions in the party-state. Several Xiamen entrepreneurs have become district rep-resentatives in the People's Consultative Committee, while a few sought Communist Party membership until the practice of encouraging promi-nent entrepreneurs to join the party was suspended following the 1989 student movement. By and large, membership in these activities is more desired by those with handicapped societal capital. In general, entrepre-neurs see membership in these political structures as onerous. First, these positions require time commitments and cannot be treated as lightly as membership in business and other civic associations. Failure to attend meetings can invite sanctions. As time is money, entrepreneurs can ill afford such obligations. Second, many entrepreneurs see party member-ship as especially problematic because, as indicated in Chapter 5, it embodies a visible commitment to principles of self-sacrifice and public

---

[14] Control was exerted by the Communist Party's United Front Department.

service that are at odds with the pursuit of self-enrichment in private entrepreneurship. The two entrepreneurs in my sample who were party members felt under greater pressure to conform to legal behavior than nonmembers.[15] One said, "As an entrepreneur you have to experiment with different ways of doing things. Some of these things might be clearly permitted by national laws but within the party there will be pressure on you not to do it" (informant no. 22). They felt that popular jealousy of their wealth was exacerbated by party membership.[16]

Participation in most of the aforementioned associations also enhances renown because of the exclusivity of membership. One must be invited to join; therefore membership indicates that one is successful and prosperous and, in some way, approved by government officials. Less well-endowed entrepreneurs squeeze membership to maximize renown. One former worker listed all seventeen of his associational affiliations and positions on his name card. The list was so long it required a fold-over sheet, so his name card resembled a small booklet. Others prominently display photographs of themselves with various high-ranking officials who are honorary members or participants in association functions.

A few former speculators and former workers sought to enhance renown by becoming registered representatives for major foreign companies. It seems that foreign companies seeking representatives contacted such organizations as the Xiamen Chamber of Commerce and even the Industry and Commerce Bureau, which then advertised the opportunity among its members. This can result in incongruous matches, for example a former speculator who ran a company trading in foodstuffs being a recognized representative for an internationally famous German pharmaceutical conglomerate. The entrepreneur listed this position on his name card and mentioned it frequently in conversation, although the only product of the firm that he seemed to be aware of was aspirin.

### Demonstrating Compliance

Another way of enhancing repute and renown is to acquire symbols of compliance with activities of various government agencies. To this end, entrepreneurs visibly demonstrate conformity with the demands of agencies. For example, some entrepreneurs have been commended by various bureaus for being "taxpaying activists" (*nashui jijifenzi*) and for "civilized business behavior" (*wenming jingying xingwei*). Their deeds are

[15] Only two members of my sample were Communist Party members and they were former functionaries. In rural areas party members accounted for about 15% of all private firm operators, but the number is much lower in urban areas because there has been less dismantling of urban administrative agencies and party organizations (Pei 1994: 110).

[16] For a related discussion, see Chapter 5 on the problems that former co-workers can cause for party members in private business.

publicized in the media and they are given banners and placards that they prominently display in their offices. Such repute is useful for several reasons. The conferral of such symbols deepens understandings between an entrepreneur and the officials of the designating bureau. Awards tend to be particularistically allocated and visibly signify an entrepreneur's favor by the designating bureau, forestalling administrative harassment by other bureaus. Furthermore, once a bureau bestows such legitimacy on an entrepreneur, it has a vested interest in assuring his continued legitimacy. For example, the Tax Bureau is unlikely to charge a designated taxpaying activist with tax evasion, as the charge would question the judgment of tax officials for bestowing the honor in the first place. Also, such displays of active conformity are closely linked to the associational strategies just described, as entrepreneurs deemed more compliant are more likely to be tapped for leadership positions in associations.

Entrepreneurs who demonstrate compliance with local government receive opportunities to enhance reputation through overseas publicity, an important consideration given that a main reason for the special economic zones is to attract foreign investment. For example, the Industry and Commerce Bureau has selected several entrepreneurs as "typical" private businesspersons to be trotted out for foreign journalists and researchers who ask to meet members of the local business community. Some former speculators, who were among the first in Xiamen to embark on entrepreneurship, have achieved some renown in the overseas Chinese and foreign press. Businesspeople whom I met in this way were blunt in expressing views; one was the only entrepreneur who encouraged me to visit him during the crackdown on private business that followed the 1989 student movement. Given the state's anti-foreign rhetoric at the time, I worried that my visit would cause trouble for him. His response revealed his strategy of augmenting reputation through publicity.

> The more my name is known the better. In the foreign and overseas communities they know my name. . . . Yesterday, a reporter from Hong Kong came to talk about the business situation. If I speak frankly, reporters will keep coming and my name will continue to be known among Hong Kong and overseas Chinese. And if anything happens to me, this will also be reported. You can say that I have become a measure to overseas Chinese of how the government treats private business. If the country destroys me, then foreign and overseas investors will think the situation is worsening and will not come. (Informant no. 15)[17]

[17] The entrepreneur Zhang Guoxi reveals a similar strategy. He told reporters from the *Christian Science Monitor,* "I'm no longer just Zhang Guoxi – I'm a symbol of reform. So it would be very difficult for officials to remove and eliminate me" (Tyson and Tyson 1995: 58).

Another way of demonstrating compliance is to make donations for community services. Some of these are at the behest of local government, such as special funds to clean buildings, repair government offices, and subsidize local school activities. This relieves pressure on local government to provide these services, thereby enhancing expectations of cooperation from the agency that placed the demand. Donations for services can also enhance entrepreneurial support in the community, as residents come to feel that they, too, can benefit from the company even if they have no direct relation with it. However, aggressive compliance is dangerous as requests for "donations" by agencies for community services can escalate dramatically. Other entrepreneurs devise their own philanthropic activities, such as providing new clothes to the elderly in the neighborhood or paying for musical instruments for local school bands. One group of young entrepreneurs in the textile business established a center to train young people in fashion design. While the design school was clearly in the interests of the entrepreneurs to train future personnel, local officials also acknowledged it as a means of reducing unemployment.

Entrepreneurs also provide benefits to the community that serve no purpose for the government but greatly enhance an entrepreneur's reputation in the community. One such activity is religious patronage. Patronage of Buddhism is considered safer than Taoism, which is still viewed as closer to superstition, or than Protestantism and Catholicism, which are stigmatized by their Western origins.[18] By contrast, Buddhism is even seen by many officials as "traditional Chinese culture," and there are few negative sanctions for patronizing it. Entrepreneurs who underwrite the monthly meals held for lay believers at local temples have their names prominently displayed as patrons of the festival. Others donate money for temple restoration and have their names carved into the new structures. One entrepreneur who donated ¥4,500 toward constructing a fence around a temple compound had his name carved into the fence three times, once for each ¥1,500 donation. Another practice is sponsoring cultural activities during festivals. In particular, entrepreneurs in the suburban villages being swallowed up by the city's growth hire opera troupes to entertain the neighborhood during festivals.

### Gift Giving

Entrepreneurs who lack networks through endowments and savings engage in incessant gift giving in all manner of social encounters. They seek to personalize all interactions to produce and enhance obligations in

[18] For a historical study of Buddhism as a source of elite status in Chinese locales, see Brook (1993). For merchant patronage of Buddhism in twentieth-century China, see Welch (1968). For Buddhism in Xiamen, see Ashiwa (1994).

Table 6.6. *Entrepreneurs in the catering,*
*hotel, and entertainment industry, by prior*
*occupation category*

| Speculator | Worker | Functionary |
|---|---|---|
| 3 | 6 | 3 |

ties. This tendency is suggested by the ownership of restaurants, night-clubs, and hotels, which are often used as venues to entertain officials. As noted in Chapter 5, some entrepreneurs number such establishments among the firms in their enterprise groups. Entrepreneurs with less advantageous societal capital endowments and savings have a greater tendency to establish such ventures (see Table 6.6). The least advantaged entrepreneurs, the former speculators, showed the greatest frequency, with 17 percent (*n* = 3) running such establishments, closely followed by former workers with 16 percent (*n* = 6). Only 7 percent (*n* = 3) of the advantaged former speculators were involved in such businesses.

The greater propensity of entrepreneurs with less advantaged societal capital to engage in gift giving was also very apparent in social practices regarding cigarettes (Wank 2000). All businessmen smoke, and many offer cigarettes to others. This offering can be seen as a strategy to elicit some goodwill and sentiment from the recipient. It can also be seen as an effort to enhance one's name by showing that one is generous and has a "broad bosom" (*xionghuai kuankuo*) and therefore is likely to behave according to the principles of upright conduct (*zuoren*). Conveying such an impression enhances trust by communicating that one will not take undue advantage of others. Entrepreneurs with the least advantaged societal capital are most active in pressing cigarettes on others. I have seen former speculators and workers tossing cigarettes to others in a room, scattering small handfuls in the laps of people seated on sofas, and sliding them across a table to those seated at the other end. They did not accept refusals, insisting that such persons take the cigarettes for later enjoyment. When I visited these entrepreneurs at their homes and companies, I noted that they were much more likely to break out a fresh pack of cigarettes. This action suggests that they hold the visitor in high regard, therefore conferring some face (*mianzi*) on the visitor and enhancing affect (*ganqing*) and obligation. Their aggressive cigarette giving contrasted markedly with the more standoffish attitude of the more prosperous entrepreneurs. Such entrepreneurs sometimes had personal valets to offer the cigarettes to visitors, inspiring awe at their power rather than gratitude and obligations to reciprocate.

## Marriage

Marriage patterns also reflect the tendency for former speculators and workers to emphasize investment strategies in regard to officialdom. One former speculator operating a trucking company had married his daughter to an official from the Transportation Bureau, which was located next door to the firm (see Wank 1995b: 159–60). This marriage presumably enhanced the cooperation of this bureau, which is crucial to the firm in matters ranging from the licensing of trucks and drivers to insider information on changes in road taxes and fuel costs. The tendency among former workers is somewhat different. Marriage is used less to create connections with officialdom where none previously existed than to ensure and amplify already-existing connections. One case involved an entrepreneur in the grain trade whose father had previously worked as an official in the Grain Bureau before his untimely death; this entrepreneur married the daughter of one his father's colleagues, who was still on active duty in the bureau. This marriage helped ensure that the entrepreneur's father-in-law lobbied within the bureau for the entrepreneur to continue to receive the special permission required from the bureau to engage in the wholesale trade of grain. Yet another instance involved an entrepreneur who ran what was reputed to be Xiamen's largest private trucking firm. This man was the son of the official who ran a public district-level trucking fleet, a connection that enabled the entrepreneur to secure leases for public trucks from the fleet. He married the daughter of an official in a similar position in an adjacent district, further expanding his trucking capacity.

I did not come across any former functionaries who had similarly married into a family headed by an official whose administrative duties were functionally intertwined with the enterprise. As previously noted, many entrepreneurs already had kin in administrative posts in the city government and elsewhere, as the superior education stemming from a bourgeois family background made them eligible for such jobs. Some former functionaries were already married into families of officials, and they were less likely to appreciate the usefulness of such marriages for building bureaucratic connections than former speculators. Also, former functionaries were less likely to feel that such marriages were needed to cement and amplify existing connections. Former functionaries appear to evaluate prospective mates in terms of whether they come from similar bourgeois family backgrounds. Such families are more likely to have overseas kin who support the foreign trade activities of this entrepreneurial path. This difference could be seen at two wedding banquets I attended, one involving a former speculator whose family originally came from a poor rural area and one a former functionary whose family had been prominent in business before 1949. At the former banquet, the bridegroom was a young official and the guests included several out-of-uniform officials from the bureau; the guests whispered among themselves about the good fortune of the entrepreneur in snaring this official as his son-in-law. At the latter banquet the bride was from the Xiamen branch of a family with businesses activities in Hong Kong; guests remarked not only on the social equivalence of the match but on its potential usefulness to the business activities of the entrepreneur.

## Converting Societal Capital into Economic Assets

The discussion in this chapter has so far established the distribution of societal capital among private company operators. There are significant variations in the distribution of advantageous societal capital, with the functionary path clearly possessing the most. This section documents that greater accumulations of advantages in societal capital correspond to greater accumulations of economic assets in business startup and subsequent prosperity. This illustrates how obligated ties, conveyed impression, and reputation are converted into money and other commodities. In regard to startup assets, former functionaries had the greatest access via societal capital to the two sources that provide the largest amounts of money: overseas kin and public resources (see Table 6.7). Fifty-nine percent ($n = 26$) of former functionaries cited overseas kin as a source of startup capital as compared with 19 percent ($n = 7$) and 11 percent ($n = 2$) of the former workers and speculators, respectively. Furthermore, for former functionaries this was the single largest source of economic capital for startup. Not only are overseas kin able to provide sufficient financial capital to establish a business, they can also serve as the guarantors of large foreign currency loans from Hong Kong banks. One entrepreneur obtained a loan of US$1 million in this way to establish a factory for assembling imported kits of medical equipment.

Also, the business family background of former functionaries enhances access to real estate, especially for those from the *grande bourgeoisie*. Such families had large houses and courtyards in the city that were confiscated in the late 1950s. Since the late 1970s, state policy has emphasized the return of confiscated real estate, and buildings are being restored to the original owners. Furthermore, my interviews suggest that the amount of real estate returned is greater if the claimant is an overseas Chinese rather than a local resident and citizen of the People's Republic. One entrepreneur whose family had owned three adjacent buildings

Table 6.7. *Entrepreneurs' sources of startup capital, by prior occupation category*

| Source of startup capital | Speculator | Worker | Functionary | Total |
|---|---|---|---|---|
| Overseas kin | 2 | 7 | 26 | 35 |
| Unlicensed trade | 14 | 9 | 9 | 32 |
| Family/friend in China | 6 | 8 | 8 | 22 |
| Moonlighting job | 2 | 12 | 1 | 15 |
| Bank loan | 1 | 2 | 7 | 10 |
| Previous job income | 0 | 2 | 5 | 7 |
| Money from public unit | 0 | 2 | 1 | 3 |
| Leasing a firm | 0 | 0 | 2 | 2 |
| Subcontracting a factory | 0 | 2 | 0 | 2 |

*Note*: Many entrepreneurs cited multiple sources of startup capital; therefore the number of sources is greater than the number of entrepreneurs in each category.
*Source*: Interviews, 1988–90.

pursued his claim in the name of a relative living in Singapore. All of the buildings were returned, even though the public units and families that had occupied the buildings had to be evicted. This contrasts with the situation of another entrepreneur, whose father had owned two buildings but who had no close overseas kin. He pressed the claim in his own name and received ownership of only one building. The other was denied him on the grounds that the current occupants could not be evicted until they had someplace else to move to.

Entrepreneurs who took the functionary path were also advantaged in deriving startup assets from public resources. There are eight instances of former functionaries receiving startup financial capital either by bank loans from state banks or as money from public units, as compared to four instances of this among former workers and just one instance among the former speculators. Also, two of the former functionaries accumulated financial capital by leasing wholesale firms, whereas nobody in the other two categories did so. Leasing also let them accumulate a network of suppliers and customers that could later be "carried over" to their private firms. Finally, many purchasing agents amassed large sums by obtaining kickbacks for placing orders.

In contrast, the other two categories of entrepreneurs relied more on their own activities to accumulate startup economic capital over a longer time period. The single largest source of startup financial capital for ex-workers, cited by 32 percent (*n* = 12), was moonlighting while still working in the public factories. Such moonlighting was usually in the construction trade, building and repairing private residences. Many of the confiscated homes that had been returned to owners in the 1970s and 1980s were in poor condition from decades of neglect. Workers skilled in welding, metalworking, and electrical wiring were in great demand and could realize large earnings. The next-largest source of startup financial capital was unlicensed trade, usually the sale of construction materials such as wire, glass, and bricks pilfered from public units. The money accumulated by such trade was smaller than that accumulated in the functionary path through unlicensed trade and kickbacks. However, compared to the ex-speculators, former workers were still relatively advantaged in securing assets from overseas kin and from public units through bank loans, subcontracting, and investments.

Of the former speculators, 78 percent ($n = 14$) cited their own illicit trade prior to getting a private business license as the main source of startup financial capital. An example of such trade was an entrepreneur who traveled frequently to Shanghai in the 1960s and 1970s to buy such personal consumer items as combs and hand mirrors that were manufactured in Shanghai but were in short supply in Xiamen. Through repeated purchases at the retail counters of major department stores, he accumulated a small stock for resale in Xiamen, a risky activity because department store clerks and railroad personnel in Shanghai were constantly on the lookout for such suspicious activity as the hallmark of speculation. The second most common source of startup funds for former speculators was money from family and friends. These amounts were minute compared with the larger amounts former functionaries received from their overseas kin, but were sometimes enough to set up a stall or shop. One person received a ¥1,000 inheritance upon the death of a relative that he used to set up a tea stand in 1980.

The greater economic value of the functionary path's societal capital is also evident in two kinds of measures. One is the greater involvement of the ex-functionaries in the forms of clientelist contracting that correspond with greater prosperity, as described in Chapter 4 (see Table 6.8). Among the former functionaries, the domestic transactions of 46 percent ($n = 20$) of the entrepreneurs were primarily with public units, as compared with 40 percent ($n = 15$) of the ex-workers and 17 percent ($n = 3$) of the ex-speculators. Former functionaries were also much more likely to engage in direct foreign trade: 25 percent ($n = 11$) did so compared with 13 percent ($n = 5$) of ex-workers and 11 percent ($n = 2$) of ex-speculators.

Also, former functionaries were the most prosperous, as measured by sales volume. In 1989, the average sales volume was ¥8,689,000 for the ex-functionaries; ¥8,597,000 for the ex-workers; and ¥3,640,000 for the ex-speculators (see Table 6.9). Former functionaries and workers had

Table 6.8. *Entrepreneurs' customers, by prior occupation category*

| Customers | Speculator | Worker | Functionary |
|---|---|---|---|
| Public & private | 14 | 21 | 20 |
| Only public | 3 | 15 | 20 |
| Foreign | 2 | 5 | 11 |

*Note*: Column totals are greater than number of entrepreneurs in each trajectory because entrepreneurs who do both foreign and domestic trade are counted twice.
*Source*: Interviews, 1988–90.

Table 6.9. *Entrepreneurs' average sales turnover in 1989, by prior occupation category*

| | Speculator | Worker | Functionary |
|---|---|---|---|
| Sales turnover (¥) | 3,640,000 | 8,597,000 | 8,689,000 |
| Turnover/years in business | 364,000 | 1,719,400 | 4,344,500 |

sales volumes about twice as large as former speculators, even though the latter had been in business the longest. The differences are more striking if sales volumes are calculated as a function of years in licensed business since 1979. For ex-speculators, with an average of ten years in licensed business at the time of my fieldwork, this translates into ¥364,000 per annum. For the ex-workers, with an average of five years in business, the value of each year was ¥1,719,400. For ex-functionaries, who averaged two years in business, each year's value was ¥4,344,500. This measure suggests that the societal capital of the functionary path has an economic value twice that of the worker path and twelve times that of the speculator path.

## Societal Capital and Risk

The risks of doing business vary by the precise mix of advantaged societal capital endowments and savings relative to societal capital investments in the activities of specific firms. One kind of risk is contractual and linked to the incentives to cooperate in market transactions. Contracts generated by invested societal capital are highly quid pro quo and less durable, increasing the possibility of malfeasance by the other parties. Another set of risks is of a more political character. One political risk is that the investment strategies involve activities that are more readily labeled as economic crimes by the state; it therefore follows that greater reliance on investments exposes an entrepreneur to a greater possibility of state regulatory actions. Another political risk is that they can generate jealousies among officialdom in local government between those inside and outside the patronage networks of a prosperous private company. Primarily because of the political risk, entrepreneurs viewed heavy reliance on invested societal capital not just as heightening uncertainties but also as downright dangerous.

Because of the greater risks in invested societal capital, those who rely more heavily on it in business have greater instability in their firms. To illustrate why this is so, let me examine more closely the downfall of Xiamen's most successful private company operator, Chen Youfu, the former stevedore whose company history illustrated the steplike sequence of clientelist contracting in private business development described in Chapter 4. As already noted, he came from a low social background and lacked any significant ties with officialdom when he embarked on business in 1979. His explosive business growth relied heavily on societal capital investments at every step in his firm's growth. He was charged with bribery and smuggling at the onset of an economic rectification campaign in 1988. Chen's downfall was rumored to have been initiated by former supporters in Xiamen, whose patronage was being devalued by his shift from local to transregional trade and by his intensified efforts to cultivate patrons elsewhere. As his Xiamen support weakened, other officials joined in the attack, including those who were jealous for having been excluded from his payroll and those who were aghast at the range of economic crimes, such as bribery and official profiteering, that his activities entailed. His heavy reliance on investment practices for producing societal capital provided much ammunition for his attackers. He was incarcerated for two years while his patrons tried to prevent a trial to save their own skins. Because of the number of high officials involved, the trial of Chen Youfu was held secretly. According to the local grapevine, he was sentenced to six years in prison.

Entrepreneurs with advantageous endowed ties to officials are less likely to suffer the fate of Chen Youfu. One reason is that they engage in fewer of the more blatantly heinous activities such as bribery and therefore their activities are less easily labeled "economic crimes." Of course, the use of family ties with officials is also an economic crime, but as this crime strikes much closer to home for the bureaucrats, they are less willing to press criminal charges of nepotism and favoritism. Also, as the

Xiamen support is more heavily secured by endowments and savings, acquiring it is less likely to generate jealousies among local officialdom. And home-base supporters are less likely to feel threatened when entrepreneurs shift beyond the locale to cultivate more geographically distant support.

# Part II

*Economic and Political Outcomes*

# 7

## Comparing Economic Performance in China and Eastern Europe

> Economic miracles include countries that had . . . competitive elections, as well as countries run by military dictatorships. . . . it does not seem to be democracy or authoritarianism per se that makes the difference but something else. (Przeworski and Limongo 1993: 65)

> Although formal rules may change overnight as the result of political or judicial decisions, informal constraints embodied in customs, traditions, and codes of conduct are much more impervious to deliberate policies. These cultural constraints not only connect the past with the present and future, but provide us with a key to explaining the path of historical change. The central puzzle of human history is to account for the widely divergent paths of historical change. (North 1990a: 6)

China's market economy since 1989 has outperformed those of post-communist Eastern European countries despite the transformation of the latter into democracies, a political regime widely held to be more conducive to market development.[1] In the years since the collapse of European communist states, China's economy has continued to grow at an average annual rate of around 10 percent, while Eastern European growth rates have been much lower, and even negative in some cases. Even as some Eastern European countries were beginning to show economic growth by the mid-1990s, China's economic performance was still markedly superior. In early 1998 China's national rate of growth in gross domestic product from a year earlier was 8.2 percent, while those of the Czech Republic, Hungary, Poland, and Russia were 8 percent, 5.1 percent, 6.9 percent, and 1.3 percent, respectively.[2] The difference is much greater when considering that China's southern coastal provinces of Fujian and Guangdong, with a population of 98 million, larger than any

---

[1] I use the term "Eastern Europe" broadly to include the European countries of the former Soviet Union and its satellites.

[2] Figures are percentage change from the previous year, as reported in *The Economist*.

153

European country's except Russia, have had growth rates almost double the national average.[3] How can the relative dynamism of China's emerging market economy be explained?

This chapter extends the institutional commodification account of China's emerging market economy to consider variations in economic performance, one of the thematic questions posed at the beginning of Chapter 2. A growing body of literature that attributes economic growth to institutional networks linking the state to private business is the explanatory starting point. I first sketch this literature's key insight on how networks of cooperation between state and business stimulate market growth. Next I examine the comparative possibilities for such networks in China and Eastern Europe and develop an explanation that emphasizes variations in the cultural content of the networks. Finally I consider questions of efficiency and equity in the operation of private business through patron–client ties.

Clarification of the character of this chapter's comparative intent is in order. The purpose is to explain the robust performance of the Chinese market economy relative to those of other communist and post-Communist orders. Eastern European economies are considered only in this respect. In other words, comparison is intended only to explain the Chinese case and is not a sustained account of the performance of Eastern European economies. Thus, I do not distinguish among the different Eastern European countries because they all underperform the Chinese economy. No attempt is made to explain, for example, why the Polish market economy is the most dynamic in Eastern Europe or why Russia's is among the least. Such comparison to illuminate a single case is in the spirit of Max Weber's broad studies of diverse religions to explain the origins of European capitalism.

## The Role of Local Government

Policies of active state participation in the economy are increasingly seen as stimulating the more rapid growth of a capitalist market economy. Such an argument has been most forcefully applied to East Asian economies, where dynamic market growth is attributed in good measure to a pronounced state presence in the economy to target industries, manage foreign competition, and control labor unrest. The sociologist Peter Evans sees successful state participation as linked to a relatively professional bureaucracy and institutional networks connecting business actors with bureaucrats. These networks are "a concrete set of social ties that

---

[3] Population figure for 1994.

binds the state to society and provides institutionalized channels for the continual negotiation of goals and policies" (Evans 1995: 12).[4]

Certain districts in Europe, such as Italy's Emilia-Romagna, Germany's Baden-Württemberg, and Spain's Valencia, illustrate cooperation between local governments and small to medium-sized enterprises.[5] These governments provide credit services and information, encourage collaboration between private firms, and support private firms to forge trade links outside of the regions. Such government–business interaction not only stems from self-interested partnership but is also embedded in a social system of cooperation that emphasizes norms of trust and reciprocity among networks of actors who share a strong regional or trade identity (e.g., Sabel 1993).

Analysts of Chinese and Eastern European private business differ markedly in their assessments of the possibilities for similar institutionalized networks in different post-communist economies. Studies of Chinese private business have already documented similar networks of reciprocity between local governments and private firms, suggesting such cooperation is already institutionalized. For example, in Wenzhou, a local township government helped local businesses producing electrical switches to meet national standards (Liu 1992). In Xiamen, the city government has encouraged trading firms to expand into manufacturing, giving tax breaks to technology ventures between Taiwanese investors and local businesspeople. The fact that many of these policies are deviations from more standard procedures and often involve particularistic allocation does not detract from the fact that these are institutionalized networks linking governments with business to enhance and upgrade commercial development in locales for the benefit of both parties, as in European industrial districts.

Observers of private business in Eastern Europe are less sanguine about the prospects for cooperation between local government and business there. Analysts of Hungary's private business see a lack of vertical as well as horizontal cooperation in private business (Gábor 1990; Szelenyi 1989). István Gábor, noting that the dynamism of private business in Italy's Emilia-Romagna and Germany's Baden-Württemberg stems from government–business cooperation, wonders if this is possible in Hungary and fears a "cooperation vacuum" (Gábor 1990: 15, n. 11).[6] Observers

---

[4] South Korea is deemed the archetype of such cooperative interaction.

[5] A classic work on such industrial districts and the type of craft approach they embody is Piore and Sabel (1984). See also Bagnasco and Sabel (1995); Perrow (1993); and Lazerson (1993).

[6] In Szelenyi's view (1989: 224), private business in Hungary cannot "form a system of its own." However, Szelenyi sees such a system as formed by horizontal links, presumably without government presence, unlike Gábor, who is also concerned with government involvement.

of Russia's market economy see local government more as an obstacle than as a facilitator of private business. According to Stephen Handelman, entrepreneurs are hampered by corrupt bureaucrats and local politicians in collusion with criminals whose "converging interests . . . undermined efforts to extend the rights of private ownership" (Handelman 1995: 22). The key comparative issue is why local networks of cooperation between government and business appear more likely in China.

## Possibilities for Local Government– Private Business Networks

The market transition and political economy accounts pursue two lines of reasoning to explain the varying performance of market economies in China and Eastern Europe. One line emphasizes variations in the degree of centralization in their planned economies prior to market reform. This is said to have created different communist era legacies that have spurred China's superior economic performance. The other line emphasizes the divergent policy process of reform. China is said to be a case of economic reform without corresponding political reform, while the post-Soviet states and other Eastern European countries are held to be cases of political reform preceding economic reform. This is said to have created an institutional stability in China that reduces transaction costs to a greater degree than in Eastern Europe, stimulating economic growth in the former. These lines of reasoning have largely sought to explain the differences in the marketization of state sectors. In this section I extend these two lines of reasoning to consider variations in the possibility for institutional networks between local state agents and private company operators. Then I offer an alternative explanation that invokes the variable of institutional culture to explain variations in the possibility for such networks.

### Variations in Statist Legacies

This line of reasoning attributes the better relative performance of China's market economy to the lesser centralization of its planned economy prior to reform as compared with other communist orders. By several measures the Chinese economy was more decentralized (see Table 7.1). One measure is state enterprise share of total economic output. On the eve of their respective reforms, China's state enterprises produced 77.6 percent of total industrial and commercial output and employed 78.4 percent (in 1978) of the total nonagricultural workforce, as com-

Table 7.1. *Share (%) of total output*
*contributed by state enterprises in selected*
*communist economies*

| | |
|---|---|
| Bulgaria (1970) | 99.7 |
| Czechoslovakia (1986) | 97.0 |
| East Germany (1982) | 96.5 |
| Soviet Union (1985) | 96.0 |
| Romania (1980) | 95.5 |
| Poland (1980) | 83.4 |
| China (1978) | 77.6 |
| Hungary (1975) | 73.3 |

*Source*: Pei (1994: 14).

pared with 96 percent and 95.9 percent (in 1985) in the Soviet Union (Pei 1994: 14–15). Another variation is scale of factories: a greater share of the Soviet Union's industrial output occurred in larger factories. In the Soviet Union, factories with over 1,000 workers accounted for 74 percent of Soviet industrial output and 75 percent of the industrial labor force, while in China factories with over 500 workers accounted for a little over 40 percent of industrial output (Naughton 1995: 40–1; see also Shirk 1993: 30). In short, in China much more economic activity took place outside the state sector and in smaller factories, many of them in the collective sector, than in the Soviet Union. In such other areas as fiscal and allocational procedures, China was also more decentralized.

In the market transition perspective, China's greater decentralization prior to reform is attributed to its shorter history of communism relative to the Soviet Union. This means that the statist institutions of central planning had less time to accumulate and power was less concentrated in the hands of central planners. Therefore the Chinese economy required fewer "structural changes" to enable the emergence of a market economy. The economist Andors Aslund writes that "less developed communist economies with a shorter history of communism, such as China and Vietnam, might be able to escape much of the duress other postcommunist countries would inevitably face" (Aslund 1995: 15). In other words, once the Chinese authorities relaxed control over the economy, the smaller state sector and less concentrated central control posed fewer obstacles to the reemergence of markets (Aslund 1995: 13–16).

The political economy perspective views decentralization as a statist legacy that constrains market organization after the onset of market reform by devolving control over resources to lower levels of the bureaucracy (e.g., Shirk 1993; Oi 1992). Applying this insight to private business suggests that differing degrees of decentralization in different countries could variably affect the networks linking private entrepreneurs and local state agents. First, greater pre-reform decentralization in China could have created denser ties between officials controlling public resources and others in society. For example, smaller enterprises had fewer management layers than larger ones, creating more routine social interactions between citizens and managing cadres in Chinese public enterprises that generate personal ties. By contrast, in the larger enterprises of the Soviet Union, citizens had fewer personal interactions with management cadres. A result is that, after market reform began, Chinese citizens who entered private business had more influence in the allocation of commodifying public resources through personal ties than Soviet ones. Second, greater decentralization in China might have been more likely to embed interactions between citizens and officials in closed social networks, enhancing the effectiveness of such community sanctions as shunning and gossip to induce greater cooperation.

The weak point of this explanatory line is that the variable of pre-reform decentralization is not clear-cut. While more decentralized in some aspects, China's planned economy was less so in others. The Chinese state exerted more control over labor mobility than in Eastern Europe as well as strong control over commerce and agricultural procurement (Naughton 1995: 43–6). Also, the greater penetration of the Maoist bureaucracy into local society down to neighborhood committees and work groups can be interpreted as the greater local control of the Chinese state rather than greater decentralization: this enabled it to more effectively suppress second-economy activity and prevented population movements in economic activity. Also, in the case of Hungary, the greater decentralization of its planned economy by some measures prior to reform (see Table 7.1) does not appear to have resulted in greater government–business dynamism in its private business. Taken together, these considerations undermine the case for varying degrees of decentralization as an explanatory variable for economic performance.

### Variations in Reform Policies

The other line of reasoning explains variation in economic performance by the different paths pursued by reformist political elites. In the Soviet Union, Gorbachev is said to have placed political reform ahead of economic reform, while China under Deng Xiaoping is seen as having pursued economic reform without corresponding political reform. In the market transition perspective, Deng's path is the classic late development strategy of an authoritarian state actively promoting economic development. The political scientist Minxin Pei likens Deng "to other Third

World autocrats, such as South Korea's Park Chong Hee, Singapore's Lee Kuan Yew, and Chile's Augusto Pinochet – men who single-mindedly focused on rapid economic development as the top priority of their governments" (Pei 1994: 209). This view attributes economic development to the state's pro-development policies of market reform.

This view is at odds with the finding in this and other studies of the loose coupling between state policies and market practices. As already noted, the state condemns many of the practices that actually occur in the market economy as "corruption" and "economic crimes." Also, as noted in Chapter 2, innovation in market practices often precedes state policies; policies can be little more than post hoc legitimation of a popular innovation that serves only to hasten the innovation's spread, as in the case of the state policies favoring cooperatives in the mid-1980s and those establishing private companies in the late 1980s. This raises the question of whether market emergence can be so heavily attributed to the policy actions of central elites. At the very least this study posits that the actions of the state need to be examined in interaction with local government initiatives and popular practices in shaping the organization and performance of the market economy.[7]

In the political economy account this line of reasoning can be extended by drawing on Susan Shirk's (1993) institutional analysis of bureaucratic restructuring in China and the Soviet Union. She argues that gradual reform in China kept intact the clientelist networks in the state while similar networks in the Soviet Union were disrupted due to the political restructuring of the state bureaucracy and shuffling of personnel. In regard to private business, this insight could be extended to argue that political reform in the Soviet Union and post-Soviet Russia undermined the personal ties between citizens and officials, while lack of political reform in China has kept such ties relatively intact. Therefore, it could be said that the Chinese reform process has preserved the routes for citizens

---

[7] The problematic analysis that results from seeing market emergence as the dismantling of communist era state control is reflected in the account of Polish private business by Simon Johnson and Gary Loveman. By the mid-1990s Polish private business had the highest rates of growth in Eastern Europe. Johnson and Loveman attribute this to Poland's Balcerowicz plan. "The plan's major achievement was to destroy the final remnants of the old economic system. Shortages were eliminated . . . most retail trade was privatized, output prices were freed. . . . These were the prerequisites of a market economy" (Johnson and Loveman 1995: 227). They attribute the swift rise of Poland's private business to the successful conclusion of the plan. This is seemingly contradicted by their account of the operation of private business, which suggests much greater links between private companies and state entities: 85% of private entrepreneurs previously worked in the state sector (1995: 112); state enterprises provide physical capital to private businesses (1995: 143); state enterprises are the initial suppliers and customers of private firms (1995: 146); entrepreneurs get scarce business licenses and rent choice real estate from local governments (1995: 191–5). But nowhere is this interaction between state, government, and private business systematically discussed.

to influence state agents, stimulating greater popular participation in the shift of public resources to the market and amplifying the aforementioned trickle-down process. By contrast, Soviet and subsequent Russian reform initiatives swept away links between citizens and bureaucrats, concentrating the commodification of public resources in collusive networks between criminals, bureaucrats, and politicians that are more impervious to popular influence.

It could also be argued that the varying reform paths have created differing state capacities to reduce uncertainties and transaction costs. In Russia and other Eastern European countries, the decline of state administrative capacity has left the state with insufficient administrative and policing monopoly to enforce legal private property rights. So-called "mafiya" gangs, which arise where central states are weak (Gambetta 1993; Blok 1974), have emerged to sell protection to private entrepreneurs. By contrast, increased decentralization notwithstanding, "the Chinese system is not realistically in imminent danger of the disintegration that has befallen the Communist countries in eastern Europe and the Soviet Union" (Li 1994: 1). In particular, the more local levels are remarkably intact (Walder 1992) and are able to enforce property rights. Although gangs have reemerged in China, they appear to operate within limits defined by local bureaucracies, and their involvement in private business does not appear to approach the scale and extent of gangs in Eastern Europe.[8]

Furthermore, while both the Eastern European gangs and the local Chinese bureaucracy guarantee property rights in manners that deviate from universal legal protection, there are important differences in their enforcement. First, mafiyas are criminal gangs that operate without the advantage of political legitimacy. They consequently have shorter time horizons, demanding large sums with less concern for the ongoing viability of the enterprises they extort from (Gambetta 1993). In Russia, the economist Anders Aslund writes that Mafiya gangs "behave like robbers ... [without] an interest in the survival of local enterprises" (Aslund 1995: 169).[9] By contrast, in China, the taxes and fees levied on

---

[8] This can be seen in the account of gang activity in Chengdu's business community. Ole Bruun documents the rise of secret societies and criminal gangs in the capital of Siquan province that extort from private shopkeepers. But he notes that many proprietors refuse to pay protection money. He also notes that these criminal elements appeared to operate at the sufferance of local authorities. "Local authorities did nothing to prevent the gangs from establishing themselves in Bin Shen, and their indifference started speculations on their own involvement. Some suggested that the police cooperated with the gangs, obtaining assistance from them in tracing hard criminals *in exchange for granting them a certain freedom to extort* from the private sector [emphasis added]" (Bruun 1993: 181).

[9] This no doubt is exacerbated by intense competition in the private protection industry. The journalist Stephen Handelman (1995) describes intense competition between private security agencies composed of former policemen, combat veterans, ex-agents of the

private firms by local governments, while burdensome, have "probably been a major factor in the growth of private business. They certainly have not been so heavy as to prevent it, and they have given local officials a direct incentive to support it" (Young 1995: 53). In other words, local governments operating with the advantage of political legitimacy have a greater long-term interest in promoting private business in their jurisdictions as a revenue source.

Such a political economy explanation of the different performance of markets and private business in China and Eastern Europe is problematic on two counts. One is that while the reform paths are clearly different as policy sequences, they are less so as organizational processes. Some have noted that the bureaucratic structures of central planning are still very much apparent in Eastern European post-communist statism, suggesting less change in political structures there than is usually supposed.[10] Even the pre-reform bureaucratic personnel remain largely unchanged, particularly at local levels: Ákos Róna-tas writes that the "personnel of ministries and local governments changes only at the top levels and many of the low- and middle-level administrators stay in place" (Róna-tas 1994: 46). If so, then attributing variations in networks linking government and business to different reform paths is not especially compelling. Scholarly reassessments of Chinese and Eastern European reform experiences as more similar than commonly supposed undermines accounts that attribute China's superior economic performance to its unique policy emphasis on economic over political reform.[11]

The emphasis on variations as structural is also problematic. Networks are seen only as connections among actors that enhance resource flows

security organs, young athletes, ethnic mafiya gangs of Chechens and Azeris, and neighborhood hoodlums and racketeers. In China too, a private protection industry has emerged, but it seems to be oriented more to protecting property than to providing bodyguards. Also the state has exerted some control over the private protection business with the "economic police management rules" of 1993. "These allow for an enterprise to install its own police station, usually with one official cop, who must then deputise sub-contracted guards to secure the premises. The deputies, often migrant labourers or ex-convicts, are paid and equipped by the company under protection. Despite the fig-leaf of state deputising, these 'economic police' owe their allegiance to whoever pays them – making them, in effect, private security forces" (Kuhn 1994: 198). An example is the twelve-officer police station funded by the tycoon Zhang Guoxi. His personal valet and bodyguard wears the dress uniform of the People's Liberation Army (Tyson and Tyson 1995: 49–50).

[10] According to Andras Sajo, "socialism still lives in Hungary. Among the causes of its survival are the retention of old attitudes; dependence on a state-run agency for management of 'privatized' firms; a judiciary rooted in the past; and still-dominant state control masquerading as 'public interest' " (Sajo 1994: 198).

[11] Andrew Walder writes that the prevailing characterization of Chinese policy as "gradualism" – economic reform without corresponding political reform – is "a moot point, because the pace of change in Eastern Europe has in the end been no faster than in China" (Walder 1995: 978).

and reduce transaction costs. The problem with this is made readily apparent by posing the counterfactual: if the policy variations described in the political economy account were held constant, then would China and Eastern Europe have experienced similar economic performance? I think not. Some sociologists and economists stress that an economy's operation reflects not only state policies but also institutional culture. As this chapter's epigraph indicates, the economist Douglass North maintains that "informal cultural constraints" rather than the "formal rules" promulgated by the state play a significant role in shaping economies. North points to the sociological view that economies are constituted in good measure by distinct cultures and civilizations (e.g., Dore 1983; Hamilton 1994). Therefore, similar state policies in different societies would not produce the same economic outcomes because of differences in their institutional cultures. Following this lead, the next section will show how variations in the institutional content of networks create different possibilities for productive networks linking government and business in different late and post-Communist market economies.

## Variations in Institutional Culture

In this section I will show how variations in institutionalized aspects of networks explain their greater functional adaptability and authority in enhancing expectations in Chinese private business, undergirding the relatively superior performance of its market economy. Institutions are both rules that delimit behavior and authority that induces compliance with the rules. Susan Shirk attributes successful Chinese economic reform to the institutional flexibility and continued authority there (Shirk 1993: 346–50). Flexibility enables adaptations to new situations, while authority ensures that rules continue to be followed. While Shirk focuses on the state sector, in this section I extend these insights to consider private business, attributing its relatively dynamic performance to the flexibility and authority of the institutional conceptions of personhood and social relations that help constitute commercial ties.

Let me also note that the image of culture in the traditional culture perspective is insufficient for such comparative analysis. The portrayal of culture as constituted by the traditional Confucian cosmology suggests uniqueness (Bruun 1993); one would have to identify variable elements in this institutional ideology to enable civilizational comparisons. Also, the claim that economic organization is patterned by norms of sharing and kinship (Lin 1995; Weitzman and Xu 1993) is too generalized for comparative purposes, as all societies have such institutions. The relevant question is, why do Chinese variants of these institutions seem especially conducive for economic activity in transitional economies?

I will begin with the classic observation from economic anthropology and sociology that economic activity is patterned by institutional categories of insider and outsider identities.[12] In economic activity, a shared insider identity can enhance trust among persons, reducing the costs of negotiating and enforcing contracts. The point I make in this section is the different ways in which insider–outsider categories are constructed in Chinese and European civilizations and the economic consequences of this. Chinese social categories are more flexible in their in-group/out-group dichotomies, enhancing the possibilities for actors to extend normatively sanctioned expectations between them. Also, Chinese social institutions carry more authority, as the basic social unit of the family is venerated. This heightens the legitimacy of economic organization by the principles and practices of family relations. In a volatile and uncertain environment, this reduces the costs of negotiating and enforcing contracts by enhancing the likelihood that cultural rules of exchange will be observed.

The contrast between European categorical conceptions and Chinese relational conceptions of personhood has been widely commented on. This contrast is made readily apparent by juxtaposing classical sociological accounts of the Polish and Chinese families. In *The Polish Peasant in Europe and America*, sociologists William Thomas and Florian Znaniecki describe the Polish family:

> The Polish peasant family . . . is a social group including all the blood and law relatives up to a certain variable limit – usually the fourth degree. . . . But the fundamental family connection is one and irreducible; it cannot be converted into any other type of group relationship nor reduced to a personal relation between otherwise isolated individuals. It may be termed *familial solidarity*, and it manifests itself both in assistance rendered to, and in control exerted over, any member of the group by any other member representing the group as a whole. . . . And again, the familial solidarity and the degree of assistance and of control involved should not depend upon the personal character of the members, but only upon the kind and degree of their relationship; the familial relation between two members admits no gradation, as does love or friendship. (Thomas and Znaniecki 1984: 65, 67)

---

[12] For example, Cohen (1969, 1971); DiMaggio (1990); Wuthnow (1987); and Weber ([1922] 1978).

Fei Xiaotong's description of the Chinese family in *From the Soil* presents a sharp contrast:

> In China, we often see the sentence "The whole family will come" (*hedi guanglin*), but few people can tell what family members should be included in the word *di* (family). In Chinese the word *jia* (family) is used in many ways. *Jialide* (the one at home) can mean one's wife. *Jiamen* (kinsmen) may be directed at a big group of uncles and nephews. *Zijiaren* (my own people) may include anyone whom you want to drag into your own circle, and you use it to indicate your intimacy with them. The scope of *zijiaren* can be expanded or contracted according to the specific time and place. It can be used in a very general way, even to mean that everyone under the sun is a *jia* (one family). (Fei [1948] 1992: 62)

This juxtaposition clearly illuminates civilizational variations in conceptions of self, family, and social relations. The Polish family is a corporate entity with clear boundaries and obligations attaching to individuals as rights of group membership. Fei Xiaotong characterizes social relations in Anglo/European civilization as a "corporatist mode of association" (*tuanti geju*) that emphasizes a group orientation with clear boundaries separating in-group from out-group and with obligations adhering equally to all members of the in-group by virtue of common membership. This contrasts with the "differential mode of association" (*chaxu geju*) in Chinese civilization, which emphasizes networks in which boundaries are not rigidly fixed but shift depending on the context, and in which obligations toward others are contingent on the identities in dyadic interactions as delimited by the specific context.

The key point is that social categories of in-group status and identity in Chinese society are more flexible in whom they actually encompass, creating the possibilities for producing trust in a wider variety of interactions and settings. The in-group category of the family contains the strongest social trust, and this trust can be more readily extended to other individuals. Institutional flexibility also means that the principles of the family can also be extended into social interactions in various spheres of social interaction. Fei observes that family lineages "carry the responsibility for political, economic, religious, and other functions" (Fei 1992: 84). This contrasts with the much more restricted extent of the Polish family bond. Thomas and Znaniecki write that the Polish family "is totally different from territorial, religious, economic, or national solidarity" (1984: 67). Here it is clear that expectations based on family loyalty are less commodious.

Let me next consider the other institutional prerequisite of authority.

Another classic sociological insight is that worship produces primordial sentiments and affiliations (Durkheim [1915] 1965). The Polish family has little religious character; it is not an object of worship and there is no ancestor cult. Thomas and Znaniecki write: "The family cannot be represented by a genealogical tree because it includes law relationship and because it is a strictly social, concrete, living group – not a religious, mythical, heraldic, or economic formation" (1984: 65). This is in marked contrast with the Chinese family, which is an object of veneration through the ancestor cult (Hsu [1953] 1981: 248–53). In the Judeo-Christian tradition legitimate authority lies in God above humans, while in the Chinese Buddhist-Confucian tradition it lies in primary social relationships, especially father–son (Fei 1992: 33–4; Lin 1988: 105–9).

The key point here is that in the Chinese context one's immediate family ties are objects of worship, whereas in the Judeo-Christian tradition they are not. The veneration of the Chinese family explains the greater legitimacy and extent of the family principle in organizing political and economic life than in a European civilizational context, such as Poland. In this regard C. K. Yang notes how popular worship is diffused into diverse areas of social life in Chinese society, "creating a general feeling of awe and respect for institutionalized practices" (Yang 1961: 298).

The greater institutional flexibility and authority of Chinese social relations is apparent when one moves one step away from the immediate family. In Poland such relationships are signified by the idiom of the "social circle" (*srodowisko*). This circle is a group of two to three dozen persons emphasizing group loyalty and mutual support in daily life. As described by Znaniecki, a person's social circle "grants him certain rights and enforces those rights, when necessary, against individual participants of the circle or outsiders. . . . He, in turn, has a social function to fulfill; he is regarded as obliged to achieve certain tasks by which the supposed needs of this circle will be satisfied and to behave toward other individuals in this circle in a way that shows his positive valuation of them" (Znaniecki 1986: 16–17). In short, the *srodowisko*, while also based on the corporatist ontology of insider status, has a distinct membership from the family.

The Polish *srodowisko* contrasts markedly with the Chinese idiom of "similarity" or "sameness" (*tong*), a comparable social institution at one remove from the family. As discussed in Chapter 5, *tong* is a grammar of relational categories that can enhance trust between two people. The key point here is that the fundamental *tong* category of "fellow villager" (*tongxiang*) enhances expectations in interactions through the primordial sense of affiliation among family members. As Fei writes, "our native place is the same as our father's native place, rather than the place of our birth or the place where we currently live. We inherit a native place just as we inherit a family name; it is like a blood relationship. Therefore, we can conclude that one's native place is only *the projection of consanguinity into space"* (1992: 123). Also, the content of *tongxiang*, as with the content of family, is context-dependent. The flexibility of *tong* is seen in Wong Siu-lun's description of compatriot (*tongxiang*) ties among Shanghainese emigrant textile entrepreneurs in Hong Kong, who stress different concepts of region in different social settings to evoke identities that facilitate trust as need be. "According to the situation, a Shanghainese can activate regional ties of various scope. His potential membership ranges from that of his native village, for instance, Xia Che village, his native county of Wuxi, his native province of Jiangsu, to the broader categories of Shanghainese, southern Chinese, Asian or Oriental, and even a member of the Third World" (Wong 1988: 111).[13] Considering the variety of other *tong* categories, such as compatriot (*tongbao*), schoolmate (*tongxue*), colleague (*tongshi*), there are abundant possibilities for imparting stronger expectations via the family principle into relationships beyond the immediate family. In all of these situations, *tong* serves as a principle for fusing identities and creating a basis for the activation of mutual obligation and shared expectations through overtones of familial solidarity and loyalty.[14]

Recent anthropological ethnographies in Poland and China document patterns of social ties outside the immediate family that bear strong evolutionary similarity to those noted earlier by Thomas and Znaniecki and by Fei. Writing in *The Private Poland*, Janine Wedel observes that "outside of their families, people have relationships within their *srodowiska....* Those of one *srodowisko* consider themselves social

---

[13] For example, an individual from Quanzhou and Zhangzhou, two cities in southern Fujian province, would probably not consider themselves *tongxiang* if they encountered each other in nearby Xiamen, but they would if they met each other in Fuzhou, the provincial capital in the northern part of the province. Similarly, individuals from Xiamen and Fuzhou would not consider themselves *tongxiang* should they encounter each other in Fujian province, but they might if the encounter took place in neighboring Guangdong province. And individuals from Fujian and Guangdong would never consider themselves *tongxiang* when meeting on the southeastern coast, but their encounter in Beijing might produce *tong* affect as southerners, while a Beijinger and Xiamener might feel *tongxiang* as Chinese should they meet in New York. Such feelings do not emerge automatically; their expression is somewhat variable depending on the calculations of their necessity in a given context.

[14] The flexibility and authority of *jia* is vividly depicted in T'ien Ju-k'ang's ethnographic account of fictive family kinship among the overseas Chinese community of Sarawak. He describes how two groups sharing the same surname of T'ien but coming from different provinces, speaking different dialects, and with no apparent genealogical link invented a fictive ancestor to enhance their joint economic endeavors. They constructed a common ancestral tomb, worshipped at it regularly, and referred to each other by intricate kinship terms (T'ien 1953: 25–6).

equals, though relationships within their circle may vary in intimacy. . . . People in varying *srodowisko* do not mix in private life. . . . It is the *srodowisko* one belongs to that indicates who one's friends are, who one's potential friends may be and how one will act" (1986: 104–5). In *Gifts, Favors, and Banquets*, Mayfair Yang observes how *guanxi* networks of family and *tong* help people cope with the demands of daily life in China. She writes:

> In the art of *guanxi*, this transformation [from unfamiliar to familiar] occurs in the process of appealing to shared identities between persons. Hence the emphasis on "shared" (*tong*) qualities and experiences that shape the identities of classmates (*tongxue*), or persons from the same county or province (*tongxiang*), colleagues (*tongshi*), as well as kinfolk, teachers and students, masters and apprentices, and so on. Familiarity, then, is born of the fusion of personal identities. And shared identities establish the basis for the obligation and compulsion to share one's wealth and to help with one's labor. (Yang 1994: 194)

These different ontologies of personhood, by constructing different parameters of normative obligation in relationships, appear more conducive to creating and enforcing personal contracts in the Chinese emerging market economy than in Poland's. Consider the comments of a Polish saleswomen regarding illicit commercial activity, as told to the Polish sociologist Wojciech Pawlik in the early 1980s: " 'If a customer I don't know approaches me,' a 26-year-old saleswomen in a clothing store told me, 'I immediately reject the proposition because I know the danger. You simply have to have your own trusted people, and this happens on the principle that your acquaintance sends his acquaintance, because it's known that in such a *srodowisko* everyone knows everyone else. So things can be "arranged" but only among those you trust' " (Pawlik 1992: 83–4).

Two things are striking in the Polish saleswoman's remarks as compared with commercial practice in China at the same time. One is that a commercial opportunity would be "immediately rejected" because it came from a stranger. A Xiamen businessperson would more likely respond to such a proposal by attempts to establish some personal link in which to nurture expectations of cooperation. One business family I knew that ran a jewelry store had a son who worked in one of Xiamen's large joint-venture department stores in the jewelry section. Whenever the son was approached by domestic tourists or peasants who wanted to sell jewelry or small amounts of gold, he referred them to his family's shop, a potentially risky act because of the restrictions on private trade in gold. It thus appears that the risk of dealings with strangers in illicit trade was not a deterrent to this Xiamen salesclerk.

The second striking aspect is that trust between two strangers is impossible unless they are physically introduced by a mutually known third party. This contrasts with Mayfair Yang's observation on how two strangers in a Chinese social context establish a bond by talking about a common acquaintance. The verbal reference to a common acquaintance "acts as a connector cable, so to speak, infusing a common current of identity into the two persons and draws them within a single circle of insideness. Mutual obligation may thus be activated" (Yang 1994: 194). Even though not physically present, the acquaintance is a symbol by which the two strangers create a common relational category in which to situate themselves.

While visiting entrepreneurs at their companies, I observed several instances of how two strangers in the Xiamen business world created some common identity, heightening expectations. On several occasions public purchasing agents not previously known to the entrepreneurs called on them while I happened to be there. With purchasing agents, kickbacks are part of doing business. However, kickbacks are illicit and subject to periodic condemnations by the state. Also, if a purchasing agent is caught taking kickbacks, the resulting investigation could lead back to the entrepreneur if the agent is compelled to identify colluders. Therefore, kickbacks have risks: purchasing agents refuse them when the political climate is bad, while entrepreneurs have to enhance expectations that the purchasing agent will not reveal the entrepreneur's name if investigated.

An entrepreneur's first step toward creating trust was to determine the purchasing agent's native place. If the entrepreneur could not tell by the agent's accent, he asked. With this information, affect was enhanced by a few well-placed and seemingly casual remarks. If the agent came from a major coastal city, the entrepreneur had likely been there and could comment on its physical beauty and social order, or could mention relatives or friends who lived there. When the native place was off the beaten path, the entrepreneur commented favorably about local products. All of this occurred quickly through chit-chat and exchanges of cigarettes, heightening familiarity by creating some shared insider status in terms of native place. The entrepreneur then deepened the bond by inviting the purchasing agent to a meal. The agent's acceptance suggested a willingness to receive further rewards, such as a kickback, while the affect and obligation produced by dining together enhanced expectations of cooperation.

In sum, the institutional categories of social relations in China appear more adaptable to the pervasive presence of the state bureaucracy and the haphazardness of formal laws that generally characterize emerging markets in communist orders. This is not to say that malfeasance does not occur in China's market economy; it does, and I heard numerous stories of breach of trust during my fieldwork. But the possibility of enhancing trust is not so lacking as to preclude new exchange relations, as it seems to be in the Polish case. Variations in the institutional culture of personal ties help to explain the greater possibilities for commodified cooperation between local state agents and private company operators, which in turn help to drive the dynamic performance of China's market economy.

## The Efficiency and Equity of Commercial Clientelism

The embeddedness of China's market economy in patron–client networks raises concerns regarding efficiency and equity. The market transition account considers the clientelization of private business in personal ties between entrepreneurs and state agents undesirable. Such networks are deemed a less efficient means of enforcing contracts than universal legal private property rights. This is because in networks, the parties have to bear more of the transaction costs, which in a functioning legal system can be externalized onto the system. The networks are also held to be less equitable because patron–client ties bias exchanges in favor of those with political power.

Let me begin discussion by noting the distinction made by the economist Harold Demsetz between a "nirvana" and "comparative" approach to economic analysis. The former evaluates economic activity against an ideal-typical market economy, whereas the latter evaluates economic activity against practically possible alternatives (Demsetz 1969). I have already criticized the ideal-typical approach to markets in Chapter 2 and proposed the comparative approach to illustrate the preference for clientelist contracting in Chapter 4. In this chapter I will consider the nirvana evaluation of patron–client ties in the performance of private business and then posit a comparative one.

### Efficiency

A main argument of the market transition perspective is that patron–client ties are inefficient because the need for entrepreneurs to cultivate relations with officials increases transaction costs.[15] World Bank economist Qingsong Lin writes that the costs of acquiring government support by paying the fees and charges levied by local state agents "has drastically impaired private enterprise's capability for self-accumulation and has restrained their development" (Lin 1990: 184). The relevant question is, impaired capability and restrained development as compared with what? Chapter 4 demonstrates why entrepreneurs preferred clientelist contracting over other practically possible contracts. No other arrangement provided such a rich resource flow in the existing context. While horizontal contracting arrangements are possible, they do not provide the same degree of profit and security-enhancing resources. Therefore, while company operators may experience increased transaction costs to ensure cooperation from local state agents, without this cooperation they would probably never have become company operators, but only small shopkeepers. Thus, if one aspires to operate a private company, patron–client ties are efficient in China's emerging market economy.[16]

Furthermore, the empirical indicators of inefficiency referred to in the market transition account are of questionable significance. For example, some see the performance of private business as suboptimal: firms are "small and undercapitalized" (Nee 1992: 10); they stop growing once they reach a certain size (Lin 1990: 184); entrepreneurs consume rather than reinvest profits (Nee 1992: 14). Yet such indicators are of questionable relevance. In light of the well-documented propensity for Chinese business to emphasize network rather than corporate strategies, the small size of any single firm is not a meaningful indicator of capitalization, growth, and reinvestment. Profits are not reinvested in existing unitary firms but into new firms linked by overlapping kinship

---

[15] For example Victor Nee writes: "Due to their restrictions on factor resources and the continuing pariah-like status of capitalists and merchants in a socialist state, private firms remain small and undercapitalized. Moreover, the pariah-like status of the private entrepreneurs encourages short-term investment decisions aimed at fast returns, liquidity, and a low rate of reinvestment in the firm's growth. To compensate for their marginal status, many private firms seek close ties with local government, often paying a 'management fee' for assistance in obtaining reliable access to factor resources and political protection or registering as a collective enterprise. Local authorities may be more willing to overlook violations of government regulations and tax evasion if the private firm has successfully cultivated good connections with local government, *although such fees and levies increase substantially the transaction costs involved in doing business* [emphasis added]" (Nee 1992: 10).

[16] This logic is similar to an anthropologist's explanation of the economic utility of economic networks among Hausa long-distance traders in West Africa based on shared ethnic identity. "It is quite true that Hausa organization of long-distance trade is 'traditional' but what [critics] overlook is that in the present circumstances this organization is the most rational, the most economic and hence the most profitable" (Cohen 1969: 188–9).

ties in management and ownership. This creates business groups (*qiye jituan*) that embody sizable investments, even though each firm unit is small.

Consider, for example Clifton Barton's description of Chinese-owned shops in Vietnam:

> The outward appearance of a shop gives no real indication of the amount of business which is transacted from it or of how many other business interests its owner is engaged in. Often a small shop with two or three employees is the front for a booming business empire controlling dozens of other enterprises operating behind closed doors in adjacent buildings or scattered through seldom visited sections of the city. Often the basis of a multi-million-dollar enterprise turns out to be an inconspicuous shopkeeper, dressed in nothing but a pair of shorts, sitting in a small, dark and very old-looking business establishment which differs not at all from scores of similar firms on the same street. (Barton 1983: 47–8)

In short, the networks of firms rather than the scale of any single company is a better indicator of capitalization, reinvestment, and prosperity in Chinese business.[17]

Also, capital flight, which is usually attributed to political corruption and economic inefficiency, does not appear to be a significant issue in China. If anything, the trend in Xiamen seems to be similar to that in pre-reversion Hong Kong, where people emigrated in order to become eligible for a foreign passport or residence permit and then returned as investors. The new status of these returnees as overseas Chinese (*huaqiao*) or as Hong Kong, Macao, or Taiwan compatriots (*tongbao*) confers various advantages such as tax breaks. In other words, individuals change their legal personal status to be eligible for more favorable legal property rights such as foreign sole ownership or a a Chinese–foreign joint venture (*zhongwai hezi*). Thus, it is not clear that capital flight is occurring on any scale; capital that does leave eventually returns, although under altered personal and firm statuses, in a process colloquially called "round-tripping."

---

[17] This is true for Chinese-owned conglomerates as well. "Usually ethnic Chinese family businesses expand by acquiring an ever-increasing number of companies rather than by expanding existing companies. The overall business group may be quite large, but its individual component companies may be relatively small. This means that ethnic Chinese feature strongly in lists of the wealthiest families or entrepreneurs but are under-represented in lists of the biggest companies" (East Asia Analytical Unit 1995: 153).

## Equity

Finally, let me consider the issue of equity. In the market transition perspective, the use of political capital for commercial advantage is deemed inequitable for several reasons. First, it is considered unfair, because those without political capital or social ties to it do not have access to necessary resources. In other words, as the allocation of the resource in question is determined by political rather than market factors, it is difficult or impossible for those who are not officials or lack ties with officials to obtain it. While this is undeniable, it does not necessarily follow that ideal-typical markets are more equitable. Certainly to those with economic capital but no political capital, horizontal markets are more equitable. But the market, too, is a structure of inequality in which those without money are denied access to desirable goods just as surely as those without access to political capital. The premise that inequalities stemming from differential access to political capital are reprehensible, while those stemming from imbalances in access to economic capital are not, is a value judgment that elides how political power is always implicated in the structure of markets.

My own findings echo those of others who find a complex matrix of officeholding, power, and opportunities for gain that complicates clear-cut evaluations of equity in the market economy. On the one hand, the commodification of political capital has actually served to equalize opportunity by enabling those who are not officials to use money to buy access to power on a scale unimaginable before the reforms. According to Connie Meany, "although one still needed good relations with officials to prosper, or even to operate, one no longer had to actually *be* an official. . . . Money could now help an individual create a network of accomplices, instead of being merely a reflection of one's connections" (Meany 1991: 137–8). But on the other hand, the market creates new inequalities. For many, excluded access to a desirable resource through lack of money is just as pronounced as in the old regime through lack of political capital. In a study of the Shanghai real estate market, David Fraser documents the high cost of private urban housing, which stood at ¥6,280 per square meter in May 1994, a figure greater than the annual salary of most public employees. He writes of "considerable frustration (which also plagued the Maoist era) over access to and cost of housing, especially among young people" (Fraser 2000). The point is that for young people, desirable housing is still out of reach, although the structure of inequality has altered. These examples illustrate patterns of inequality and equality that considerably complicate evaluations of the equity of political capital relative to economic capital.

Also, it must be kept in mind that unequal distribution of access to political capital through patron–client ties may maximize efficiency in China's market economy, as mentioned in Chapter 2. As patrons have to be continually rewarded to ensure their support, the capacity to muster revenue is placed at a premium, ensuring that only the most profitable companies survive in the long run. Furthermore, what may be considered more equitable may actually be less efficient and vice versa. For example, *nomenklatura* privatization, in which an enterprise is sold in a sweetheart deal to the existing management, can be quite efficient, as management then has a monetary incentive to restructure the firm or, if unable to do so, to sell it to managers that can. However, *nomenklatura* privatization was seen as highly inequitable in Hungary in 1989 and was discouraged in the state's privatization efforts (Clague 1992: 7). Thus, principles of equity and efficiency can work at cross purposes.

The preceding discussion of equity highlights the importance of perceptions of equity in legitimating economic activity and the need to examine the content of these perceptions to explain the persistence or decline of practices. Christopher Clague usefully distinguishes two views of equity. *Ex ante* equity refers to equality of opportunity to be gainers or losers, while *ex post* equity means that there are no excessive windfall gains and losses (Clague 1992: 18). Findings from fieldwork in locales in China suggest a greater popular sensitivity to *ex post* rather than *ex ante* equity. For example, in Chen village near Hong Kong, Anita Chan, Richard Madsen, and Jonathan Unger observed how the flow of gifts that villagers proffer to their Communist Party secretary is not considered corruption.

> Villagers reason that a man with the qualifications and connections to be a party secretary would, were he to resign, be able to make an excellent living in the private sector. The post of party secretary pays only ¥1,500 a year, far less than the income of the average family, so it is deemed acceptable that he should see to his own interests and make up the difference through private donations. A livelihood that is on a par with that of the village's most successful entrepreneurs is almost considered his due. (Chan, Madsen, and Unger [1984] 1992: 286–7)

As long as the party secretary keeps his demand for gifts and money at a level deemed reasonable by the community, he can keep a reputation as relatively incorruptible. Cadres are considered corrupt only when their demands grossly exceed community values of acceptable levels of payoff. In other words, corruption is defined not as the use of political power for private gain but rather by the size of the gain.

The use of political capital for commercial gain is also judged inequitable by the market transition account because "it rewards arbitrary grabbing of control rights and openly acknowledges that politicians are not working in the public interest" (Boycko, Shleifer, and Vishny 1995: 59). However, this overstates the case because the usurping of control over public resources by local officials is not only for personal gain. My observations, along with those from other locales in China, suggest that the funds generated when officials profit by use of political capital may not only line the pockets of officials but also provide benefits for their public units. As noted in Chapter 4, a sizable portion of the funds also goes into the second budgets of public enterprises and agencies, which are used for everything from enhancing benefits to the personnel of specific public units in the form of wage bonuses and new housing to projects designed to promote regional development. In other words, political capital is embedded in processes of redistribution that can benefit not only officials as persons but also communities they reside in (see also Oi 1994: 74–6; Anagnost 1989: 220–3).

Furthermore, my observations from Xiamen suggest that the affective aspect of patron–client ties lets officials apply pressure on entrepreneurs to redistribute private wealth to the community. This might be less efficient but more equitable. Particularistic allocation of licenses, dispensations, leasing contracts, and so on may be less efficient in that the criterion for allocation is whether or not the entrepreneur is known to the official who is doing the allocating rather than whether or not the entrepreneur offered the best price or is the best possible manager. But in terms of equity, it might create a greater distribution of wealth to the community. This is because the entrepreneur is under obligation to reciprocate in the form of side payments that are off the books and can therefore go into the second budget rather than being collected as tax revenue by the central state. Such a distribution would have been less likely if the payment had been through an ideal-typical market transaction in which entrepreneurs have no obligation to sellers after the spot transaction is completed.

## Conclusion

This chapter has extended this study's claim that social networks are institutional elements of China's emerging market economy through a comparative analysis. Greater leverage in explaining the dynamic performance of China's market economy relative to other post-Communist economies is gained by considering not only the varying structural possibilities for certain types of social networks between government and business but also their manner of institutionalization. Chinese social networks appear to have greater institutional flexibility in extending claims based on family solidarity to persons outside the immediate family and authority because they are objects of veneration. Also, I have underscored concepts of efficiency and equity that take into account the context in which means and ends are defined and considerations of fairness are held. Evaluations of efficiency are less meaningful if the historical, social, and political contexts that shape means and ends are ignored. Popular perceptions of equity that redefine and legitimate the commodification of state power in accordance with community norms help to explain why patron–client ties are so routinized in commercial life, even though they are routinely condemned as corruption by the state and inefficient and inequitable by conventional economic theory.

# 8

## *The Transformation of Political Order*

The demise of Eastern European communism in 1989 has been "celebrated by many as the final proof . . . that the unrestrained operation of the market for capital and labour constitutes the material base of democracy" (Rueschemeyer, Stephens, and Stephens 1992: 1). If this is so, then China must pose the biggest challenge ever to this proof, because the most rapidly growing market economy in the late twentieth century is also one of the few remaining communist party-states.

This chapter examines the political consequences of China's emerging market economy, the other thematic question posed at the beginning of Chapter 2. The key issue is whether or not the commercial patron–client ties in private business described in previous chapters are also fault lines of alliance and conflict in the polity. By examining this issue we can also answer the question in Chapter 4 on the possibility of collective action by entrepreneurs against potential patrons. Transformations in the polity as they appeared at the end of the first market reform decade are the subject of this chapter, while trends in the second decade are described in Chapter 9 by drawing on more recent fieldwork.

The timing of the fieldwork spotlighted political behavior that I might otherwise have not noted. As mentioned in Chapter 1, two events occurred that posed the most severe crises for private business since its revival in 1979: the economic rectification campaign launched in September 1988, shortly after I began my fieldwork, and the student movement of mid-1989. The former was a mobilizational campaign that targeted the blurred boundaries of public and private property rights in the market economy. It merged into the crackdown that followed the student movement; it did not run its course until the early 1990s. The student movement erupted in spring 1989 and reached its bloody climax in Tiananmen Square on June 4. The severe political repression that followed included a campaign against corruption and tax evasion in private business. This heightened tension during 1988–90, casting political orientations and actions into sharper relief than would have been apparent in less troubled times.

This chapter presents a scenario of political change that is grounded in the organization of commercial clientelism described in Part I. To sharpen the picture, I juxtapose it with the scenarios of the political consequences of private business found in the market transition, political economy, and traditional culture perspectives. The market transition account tends to see market reform as causing a disjuncture in polity as the autonomy and legality ushered in by the rising market economy replaces the dependency and clientelism of the communist era. The traditional culture and the political economy accounts emphasize continuities in the polity through, respectively, enduring traditional authority and bureaucratic structures in the market economy. The scenarios developed in this chapter emphasize the transformation of political interests and strategies *within* a clientelist economic system.

The organization of the chapter is as follows. First, I briefly recount how state monopoly and patron–client ties constituted two axes of the polity in the classical communist system: one axis is state–society relations and the other is center–local relations. Second, I evaluate extant scenarios on the consequences of private business for state and society relations and describe an alternative clientelist scenario. Third, I consider the consequences for center–local relations. Fourth, I sum up the political transformation of the clientelist system.

## The Classic Communist Order

The patron–client networks that grew up in communist planned economies also came to constitute an institutionalized political order (Oi 1985, 1989; Walder 1986). They did so by enhancing the state's monitoring and sanctioning of agent and constituent compliance with central policies and goals. Monitoring is the capacity of a central authority to receive information about the degree of agent and constituent compliance (Hechter 1987: 49–52). In communist states it is manifested in security police surveillance, residency restrictions, networks of informants, small-group sessions of study and criticism, and party-controlled mass organizations. The capacity to monitor varies according to the degree to which effective institutions of surveillance exist and according to the willingness of the central authority to bear their costs.

Sanctioning is the use of selective incentives by superiors to induce compliance from subordinates. Superiors give incentives as rewards to the loyal and deny them to punish the noncompliant. Effectiveness varies by the degree to which incentives are desired and excludable. An excludable incentive is a collective good that is not available in markets but rather is forthcoming by membership in an organization. It follows that the more desirable and excludable are the goods possessed by an organization, the greater the possibility for solidarity among its members and their compliance with its authority (Hechter 1987: 38–9). In communist party-states these goods are career opportunities and material rewards, such as Communist Party membership and better housing.

In the decades before market reform began in China in 1979, client dependence on patrons constituted the polity in two ways. First, at the local borders of state and society, dependence gave rise to political machines in the work units where citizens and officials interacted on a regular basis and distribution of opportunities and goods occurred. Local officials doled out resources to selected citizens in exchange for political loyalty, enhancing the monitoring capacity of those officials. Loyal citizens, known as activists (*jiji fenzi*), created networks of informers for officials and helped to implement policies locally by taking the lead in public displays of compliance. This also created cleavages in the local society between clients and nonclients, reducing the likelihood of organized popular protest and resistance. Indeed, popular frustration with the system was often vented on activist clients rather than local agents of the state.

Second, within the bureaucracy, dependence enhanced lines of authority within the state structure, linking local agents and units with the central state. Officials' living standards, consumption patterns, mode of transportation, schooling opportunities for offspring, and so on were all tied to specific ranks within the bureaucracy (Vogel 1967). The movement of an official to the next higher rank depended on screening by immediate superiors.[1] Subordinates responded by conforming to the expectations of superiors. The implementation and enforcement of central state policies to coordinate society was therefore embedded in chains of particularistic dependence and personal loyalty within the state bureaucracy. The next two sections examine, respectively, the consequences of the rise of private business for state–society relations and for center–local relations.

## Shifting State–Society Relations

What have been the consequences of market reform for local relations between state and society? The market transition perspective posits the civil society scenario, which sees the emerging market as the domain of society, its emergence therefore enhancing the power of society at the expense of the state. Civil society is the antithesis of the communist state

---

[1] Surveillance for loyalty affected officials even more than citizens, and purges in the bureaucracy eliminated suspected deviants (Walder 1994a: 309).

in political organization, just as the market is the plan's antithesis in economic organization (Hankiss 1988; Vadja 1988).[2] The scenario's classic application to private business is Ivan Szelenyi's analysis of private entrepreneurs in rural Hungary. The private business class is a force for expanding civil society because entrepreneurs have a strong interest in economic freedom. Indeed, Szelenyi defines entrepreneurship as an economic "strategy of emancipation" from communist state control (Szelenyi 1988: 57). People become entrepreneurs to gain autonomy denied them in public employment, and so entrepreneurship is an "active strategy of resistance" to state control (Szelenyi 1988: 64). In Szelenyi's scenario, the entrepreneurs will form horizontal alliances with other subordinated groups, such as intellectuals and workers, to further their emancipation by extracting further concessions from the party-state (1988: 218). In China, too, some see a similar process of a rising civil society "flourishing in the fertile soil of autonomous economic activity" (Gold 1990b: 31; see also Pei 1994; Tong 1994). Market reform in China gives society a high degree of economic and civic freedom as well as material resources. Minxin Pei terms this a "societal takeover" that paves the way for more far-reaching political change in alliances between the new entrepreneurial groups and fledgling democratic opposition groups to gain entry to the political process (Pei 1994: 116–17).

The political economy account views the emerging market as enhancing local government's bureaucratic domination of societal groups in jurisdictions. This is expressed in the concept of "regional corporatism" proposed by the sociologists Anita Chan and Jonathan Unger. They see economic reform as decentralizing power to local governments by enhancing their control over resources in their jurisdictions. Local governments exert control over social groups through the various associations in their bailiwicks, often at the expense of higher authorities (Unger and Chan 1995: 47). In this vein Susan Young sees the Industry and Commerce Bureau as enhancing its power through the rise of private business; the planned economy is the purview of central ministries, while the market economy is controlled by local governments. She regards the activities of the bureau to encourage private business, such as building produce markets and renting stalls to private businesses, as both implementing central policies and "empire-building" (Young 1995: 124). Similarly, Ole Bruun points to continuities in the traditional culture of authority. As the emerging class of private business proprietors values bureaucratic access above all else as the route to status and wealth, their

---

[2] As one Polish intellectual writes: "It is here [civil society] that ideas and values inimical to the system of state and economy domination incubate and develop, and eventually lead to the creation of a new 'historic bloc'. . . which challenges the old 'bloc'" (Pelczynski 1988: 368).

values do not challenge state domination but merge with the interests of street-level officials. This further entrenches street-level bureaucracy so that its domination in locals "appears to remain qualitatively unchanged by the switch to a market economy" (Bruun 1993: 210).

The scenario I posit of shifting state and society relations emphasizes the relational and particularistic construction of political interests. Rather than see entrepreneurs' interests as determined by class location, as in the market transition account, I show how they are shaped by the social relations of doing business. This relational view of interests is expressed by Mark Mizruchi: "it is their relations with other firms that determines both how firms perceive their interests and the ways they act upon them" (Mizruchi 1992: 79; see also Thelen and Steinmo 1992: 7–10). In other words entrepreneurs have an interest in promoting the stability of the social relations of their business and act accordingly to preserve and redefine their relationships. As these social relations vary by an entrepreneur's societal capital, it follows that political interests reflect the particularistic relations of specific entrepreneurs; in this particularistic emphasis I differ from the traditional culture account. Finally, I differ from the political economy and traditional culture accounts on the question of the changing power configuration. These two perspectives see entrepreneurs as experiencing continued dependencies on lower-level state actors. While not denying the local state domination through its ongoing administrative monopoly, my emphasis is different: I show how entrepreneurial strategies in networks also shape the local polity.

### The Political Interests of Entrepreneurs

The political interests of Xiamen's entrepreneurs can be discerned from their attitudes toward the 1989 student movement. From its beginning in April through its aftermath in the late summer, the student movement came up in my conversations with twenty-nine entrepreneurs. The student movement targeted bureaucratic corruption and the windfall economic gains of the families of the political elite during market reform; one of its rallying cries was the term "democracy."[3] The civil society scenario expects that the entrepreneurs would support such a popular movement because they have similar interests in enhancing freedom. Yet only two entrepreneurs acknowledged having taken any actions in support of the students. One of these two had given money to a student, the daughter of a close friend, who solicited contributions to send to local student representatives in Beijing. The other permitted a student he employed as a part-time translator to use the firm's telephone to call local

---

[3] For the movement in Fujian province, see Erbaugh and Kraus (1990).

colleges in organizing a demonstration. In both cases entrepreneurial support was forthcoming in the context of a preexisting personal relationship. Therefore the degree to which these actions indicated support for the student movement or the pull of personal ties is unclear; they reveal little of entrepreneurial political values and interests.

Entrepreneurs expressed little sympathy for the movement, even in May when the movement was receiving widespread coverage in the Chinese media and people were astonished at how far it had gone in publicly challenging the central authorities in Beijing. The best that any entrepreneur said about the students was that their demands for change through actions by the national leaders were based on pure and noble sentiments but were politically naïve. One entrepreneur said: "The students don't understand reality. They have a high political consciousness but little understanding of practical politics. The more you tell the Communist Party to do something, the less it is willing to do so. It feels that it founded the country and knows what is best" (informant no. 20).

The entrepreneurs expressed the common value of the need for stability. This appears to be the core of their political ideology. As one said, "People's livelihood is connected with order. Only by having stability can there be order" (informant no. 22). Political change should be gradual and come from above as a reform (*gaige*) rather than pushed from below as a transformation (*gaizao*), because the latter is more likely to reflect a breakdown of central authority and lead to chaos. The main problem, therefore, is not lack of democracy but rather lack of wise leaders who listen to the people and respond to their needs. One businessman put it as follows: "people want a good emperor, not a democratic environment" (informant no. 10).

The belief that only a wise leader can make decisions for the greater good is heightened by the belief that "autonomous" groups only make demands on behalf of sectarian interests. Some people said that the students were protesting to ensure themselves better job assignments upon graduation. Others said that workers joined the movement to protest their low salaries. Furthermore, autonomous groups are suspect because it is not clear whom they represent. Regarding the coordinating organizations that emerged for the student movement, the Students' Autonomous Union and the Workers' Autonomous Union, one entrepreneur said, "We don't really understand what these two organizations are. According to official reports, the burning of cars, the fighting, and other violence was done by these two organizations. It is clear they orchestrated the violence. As soon as they set things off in Beijing, they ran off to stir people up elsewhere" (informant no. 15). Some people said that national leaders manipulated the students, using them as pawns in factional politics. Others saw the hand of foreign elements, a perception heightened by the movement's use of foreign symbols such as the Statue of Liberty (renamed the Goddess of Democracy) and the flight abroad of many movement leaders after June 4.

A preference for enlightened authoritarianism is strengthened by the widespread belief that democracy is not compatible with the Chinese context. Some opined that democracy undermines strong, decisive leadership by releasing a cacophony of voices that only confuses decision makers: it is coterminous with "anarchy" (*wuzhengfu zhuangtai*). Others saw democracy through a nationalistic lens as a foreign political ideology that had no roots in Chinese political culture. A few better-educated businesspeople saw some benefit to democracy: it would be possible to vote corrupt officials out of office. Yet they also held to the elitist view that democracy was unsuitable for China's polity except as a very long-term project. In their view, democracy requires an educated populace that can read and discuss political issues, a favorable condition not yet found in the large semiliterate peasant population.

Only on the issue of corruption was there significant variation in the entrepreneurs' political orientation. I came to realize that this variation reflected differences in their social networks with officialdom. These differences emerged when, surprised by the entrepreneurs' lack of enthusiasm for the student movement, I pushed them by mentioning that the movement's goals of ending bureaucratic corruption and nepotism in the market economy could improve their business environment. The responses of private entrepreneurs running the smaller businesses – private shops and the least prosperous companies – indicated mere skepticism concerning the anti-corruption platform. They believed that, while corruption is a problem, it is inevitable and nothing would come of the movement's call for stronger anti-corruption measures. As one said, "You can't expect the government to reform itself. It is corrupt from top to bottom. Why, the biggest profiteer is Zhao Ziyang's son! How the students can even think of asking him to end corruption is beyond me. As the saying goes, 'when those above behave unworthily, those below will do the same (*shangliang buzheng, xialiang wai*)'" (Informant no. 9).

Those running the most prosperous firms held a very different view. They did not agree with the platform because they felt that corruption was not a problem but rather part of the business process.

> Some businesspeople blame all their problems on bureaucratic corruption. But this is wrong. It is not a question of whether officials are honest or not. It is a question of the businessperson's skill. If you know how to conduct (*zuoren*) yourself, you can work things out. If you have a problem with

an official, you deal with the matter personally. You can't solve business matters by asking the government for more policies. (Informant no. 19)

Some of these prosperous entrepreneurs even criticized the students for raising the issue of corruption in the first place. One said, "The students should not cause a ruckus over this [corruption]. Who asked them to do so? They get money from the government for college. If they were really patriotic they would stay in school and study hard" (informant no. 19).

The interests of the entrepreneurs do not fit those expected by the civil society scenario. First, the attitude of the entrepreneurs as a group reveals no inherent values of freedom stemming from class position but rather a concern for stability that reflects business considerations.[4] Entrepreneurs showed at best only a lukewarm sympathy for the student movement's ideals. They were more concerned about the students' actions destabilizing the environment in which they operated. Their fear of the movement as representing hidden interests embodies a suspicion of sectarian movements. They tended to associate stability with the order created by strong state institutions.

Second, the entrepreneurs' varying reactions to the student movement's anti-corruption platform suggest that they might have fewer group interests in common than presupposed by the civil society scenario. Their interests are also shaped by the specific kinds of relationships that each forges in the market economy. Those operating the larger firms, mostly former functionaries and, to a lesser extent, former workers, already enjoyed support from officialdom through personal ties. For them, corruption was not really an issue because they had the necessary *guanxi* with officialdom to work out problems. More significantly, this suggests that as the scale of their business grows, entrepreneurs are increasingly inclined to seek solutions through personal ties with officialdom and less likely to seek solutions in collective action. Thus the differences in their interests produced by varying social constraints mitigate the kinds of alliances among entrepreneurs necessary for collective action.

## The Political Alliances of Entrepreneurs

The cleaving of entrepreneurs as a social class by the kinds of trade networks they forge is seen in their behavior regarding an "independent"

---

[4] This parallels Robert Manchin's (1988) survey finding from Hungary that people there engaged in private economic activities are not particularly likely to hold values conducive to civil society.

business association designed to lobby on their behalf. The establishment of such an association, called the Xiamen City Civic Association of Private Industry and Commerce (*Xiamen Shi Siying Gongshangye Gonghui*), was permitted by a proviso in the 1988 Private Enterprise Interim Regulations that private firms could establish their own association. However, the regulations did not stipulate which bureau should sponsor it. Xiamen's private business elite, those running the largest or oldest private companies and shops, sought a sponsoring agency that would work actively on their behalf. They wanted to avoid sponsorship by the Industry and Commerce Bureau (hereafter referred to as the Bureau), which issues private sector business licenses, regulates private business in matters such as entrepreneurial compliance with family planning policies, and cooperates with other bureaus in such matters as tax collection and the confiscation of counterfeit goods. They turned instead to sympathetic personnel in the recently revived Xiamen Chamber of Commerce (hereafter referred to as the Chamber), which has no regulatory functions regarding private enterprise.[5]

In 1988 the Xiamen City Civic Association of Private Industry and Commerce was established as an affiliate of the Chamber.[6] Its stated purpose as expressed in its bylaws was to help entrepreneurs acquire management skills, establish business contacts, obtain information, and protect their legal rights, and to represent them in dealings with government bureaus. The entrepreneurs elected officers from among themselves and hired their own staff. The Civic Association moved quickly on behalf of its members. It lobbied the city government to reduce taxes on the business profits of licensed private firms from the ostensible national rate of 35 percent to the 15 percent rate enjoyed by public enterprises in the

[5] The Chamber is a descendent of the business associations established by the Qing dynasty in the early twentieth century. Chambers provided the business community with some autonomy through self-regulation. In 1953 they were amalgamated into the All-China Federation of Industry and Commerce (*Gong Shang Lian*) under the control of the Communist Party's United Front Department. The Federation was active in the criticism and reeducation of former capitalists during the nationalization of private business in the 1950s. The Federation ceased functioning altogether during the Cultural Revolution. Revived in 1979, its first task was to rehabilitate the reputations of businesspeople who had been persecuted during the Cultural Revolution. Local Federation branches have also begun to help the businesses created since 1979. The revival of the Xiamen branch has been especially noteworthy. The first local branch to adopt its prerevolutionary name, it is now once again called the Xiamen City Chamber of Commerce (Xiamen Shi Shang Hui). Partially self-supporting, it runs commercial establishments and serves as an umbrella organization for specialized business associations for overseas and Taiwanese investors, private businesses, and specialized trades. For other discussions of revived private business associations in China and issues of civil society and local corporatism, see Nevitt (1996); and Unger (1996).

[6] The first association for private firms was established in Fuzhou, followed by Wenzhou and Guangzhou, with Xiamen's being fourth (interview, United Front Bureau, Xiamen branch, spring 1989).

special economic zone. The Civic Association also lobbied on behalf of individual members. In one case, one of the Civic Association's four elected officers ran a joint venture company with a rural township government. A township official absconded with the firm's cash, and the entrepreneur was unable to pay back a bank loan for the purchase of a truck. When the bank moved to repossess the truck, the entrepreneur sought the intervention of the Civic Association to hold the township government, rather than the firm, responsible for the loss.

From the start, the Civic Association was the focus of intra-bureaucratic conflict. Chamber officials considered themselves the rightful sponsors of the Civic Association because their national organization, the All-China Federation of Industry and Commerce, had supervised businesspeople as a social group since the 1950s. On the other hand, Bureau officials considered themselves the rightful sponsors because they issued private business licenses. Bureau officials saw the Civic Association as a challenge to their regulatory authority. This was a well-grounded concern, because entrepreneurs frequently had expressed anger at the arbitrary fees for annual license renewal that were used to punish uncooperative entrepreneurs. For example, the licensing fee that was demanded from one entrepreneur doubled to ¥500 after he joined the Civic Association. The matter of licensing fees also points to a key concern in the conflict: whichever organ became the sponsoring agency could obtain income from the entrepreneurs through fees, donations, and various charges.

The Bureau moved to suppress the Civic Association. It harassed members by summoning them to meetings at short notice, raised their licensing fees, and warned nonmembers against joining. The leading officer of the Civic Association was among the first local targets of the 1988 economic rectification campaign. In early 1990, the Bureau inaugurated its own private business association. The leading entrepreneur of the Bureau-sponsored association was the son of a city official. His polished manner, easy projection of authority, and high level of education, which included graduate study in the United States, contrasted with the Civic Association's rough-hewn officers, three of whom were former speculators and one a former worker. When I left Xiamen in the summer of 1990, the Civic Association had ceased functioning, its fate apparently sealed by a decision from the central state's support of the Bureau-sponsored association.

I found much variety in the reaction of member entrepreneurs to the suppression of the Civic Association. Those running the least prosperous firms were upset by its suppression. They were mostly former speculators running small companies and just expanding into the wholesale business. Lacking networks with local officials to cope with local administrative problems, they hoped that the Civic Association could help them to compensate for this deficiency. This view is expressed by an entrepreneur who was a member of the Civic Association's executive committee:

> There was already a Self-Employed Laborers Association. But the head of this association is also the head of the Industry and Commerce Bureau, so it is but an appendage of the Bureau. The Bureau's view is that it should control private business. If it was concerned about us and wanted to protect us from those who make trouble for us, this would be fine. But the Bureau only wants to tell us what to do. So the Civic Association seemed like a good idea. If private businesspeople manage the Civic Association, then it can talk on our behalf with the Bureau if it does something like confiscate our merchandise for no reason. (Informant no. 20)

By contrast, those who operated the most prosperous companies were former workers and functionaries and less concerned about the Civic Association's suppression. They were already established in the wholesale trade and had significant support from local officialdom. To the extent that they were seeking bureaucratic backing, it was to support their interregional trade outside the jurisdiction of the Xiamen municipal government, and the Civic Association was of little use in this regard. As one entrepreneur said:

> The Civic Association can't solve my problems. For example, when I hire a truck to haul something to Guangzhou, it goes through many checkpoints on the way. These belong to the traffic police, the Tax Bureau, the Industry and Commerce Bureau, and so on. They use their authority to stop trucks and fine them as they please. This costs me a lot. The Guangdong provincial government knows about this but doesn't do anything, so what does the Xiamen municipal government think that it can do? (Informant no. 36)

Another reason for their differing responses is linked to the extent of their business affiliations with public units. Entrepreneurs running the more prosperous companies actively reduced their commitment to the Civic Association, which tagged them as "private," since they had more affiliations with public units than the less prosperous firms and therefore more of their income came from activities conducted under a public legal status. They had joined the Civic Association in the heat of the favorable political climate for private business in 1987 and early 1988. But in late

1988 central state policies became much less supportive. So the operators of the most prosperous firms began actively distancing themselves from the Civic Association. In a conversation with me following the student movement in 1989, one of its officers even refused to acknowledge his membership.

In sum, there were different entrepreneurial responses to the Civic Association's suppression. This supports the aforementioned finding in regard to the civil society scenario, that entrepreneurs shared little common group interest; rather, their orientations toward forging horizontal alliances with other entrepreneurs varied according to their different relations in the market economy. Relations with officials cross-cut entrepreneurs as a group, reducing their class identity and the possibility for a unified bargaining position as a political interest group.[7]

These differing responses also suggest a local polity that differs from the local corporatist scenario of the political economy account. Entrepreneurs' actions call into question the effectiveness of the corporatist strategy of local governments, if that is indeed what they are pursuing. Far from asserting control over the entrepreneurs, we see entrepreneurs deftly using state-sponsored associations to pursue their own interests. One strategy is an associational one of "political amphibiousness," a concept posited by X. L. Ding (1994b) to express how societal actors can pursue their interests within the framework of state-dominated institutions and be working from the inside to reshape the function and agenda of these institutions. This is seen in the participation of the less prosperous companies in the Civic Association. First their operators played on splits within the state bureaucracy to find a bureaucratic sponsor for the Civic Association that would be more suitable for their purposes. Then they used the Civic Association as a vehicle for lobbying government agencies and enforcing their interests in their business problems. The other strategy, pursued by the most prosperous entrepreneurs, was to use participation in state-sponsored business associations to pursue agendas in networks with strategically placed officials. They favor other associations such as the Young Factory Director and Managers Association, which provided numerous opportunities to meet officials at the city government level and higher. This is not political amphibiousness, because the function and agenda of the association are not reshaped. Instead, entrepreneurs take advantage of its formal function and agenda to produce obligated ties with officials as well as enhanced reputation through membership.

---

[7] Similarly, Ole Bruun writes that private business exchanges with officialdom "actively discourage all potential alliances along horizontal lines expressing stratum, class, or common business interests" (Bruun 1993: 141).

## Shifting Center–Local Relations

This section describes the consequences of patron–client networks at the borders of state and society for center–local relations within the state structure. The market transition account sees center–local relations as increasingly characterized by legal-rational principles of administrative and personal conduct by local state agents. This stems from the central state's need for standardized administrative procedure to regulate markets; it therefore seeks to institute a "a public bureaucracy akin to Weber's ideal type of the legal-rational bureaucracy, capable of stable, methodological, rule-governed action based on written documents and files, strict subordination to higher bureaucratic levels, and the separation of the office from the personal interests of the officeholder" (Nee 1989b: 178). This professionalization of the bureaucracy is accompanied by the increasing imperviousness of its staff to societal influence. This legal-rationalization scenario is belied by the political economy account. Susan Young observes that "cadres appear to be resisting efforts to turn them into Weberian bureaucrats" (Young 1995: 124) and sees the interests of the central state and local staff as diverging rather than converging. The interests of local government lie "not in further reform but in the maintenance of the disorderly, experimental, transitional stage . . . [because this] gives the greatest degree of local or personal discretion" (Young 1995: 123). Local officials selectively implement central policies toward private business to enhance their control over it, often at the expense of higher authorities. Yia-ling Liu describes how the central state sends outside work teams to discipline local officials in rectification campaigns reminiscent of the Mao era. She characterizes the center's alternating emphasis on regular administration and extraordimary campaigns as "sporadic totalitarianism" (1992). Within the traditional culture account, Ole Bruun holds to a compatible view; political contestation in communities centers on the local bureaucracy, generating values that inhibit central attempts to institute the rule of law and precluding the emergence of democratic values, reinforcing officialdom's hierarchy (Bruun 1995).

I propose a dynamic scenario of the consequences of commercial clientelism. In contrast to the aforementioned legal-rationalization scenario, which privileges the policies of the central state or the traditional culture account's emphasis on the strength of local societal values and practices, I examine how the polity is shaped by the interaction of central policies and initiatives, local government practices, and entrepreneurs' business strategies. I also differ from the sporadic totalitarian scenario, which views center–local relations as cycles of local deviations and central despotic interventions, a pattern that predates the reform era. The mechanistic and enduring character of this cycle prompts the question of how the polity changes. My explanation is more dynamic. Shifting central state intervention strategies elicit responses in patron–client networks, constraining subsequent central actions and the character of further local responses. Commercial clientelism therefore transforms center–local relations within a clientelist system. I will show how expanding popular influence in the lower state structure through commercialized patron–client ties alters center–local relations. Shifting central state strategies of intervention stimulate local strategic responses in patron–client networks, constraining subsequent central state actions, patterning the evolution of center–local relations.

### Central State Strategies for Obtaining Local Compliance

To the central state, networks of officials and entrepreneurs are a compliance problem. It defines as "corruption" and "economic crimes" many of the exchanges that occur in networks. The networks siphon income away from the central state in covert exchanges. Losses to the center are incurred through the sale of assets such as land use rights below market prices; making bank loans to people and organizations that do not repay them; the sale of publicly owned commodities below cost; and the evasion of taxes. Another problem is that networks, being concealed, circulate goods and cash in ways not measurable by state monitoring institutions, undermining central state attempts at macroregulation. One example is the state's inability to check inflation, induced in part by uncontrolled bank lending at the local level and the concealed incomes of public units and private firms; this weakens state efforts to control money supply. Therefore, central state governance of the market economy since 1979 has proceeded via several institutional strategies to ensure policy compliance.[8]

One state strategy is to induce the compliance of local agents and constituents. This is done by invoking the legal-institutional trappings of a market economy as embodied in commercial law, legal property rights, contracts, and business licenses. These institutions, often resembling practices in such neighboring capitalist orders as Japan, pre-1997 Hong Kong, and Singapore, operate in the ordinary activities of administrative agencies, and have been promulgated in successive policy waves. They have induced some compliance that is quasi-voluntary because it is spontaneously forthcoming through fear of punishment for noncompliance. Both entrepreneurs and officials question themselves: what is the

---

[8] The three state strategies are based on Levi's (1988) account of state strategies to ensure compliance in taxpaying.

likelihood of being caught? Are the gains from noncompliance larger than the likely punishments if I am caught?

Induced compliance is impelled by routine administration. For example, licensing makes economic activities visible to state regulatory agencies because businesses must keep account books for official inspection and licenses can be revoked for noncompliance. Furthermore, the licensed business scope stipulates the goods that an entrepreneur can legally trade, increasing the likelihood that he or she will focus on these goods rather than more risky nonlicensed ones. The institutions of banking and contracts also heighten monitoring and sanctioning. For example, bank accounts create records of private business transactions, and the accounts of the noncompliant can be frozen.

State-sponsored business associations induce compliance through their techniques of intragroup surveillance. A case in point is the Self-Employed Laborers Association, set up in the early 1980s by the Industry and Commerce Bureau with mandatory participation for private shopkeepers. The association has been used to enhance tax collection. So-called "small taxation groups" (*nashui xiaozu*) have been established, each consisting of about ten neighboring shops. Every month the small-group leader reports the estimated business volume of each member to the local bureau substation. This provides the bureau with an independent check of the monthly self-reported income that each shop proprietor is required to make. Another example of intragroup surveillance is the trade associations organized by the Chamber of Commerce. Each trade association is composed of all the significant state, collective, or private sector firms in a certain line of business; by 1990 trade associations for the catering and electrical appliance industries had been established. Each association provides administrative agencies with information on the profit rates of its type of business and the estimated business activity of its members. Such intragroup monitoring has been established among officials too. For example, the regulations of the Tax Bureau and the Industry and Commerce Bureau stipulate that officials visit entrepreneurs in groups of two or more to inhibit individual officials from soliciting bribes and gifts.

Institutions that reinforce society-wide monitoring of businesspeople and officials have also been established. At the beginning of the massive anti–tax evasion campaign that began in August 1989, special hot lines were set up in the Tax Bureau for people to anonymously "inform on, expose, and stop the behavior of . . . tax cheating and other violations of the tax regulations" by entrepreneurs (*Xiamen Daily* 1989c). A similar hot line to report corruption within officialdom was established at the onset of the economic rectification campaign in September 1988. The media appealed to citizens to report such cases of corruption as bribery, illegal income, embezzlement of public funds, dereliction of duty, racketeering, official profiteering, and pressing fraudulent charges (*Xiamen Daily* 1988c). Societal monitoring enables the state to expand its information-gathering capacity by tapping popular feelings of envy toward rich entrepreneurs and corrupt officials.[9]

A second state strategy is to obtain compliance through coercion. State bureaucratic energy is concentrated on specific deviant practices that have defied more routine administrative solutions. This is coercive because it subjects all the members of a given population to monitoring, punishing those found to be transgressors, including evaders of the monitoring process. It draws on the communist legacy of mass campaigns to implement central policies by mobilizing all the resources of key bureaucratic agencies to achieve central goals, which since 1979 have been dominated by the creation of a market economy.

Campaigns unfold according to a stereotyped script. An example is the comprehensive tax investigation campaign (*shui shou da jiancha*) to target tax evasion that was launched in August 1989.[10] As a standard operating procedure, the Tax Bureau ratchets up the business tax on entrepreneurs by 10 percent to 20 percent annually on the assumption that this amount is routinely evaded. In comprehensive investigations the increase is much larger and is assessed retroactively. During the 1989 campaign, the Tax Bureau assumed that entrepreneurs had evaded taxes on about 75 percent of their income for the previous year (Gold 1991: 98). Tax officials teamed up with police from the Public Security Bureau to quash resistance by surprise raids on private businesses to seize account books (*Xiamen Daily* 1989b). Transgressors who turned themselves in were promised leniency (*Xiamen Daily* 1989c). Mass rallies were held in November 1989 to sentence the transgressors. Lenient punishment was payment of back taxes; normal punishment was payment of back taxes and a fine of two and a half times the amount of evaded taxes; harsh punishment consisted of a jail sentence and payment of back taxes and fines (*Xiamen Daily* 1989k).

Economic rectification (*jingji zhengdun*) campaigns and clean government campaigns (*lian zheng*) can occur simultaneously, much like the three-anti, five-anti (*sanfan wufan*) campaigns in the early 1950s, the former targeting corruption among officialdom and the latter economic crimes in private business.[11] In the early 1980s, economic rectification campaigns targeted smuggling and profiteering. Subsequent campaigns

---

[9] These hot lines are based on a similar practice in Hong Kong (interview, Tax Bureau, spring 1990).

[10] The launching of this campaign so soon after the 1989 student movement suggested to the entrepreneurs that it was part of a central state effort to punish them for their alleged support of the student movement.

[11] The three antis were corruption, waste, and obstructionist bureaucracy among officialdom. The five antis were bribery, tax evasion, theft of state property, cheating on government contracts, and stealing state economic secrets.

have focused on distinguishing legal from extralegal market behavior. A major campaign in 1985–6 targeted so-called suitcase companies (*pibao gongsi*), firms that exist on paper but lack assets. Such firms were said to be characterized by the "four withouts" (*si wu*): without capital, without a business site, without qualified staff, and without clear business scope (*Xiamen Daily* 1988a). The campaign reduced the number of trading firms nationally by 40 percent, from 300,000 to 180,000 (Jiang 1989: 16), and in Xiamen by 44 percent, from 1,371 to 765 (*Xiamen Daily* 1988b). Clean government campaigns focus on corruption in the bureaucracy. They aim at favoritism in administrative procedure, moonlighting and shareholding in private firms, profiteering, appropriating confiscated commodities and fines for personal use, soliciting bribes and attending banquets, and racketeering and extortion. Punishments range from warnings placed in personnel dossiers to expulsion from the Communist Party to execution for serious transgressions that involve large amounts of money or repeated violations.

A third state strategy emphasizes voluntary compliance. It is manifested in state efforts to propagate certain values that stimulate compliance as a matter of course. Since 1979, the central state has pursued propaganda activities in the business community that stress compliance with state policies as expressions of patriotism and the duty of citizenship. This intervention aims to make compliance voluntary and spontaneous: people should adhere to the rules because they see it as the proper, fair, and patriotic thing to do. To this end, the state promotes professional ethics in the media and by special activities in administrative agencies. State-defined business ethics (*shengyi daode*) encourage entrepreneurs to have a legal sensibility, practice civilized trade, give polite service (e.g., *Xiamen Daily* 1988e, 1990), and cultivate a taxpaying consciousness (e.g., *Xiamen Daily* 1989d). They are told that their obligations to the state are a kind of contract; the state provides services in exchange for citizens' compliance. For example, a *Xiamen Daily* (1989f) article exhorted private entrepreneurs to keep in mind that the social stability of the business environment is dependent on the army's protection of the country against outside enemies and the maintenance of domestic order by the police.

Efforts to induce voluntary compliance are also aimed at officials. Codes of ethics are promulgated for specific bureaus that distinguish proper from corrupt behavior, like the "Eight Imperatives and Eight Prohibitions" code of the Industry and Commerce Bureau mentioned earlier.[12] Officials are also reminded of the state's concern for their welfare, such as providing housing, medical care, and education, and

---

[12] See Chapter 5, note 16, for the code's content.

exhorted to be responsible in complying with the demands of the solicitous state. Officials are also reminded of their professional ethics and their duty to serve the state.

The state also seeks to shape people's perceptions that their activities are linked to broader projects, such as nation-state building and societal development. They are told that their efforts are crucial to national endeavors, such as the Four Modernizations (science, industry, agriculture, defense), to create a strong and rich country. The state organizes speech contests in local administrative agencies and at meetings of entrepreneurs on such themes as "expressions of patriotism" (*aiguo de biaoxian*). People are told that they should obey regulations and laws because that is how public order is maintained and societal development is enhanced. Finally, appeals are made to entrepreneurs to "fulfill responsibility to society" (*dui shehui fuzeren*). Such responsibility is manifested not only by compliance but by active contributions. The state encourages entrepreneurs' philanthropy through such activities as providing money for widows, orphans, and the handicapped as well as contributions to the construction of schools, roads, and sports centers and the purchase of government bonds (*Xiamen Daily* 1988d, 1989i). An added benefit of philanthropy to the state is that this private provision of public goods gives it a nonrevenue source of income by freeing up funds that it would otherwise have to use to provide these goods.

Another technique to encourage voluntary compliance is to issue status-enhancing rewards to compliant officials and entrepreneurs. It is expected that people will act in ways that are socially desirable if they receive recognition that will raise their status in the community as a result of that action. This state strategy dovetails with the attempts of entrepreneurs with less advantaged societal capital to enhance it by acquiring symbols of legitimacy, as described in Chapter 6. To this end entrepreneurs and officials are invited to join the Communist Party and become representatives in the local People's Congress (e.g., *Xiamen Daily* 1987a). Businesspeople are given titled positions in new business organizations, designated as model entrepreneurs, and recognized in the media. They are also rewarded for compliance with specific policies. For example, as mentioned in Chapter 6, entrepreneurs who pay taxes according to the law are designated "taxpaying activists" (*nashui jiji fenzi*) and receive red and gold banners to hang in their offices and have their achievements publicized in the media. Parallel techniques of status enhancement for officials include job promotions, recording exemplary behavior in their personnel dossiers, and opportunities for travel and further education. This strategy of status enhancement presupposes that those rewarded will likely comply in the future, while publicizing their activities in the media illustrates the state's definition of desirable behavior for others.

Another technique of voluntary compliance is to seek to delegitimate practices that the state sees as reducing compliance. Banqueting is a case in point. Because it generates strong obligations that can undergird cooperation between entrepreneurs and officials, the state discourages banqueting and traditional rituals and festivals that involve banqueting. One such event is the annual ghost-feeding ritual called *Pudu* in southern Fujian province.[13] Before and during the festival an intensive propaganda campaign is launched through the state-run media and wall posters to discourage participation. The Self-Employed Laborers Association convenes meetings in which businesspeople publicly swear to forgo participation, a practice that occurs in public units as well. The state exhorts citizens to shun participation in the ghost-feeding festival because it is a feudal superstition (*fengjian mixin*), it wastes resources that could be used for national development, and the increased drinking creates public disorder and traffic accidents (*Xiamen Daily* 1987b, 1989h).

### Local Responses and Strategic Interaction

Variations in the effectiveness and efficiency of each compliance strategy constrain the central state, resulting in shifting emphases among the strategies. Routine institutions for monitoring and sanctioning the market economy that emphasize induced compliance are efficient, because they are part of routine administration and do not require the extra expenditure of resources. However, they appear less effective, as it is relatively easy for firms and people to evade monitoring, and sanctions are relatively light, such as a fine or reduction in licensed business scope. The strategy of voluntary compliance is more efficient for the state because, as compliance is spontaneous, fewer resources are expended on monitoring and sanctioning. However, the lack of monitoring and sanctioning institutions also renders it the least effective strategy to obtain compliance.

The more limited effectiveness of induced and voluntary compliance pushes the state to campaign intervention. For the central state, bureaucratic campaigns are the most effective strategy, as almost all members of a potentially noncompliant group are placed under tighter surveillance. Indeed, all firms in a jurisdiction may be investigated. This can markedly reduce problematic behavior. However, coerced compliance is also the least efficient strategy. It consumes a tremendous amount of the bureaucracy's administrative capacity and diverts attention from other matters. Also, because much commercial activity occurs in targeted ac-

---

[13] During the seventh lunar month, all ghosts (souls) suffering in the underworld are released for a month of freedom. Eating is important in this festival as a symbolic feeding of these ghosts. People invite persons who are potentially useful to them to dine (see Weller 1987).

tivities, their suppression can create an economic slump that becomes a problem in itself. For example, state attempts to eliminate dubious commercial loans to enterprises might lead to bankruptcies, increased unemployment, and disruptions in the supply of commodities. Finally, campaigns only suppress rather than eradicate targeted problems. This is because the problems also stem from broader institutional structures within the state that create uncertainties and incentives not addressed by the campaign. To the extent that a campaign does not change these structures, the uncertainties and incentives that gave rise to the problem remain. As continued campaign-style suppression of the problem is impossible because of the expense, targeted behavior tends to reemerge after a campaign has run its course. In fact, targeted behavior often reappears with redoubled vigor because another campaign is not expected for a while and officials are preoccupied with other matters.[14] The result is incessant campaigns against such perennial problems as suitcase companies and banqueting officials.

Central state shifts among these strategies can heighten local perceptions of the value of cooperation between entrepreneurs and officials. The shifts stoke entrepreneurs' perception that central state policies are unstable, thereby reinforcing their demand for supporters in officialdom to protect them from these uncertainties by warnings of impending campaigns and investigations, and intercessions to reduce punishments. Also, campaigns often target practices that stimulate the local market economy and provide benefits to officials and public units. By doing this, campaigns can also inadvertently enhance local cooperation by pushing officials to side actively with entrepreneurs in circumventing or sabotaging new central initiatives.

The case of cooperative companies illustrates these constraints. The economic rectification campaign that ran from 1988 to the early 1990s targeted trading firms that blurred the distinction between public and private property rights.[15] Cooperative firms were a target. Previously, cooperatives were portrayed in the media as private solutions to such public problems as unemployment and scarcity of consumer goods, and their operators were lauded as heroes. Suddenly they were accused of using public advantages for private gain and were branded "false collectives" (*jia jiti*), and their operators were vilified for duplicity for "displaying a sheep's head but selling dog meat" (*gua yangtou mai*

---

[14] For example, after the 1985–6 economic rectification campaign against commercial firms, their number plummeted from 300,000 in 1984 to 180,000 in 1986; but by 1987 the number had climbed to 360,000 and then to 470,000 in 1988 (Jiang 1989: 16).

[15] It targeted "companies where there is no separation between political administration and enterprise ... companies set up by party organizations ... [and] problems such as officials in party and administrative posts and retired officials holding full- and part-time jobs in enterprises" (*Xiamen Daily* 1988a).

*gourou*).[16] A campaign was launched to determine which cooperatives were "false" and which were "socialized." Such a determination required detailed knowledge of the allocation of profits in each cooperative. The various public units that sponsored cooperatives refused to go along with the administrative agencies implementing the campaign because they feared the loss of such gains as the monthly management fees paid by cooperatives. This aspect of the campaign apparently went nowhere; the ambiguous status of the cooperatives in my sample remained unchanged.[17] In sum, campaign-style intervention, while effective in the short run, can be counterproductive for the state in the long run. It raises the awareness of officials and entrepreneurs of shared interests, reinforcing the values of mutual support and localism that undergird their cooperation.

The most immediately apparent consequence of a campaign is not to eliminate the targeted practice but rather to shift competitive advantage further toward entrepreneurs whose social networks with officialdom are embedded in more durable ties. These norms contain stronger obligations, ensuring that state agents will exert themselves on behalf of entrepreneurs, and they involve fewer practices readily labeled as corruption. Indeed, the cases of private entrepreneurs accused of economic crimes that appear in the media seem disproportionately to involve those from low social backgrounds, such as former speculators, who can be easily accused of more blatant economic crimes like bribery (e.g., Hershkovitz 1985).

When I concluded my fieldwork in mid-1990, state strategies of control increasingly appeared to be relying on intragroup monitoring, such as the use of trade associations.[18] The burden of monitoring is delegated to those being monitored, enhancing efficiency. Once the institutional framework is erected, it needs few resources to sustain. It is also relatively effective: surveillance is by peers who understand the conditions of a market segment, so information is likely to be accutate. Compliance is further enhanced because each firm operator knows the information is more accurate, thus increasing the chance of being caught for noncompliance. Finally, intragroup monitoring is institutionalized in routine administrative procedures and does not disrupt commercial activity as does a

---

[16] See Lin (1989) for an example of this later view of cooperatives as problems rather than solutions.

[17] The willingness of Industry and Commerce Bureau officials to talk about cooperative firms during my initial interviews in 1988 and early 1989 gave way to a marked avoidance of the topic in later interviews, a sure sign that the rectification of cooperatives was not going smoothly.

[18] This accords with the argument by some China analysts that the Chinese state is emphasizing corporatist techniques of control. Jonathan Unger and Anita Chan (1995) provide a succinct statement of this position and an overview of the relevant literature.

campaign. A limitation of intragroup monitoring is that firm operators might collude to control the information given to the authorities, while those supported by highly placed officials can still act with impunity.

Intragroup monitoring is also more efficient and effective than intrasocietal monitoring. With societal monitoring, the ongoing participation of citizens requires ongoing exhortation through the media and public rallies. It is ineffective in that the information received from anonymous informants may be inaccurate and therefore have little relevance to state goals. The importance of this latter point became apparent in my conversations with both entrepreneurs and officials regarding the telephone hot-lines instituted in 1988 to report private business corruption. In the view of the entrepreneurs, anonymous informers were either fellow entrepreneurs or jealous citizens whose reports reflected business competition or popular jealousy rather than an entrepreneur's degree of compliance. Consequently, entrepreneurs saw little reason to modify their behavior.

In sum, the logic of relations between center and local is driven by the interaction of central initiatives and local responses, which constrain further central initiatives. To the central state, the local networks between entrepreneurs and officials, by capturing resources that the central state perceives as its due, create a compliance problem. However, the state is limited in how it can intervene. One constraint is the durability of the local networks. Networks are bundles of tactics that local actors can improvise on in the face of state intervention. While tactics emphasizing money *guanxi* can be readily targeted, those emphasizing affective ties with officials are more impervious to central intervention. The other constraint for the state is that the most effective strategy, the mobilization campaign, is also the least sustainable because of such high costs as the excessive use of bureaucratic capacity and the economic slump that occurs when exchange networks are suppressed. This leads the state to alternate among intervention strategies, creating uncertainties in the market economy that heighten entrepreneurial perceptions of the importance of networks, increase the commercial value of the protection that officials can provide from campaigns, and shift advantage to ex-functionary and ex-worker entrepreneurs, who have more advantaged accumulations of societal capital.

## Institutional Transformations in the Polity

The preceding discussion of the dynamics of relations between state and society and center and local suggests several transformations occurring within a clientelist political system. This constitutes continuity with the past, as the networks are still patron–client ties. However, it also constitutes much change, as the relations of power are much altered.

### From Political Machine to Development Coalition

Political machines in Xiamen have dramatically eroded, reflecting both the declining old form of citizen dependence on officials and the subsequent growth of new dependencies of officials on entrepreneurs. Entrepreneurs no longer depend on officials for basic needs, because they can now purchase such necessities and luxuries as housing, consumer appliances, and cars and such welfare benefits as health care and education in the market economy.[19] Obviously, entrepreneurs no longer depend directly on officials for career opportunities either, because they run their own firms. Some of the opportunities that officials still control, such as Communist Party membership and appointment to leading positions in new business associations, are sought only to the extent that entrepreneurs lack effective social networks with officialdom. Rather, it is officials who now depend increasingly on entrepreneurs for material benefits in the form of gifts, salaries, and dividends. Entrepreneurs also give officials career opportunities as employees, managers, advisors, and board members in their companies.

Changing relations of dependence are found also in shifting flows of information. Previously, client-citizens served as informers for officials, providing helpful information on local responses to new policies, the behavior of others, and possible pockets of resistance. This information helped officials to monitor and govern their jurisdictions. But now it is officials who serve as entrepreneurs' ears in the bureaucracy, giving them timely information on commercial opportunities, policy changes, and regulatory actions.

The increasing dependence of officials is visible also in altered patterns of competition. Previously, citizens competed to enter officials' patronage networks. Successful ones received material benefits and entrance into the political elite through party membership. In contrast, now officials also compete with each other for links to larger private companies, with successful ones becoming shareholders and managers. As the bureaucracy is vast, it is relatively easy for entrepreneurs to find willing supporters in officialdom. This is illustrated by the response of an entrepreneur who exported products to my comment that it must be difficult to find

---

[19] In my sample of 100 entrepreneurs, 39 had bought houses or apartments or had them under construction; 30 owned houses that had been confiscated from their families in the 1950s and 1960s and returned to them in the 1980s; and 31 still lived in public housing, most of these intending to purchase private housing. Regarding vehicle ownership, 46 entrepreneurs had motorcycles and 32 had cars, trucks, and/or vans.

state foreign trade corporations to sponsor his foreign trade. He said that there were hundreds of such corporations in Xiamen: "Officialdom doesn't choose us, rather we choose them" (informant no. 69). The competition among officials can be seen in the capacity of entrepreneurs to extend influence to much higher levels of government than previously. In the pre-reform era, one's *guanxi* was primarily with grass-roots officials, while petitioning officials at higher levels often required an intermediary. Now entrepreneurs socialize with district heads, bureau chiefs, state enterprise managers, and city mayors, cultivating personal ties with these prominent and powerful cadres.

The decreasing dependence of private entrepreneurs on officials does not necessarily mean that businesspeople are more autonomous in the sense of a declining need to bargain with officialdom. It must also be kept in mind that even as the scope of state agents' control over resources declines, they still monopolize the means of administration and information in the realm. Therefore, having bureaucratic supporters is crucial for business success. Instead, the relative bargaining position of entrepreneurs is much enhanced. Networks have become more open-ended, fluid, and easily exited by both parties, while power asymmetries are muted by the highly complementary character of commercial calculations in exchanges.

These new relationships can best be described as development coalitions. Coalitions differ from political machines in several key respects. First, political machines tend to be intraorganizational and provide benefits that are highly excludable, as epitomized in the work unit system of control and distribution. In contrast, coalitions are interorganizational alliances between discrete entities to achieve a more precise range of goals. Although the ideal is a long-term partnership, coalitions can be more easily dissolved when goals are not met and members desire new partners. This characterizes the more fluid relations between government entities and private firms oriented to producing commercial profit. Second, participation in political machines is often coerced, as there are no alternatives for securing a resource. In China's planned economy, coercion was amplified by the difficulty of transferring out of work units. In contrast, entrance and exit in a coalition are easier, though the ideal is a long-term alliance, as this reduces costs of cooperation.

Finally, local coalitions differ from political machines in regard to support for central authority. In political machines, local state agents generate constituent support for the center by deviant means. This differs from coalitions, which are alliances to further the members' goals, often at the expense of nonmembers. This is true of the relations between private companies and public units to reap commercial benefit from public resources at the expense of the central state. Coalitions therefore embody two significant changes. One is the orientation of agents. Their concern for implementing the goals of the central authority in society is increasingly displaced by the desire to forge beneficial alliances with constituents. The other change is that in a coalitional order, the explicit policy intentions of the central authority are less likely to be implemented locally. Coalitions may even seek to oppose or circumvent central preferences.

### From Loyalty to Venality of Local Officialdom

The declining scope of dependency has eroded authority relations in the bureaucracy. Previously, officials complied with the requests of superiors to gain the rewards and opportunities that superiors controlled. Dependence therefore enhanced officials' loyalty because the rewards were highly excludable and there were no alternatives for obtaining them other than by exhibiting compliance. Now the value of statist rewards has declined dramatically. The potential rewards in the market economy now far exceed the rewards for loyalty to superiors within the state structure. Consequently, officials' loyalty to superiors is changing to venality of office as they seek to profit by selling their control over the means of production and administration to bidders in the market economy.[20]

In the late 1980s the monthly salaries of officials in Xiamen were several hundred yuan, including the special economic zone subsidy for public employees.[21] In contrast, employees who work in private companies enjoy base salaries of several times this amount. With bonuses and commissions, some can realize monthly incomes dozens of times greater than their previous public salaries. Entrepreneurs also entice officials and other talented public employees by giving them one-time lump-sum payments when they go to work in the private company that are equal to the sum of the public wages they would have earned had they remained in public employment until retirement. Private businesses also provide medical insurance and pension plans to core employees comparable to benefits in the public sectors.

The shift from loyalty to venality does not necessarily mean that officials are more corrupt now than before. Deviant administrative practices were as much a part of the political order before the reform era as during it. However, the character of deviant behavior has changed, reflecting the above changes in the incentive structure. In the planned economy, deviant behavior was moral hazard: the concentration of individual efforts on fulfilling quotas, which superiors used to measure

---

[20] Officials' shifting orientation is suggested by the fact that 70% of economic crimes in 1987–8 were committed by officials (Chang 1989: 25).

[21] This subsidy was around ¥70.

performance (Eggertsson 1990: 45). In order to please superiors, local officials often filled the quotas that came down from above with falsified information.[22] This deviancy is best described as a form of opportunistic overcompliance (Goldstein 1991). By contrast, venality is opportunistic noncompliance with central policies. The deviant practice of officials to exceed quotas in order to gain rewards from superiors has been supplanted by deviant practices to circumvent and sabotage more stringent central policies in order to gain rewards by stimulating private business locally.

Some analysts have highlighted the functional aspects that venality of office serves in mediating authority relations within the state structure. According to Ezra Vogel (1989: 422), higher-level officials tolerate the venality of lower-level officials as a way of buying their support for implementing the reform policies. Others (Chan, Madsen, and Unger [1984] 1992: 287, n. 13) maintain that the central state tacitly accepts venality in lieu of raising officials' salaries. Such views, by suggesting that venality of office is a new kind of compliance strategy by the central state toward lower officialdom, overlook one crucial point. Whereas the loyalty of the planned economy emphasized bargaining relations within the bureaucracy, venality emphasizes bargaining relations across the local boundary of state and society. This has had profound consequences for the capacity of the central state.

The capacity of a state to coordinate society rests on the responsiveness of the lower bureaucracy to the center (Mann 1986; Skocpol 1985a: 15–17). The earlier relations of dependence ensured responsiveness by creating vertical chains of loyalty in the bureaucracy that induced local officials to assiduously implement policies that came down from above, and gather information about the local society and economy for superiors. Dependence also created a cleavage in the local society between citizens inside and outside the patronage networks of the local political machines, preventing organized popular resistance to state actions. The decline of valued excludable resources and the rise of new opportunities in the market economy have led to a shifting orientation for officials. They have decreasing incentives to seek rewards through compliance in implementing and enforcing central state policies. Instead, as the value of statist incentives declines, officials are now increasingly likely to seek rewards through local forms of cooperation with constituents that, as just noted, willfully circumvent and even sabotage central policies. The

---

[22] This type of deviance caused some of communism's greatest disasters, such as the overprocurement of grain after false reporting of grain production in the USSR and China led to the collectivization famines of 1929–33 in the former and 1959–61 in the latter, which in turn led to the escalating search for and elimination of the class enemies who had supposedly caused these disasters (Walder 1994: 309). In each case, local officials assiduously implemented central policies, albeit in an exaggerated fashion.

central state therefore finds local officialdom less responsive and its directives less assiduously implemented.

As state infrastructural power erodes, new areas of autonomy are emerging in the polity. However, this is not the autonomy of society from the state, as in the civil society scenario. Instead it is the autonomy of communities of networks between local state agents and societal constituents that are increasingly developing their own economic strategies without direct reference to the center. As rewards controlled by the state hierarchy diminish, agents increasingly seek new founts of resources locally in cooperation with constituents. The new willingness of agents to cooperate creates possibilities for entrepreneurs, driving the expansion of private business and the market economy. Local expansion of the market economy in turn further reduces local officialdoms' reliance on the center, undervalues state rewards, and fuels cooperation across local state–society borders.

## The Pluralization of Power

The expansion of a market economy in a one-party state is likely to increase patronage (Flap 1990: 240; Meany 1991) as political authorities search for new means of support (Shefter 1994) by using the new administrative levers at their disposal. This can lead to such hallmarks of a clientelist polity as officialdom's preferential proffering of licenses, loans, and special dispensations from state regulations to clients engaged in business. Rather than view this expansion of patronage as propping up the system and hindering further political evolution, the expansion and commercialization of patron–client ties may also be considered a pluralization of the polity.[23] Such pluralization does not occur through the formal trappings of electoral democracy, such as competitive parties and popular voting, but rather through the shifting power distribution and bargaining relations within networks. The changing character of patron–client ties reflects increased competition among local state agents to gain clients and their heightened responsiveness to constituents' demands. It also reflects the capacity of certain citizens to exercise a great deal more influence on the decision-making process in local government. However, the application of policies and delivery of benefits continue to be based on particularistic criteria.

This form of pluralization varies by local social structures. For example, both strong and weak village governments are found in the two

---

[23] For this view see Boissevain (1966); Powell (1970); Weingrod (1968, 1977); and Silverman (1970).

counties adjacent to Xiamen (Nee 1990: 18–21). Also, the process of variation does not support the view, widespread in Western political and economic discourse, that embeddedness in transnational flows of market capitalism enhances the prospects for a democratic political order. In fact, the data from Xiamen, when taken together with the other local studies mentioned in Chapter 4, suggests practically the opposite. In regions less connected to transnational flows, a more absolute erosion of clientelist networks may occur. The local polity of such regions may approximate a civil society scenario in which the control of local officialdom over resources declines and clientelism gives way to a more egalitarian order of self-employment and small private business (Szelenyi 1988: 16–18). This polity seems apparent in North China's Xiajia village, with its farming households (Yan 1995). A coalitional-type polity, such as in Xiamen, is visible in Chen village adjacent to Hong Kong. Villagers' personal ties with overseas kin, giving them access to financial capital and foreign markets, do not so much enhance autonomy from local officialdom as augment capacity to bargain for administrative support (Chan, Madsen, and Unger [1984] 1992: 287). A third configuration is apparent in the corporate polities of southern Jiangsu's industrializing villages (Oi 1989: 1992). Local rural government plays a key role in mobilizing local resources for production and providing links outside the locale.

The case of Taiwan, less than 100 miles from southern Fujian, suggests a further possible evolutionary course. It shows that political and economic clientelism do not necessarily diminish with economic development and democratization. The Nationalist Party on Taiwan has extended special economic privileges to local factions that support it in the electoral process; these privileges include special bank loans, contracts for public works projects, and conduct of dubious and illegal activities such as gambling and the use of public office for private gain (Wang 1994: 185). This has been crucial for the Nationalist Party to gain the support of local elites (Wu 1987). This suggests that a one-party state like China's committed to the development of a market economy can maintain a clientelist politico-economic system for a long time without appreciably harming the market development, in effect "strik[ing] a satisfactory equilibrium between clientelism and a market economy" (Wang 1994: 201).

# 9

## Epilogue: Evolutionary Trends in the 1990s

A market economy is not capitalism because there are markets under socialism too. (Deng Xiaoping, 1992)

Returning to Xiamen for several weeks in 1995, I revisited people I knew and met new entrepreneurs. The economic depression that began in 1989 was already history; people attributed the change to Deng Xiaoping's much publicized southern tour (*nanxun*) in 1992, when he visited Guangdong province and urged greater boldness in market reform (Zhao 1993). To many this tour clarified the state's commitment to market reform, reducing uncertainties that grew out of the political suppression of the 1989 student movement. One immediate result of Deng's action was the resumption of bank lending, pouring financial capital into the market economy and fueling a new commercial boom.

I noted new elements in the configuration of business, trust, and politics, suggesting an evolution of commercial clientelism. Among these new elements were policies of corporate ownership; the emergence of a new entrepreneurial path for formerly high-ranking officials; new patterns of government–business cooperation to promote translocal trade; and the rising prominence of regional idioms. As economic reform policies proceed, the comparative advantage of locales is based less on special privileges obtained from the central state than on position in translocal market flows.

## Evolving State Monopoly

In the late 1980s I observed how legacies of the planned economy encouraged the clientelist organization of market transactions in private business; in 1995 I observed evolutionary trends in these legacies that embodied both continuities and changes. One trend is that, although the state's direct monopoly over material goods was still declining,[1] limited rationing had been reinstituted for some basic consumer items such as grain. Furthermore, regulatory forms of state control over allocation continue to increase. The licensing system for authorizing private companies to trade specific products was still intact, while items such as cotton, sugar, and cooking oil, which had undergone sharp price increases, were now subject to price controls. During my visit new price controls were announced on consumer items; traders found to be selling them above an average market price were to be punished.

State monopoly through multiple price categories has continued in certain key goods, most spectacularly in real estate. In fact, real estate development had become a huge industry. Speculation in residential housing is linked to state policies to privatize housing by selling it to the occupants. As public employees lack money to pay the market price for their housing, special low prices are set to enable occupants to afford it. The difference between the market and administrative price can be huge, with ratios from 15:1 to 20:1 in the cases I heard of.[2] There are also low prices for special categories of individuals such as poor households (*kwunnan hu*). Other forms of real estate speculation concern access to choice land for shopping centers and office complexes.

Information on real estate and the supply and demand of goods by state enterprises still flows in bureaucratically mediated networks, although the commercial value is much greater than before. This is linked to the emergence of a new entrepreneurial career route of formerly high-ranking officials who have left their public posts since 1992 to start private businesses, a practice called "diving into the sea" (*xia hai*).[3] Those I met use personal ties in higher levels of officialdom to broker between market segments, creating much greater turnovers and profits than was considered possible in private business just a few years earlier. They also use ties to state enterprises to establish corporate joint ventures with public units. Some belong to the new breed of corporate tycoons.

A second trend is that ambiguous meanings and sudden changes in central state policies still create uncertainties in commercial activity. For example, while the media announcement of the aforementioned price controls described the formula for determining average market price and the sanctions for selling above it, there was vagueness about which goods

---

[1] The proportion of industrial production allocated by central planning declined from 90% of all products at the beginning of market reform to around 12% by the early 1990s (Kumar 1994: 323).

[2] I found one instance where a public apartment with a market value of ¥200,000 was sold to a public unit employee for ¥10,000. Another apartment with a market value of ¥600,000 was sold for ¥40,000.

[3] By mid-1992 as many as 120,000 people were reported to have left public administrative positions to work in the private sector (Meyers 1994: 6).

would be affected. Consequently, the new regulations give local state agents even more leeway in identifying entrepreneurs as transgressors of this or that regulation. There are also sudden regulatory changes in the goods that private firms may legally trade. For example, in March 1995, it was announced that private businesses could no longer trade sugar wholesale beginning on April 1, and that private firms licensed to do so would have this authority revoked. Illegal profiteering by private sugar traders was said to have caused the price of sugar to appreciate from ¥2,600 per ton in 1992 to ¥4,500 in 1995, well above the international price of about ¥3,300 per ton. Judging from media reports, illegal profit was derived by some firms that transacted large volumes, including one that sold 100,000 tons of sugar in 1994 (*China Daily* 1995a: 2). However, the point at which legal transactions became illegal attempts to corner the market was not explained in the policy. Nor was it explained why cornering the market was wrong if it merely reflected market principles. This exacerbated uncertainty.[4]

Despite the continuing profusion of laws and rules, regulation by campaign-style injunctions continues with two new twists. One is the announcement of regulatory campaigns followed by nonimplementation for fear of their negative economic consequences. This was first evident in a 1993 campaign against rampant bank lending, which was soon called off because of state fears that the sudden drying up of financial capital would cause a new economic slump. What is intriguing is that previously, such fears of an economic slump were confined to local governments seeking to blunt campaigns' local implementation sufficiently to avoid harming the businesses within their jurisdictions. Now the placing of commercial profit above regulatory order even characterizes the central state's handling of its own control levers.

Another innovation is a narrowing of scope of campaigns as compared to previous ones. For example, in March 1995, a national campaign targeting so-called suitcase companies was announced in which all 8 million commercial trading firms in China were to be investigated. The target was companies characterized by the "three withouts": those without the amount of capital registered in their license; those without a proper business site; and those trading in goods outside their legal business scope (*China Daily* 1995b: 1). One entrepreneur jokingly noted that this campaign signified progress in creating a market economy, as the "three withouts" targeted in the current campaign were one less than the "four withouts" targeted in a similar campaign a decade ago (see Chapter 8).

---

[4] For similar uncertainties over a decade earlier, see the career of the "God of Fortune" mentioned in Chapter 2, note 23.

A third trend is the waning of conscious distinctions between legal public and private property rights. The state media, officialdom, and entrepreneurs increasingly use terms that encompass both private and certain public firms such as "nonstate" (*fei guoyouzhi*) and "popularly managed" (*minying*). These terms refer to private companies, jointly managed firms, cooperatives, and corporations. This declining attention to public and private status reflects not the increasing clarity of legal property boundaries but rather the greater legitimacy of arrangements that do not conform to legal distinctions between public and private property. The emergence of such categories as "popularly managed" that do not distinguish public and private legitimately encompasses both the popular ideology of a personal network economy in which bureaucratic authority is commodified and the state ideology of a "market economy with Chinese characteristics" that is neither capitalist nor socialist but a blend.

The decreasing urgency to draw a clear line between "public" and "private" property is also apparent in the 1994 Company Law, which appears to eliminate the legal public–private distinction in companies that are limited-liability corporations.[5] These companies have the status of a legal person and are managed by a board of directors elected by the shareholders rather than appointed by the state. An individual, such as the chairperson of the board of directors, is designated as the legal individual representative who signs contracts on behalf of the firm. However, in these firms bureaucratic power and influence continues to be converted into commercial gain. I heard of a number of practices I had been told of half a decade earlier, only the scale was much greater.

## Power and Entrepreneurship

Forms of state monopoly continue to reproduce the opportunity structure encapsulated in the local maxim "favorable climate, advantageous position, harmonious relationships," described in Chapter 3. The greatest sources of profit and protection still lie in officially brokered opportunities. As earlier uncertainties over the state elite's commitment to the market economy recede, entrepreneurs have become bolder in seeking them.

---

[5] Limited-liability corporations now appear to constitute a third property category. Companies with from three to fifty investors and registered capital of ¥500,000 can become limited-liability corporations. Those with at least ¥10 million in registered capital and over fifty investors can become incorporated limited-liability companies. Firms can raise capital by selling shares to the general public, and those with over ¥30 million in registered capital can be listed on the stock exchange.

### The Rise of a Cadre Entrepreneurial Path

In the five years since I had been in Xiamen, a new group of entrepreneurs had emerged composed of people who had once been high-ranking officials. These entrepreneurs have benefit-rich personal ties in the state structure through prior holding of higher office. Lucrative opportunities for them stem from several sources. One is a credit crunch that began in 1993 when the central state cracked down on rampant bank lending. This created the triangular debt (*san jiao zaiwu*) phenomenon: since the state stopped lending them money, state enterprises suddenly lacked cash. Consequently, needing money to pay for goods and their employees' wages, many state enterprises gave the goods they produced to well-connected people who were able to sell them for cash. These people then remitted the cash to the enterprises, after, of course, taking nice commissions for themselves.

The other opportunity for these individuals stems from a proviso in the 1994 Company Law that public enterprises can be reconstituted as limited-liability companies. Although the law stipulates that the state should be compensated at the fair market worth for the assets of the public enterprises, it is exceedingly difficult for the state to ascertain what this worth is because of the widespread underreporting, undervaluation, and concealment of the assets and their rates of return. Thus, high-ranking officials resign to set up private companies that then enter into corporate partnerships with state enterprises, shifting public assets that they formerly controlled or that are controlled by others they know into their limited-liability corporations. Once ensconced as corporate managers, they can continue to draw on their ties in the bureaucracy for profit and to forge new commercial activities. Although the managers and shareholders do not own the corporations, they gain through salaries, dividends, and management perks.

These entrepreneurs began business with significant financial and societal capital savings through their prior experiences of holding high office. They are unlike members of the previous functionary path to entrepreneurship, who controlled few public resources despite having previously worked in the state bureaucracy. They are also unlike the entrepreneurs in all the other paths in that they are less likely to be Xiamen natives. Thus, many begin business with networks that already extend well beyond any local jurisdiction. Some have chosen Xiamen as a business site because they deal in coal and other minerals and in construction materials such as steel, cement, and glass that are exported, primarily to Hong Kong and Southeast Asia.

One such entrepreneur was a former high-ranking officer in the People's Liberation Army in his mid-forties. He left the army in 1993 when a former classmate working in the coal mine administration in Shanxi province told him of a state mining enterprise seeking cash to upgrade its mining equipment and develop new mines. He obtained a ¥6 million bank loan by tapping personal ties with former comrades-in-arms who had returned to their native villages, where, as former soldiers, they came to occupy positions in rural governments. These former comrades-in-arms let him use village lands as collateral for the bank loan.[6] He then set up a private company to enter into a public-private partnership with the state coal mining enterprise, basing his company in Xiamen to facilitate exports. After investing the ¥6 million, he and the state enterprise split the profits from selling the coal. In 1994, he had a sales volume of ¥400 million and expected it to be ¥1 billion in 1995. His company was now a limited-liability corporation; he is the chairman, and the major shareholders are his private company, firms managed by his former army comrades, and other firms associated with the state mining enterprise. The coal mining operations sold by the state mining enterprise to the corporation were significantly undervalued.

Another businessman, also in his mid-forties, was formerly an official in the central Heavy Industry Bureau. He resigned his job in 1993 to pursue business with a steel factory in Manchuria. The steel factory was desperate for money to pay its workers wages. It gave him 1,000 tons of steel to sell on consignment; the entrepreneur would have to pay for the steel only after he sold it. Former bureau colleagues in Fujian province told him of opportunities to sell it in the special economic zones. After selling the steel to a Hong Kong construction firm, he took out a private business license and set up a joint venture with a state steel manufacturer. He now trades in lots of 6,000 to 10,000 tons of steel. Some trade is with Hong Kong and overseas Chinese firms, as this provides him with the cash to pay the state enterprise for the steel. Other trade is barter with state construction and real estate development firms: steel is exchanged for legal title to apartments and villas in complexes they construct, which the entrepreneur then sells.

Finally, another entrepreneur, also in his mid-forties, is currently a prominent official in the Xiamen city government. His business developed in response to a situation that has existed since 1993, when central policy austerity measures forbade state enterprises from giving their employees cash bonuses for holidays (*guojiefei*) during Spring Festival. State enterprises have responded by giving bonuses to their employees in the form of watches, home appliances, and other gifts. This entrepreneur supplies these gifts to state enterprises, relying on his networks through-

---

[6] This entrepreneur told me that loans could be obtained in the mid-1990s for 65% of the market value of real estate put up as collateral.

out the city government to obtain orders. In 1993 he also started a private business in the name of a relative. Although the official has no formal position in this firm, he is its de facto entrepreneurial manager. Since state enterprises in Xiamen own much real estate, he accepts payments in this commodity that can be sold for profit.

### The Earlier Entrepreneurial Paths

Some entrepreneurs whom I had previously met were also faring well in general. Many of those without significant bureaucratic connections are trading in textiles, home appliances, and other goods that require less official brokerage. Some are expanding through the multiplication of small shops in a variety of locations. One entrepreneur has been quite successful, parlaying his textile business into dozens of small boutiques in Fujian and Zhejiang provinces and in Shanghai. Others are moving into manufacturing, emphasizing products that are not officially brokered. One entrepreneur has been in the seafood business for many years. He used to buy eels and shrimp in the region and sold them to state foreign trade companies, which in turn sold them to Japanese businesses. In 1992 he invested in an eel farm and persuaded Japanese buyers to buy directly from him. He has developed several other export seafood farms and reaped a profit of ¥8 million from these activities in 1994. Other entrepreneurs are moving into high technology items, which are also not officially brokered. For example, one entrepreneur who previously dealt in handicrafts and construction materials is negotiating with a Russian factory through a Russian language teacher at a local university to market Russian computers in China. However, he is clearly hampered by a lack of knowledge of Russian or computers.

Some entrepreneurs from the speculator and worker paths are investing in poorer hinterland regions. They take advantage of the tax holidays and preferential treatment by the local rural governments that outside investors can enjoy. Several entrepreneurs told me that the perks they receive in these inland areas are similar to those received by overseas Chinese investors. A number of private companies from Xiamen are investing in Longyan, an old revolutionary base area in western Fujian, which has many untapped natural resources. Companies that invest there get a two-year tax holiday. This has stimulated ¥65 million in investments from Xiamen businesses in developing coal, cement, lumber, and bamboo-producing ventures.

Other entrepreneurs are venturing into activities that are more officially brokered. The auto trade is a case in point. Private companies that had previously sold car parts are now dealing in cars. Some sell such foreign luxury cars as the BMW, Mercedes Benz, and Lexus. I was told by the manager of one company that many such cars are smuggled ashore intact in Guangdong or imported in pieces and reassembled domestically to avoid the high duty on imported cars. Although car licenses are still in restricted supply in Xiamen, restrictions are bypassed by purchasing the unused car license quotas of public units and foreign-owned firms. Real estate is another example. Ties with officialdom are needed to get choice real estate and bank loans for development. One practice is to obtain control over a piece of real estate via personal ties. With the real estate as collateral, a bank loan can be obtained to draw up blueprints for a residential complex. Apartments are sold before construction even begins, as there is much demand because of popular worries of rising prices and the privatization of public housing. This money is then used to build the complex, and an entrepreneur profits without investing any prior financial capital.

The most spectacular way that the businesspeople who took the earlier paths to entrepreneurship continue to benefit from state power in the mid-1990s concerns use of the 1994 Company Law to reconstitute cooperative companies as limited-liability stock corporations. This has enabled some entrepreneurs who were never officials to raise huge amounts of financial capital by public stock offerings that they use to increase their sources of profit and security in the state bureaucracy. Such development can be seen in Xiamen's largest private company, described in Chapters 4 and 6, which was operated by the former stevedore Chen Youfu until his arrest in 1988 on charges of bribery and smuggling. As Chen had invested heavily in real estate in the 1980s, the company did not go bankrupt while he was in prison. Upon release in 1992 he threw a big party in Xiamen, inviting over 100 officials and important people. In 1994 his was among the first private companies in China to make a public offering of stocks, reputedly raising ¥25 million in capital. By 1994 his enterprise group had over fifteen separate firms. He has invested money in a project to build a new bridge across the Xiang River in Changsha, Hunan province's capital, is involved in developing 300,000 square meters of real estate in and around Shanghai's Pudong Zone, and is building a corporate tower in Xiamen. Also, Chen is assiduously acquiring the trappings of Communist legitimacy; his corporation has a workers' union and a Communist Party branch. Other entrepreneurs joked to me that all the firm needed was the addition of a Women's Federation (*Fulian*) branch to be considered a public unit.

Another trend in the 1990s has been the merging of overseas Chinese kin networks with domestic clientelist ties. A number of former functionaries and workers have been sponsored by their kin to emigrate to Hong Kong and the Philippines, where they have gained valuable experience working in the companies of overseas relatives, and have returned to the mainland with a Hong Kong identity card or foreign passport and new human capital skills. They have several options upon return. They can form a Sino-foreign joint venture with themselves as the foreign party and a family member who has taken over their original private company. Such ventures bring tax holidays, easy access to bank loans, and increased prestige, which is valuable when dealing with officials. One such businessperson commented: "When I was a private entrepreneur, the banks would ignore me when I sought loans. But now that I am an overseas investor (*waishang*), bank officials even visit me to offer me loans."

Other returnees set up Sino-foreign joint ventures with local governments to obtain choice real estate and protection from the enforcement of labor and environmental regulations. One such entrepreneur emigrated to the Philippines in 1985 and then returned to Xiamen in 1988. He drew on his earlier ties with district government officials to set up a department store in Xiamen in the early 1990s, expanding to other cities in Fujian in 1994. He has also drawn on the expertise of his father, who ran a shoe factory before the revolution, to reenter the traditional family business and become a partner in several township enterprises in adjacent Tongan county that produce shoes for domestic and foreign sale. Another businessman ran a private textile factory in the nearby city of Shishi before emigrating to Hong Kong, where he worked for several years in his siblings' real estate development company. In the late 1980s he returned to Xiamen to supervise a US$60 million project developed by his family's Hong Kong development firm in partnership with the public Xiamen City Real Estate Company. One of his brothers-in-law in Xiamen is an official in the City Real Estate Company, ensuring access to choice land. His company is also heavily invested in Shanghai real estate.

I also heard of entrepreneurs who had left business because of regulatory and legal problems, although none who had actually gone bankrupt. One entrepreneur had previously embarked on her entrepreneurial career by leasing a district trading firm. While leasing the firm, she used bank loans obtained for her by the firm's legal public owner to buy several luxury villas in a new suburban estate. According to the person who told me this, problems arose when she tried to scuttle the firm and shift the real estate over to a new private company she had founded. Officials in the sponsoring unit of the leased firm saw her as trying to appropriate the property in violation of a previous understanding and sought to block the property transfer, claiming that the villas belonged to the leased firm and therefore the public unit. According to my source, the entrepreneur responded by simply selling off the few assets she had left, transferring her funds to Hong Kong, and emigrating to Australia, where she had already sent her children to college.

Finally, Xiamen is attracting successful private entrepreneurs from elsewhere in Fujian. Just as Xiamen-based entrepreneurs seek to expand beyond their regional economy by seeking opportunities in such national market centers as Shanghai and Guangzhou, so entrepreneurs from the Minnan hinterland are coming to Xiamen to seek new opportunities beyond their local markets. Many of the new private companies established in Xiamen since 1992 are by capital investments from the hinterland. One source is Longhai county, where easy water access to Xiamen's harbor has led to the proliferation there of factories producing such exports as chopsticks, plastic sandals, and umbrellas. Another source is Shishi city, in nearby Jinjiang county, with extensive overseas kin connections and a government famous for its pliability to local interests: in the 1980s Jinjiang's private textile factories produced a huge volume of jeans and other popular fashions. These entrepreneurs are already familiar with Xiamen, as they have been producing for sale or transshipment in the Xiamen market and also have kin in Xiamen. According to native Xiamen businesspersons, these nonnative entrepreneurs, distinguished by their local accents of the Minnan dialect, are said to support each other by loans and information, giving rise to dark talk of the Longhai and Shishi cliques (*bang*). In particular, such talk raises fears that the gangs, reportedly rife in Shishi and alleged to work hand in glove with the local government to maintain order there, will expand to Xiamen.

### The Chamber of Commerce

One surprise I found concerned the Xiamen City Civic Association of Private Industry and Commerce, sponsored by the Xiamen Chamber of Commerce. When I left Xiamen in 1990 the Civic Association had ceased activities and a rival Private Business Association, sponsored by the Industry and Commerce Bureau, had been created, a situation described in Chapter 8. When I returned in 1995 I found that the rival Private Business Association was moribund. Entrepreneurs and Chamber of Commerce officers told me that a 1992 directive from the central state had declared that administrative units, such as the Industry and Commerce Bureau, could not both regulate and represent such societal groups (*shehui tuanti*) as private company operators. The Civic Association thereupon resumed operations by first holding social events, such as Spring Festival parties. Its next step was to invite leading officials of the Industry and Commerce Bureau and other relevant bureaus to be its paid advisors, ensuring cooperation from formerly antagonistic officials by spreading benefits around. However, a 1994 directive from the central state made it against regulations for officials from administrative bureaus to be advisors to societal groups, creating a new obstacle in the efforts of

Civic Association to ensure harmonious relations with administrative bureaus.

The Chamber of Commerce responded by creating chambers at the lower level of urban district governments. By 1995 each district had its own chamber and the main chamber was renamed the Xiamen City General Chamber of Commerce (*Xiamen Shi Zong Shang Hui*). While the General Chamber has continued its emphasis on trade associations that combine public and private firms in a particular industry and attracting overseas investment, the district chambers emphasize nonstate businesses, and can be considered as together being the successor of the Civic Association.[7] Each district chamber has about 100 members. Their officers are private businesspeople appointed on the basis of the amount of their financial contribution to their district chamber. Each district chamber also includes district government officials as advisors, an arrangement that mirrors the practices of the General Chamber. These officials receive honorariums for speaking at district meetings. According to entrepreneurs, district officials are more enthusiastic participants in chamber activities than city-level officials. District chambers work actively on behalf of their members. Each has established a mutual aid fund (*huju jijinhui*) endowed by members' donations to guarantee bank loans to members.[8] District chambers also coordinate entrepreneurial philanthropy to maximize publicity and prestige and have plans to construct headquarters to provide greater visibility and prestige.

The General Chamber has continued to actively support private companies. However, it no longer only lobbies the Xiamen government but also pressures local governments elsewhere on behalf of Xiamen entrepreneurs. This shift is in keeping with the spirit of the Glorious Enterprise (*Guangcai shiye*) policy, a 1992 central initiative to encourage investment flows from richer regions to poorer borderlands, revolutionary base areas, and minority districts.[9] For example, in 1994 the Xiamen General Chamber of Commerce led a group of private entrepreneurs to the Longyan region to negotiate special concessions. It obtained favorable terms of trade for private real estate investors from Xiamen. In the old revolutionary base areas of Longyan, the Xiamen group arranged a deal whereby the ratio of payment of profits between investors of financial

---

[7] By 1995 the General Chamber had five new trade associations for the following business lines: electrical appliances, machinery, textiles, rubber and plastics, and general merchandise. In addition, associations were being set up for personal care and beauty products and for handicrafts.

[8] In one of Xiamen's larger districts, the amount was ¥400,000.

[9] My understanding of this policy is derived from interviews with officers of the Xiamen General Chamber of Commerce and the following published sources: Sun et al. (1994); Liu et al. (1995); Xiamen City Glorious Enterprise Promotion Office (1995).

capital and investors of land would be 80:20 in favor of the Xiamen financial investors. The General Chamber also lobbies on behalf of specific entrepreneurs in negotiations with other local governments. Through Chamber mediation, one businessman was given a very unusual privilege: he was authorized to sell gold in Longyan. District chambers have also worked on behalf of private companies in Glorious Enterprise activities. The Siming district chamber has established connections with the Guiyang city government in impoverished Guizhou province to assist Xiamen entrepreneurs in purchasing unprofitable public firms and to coordinate their donations to Guizhou schools.

## Neomercantilism in Business–Government Networks

I noticed a distinct new pattern of private business–local government cooperation. During the 1980s local market economies were stimulated by the differences between more restrictive central policies and local variances from them. Locales with greater deviations tended to have a more liberal climate and dynamic market, enhancing local wealth accumulation. These privileges and deviations were a competitive advantage that enabled activities not found elsewhere to flourish. In Xiamen some deviations were concessions granted from above by the state, such as the special economic zone policy that authorized lower business taxes and import tariffs than other places. Other deviations were adopted by the local government, such as licensing private trading companies, which hastened the circulation of commodities through Xiamen. Yet other deviations were popular practices such as smuggling, labeled economic crimes by the central state and variously tolerated by local governments.

By the mid-1990s rates of wealth accumulation through local policy deviations were in decline. This is because such accumulation depends on the existence of more restrictive central policies, thereby creating advantages for locales with looser practices. But by the 1990s many original policy advantages of the special economic zones have been given to other cities as well, most notably Shanghai. As the importance of policy privileges declines, technical and geographic considerations figure more in cost calculations. The local worry is that overseas Chinese and foreign investors will now bypass Xiamen because of its geographical isolation, lack of an industrial base, and relatively small population, and instead favor Shanghai and its Yangzi River hinterland or Guangzhou and its Pearl River hinterland.

This has fueled widespread concern in Xiamen that the local market economy is falling behind in competition with other regions. The secretary of the Xiamen General Chamber of Commerce expressed this concern in a conversation with me. "Xiamen is a special economic zone with favorable policies and so they [local business people] have become lazy. They just hang out a sign, waiting for customers to come to them. But the market economy is developing quickly and you cannot keep running in place. If you don't go and try to make opportunities you will fall behind." The secretary and others fret that the main industries in Xiamen are shifting toward real estate speculation and an entertainment sector of restaurants, karaoke bars, saunas, and prostitution.

The fear is that Xiamen will share the fate of nearby Shishi city. In 1980, Shishi was a small out-of-the-way town along the coast north of Xiamen. It was noteworthy for the high proportion of locals with overseas relatives in the Philippines, a historical legacy of out-migration from this once impoverished area. Many of these overseas relatives were in the textile business, and when market reform began they gave their kin in China the financial capital to enter the textile trade. Thousands of small factories were founded in the early 1980s that manufactured jeans and other popular garments. Many hired far more than the seven-person legal limit, a practice actively encouraged by their village and township governments. Also, local officials turned a blind eye to the smuggling of home appliances in Taiwanese fishing boats. The narrow streets of Shishi were lined with small shops piled high with bales of blue jeans and boxes of smuggled VCRs and thronged with buyers from all over China. This gave Shishi the nickname of "popularly run special economic zone" (*minban jingji tequ*), a reference to the mix of popular practices and local government deviations from central policies that stoked its business climate. However, by the early 1990s this political comparative advantage had evaporated because such practices as large workforces were no longer widely proscribed and Shishi's technical weaknesses, such as high labor costs and poor transportation links, sent the textile industry into decline, while the wider availability of home appliances elsewhere undercut the smuggling industry.

When I visited Shishi in 1995 I found the situation much changed. The town had been administratively upgraded to a city, and broad avenues flanked by twenty-story buildings now covered former agricultural fields. However, the city was still not connected to anywhere by a major road and lacked the hustle and bustle I noted over half a decade before. In 1995 there were only trickles of customers in the streets; as night descended, the high-rise buildings remained mostly darkened, lacking tenants. This cooling of the economy was reflected in the drop in local real estate prices from a high of over ¥1,500 per square meter in the early 1990s to less than ¥800 in 1995, a trend counter to that of Xiamen and other major urban centers along the coast. Several textile entrepreneurs whom I visited subcontracted with the Foreign Trade Bureau to produce luggage and sneakers for export. Such business was steady but did not generate the large profits of earlier trade patterns. Several operators of transportation companies I knew told me that the once-booming market for transporting tourists, customers, and products between Xiamen and Shishi had evaporated.

In Xiamen a new kind of cooperation between business and government might forestall the fate of Shishi's private firms. Best termed "neomercantilism," it involves Xiamen's city and district governments' negotiating with authorities in other jurisdictions on behalf of Xiamen entrepreneurs. I had noted inklings of this trend in the 1980s with the trade and study missions to Hong Kong and abroad organized by the city government, the Chamber of Commerce, and the Young Factory Directors and Managers Association. However, in the 1990s such trade and study missions now venture into the domestic hinterland where Xiamen authorities lobby local governments to give concessions for Xiamen-based companies. This neomercantilism has its characteristic features. One is the emphasis on bargaining between local governments. Policy concessions are less forthcoming from the center because there are fewer restrictions; they are now granted by authorities in a locale to the business interests of another locale. A second is the more active role of local government in seeking outside investment. Whereas previously local governments did little more than tolerate deviant practices within their jurisdictions to create a more liberal market environment locally, they now actively seek concessions to benefit their local businesses that venture into other jurisdictions.

Neomercantilist cooperation between the Xiamen city government and Xiamen private companies is visible in the city's various programs. The government has lobbied local governments in the interior of Fujian province to give special tax and regulatory concessions to private companies from Xiamen that invest in these regions. Indeed, the aforementioned Glorious Enterprise policy can be considered little more than central recognition of new business links and investment flows and an attempt to derive political legitimacy from these growing trends. Neomercantilist initiatives also coexist with the previous emphasis on local deviations from central policies. For example, the Xiamen government circumvented national restrictions on foreign trade by private businesses by creating a special bonded district within the special economic zone. Private companies may establish import-export branches in this district; the city government looks the other way when commodities are moved in and out of the district as long as various fees are paid. This has made Xiamen more attractive to businesses elsewhere, as seen in the increasing number of Xiamen's private entrepreneurs who are not native to Xiamen.

In neomercantilism locales and activities are not defined by the degree of liberalization vis-à-vis state policies but by their position in translocal commodity exchanges. One exchange flow is between northern and southern regions. Much heavy state industry lies in the north, particularly in Manchuria, while much market purchasing power is in the south, leading to exchange flows of industrial products for cash. Another flow is between the coast and the hinterland. The hinterland contains raw materials and human labor, while coastal regions demand these resources. Also, enterprises from the domestic hinterland seek opportunities in Xiamen; the number of branch firms in Xiamen increased from about 500 in the late 1980s to several thousand by the mid-1990s, and many new private companies were founded by entrepreneurs and financial capital from the hinterland. Yet another pattern of exchange is that between China and the international economy, largely mediated by the overseas Chinese diaspora. In this exchange, Xiamen is a key node in exchanges across national boundaries, mediating flows of industrial products from North China to buyers in Pacific Rim countries and the flow of such labor-intensive products as textiles, toys, and appliances and foodstuffs such as seafood and canned goods to the United States, Japan, and elsewhere.

Neomercantilism depends on a national market of some sort for its smooth operation; regionalism is therefore a force for integration rather than fragmentation. As the prosperity of locales becomes more deeply embedded in criss-crossing exchange flows, government and business actors are increasingly reluctant to see it disrupted by political fragmentation. Indeed, people in Xiamen mentioned the former Soviet Union as an example of how political fragmentation disrupts economic flows, hindering prosperity. Politically, the paradox of neomercantilism is that it reflects the increasing autonomy of locales from the center while simultaneously stimulating the importance attached by local political and business elites to maintaining the larger political entity of China governed by the center. The heightened autonomy of locales in neomercantile practices does not threaten to fragment the state; instead, it reconstitutes it through lower-level networks of transregional market exchanges and bilateral negotiations between the more local layers of government. This process is a manifestation of what some analysts have termed "Chinese-style federalism," which emphasizes economic flows between regions and competition and experimentation between and among local government jurisdictions that are relatively autonomous from central state control (Montinola, Qian, and Weingast 1995; see also Huang 1996).

## The Rise of Regional Idioms of Cooperation

Neomercantilism is undergirded by an institutional ideology of regionalism within locales that spurs the formation of development coalitions between officials and entrepreneurs oriented toward expanding business opportunities in other locales. While I had noted regional idioms during my earlier fieldwork, they were much less pronounced than the personal idioms of *guanxi* at that time. In 1995, they had become much more prevalent in the manner by which Xiamen's successful company operators, officers of the Chamber of Commerce, and agency officials explained and justified their behavior and cooperation. *Guanxi* was now often seen as the idiom of the traditionally minded and less prosperous private shopkeeping *getihu*.

An analytic distinction can be made between several idioms of regionalism, although they are frequently intertwined in actual speech. One set refracts central state ideology as expressed in policies and utterances of national leaders to legitimate local practices so that deviations that violate the letter of state policies are reframed as compliance with them. This idiom makes a distinction between the policy's spirit (*zhengce jingshen*), which reflects the desired outcomes that leaders would like to see happen, and a policy's stipulations (*zhengce tiaoli*), which are practical measures intended to achieve desired outcomes.[10] In implementing a policy, it is more important to try to accord with the spirit rather than the stipulations. In regard to market reform policies, it is more important to stimulate economic development than to conform to the policy's stipulations of how this should be achieved.

This idiom was apparent during conversations with officialdom and entrepreneurs. Officials stressed that central policies are general guidelines for establishing a general understanding (*renshi*) that should guide actions, but that it is not necessary to adhere to them rigorously because the state elite does not have intimate knowledge of local conditions (*difang tiaojian*). Local policy making is not only reasonable (*heli*), but, as one tax official said, "a matter of course" (*li suo dang ran*). They justified this view by references to the endorsements of expediency associated with Deng Xiaoping through his various statements, such as the one about it not mattering if a cat is black or white so long as it catches mice, and his various definitions of the Chinese commercial economy, such as "socialism with Chinese characteristics," a "socialist market economy," and a "market economy with Chinese features." Thus, the state's patriotic and nationalistic appeals for compliance with its policies

---

[10] This recalls Franz Schurmann's ([1966] 1968) classic distinction between ideology as practical strategy and as world view.

is refracted locally as regionalism that stresses the primacy of local interpretations in fulfilling the state's goals.

In a similar vein, entrepreneurs justified giving money and gifts to officials as fulfilling the spirit of market reform. Again this view plays off several thematic slogans propounded by the state elite. The state's frequent trumpeting of the need to raise living standards and prevent large income inequalities (*liang jieji fenhua*) is cited, only partially in jest, as necessary to prevent officials from falling behind. As one entrepreneur said, "If you want to get rich, you have to let officialdom be well off also. Otherwise they will fall behind" (informant no. 17). And some entrepreneurs maintained with tongue only partially in cheek that giving officials electric home appliances promoted individual modernization (*geren xiandaihua*) in small fulfillment of the state project of achieving the Four Modernizations (*Sige Xiandaihua*) in agriculture, industry, science, and defense. What is labeled as corruption by the state in its rhetoric of corruption and economic crime can be reframed as an expression of conformity and compliance with the state's rhetoric of economic development.

A second set of idioms is that of natural resources (*ziran tiaojian*), which depicts commercial activity as a natural outgrowth of local geography and therefore serves a legitimating function. Locals repeatedly told me that Xiamen is a natural site for commerce. They pointed to its beautiful deepwater harbor, one of the few along the South China coast. They also see Xiamen as a natural site for an entrepot between the hinterland and the international economy and as the port of embarkation for many overseas Chinese. There is much talk of how the cities of Xiamen, Taipei, and Guangzhou form the urban points of a "regional economic triangle" (*sanjiao jingji qu*) that might someday become another "Special Administrative Region" (SAR), in the image of Hong Kong since its 1997 return to Chinese sovereignty. Also, Xiameners often mention their geographical proximity to Taiwan, noting that Xiamen is closer to Taiwan's industrial city of Kaohsiung than it is to the Fujian capital of Fuzhou.

The legitimating logic of these idioms has two steps. First, Xiamen is represented as a natural site for commercial wealth accumulation because of its geographic features, such as its natural deepwater harbor, its proximity to Taiwan, and its coastal location midway between Guangzhou and Shanghai. Second, the commercial potential was obstructed by prior decades of central state policies that cut off transnational trade contacts and private business. These two propositions establish that it is the policies of the central state that have blocked natural commercial activity in Xiamen, while local initiatives, be they deviations by local governments or popular practices in the networks of entrepreneurs and officials, help release the region's economic potential.

A third set of idioms is that of local tradition or custom (*difang zuofeng*), which relativizes Xiamen's local business practices by comparisons with those of other places. Through such comparison Xiamen's practices appear in a favorable light, recasting questions of right and wrong as questions of degree. The market in the hinterland is seen as heavily embedded in personal ties and considerations, hindering profitability. One entrepreneur said, "In the interior everything is done by *ganqing*. Doing business is really troublesome because it takes so much time" (informant no. 84). This extreme of personalistic exchange is juxtaposed with the extreme practicality (*xianshi*) of Taiwanese businessmen from Taiwan, who are said not to recognize human sentiment. One entrepreneur recounted his negotiations with a Taiwanese businessman to establish a joint venture "When he went to Hong Kong he asked if there was anything he could buy for me. I said I couldn't think of anything as I have everything that I need. So the next time he came he didn't bring anything. But to establish business relations he should still have brought something" (informant no. 15). Furthermore, the Taiwanese businessmen did not understand face (*budong mianzi*), because his question positioned the entrepreneur as a supplicant, and so the entrepreneur's refusal was an attempt to preserve face. Statements such as these securely locate Xiamen's business practices between the extremes of affect and practicality, implying that its entrepreneurs and their practices are reasonable, striking a good balance between the concerns of profit and upright conduct (*zuoren*).

Another axis of comparison runs north–south and focuses on issues deemed by the state as issues of the fundamental consciousness (*yishi*) that guides action. The market economy toward the north in Jinjiang and Wenzhou is characterized by Xiamen businesspeople and officials alike as "peasant entrepreneurship." Peasants are said to have a low cultural level and do not recognize obligation to pay taxes, engaging instead in chaotic practices that contrast with Xiamen's more civilized business (*wenming jingying*) behavior. In the market economy in the more urban and southerly climes of Guangdong province, businesspeople are said to worship profit above all else, in contrast to Xiamen entrepreneurs who see business as a means to cultivate higher tastes. For example, one entrepreneur said in regard to business in the Shantou Special Economic Zone in Guangdong, "Shantou people raise up the cultural level of their children only enough to teach them how to make money. This is very different from Xiamen businesspeople, who raise their children to learn music and go to good schools" (informant no. 22). Yet another comparison reflects state efforts to institutionalize a "legal consciousness." This can be seen in the comments of Xiamen University's law dean to a *Far Eastern Economic Review* reporter. "Fujian takes full advantage of the rules, doing everything that is allowed. Shanghai lobbies to rewrite the rules in its own favor. But Cantonese go one step further; they'll try anything that's not prohibited" (Kaye 1995: 25). This north–south comparison, too, represents business life in Xiamen as well balanced in comparison to the existing extremes.

Taken together, these idioms institutionalize local practice in ways that are similar as well as distinct from *guanxi*. Like *guanxi* it has overtones of consanguinity, as regionalism draws on the idiom of nativism (*tongxiang*), which, as noted in Chapter 5, is the projection into space of consanguinity. Also like *guanxi*, as well as other idioms of social trust such as reputation (*mingyu*) and impression (*yinxiang*), it refers to relations and identities that cannot be reduced to business concerns but can institutionally undergird them. However, its orientation transcends the purely dyadic orientation of *guanxi*. It does not displace more narrowly particularistic idioms of interaction but rather amplifies them to further enhance cooperation and legitimate actions that do not conform with state policies. The expanded repertoire of particularistic interaction is a further institutional evolution of commercial clientelism.

## Conclusion

In the evolution of the market economy in the first half of the 1990s, I observed the intensification of trends I had noticed during my earlier research. During the course of the first decade of market reform, each wave of new entrepreneurs was characterized by people who were increasingly well placed in terms of the state hierarchy. From the first path to entrepreneurship of the speculators, who had almost no capacity to project influence into the bureaucracy, the decade ended with the emergence of lower and moderately ranked functionaries who began their entrepreneurial careers with support from officialdom acquired by ties of kinship and close friendship. By the mid-1990s a new wave of entrepreneurs had emerged: they were fairly high-ranking officials, many with two decades of public service. They were able to project influence through the significant ties acquired during their bureaucratic careers and were doing business on a scale unimaginable only a few years earlier.

This suggests a different image of economic reform from that found in extant perspectives. The market transition account sees the emerging commercial economy as increasingly approximating the ideal-typical model of a market economy: private property rights become increasingly clarified and transactions are increasingly horizontal. The evolution of private business in Xiamen confounds this. While the market is clearly growing, as seen in increasing commercial wealth and transregional integration, it is not converging on an ideal-typical market. Rather, such processes as the emergence of a cadre entrepreneurial path and translocal patterns of business–government cooperation signify an intensification of the commercial clientelism documented in Part I of this study. Thus, rather than a chaotic and liminal stage of a "partial transition" that is neither market or plan, we can see the deepening and institutionalization of a market economy organized through an equilibrium in which competition consists in good measure of capacity to obtain particularistic support from state agents in commercial endeavors.

The institutional trends described in this chapter also expand on those posited in the traditional culture and political economy accounts. The traditional culture account sees popular norms and identities as providing some exchange stability within communities of face-to-face interactions. This study shows how this traditional culture can evolve to support exchanges that transcend locales as well. Finally, while the political economy account emphasizes the decentralization of control over resources to more local levels, I have shown how private entrepreneurs continue to manipulate this decentralizing state authority in network strategies to cultivate business support with local officialdom all the way up to provincial governors.[11] The more authority is decentralized, the more entrepreneurs obtain it for use in business, and so the upward mobilization of popular influence parallels the decentralization of authority within the state structure.

---

[11] For example, the entrepreneur Zhang Guoxi numbered the governor of Jiangxi province among his active supporters (Tyson and Tyson 1995: 58).

# Final Insights

In this study I have offered an explanation of how market values emerge in a centrally planned economy and communist party-state and the economic and political consequences of this as seen through entrepreneurial private business in southeast China. In this final chapter I shall recount and reflect on some of the study's key themes. First, I will summarize the processes of commodification in economy, networks, and polity. Second, I will consider change and stability in the commercial clientelism that undergirds private business. Finally, I will consider this study's implications for viewing China's capitalist transformation.

## Commodification as System Transformation

The key premise of this study has been that economic reform causes a transformation in the communist system rather than its outright decline and replacement by a market order. I have termed this transformative process commodification, as it signifies the introduction of standard price calculations into a communist system of centralized redistribution. Commodification refers to several intertwined processes that are centered on the state's lower bureaucracy, which is the site of actual redistribution and routinized contact between officials and citizens.

First, there is commodification of the vast resources controlled by the state as these resources come to be perceived in terms of market price. State market reform policies have diminished some elements of the bureaucratic monopoly over material resources while maintaining others, as in real estate, and creating new administrative monopolies, as in commercial licensing and foreign trade. Local state agents shift the public resources they control toward commercial activities. Some agents become entrepreneurial, turning the resources at their disposal into commercial enterprises, while others profit by selling the public resources at their disposal to firm operators. The shift of public resources for commercial profit creates an opening for private entrepreneurs to seek access to them. This utilitarian approach to state power is not new, as barter exchanges between officials and citizens centered on bureaucratic redistribution also characterized the old order. What is new is the role of money and markets in enabling resources to be priced by supply and demand. Therefore the exchange values contained in transactions between citizens and officials have mushroomed.

These resources constitute the "primitive accumulation" that stimulates business startup, drives subsequent growth, and provides security. The multifaceted forms of value in bureaucratic resources as both sources of profit and protection mean that the sale of state power will not decline simply with the decrease of state control over material goods through the practices of administrative pricing. For even as the outright sale of bureaucratic-controlled material resources declines, commodification has proceeded apace in the expansion of the state's licensing and regulatory monopoly. For state power to be decreasingly perceived as a commodity depends on factors that lie outside the realm of purely economic consideration. For example, state institutionalization of more universal codes of behavior through an effective legal system could reduce the more particularistic demand for protection services from specific officials and state agencies. These are political decisions.

Second, commodification refers to the transformation of particularistic networks of access to commercially valuable resources in the state. For private entrepreneurs, commodification proceeds in the networks they mobilize to influence officials' discretion in their favor. The social background of entrepreneurs constrains business strategies and advantage in the competition for bureaucratic access. The competitive stance of any entrepreneur is the sum of his or her economic and noneconomic capital – obligations, reputation, and impression – that can be mobilized to influence the discretion of local state agents. During the 1980s and 1990s there have been four distinct entrepreneurial paths, each mobilizing successively more valuable forms of capital to gain access to greater degrees of state power for commercial ends.

In commodified networks, the use value of a tie in terms of the relational identity of transacting partners enters into the exchange value of the market transaction. This, of course, is nothing new, as utilitarian *guanxi* networks proliferated before economic reform as well. However, the injection of money has created new practices such as money (*jinqian*) *guanxi* while diminishing the utility of older forms, such as emotive (*ganqing*) *guanxi*. Money *guanxi* is less identity-specific than emotive *guanxi* because constant quantitative pricing enhances calculability in transactions and is less time-consuming than transactions embedded in emotive *guanxi*. This has led to the proliferation of new bargaining relations between citizens who are entrepreneurs and local government officials. These relations are more fluid than the old barter relations as entrepreneurs increasingly shop around for better deals while officials increasingly compete with each other for wealthy clients. In short, money *guanxi* represents a significant decline of the power of officials to determine unilaterally the terms of exchange within particularistic transactions. It has shifted more power from those who wield state power to those who seek state power, a process that approximates movement from a sellers' to a buyers' market.

Third, commodification also indicates new patterns of contestation over legitimacy. These kinds of exchanges between private entrepreneurs and officials are called "corruption" and "economic crimes" by the state. The state condemns them, because they threaten to institutionalize a market organization that confounds central monitoring and undermines the state revenue flows. Condemnation further constrains the market economy by turning it into an arena of political contestation for asserting legitimacy.

While state condemnation of particularism and recourse to *guanxi* are nothing new in China's post-1949 history, commodification appears to have significantly altered the state's perceptions of particularism and affected its efforts to eliminate it. As the market economy has expanded apace, central campaigns targeting activities deemed graft and corruption have become less virulent. This can be seen in the sudden halt of the 1993 campaign against corrupt bank loans, as noted in Chapter 9. It can be surmised that the campaign was called off to prevent the kind of boom-and-bust cycles that characterized state intervention in the economy in the 1980s. In other words, commodification also enables the state to measure the consequences of actions in monetary and other quantifiable forms of accounting. This has injected new calculations of expediency on the part of the state in the contestation among various actors over legitimate behavior. This further suggests that diminishing state campaigns against corrupt practices and particularistic allocation do not signify a further advance to a more standard market economy but rather the gradual acceptance of the practices of commercial clientelism as being expedient for economic growth.

## Commercial Clientelism as Market Equilibrium

State power is now bought and sold. Officials view their new commercial regulatory powers as a way to line their pockets and fill local government coffers through particularistic administration. Entrepreneurs view their tax bills as the opening round in bargaining to decide how much revenue they will hand over. Much of this activity proceeds in the clientelist ties described in this study. The key question is whether this sale of state power will give way to something more approximating a standard market economy, in which the sale of state power is much less prominent. To answer this question requires first identifying those elements that cause bureaucratic commodification to persist. Then it is possible to speculate on sources of change.

Commercial clientelism has achieved a stable equilibrium because it reflects a convergence of interests. Local governments are able to acquire incomes in the face of declining central support, enabling them to buttress and even amplify their power in jurisdictions. Entrepreneurs are able to manage their dependence on the state by acquiring modicums of power to advance their own enterprises. This local government–business cooperation may stimulate the development of the local economy. Such development is also in the interests of the central state. The commercial activities of local governments enable them to fund their own projects and provide public services in jurisdictions, reducing pressure on the state to fund them. The dynamism of local economies provides the central state with increasing tax revenue. This convergence of interests is possible because of the rapid growth of the economy. Thus even as the state's relative share of national wealth declines, its absolute income rises annually, letting it fund its projects, such as supporting unprofitable state-owned enterprises and modernizing the military to project power internationally.

This logic of economic growth contravenes the contention of the market transition account that the growth of the market economy generates pressures for systemic transformation, such as the need for bureaucratic-legal administration. Instead, it appears that the growth of the market economy can also perpetuate an economy driven by particularistic access to state power; as long as entrepreneurs, local governments, and the central state can continue to reap benefits from it, there is little incentive for the state to seek to promote radical systemic change. The rising business middle class does not appear to be a force for change as its potential class-based interests are undermined by cross-cutting cleavages that reflect the relation of different segments of this class to state power. Nor is China's increasing integration into the international economy necessarily a clear-cut force for change. Much of the pressure for the Chinese state to vigorously promote greater transparency and universalism in the economy comes from other states and non-Chinese foreign investors, who constitute only around 20 percent of the foreign capital being invested in China. The other 80 percent comes from Chinese abroad and from the process of "round-tripping" by domestic China as described in Chapter 7. These business interests are much less opposed to the particularistic practices in the Chinese economy, especially as such practices give "ethnic" Chinese an advantage in commercial competition with non-Chinese in China. The importance of these links can be seen in the fact that many of the leading Chinese overseas businesspeople have cultivated their own personal ties with the Chinese leadership.

This suggests a somewhat different perspective on systemic change in China. One is that radical change may also come from economic crises rather than continued growth, spurring elites on to greater measures that change the system in order to save the system, much like the New Deal in the United States in the 1930s. Such change could just as likely lead to new versions of authoritarianism as to democracy. Second, it is important to note the far-reaching evolutionary transformations that are occurring within the processes of commercial clientelism. This is seen in the increasing civilianization of the economy, the greater share of economic production and wealth produced outside the formal state structure, without a corresponding increase in civil society. This is also seen in greater pluralization by the intensified cooperation between state and society actors in jurisdictions. Much of the market dynamism in locales has depended on this cooperation. In the 1980s this cooperation consisted of deviant actions by local government that created a more hospitable commercial climate relative to other locales. As central state policies have become less restrictive in the 1990s, the capacity to generate advantage through local deviations has declined and cooperation has increasingly depended on neomercantilist practices that project cooperation beyond local jurisdictions.

## Capitalism and Bureaucracy

This study has presented an image of China's transformation in the late twentieth century that does not lend itself to the common view of economic reform in communist orders as movement toward a standard market economy and democratic political system. Rather, it supports an alternative tenet that the rise of market capitalism and expansion of state bureaucracies go hand-in-hand (Polanyi [1944] 1957; Tilly 1984; Wallerstein 1974; Weber [1922] 1961). Bureaucratic states facilitate coordination and interregional trade, which in turn stimulates the growth of these states by placing new regulatory demands on them and generating the resources to meet them. This does not mean convergence on a standard configuration because the character of the market capitalism that emerges is constrained by the historically contingent organization of the state bureaucracy, its relations with commercial actors in society, and the institutional culture (Evans 1995).

The trenchant issue therefore is not how the party-state will retreat from the economy but rather how it will come to constitute the emerging market economy. At the beginning of the twentieth century China was an agrarian empire ruled by a small corps of officials staffing a bureaucracy that penetrated no deeper in society than the county level. Political centralization during the first half of the century was checked by ongoing warfare. For several decades after the Communist Party took power in China, the party-state bureaucracy grew to immense proportions by recruiting millions of new personnel and incorporating within its purview all the structures of central planning, resulting in huge economic accumulations and gains. Centralized redistribution and political monopoly enabled the state to pursue various goals, such as restoring domestic order, fending off foreign military challenges, and establishing new forms of social justice. These structures also gave rise to a pervasive use of networks to facilitate allocation and political support.

The kind of market economy and state bureaucracy that is emerging with China's turn to a commercial orientation since 1979 reflects this legacy of networks. At the onset of economic reform, the state structure is the main integrative structure in the realm, given the lack of markets. It is rational, then, for new commercial actors to use this structure to enhance efficiency and for state agents to use the resulting new links for new forms of support. As they build on preexisting institutional routines, the character of commercial activity continues to reflect a strong bureaucratic presence. For new commercial actors, the pervasiveness of particularistic links to the state structure is evidence not of a distorted market economy or dysfunctional state but rather of the twin processes of an emerging market economy and the reconstruction of the state bureaucracy.

Given the vastness of China, several patterns of economic and state reconstitution can be clearly discerned, each characterized by a specific pattern of institutional interaction with the state bureaucracy. The entrepreneurial private business visible on China's southeast coast operates in a symbiotic clientelism that links businesses to local governments. This study has also hinted at other forms of capitalism: the state capitalism of the conglomerates attached to various ministries and provincial governments that enjoy favorable access to loans from state banks; the crony capitalism of the offspring of central government officials; the entrepreneurial capitalism of local rural governments that promote rural industrialization; the relatively egalitarian petty *bourgeoisie* capitalism of villages that specialize in private agricultural commodity production; the diaspora capitalism of Chinese overseas that emphasizes flexibility and lobbies various levels of the governments for favorable concessions; and possibly a "mafiya" capitalism in those border regions where smuggling and drug dealing proliferate.

The symbiotic clientelism in which private business operates not only reflects the utility-maximizing interests of entrepreneurs and state agents but also constitutes broader economic and political structures. For entrepreneurs, these ties are of ongoing benefit, even as the earlier emphasis on profit seeking in public assets controlled by the bureaucracy gives way to enhancing security and information through ties to local governments. The ties are also innovations by which local governments obtain support, enabling them to forge new links to the market economy, which, in the southeast region, include links to the financial capital of Chinese overseas. These strong local webs of affiliation are development coalitions that heighten the autonomy of locales from the center and the bargaining position of certain societal economic actors vis-à-vis local state agents. One should not, of course, be too starry-eyed about this symbiosis. Although it has stimulated business, the mutually beneficial exchanges have occurred in the context of China's historically unprecedented economic growth. During economic stagnation, the relationship could turn predatory, with local government extracting more value than it gives private business in return.

The particularistic ties and bureaucratic power that pervade China's emerging capitalism is the social process by which market values emerge in the redistributive command economies and one-party states of former communist orders. These ties embody commercial transactions, contractual expectations, and property enforcement that construct the market economy and facilitate its emergence. They embody political processes of interests, bargaining, and alliances that are reconstituting state and society. They will not simply erode over time in proportion to the transition to a market economy because they constitute the very process of historical transformation.

*Appendixes*

# Appendix A: Glossary of Chinese Terms and Place Names, with Corresponding Chinese Characters

## Terms

***ba guanxi laguolai*** 把關係拉過來　to carry over a relationship; to use a preexisting tie for new ends

***babing*** 把柄　to have a handle or grip (against somebody)

***bang*** 幫　clique

***bangmang*** 幫忙　assistance

***bangzhu lianluo*** 幫助聯絡　helping to put someone in touch with someone

***bao*** 報　reciprocity

***baochou*** 報酬　reward; compensation

***baoen*** 抱恩　to reciprocate for the kindness one has received

***baohusan*** 保護傘　protective parachute

***baoshou*** 保守　conservative

***beidong*** 被動　passive

***bendiren*** 本地人　native

***biao*** 表　maternal cousin

***bifeng*** 避風　sheltering from the wind

***bifengchu*** 避風處　wind shelter

***budong mianzi*** 不懂面子　not to understand face; not to be properly aware of status and propriety in social relations

***bukekao*** 不可靠　unreliable

***bumen bande*** 部門辦的　bureau-run

***buwending*** 不穩定　unstable

***caigouyuan*** 採購員　purchasing agent (of a state factory or enterprise)

***chaxugeju*** 差序格局　differential mode of association

***chengbao*** 承包　to contract

***chuangzao jihui*** 創造機會　to create an opportunity

***chuanmen*** 串門　to drop by for a visit

***chuchou*** 出醜　to make a fool of

***chumian*** 出面　to appear personally; to act on behalf of

235

*dai hong maozi* 戴紅帽子   red-hatting; a private firm posing as public

*dai xiao maozi* 戴小帽子   wearing a small hat; minimizing apparent scale of business to avoid attention

*daixiao* 代銷   to sell on consignment

*dang laoban* 當老板   being the boss

*dedao zhichi* 得到支持   to obtain support

*difang bande* 地方辦的   locally run

*difang tiaojian* 地方條件   local conditions

*difang zhengfu* 地方政府   local government; any level of government lower than the center

*difang zuofeng* 地方作風   local practice

*dingdan* 訂單   order form

*diu lian* 丟臉   lose face

*dixia hei gongchang* 地下黑工廠   underground, "black" factory; illegal enterprise

*Duanku Laoban* 短褲老板   Boss Shortpants

*dui shehui fu zeren* 對社會負責任   to fulfill (one's) responsibility to society

*duzi* 獨資   solely owned; single proprietorship

*fang* 房   family branch; male descent group (father and sons)

*fei guoyouzhi* 非國有制   nonstate ownership

*fengdu* 風度   poise; bearing

*fengjian mixin* 封建迷信   feudal superstition

*Fu Lian* 婦聯   Women's Federation

*fuza* 複雜   complicated

*gaige* 改革   reform

*gaizao* 改造   transformation

*gaizhang* 蓋章   to affix an official seal of approval

*ganqing* 感情   affect; emotional feeling

*ganqing guanli* 感情管理   emotive management; manipulating sentiment to enhance authority in an employment relationship

*ganqing guanxi* 感情關係   an affect-based relationship

*gao tuzhengce* 搞土政策   local policy making

*gei mianzi* 給面子   to give face; to augment another's social prestige

*geren xiandaihua* 個人現代化   individual modernization

*getihu* 個體戶   private family business; petty private entrepreneur

*Geti Laodongzhe Xiehui* 個體勞動者協會   Self-Employed Laborers Association

*gongan paichusuo* 公安派出所   police substation

*gonggong jilei jin* 公共積累金   public accumulation fund

*gongjiade* 公家的   public

*gongren* 工人   worker

*gongsi* 公司 company; corporation

*gua yangtou mai gourou* 掛羊頭賣狗肉 hanging up the sheep's head to sell dog meat; duplicity

*guanban jiti* 官辦集體 officially run collective

*guandao* 官倒 official profiteering

*guangcai shiye* 光彩事業 glorious enterprise

*guanka* 關卡 strategic pass; an official who must be dealt with (i.e., cannot be bypassed) in the business process

*guankao* 掛靠 to hang and lean on; to hide a private firm behind the façade of a public organization

*guanxi* 關係 relationships; social connections

*guanxin* 關心 concern

*guanxixue* 關係學 the art of connections

*guojia bande* 國家辦的 state-run

*guojiefei* 過節費 holiday bonus

*guwen* 顧問 advisor

*hediguanglin* 闔第光臨 the whole family will be present

*hefa* 合法 to accord with the rules; legal

*hehuo* 合夥 to form a partnership

*hei hukou* 黑戶口 illegal residence

*heli* 合理 to accord with reason or popular opinion

*hengxiang lianxi* 橫向聯繫 horizontal linkages

*hezi* 合資 joint investment; joint venture

*hongbao* 紅包 red envelope for giving money gifts; bribe

*hong yan bing* 紅眼病 red-eye disease; envy

*hou* 厚 thick (in regard to degree of blood and obligation in a relationship)

*houlu* 後路 route of retreat

*huan koudai* 換口袋 pocket-swapping; using public property for private ends; changing the legal registration of property from public to private by dubious means

*huaqiao* 華僑 overseas Chinese; Chinese who live abroad without changing citizenship (especially in Southeast Asia)

*huikou* 回扣 sales commission

*huilu* 賄賂 bribery

*hutong xinxi* 互通信息 exchange information

*huxiang liaojie* 互相了解 mutual understanding

*huzhu jijinhui* 互助集金會 mutual aid fund

*jia* 家 family

*jia jiti* 假集體 false collective

*jiamen* 家門 kin

*jiaoyou* 交友 make friends

*jiazu* 家族 lineage

*jiben hege* 基本合格    basically qualified

*jiedao weiyuanhui* 街道委員會    street committee (the lowest level of urban government)

*jiji fenzi* 積極分子    activist in complying with state policies

*jijiao* 計較    hassling over trifles; petty

*jilei* 積累    savings (societal capital acquired through life experiences)

*jingji zhengdun yundong* 經濟整頓運動    economic rectification campaign

*jingying bu* 經營部    business department

*jingying fanwei* 經營範圍    licensed business scope

*jinqian guanxi* 金錢關係    money connections; instrumental social relationships

*jishu gong* 技術工    technician

*juedui hege* 絕對合格    decidedly qualified

*jumin weiyuanhui* 居民委員會    residents' committee

*kaifang* 開放    liberal

*kaoshan* 靠山    backer; patron

*kunnan hu* 困難戶    hardship family

*lao xiang* 老鄉    compatriot

*laoshi* 老實    honest; naïve

*li suo dang ran* 理所當然    as a matter of course

*lian* 臉    face (public recognition of one's moral integrity)

*liang jieji fenhua* 兩階級分化    inequality between social classes

*lianlei* 連累    to be implicated

*lianluo* 聯絡    get in touch with; make contact with

*lianying* 聯營    joint venture

*lianzheng yundong* 廉政運動    clean government campaign

*ling* 靈    efficacious

*linju* 鄰居    neighbor

*linshi hukou* 臨時戶口    temporary residence permit

*liuzhe* 留彤    keeping (for later use)

*liyong guanxi* 利用關係    utilitarian relationships

*meiyou mianzi* 沒有面子    to have no face

*mianzi* 面子    face (in the sense of social honor)

*Min Jian Dang* 民建黨    Democratic National Construction Party, a party composed mostly of businesspeople

*minban jingji tequ* 民辦經濟特區    a people's Special Economic Zone

*minban jiti* 民辦集體    people-operated collective; a cooperative (a collective firm founded with private capital and operated independently of government)

*mingqi* 名氣    fame; reputation generated by public knowledge of one's deeds and exploits *mingsheng* 名聲   renown; reputation stemming from family name

*mingyu* 名譽   repute; reputation generated by observing community standards and norms

*minjian zuzhi* 民間組織   people's organization; organizations managed by the Communist Party's United Front Bureau; government-organized nongovernmental organization

*minying* 民營   people-run organization or enterprise

*nanxun* 南巡   Deng Xiaoping's 1992 southern tour

*nashui jijifenzi* 納稅積極分子   taxpaying activist

*nashui xiaozu* 納稅小組   tax-collecting small group

*nei* 內   inside

*neibu* 內部   considered internal to the organization

*neibu chuli* 內部處理   selling internally at reduced price

*neidiren* 內地人   native

*neilian qiye* 內聯企業   representative company

*pibao gongsi* 皮包公司   suitcase company; a company with assets that exist only on paper

*piwen* 批文   to write comments on an official document

*pu houlu* 鋪後路   paving a route of retreat

*Pudu* 普渡   Ghost Feeding Festival; All Souls Festival

*qi hou, di li, ren he* 氣候，地理，人和   favorable climate; advantageous position; harmonious relations

*qingnian* 青年   youth

*qiye jituan* 企業集團   enterprise or business group; three or more firms connected by overlapping kinship and financial ties in ownership and management

*quan* 權   power

*quanli* 權力   power of office

*quanli fen* 權力份   power share; the power an official invests in a company in exchange for commercial shares

*quanli hu* 權力戶   power family

*renqing* 人情   sentiment; human feeling

*renqing zhizhao* 人情執照   human sentiment license

*renqingwei* 人情味   the flavor of human sentiment

*renshi* 認識   consciousness

*rongbi* 榮筆   to honor (somebody) with one's signature

*Sanfan wufan* 三反五反   Three anti, five anti; campaigns against bureaucratic corruption and capitalist business in the early 1950s

*sanjiao jingji qu* 三角經濟區   delta economic region

*sanjiao zhaiwu* 三角債務   triangular debt

*shangdian* 商店   shop

*shanghang* 商行   trading emporium

*shangliang buzheng, xialiang wai* 上樑不正，下樑歪    If the upper beam is not straight, the lower beams will go aslant; when those above behave unworthily, those below will do the same

*shehui liutong* 社會流通    societal circulation

*shehui quanzi* 社會圈子    societal circle

*shehui tuanti* 社會團體    societal group

*shehui ziben* 社會資本    societal capital

*sheng* 生    raw; unfamiliar

*shengyi daode* 生意道德    commercial ethics

*shi* 市    city

*shili* 勢力    power and influence

*shu* 熟    familiar

*shuishou da jiancha* 税收大檢查    massive campaign to counter tax evasion

*si wu* 四無    four withouts

*sige xiandaihua* 四個現代化    four modernizations

*songli* 送禮    gift giving

*taizi dang* 太子黨    princes' party; entrepreneurial offspring of central party elite

*tang* 堂    paternal cousins

*tanzi* 攤子    stall

*taotai* 淘汰    fall by the wayside

*teshu youdai* 特殊優待    special treatment (favoritism)

*ti ni jianghua* 替你講話    speaking up on behalf of

*ti ni xiang banfa* 替你想辦法    to think of a way for somebody

*tianshengde* 天生的    congenital (literally); societal capital that one acquires by birth into a family of a particular economic class or bureaucratic rank

*tianzi* 天資    endowment; (same as above)

*tigong xinxi* 提供信息    providing information

*tinghua* 聽話    obedient

*tingxin liuzhi* 停薪留職    unpaid leave of absence

*tong* 同    same; sameness

*tongban* 同班    classmate

*tongshi* 同士    colleague

*tongxiang* 同鄉    person from same native place; compatriot

*tongxin* 同心    united hearts; unity of purpose

*tongxue* 同學    schoolmate

*toujidaoba* 投機倒把    speculation; buying to resell for profit

*touzi* 投資    to invest; investment; societal capital acquired after the onset of a business career

*tuanti geju* 團體格局    organizational mode of association

*wai* 外    outside

*waibu* 外部 external to the organization

*waidiren* 外地人 nonnative

*waijia* 外嫁 to marry outside the family or lineage (always refers to a female)

*waimao* 外貿 foreign trade

*waishang* 外商 foreign businessperson

*weichi xianzhuang* 維持現狀 maintain the present situation

*wenhua shuiping* 文化水平 cultural level

*wenming* 文明 civilized

*wenming jingying* 文明經營 civilized business conduct

*wumen jingying* 無門經營 no door business; to close down a store, giving the appearance of being out of business, while carrying goods directly from producer to consumer

*wuzhengfu zhuangtai* 無政府狀態 anarchy

*xia hai* 下海 leaping into the sea; resignation of officials to work in private and foreign companies

**Xiamen Shi Siying Gongshangye Gonghui** 廈門市私營工商業工會 Xiamen City Civic Association of Private Industry and Commerce

**Xiamen Shi Zong Shang Hui** 廈門市總商會 Xiamen City General Chamber of Commerce

*xiandaihua* 現代化 modernization

*xiangzhen qiye* 鄉鎮企業 village and township enterprise

*xianshi* 現實 practical

*xiao baogao* 小報告 small report; to inform on

*xiao jinku* 小金庫 small treasury; slush fund; hidden budget

*xiao jiti* 小集體 small collective; a collective operated by the lowest levels of government (below the district in urban areas)

*xiao ren* 小人 small person; an insignificant person

*xin* 心 heart

*xinli goutong* 心理溝通 heartfelt collusion

*xionghuai kuankuo* 胸懷寬闊 having a broad bosom; being generous

*xitong* 系統 system (a demarcated organization within the bureaucracy like the army or a ministry)

*yao kao shehui huanjing* 要靠社會環境 the need to depend on the social environment

*ying* 硬 hard; solid (measure of degree of bureaucratic power)

*yinxiang* 印象 impression

*yishi* 意識 consciousness

*yitiao long* 一條龍 a single dragon; a vertically integrated firm

*zhaogu* 照顧 to take care of; to show special favor toward

*zhengce jingshen* 政策精神 spirit of a policy

*zhengce tiaoli* 政策條例 letter of a policy

***Zhengce Yanjiu Suo*** 政策研究所   Policy Research Institute
***zhengfu bande*** 政府辦的   government-run
***zhenggui*** 正規   standard
***zhi an fei*** 治安費   security fee
***Zhi Gong Dang*** 致公黨   political party of mostly overseas Chinese and their relatives
***zhixiang lianxi*** 直向聯繫   vertical linkage
***zhongwai hezi*** 中外合資   Chinese–foreign joint venture
***zhongyang bande*** 中央辦的   centrally run
***zhudong*** 主動   active
***zibenzhuyi de weiba*** 資本主義的尾巴   tail of capitalism; term applied to private petty traders from 1950s to 1970s
***ziji gan*** 自己幹   doing it on one's own; private entrepreneurship
***zijiaren*** 自家人   one of the family
***zijiren*** 自己人   one of us
***ziran tiaojian*** 自然條件   natural conditions
***zou zai zhengce de bianshang*** 走在政策的邊上   walking on the edge of the policy; legally ambiguous (but more profitable) business
***zuo gong*** 做工   labor
***zuo shengyi*** 做生意   doing trade
***zuoren*** 做人   proper behavior; upright conduct

## Places

Changsha 長沙
Chaozhou 潮州
Chongwu 崇武
Foshan 佛山
Fuzhou 福州
Guangxi 廣西
Guangzhou 廣州
Guiyang 貴陽
Guizhou 貴州
Gulangyu 鼓浪嶼
Hainan 海南
Huian 惠安
Jimei 集美
Jiangsu 江蘇
Jinjiang 晉江
Jinmen 金門
Kaiyuan 開元

Kaohsiung 高雄
Longhai 龍海
Longyan 龍岩
Lujiang 鷺江
Minnan 閩南
Quanzhou 泉州
Sanming 三明
Shandong 山東
Shanghai 上海
Shantou 汕頭
Shanxi 山西
Shenyang 沈陽
Shenzhen 深圳
Shishi 石獅
Siming 思明
Sichuan 四川
Taigu 太谷

Taiyuan 太原
Tongan 同安
Wenzhou 溫州
Xiamen 廈門

Xinglin 杏林
Yangzi 揚子
Zhangzhou 漳州
Zhejiang 浙江

# Appendix B: Fieldwork in Xiamen's Business Community: A Methodological Essay

The key observations of this study were derived from fieldwork within the community of private business operators in Xiamen. Therefore it is fitting that I describe this fieldwork in more detail, recounting the diverse factors, such as institutional affiliation, perceptions of others, problems of documentation, and serendipity (Lofland and Lofland 1995; Schatzman and Strauss 1973), that characterized it. This appendix describes the conduct of the fieldwork as it pertains to the sample of one hundred entrepreneurs that yielded the study's core data.

## Meeting Entrepreneurs

My sponsoring institution in Xiamen was Lujiang College, a community college newly founded to train white collar personnel for government agencies and commercial enterprises in the Xiamen Special Economic Zone. The college was very supportive of my research. Doing research under the sponsorship of a local unit as opposed to a more prestigious nationally ranked unit has its advantages for conducting ethnographic fieldwork in a single locale without the need for coordination across government jurisdictions. One advantage is that there are likely to be few foreign researchers in such a unit and therefore fewer bureaucratic structures and routines to restrict them. Also, local units are less concerned with implementing more restrictive central policies toward foreigners, because they take their orders directly from local, and often more tolerant, governments. This gave me much freedom of movement. I lived in faculty housing where people could visit me without signing their names in a security register, as was standard practice elsewhere. I also had a telephone in my apartment and could make and receive calls directly, which was very useful in letting me arrange my own research activities. Another advantage is that local units often have denser ties in the local communities. Almost all of the students at Lujiang College were from Xiamen city and many of the faculty were long-term residents as well, possessing local connections and knowledge of Xiamen politics and culture.

I met entrepreneurs in several ways. Some were introduced by various government bureaus, especially the Industry and Commerce Bureau, the United Front Bureau, and the Tax Bureau. These agencies invariably introduced me to entrepreneurs they had designated as "typical" business people to be trotted out for visiting journalists and academics. During our first meeting, at which officials were present, their comments hewed to the official line and were sprinkled with slogans from the state media. However, in my follow-up visits without officials, these entrepreneurs were talkative and frank. Toward the end of my stay, the head of the private enterprise section of the Industry and Commerce Bureau gave me the telephone numbers of all licensed private companies in Xiamen and carte blanche to arrange my own interviews.

I also met entrepreneurs through introductions provided by three local research assistants. These were young men whose full-time jobs in public units made them useful to entrepreneurs. One worked in the public insurance company as a claims assessor, another for the public television station selling advertising space, and the third was in charge of a student employment agency that placed college students in private businesses in such positions as restaurant personnel and language translators. These three persons all introduced me to entrepreneurs they knew and conducted follow-up contacts on my behalf.

Chance encounters also played a part. I met one entrepreneur on the overnight ferry ride from Hong Kong to Xiamen. In a few cases entrepreneurs I knew introduced me to other entrepreneurs. Participation in social occasions such as the Spring Festival party sponsored by the Xiamen Chamber of Commerce also provided opportunities. Some local residents I knew had relatives and friends in business to whom they introduced me. To underscore the role of serendipity, let me give two examples. In one instance a research assistant took me one morning to visit his cousin who sold pornographic videos. Although quite young, the cousin had done well enough to buy his own apartment. When we entered we found the cousin, his younger brother, and a young man in the uniform of a Tax Bureau official asleep in a room strewn with cigarette butts and empty beer bottles. After waking them up we spent the morning in conversation, which gave me much insight into the personal interaction between the businessman and his friend the tax official. In another instance I visited a luxury housing estate for an interview at a private company supposedly located there. I arrived by taxi and alighted just as a thunderstorm broke. Dashing to the address, I discovered that the company had moved elsewhere and the townhouse was now occupied by a state foreign trade corporation from an inland province. All the employees were out except for the manager, a man about five years older than I. The heavy monsoon rain disrupted telephone service, prevented employees from returning, and precluded my departure. So the manager and I spent the afternoon sipping tea; our wide-ranging chat gave me my first insights into the organization of foreign trade.

My age and foreignness were assets. At the time of the research I was in my early thirties, old enough not to be so easily taken for a callow youth (*qingnian*) but young enough to be forgiven for asking naïve questions. Many of the entrepreneurs were also in their early thirties, particularly former workers, and this enhanced feelings of closeness. My position as a foreigner also contributed to the willingness of the businesspeople to be interviewed by me. Some who might have felt they gained face by a visit from a foreign scholar were flattered by the attention, some were simply curious to talk to an American, others felt a duty to educate me about the local ways. I always introduced myself as a graduate student writing an academic dissertation for an American university, but businesspeople interpreted my fieldwork in their own way. Many saw me as a market researcher for a large American company writing a business report of some kind. Some tried to get market information from me, tried to scout out possibilities for partnerships, or simply saw me as a future business contact.

Entrepreneurs were generally of two minds regarding my inquiries. Some told me that the situation of private business in a communist country such as China was too complex (*fuza*) for an outsider to fathom; others felt that business was pretty much the same everywhere and were puzzled why I remained so long in Xiamen. Whichever view they held, entrepreneurs always treated me hospitably. Some were busy and our meetings had to be rescheduled, but almost no one refused to be interviewed. Many, however, requested that I not write anything that could harm them and some asked that I conceal their identities.

## Interactions and Observations

Interactions with the entrepreneurs were of three sorts. First there was the formal interview. In as conversational a manner as possible, I asked a set of questions memorized in advance. Some questions sought factual data on family background, life history, and personal situation; others inquired of enterprise activities and organization; yet others probed social, political, and personal attitudes. I made a point of asking all the questions in the first two categories, which provide the statistical data on the sample that are used to support the qualitative observations. The questions on social, political, and personal attitudes were variable, depending on the personal dynamics of the situation and the entrepreneur's willingness to talk on certain topics. Interviews were conducted by myself in Mandarin Chinese. Although it is not the local dialect, entrepreneurs use it in daily business dealings and speak it fluently.[1] All of the entrepreneurs were revisited by me in at least one follow-up contact.

The second sort of interaction was the more informal interview in the form of a chat and conversation, often at the entrepreneur's home or at a restaurant. Such socializing enabled me to discuss many topics more informally. An especially insightful form of socializing was visiting entrepreneurs at their homes and offices on Sundays, when they were more relaxed and willing to talk. During these visits I could note the kinds of people who visited them, a clear window on the range of the entrepreneurs' own social interactions (cf. Wank 1995b: 159–60). I also invited some entrepreneurs to my apartment for beer and conversation. These kinds of interaction also built rapport. One especially intriguing type of data derived from this kind of interaction was the entrepreneurs' comments and gossip about others in the business community. This helped me understand the positively and negatively valued behavior in the community.

The third sort of interaction was limited participant observation in business activities and more diffuse concerns. I accompanied one businessman on short business trips, served as an interpreter in several meetings between local entrepreneurs and foreign businessmen, and participated in company opening celebrations and Spring Festival parties held by private companies and associations such as the Xiamen Chamber of Commerce. I also lived for a week with one business family. Many invited me to dinners, festival celebrations, and wedding parties, and to accompany them on visits to their ancestral villages. The insights I gleaned from these kinds of interaction helped me see how entrepreneurs integrated business with other aspects of their lives and their relations with other members of the community.

Observations of the business community were also obtained by interactions with other community members. Most important were my research assistants. They were also participants in local business life and shared their personal experiences with me, giving me much insight on how entrepreneurs sought to cultivate relations with them. Also, as they knew the businesspeople they introduced me to, they provided much helpful background information. I often asked them to inquire about specific things in their own subsequent contact with businesspeople. This could be something as specific as the identity of someone I had noticed

---

[1] I also studied the local dialect for three months upon arriving in Xiamen and found it useful for exchanging pleasantries, but I did not become proficient enough to interview in it.

during a Sunday social visit to the house of an entrepreneur or as personal as a detailed account of their investments or as general as questions of motivation and values. Yet another source of information was locals who, while not in business themselves, had family members or close friends who were and told me about their activities.

## Verification and Documentation

One of the problems of doing fieldwork on business-related matters is how to ensure that the information one receives is accurate. Chinese businesspersons, like those elsewhere, keep their cards close to their vests. They do not reveal aspects of their activities that might disclose competitive secrets. The dubious and illegal character of much business adds yet another layer of information manipulation. Also, they exaggerate their business to convey an impression of success, talking of their grandiose plans as if they were already-existing business operations. It is necessary to constantly evaluate the data for accuracy, separating fact from fiction.

To evaluate the data, I emphasized consistency across observations rather than the absolute veracity of any one observation. I used the "triangulation method," which emphasizes multiple points of reference to establish the veracity of data (Ding 1994: 207; Walder 1986: 256–7). First, I accumulated a broad enough sample of entrepreneurs so that unusual data could be spotted among the more general trends. Once such a datum was spotted, the question was if the datum was inaccurate or indicated a phenomenon I did not know about. Second, I could use follow-up interviews and visits with entrepreneurs to assess the consistency of data. Unusual data from an entrepreneur in an earlier visit could be explored during follow-up visits. I made at least one follow-up visit to each entrepreneur, and further visits were made by me or a research assistant. Also, my research assistants, other entrepreneurs, and locals themselves could verify information about specific entrepreneurs. Third, the national and local media formed the third point of reference. In the 1980s the press became more open in its reporting, letting me assess the local and more specific information I gleaned on the business community with the more generalized situation depicted in the media.

I also used triangulation to judge the consistency of the data on company prosperity reported in Chapter 4. To minimize the probability that entrepreneurs would lie about their firms' financial situations, I avoided more sensitive questions about profits, which are taxed, and asked instead about sales turnover, which is not. Nevertheless, I do not claim that the figures I obtained from each company in interviews are accurate, because some entrepreneurs probably misrepresented sales turnover as well. Instead, my claim is that the data provide a scalar measure of relative prosperity, and consistency within the sample is more important for my purposes than absolute accuracy for any one company. To assure consistency, I checked that each company's sales turnover accorded with other wealth indicators such as luxuriousness of interior decorations, number of cars, and general reputation. I also checked the reliability of the figure for each company in follow-up contacts weeks or months later, when I again asked the sales turnover. Because of inconsistencies, I eliminated thirty-one firms from the sample used in Chapter 4, leaving a total of sixty-nine private companies from my larger sample of one hundred firms.[2]

I have also spent much time thinking about how to document the data. The freewheeling character of ethnographic fieldwork ensures that much research activity occurs outside of officially approved contacts and could conceivably be labeled as crimes like "divulging state secrets" or "collusive contact with foreigners." Although I think this unlikely, I cannot be sure. The principle for documenting the data from interviews is to ensure that my informants cannot be identified. Toward this end all names in this study are aliases and small details have been changed in the entrepreneurs' backgrounds, such as age and enterprise activities. Also, I do not indicate the dates of interviews, because this could also result in entrepreneurs' being traced if any surveillance agencies have a daily record of my activities. This caution extends to my interviews with officials as well. Although initial meetings were officially arranged, subsequent contacts involved informal meetings, such as spontaneous social visits to bureaus and chats with officials in my apartment or in restaurants. These contacts were not formally approved and officials could conceivably be sanctioned for them. Therefore, I have not indicated specific dates for contacts with officials either.

## Fieldwork as Enterprise

In key regards, my efforts to advance the research were a form of participant observation in running an enterprise. My research assistants and several entrepreneurs noted parallels between my research and commercial enterprise. My assistants commented that I was maximizing the number of informants and interviews. Several entrepreneurs, noting my

[2] One kind of inconsistency was a noticeable lack of correspondence between the professed sales turnover and other indicators of prosperity. Another kind of inconsistency was a large discrepancy in the professed sales turnover between the first and follow-up visits.

extensive networking in the business community, commented that I, too, sought *guanxi* and information. Others noted that I, as they, was "doing it on my own" (*ziji gan*) by arranging my own activities. I also had a business license and business scope, in the form of permission from the Ministry of Education to conduct research on private business. The maxim "favorable climate, advantageous position, harmonious relations," by which entrepreneurs summarized the opportunity structure they faced, applied to me as well.

Much of my efforts were directed at ensuring harmonious relations. I had to encourage the Foreign Affairs Office of Lujiang College engaged in the time-consuming process of getting the various stamps of approval for interviews in bureaus, galvanize my research assistants with a mixture of emotional and material incentives, and cajole officials and entrepreneurs into talking with me. My official mentor, the president of Lujiang College, also helped by arranging a meeting that included the college's economics faculty, leading officials from a variety of economic regulatory agencies, and myself. He introduced my research as part of his project and urged the officials to assist me. From my perspective, he "stuck out his face" (*chumian*) on my behalf, bestowing his high position on my enterprise to heighten cooperation from state agents.

I also had to deal with changes in the political climate. Following the 1989 student movement, the government warned locals in internal directives not to divulge economic secrets to American spies, and my American funding agency withdrew its sponsorship for American graduate students and academics whom it was supporting in China. At the time, these changes seemed to dampen the prospects for completing my project. Fortunately, my mentor agreed that I could continue my research even though my American funding agency had urged leaving the country. I was later told by several officials that it was his status as a former vice-mayor that enabled me to continue fieldwork without interference from local authorities. I also acquired some helpful reputation (*mingqi*) when the college president, in an interview on the Fujian province radio station about the remarkable fact that Lujiang College students had not joined the student movement, mentioned that the college's visiting U.S. researcher had remained in Xiamen despite the urgings of the U.S. embassy for its citizens to evacuate China. At the time, any action that could be interpreted as evidence of a foreigner's trust in the stability of China was useful propaganda to counter reports of the rapid departure of foreign and overseas Chinese investors from Xiamen to Hong Kong. Just as a businessperson recognized as a model taxpaying activist is unlikely to be soon charged with tax evasion, so the city government was less likely to interfere with the activities of a publicized model of foreign trust in China's political stability.

I also had to worry about securing my accumulation of data. I was unsure how the local authorities would judge my work, because it was on a topic that had become politically sensitive; furthermore, following the student movement, foreigners and especially U.S. citizens were considered potential spies and agitators. So like the dual account books of entrepreneurs, I kept two data files. The first consisted of publications purchased at local bookstores for which I had receipts, and write-ups of interviews formally arranged by authorities. The second contained publications given to me by various people, my journals, and my notes and interview write-ups (the interviewees being identified in code) on my self-arranged field activities. The first file I left prominently on my desk and shelves with easily understood identifying labels so that it would be found if my room were searched by authorities. I kept data from the second file on computer disks; second-file publications were stored at the homes of other foreigners living in Xiamen. I periodically carried parts of the second file out of China during visits to Hong Kong.

The comparability of my research enterprise with the commercial enterprises I sought to comprehend underscores how the market is embedded in broader social institutions. The social relationships of my research gave me insight into the webs spun by entrepreneurs to promote business. Our respective enterprises reflected the seeming contradiction of the increasing autonomy of people to coordinate activities of their own choosing and the pervasive presence of the state and its bureaucratic structures in constraining the organization of these activities and the behavior necessary to further them.

# Bibliography

Alexander, Gregory S., and Grazyna Skapska (eds.). 1994. *A Fourth Way?: Privatization and the Emergence of New Market Economies*. New York: Routledge.

Amsden, Alice. 1989. *Asia's Next Giant: South Korea and Late Industrialization*. New York: Oxford University Press.

Anagnost, Ann. 1989. "Prosperity and Counterprosperity: The Moral Discourse of Wealth in Post-Mao China." In *Marxism and the Chinese Experience*, ed. Arif Dirlik and Maurice Meisner, 210–34. Armonk, N.Y.: M. E. Sharpe.

*Annals of Xiamen City Real Estate (Xiamen Shi Fangdichan Zhi)*. 1989. Xiamen: Xiamen University Publishing House.

Appadurai, Arjun. 1986. "Introduction: Commodities and the Politics of Value." In *The Social Life of Things: Commodities in Cultural Perspective*, ed. Arjun Appadurai, 3–63. Cambridge University Press.

Archer, Margaret S. 1988. *Culture and Agency: The Place of Culture in Social Theory*. Cambridge University Press.

Ashiwa, Yoshiko. 1994. "Transnational and Local in the Revival of Buddhism in China." Paper presented at Association of Asian Studies Annual Conterence, Boston (March 23–27).

*Asia 1988 Yearbook*. 1989. Hong Kong: Review Publications.

Aslund, Anders. 1985. *Private Enterprise in Eastern Europe: The Non-Agricultural Private Sector in Poland and the GDR, 1945–1983*. London: Macmillan.

1989. *Gorbachev's Struggle for Economic Reform*. Ithaca, N.Y.: Cornell University Press.

1995. *How Russia Became a Market Economy*. Washington, D.C.: Brookings Institution.

Ba, Shan. 1989. "Zhongguo Getihu" (China's *Getihu*). *Hainan Jishi*.

Badaracco, Joseph L., Jr. 1991. "The Boundaries of the Firm." In *Socio-Economics: Towards a New Synthesis*, ed. Amitai Etzioni and Paul R. Lawrence, 293–327. Armonk, N.Y.: M. E. Sharpe.

Bagnasco, Arnaldo, and Charles Sabel (eds.). 1995. *Small and Medium-Size Enterprises*. London: Pinter.

Baker, R. H. 1982. "Clientelism in the Post-revolutionary State: The Soviet

253

Union." In *Private Patronage and Public Power: Political Clientelism and the State*, ed. C. Clapham, 36–52. London: Pinter.

Ball, Alan, M. 1987. *Russia's Last Capitalists: The Nepmen, 1921–1929*. Berkeley: University of California Press.

Bannan, Rosemary. 1992. "Little China: Street Vending in the Free Market (1989)." *Journal of Developing Societies* 8: 147–59.

Barth, Frederik. 1972. "Introduction." In *The Role of the Entrepreneur in Social Change in Northern Norway*, ed. Frederik Barth, 5–18. Bergen: Universitetsforlaget.

Barton, Clifton A. 1983. "Trust and Credit: Some Observations Regarding Business Strategies of Overseas Chinese Traders in South Vietnam." In *The Chinese in Southeast Asia*, vol. 1, *Ethnicity and Economic Activity*, ed. Linda Y. C. Lim and L. A. Peter Gosling, 46–64. Singapore: Maruzen Asia.

Bates, Robert. 1981. *Markets and States in Tropical Africa: The Political Basis of Agricultural Policies*. Berkeley: University of California Press.

Baumann, Z. 1979. "Comment on Eastern Europe." *Studies in Comparative Communism* 12: 184–9.

Bergère, Marie-Claire. (1986) 1989. *The Golden Age of the Chinese Bourgeoisie 1911–1937*. Cambridge University Press.

Bernstein, Thomas P. 1977. *Up to the Mountains and Down to the Villages: The Transfer of Youth from Urban to Rural China*. New Haven: Yale University Press.

Bian, Yanjie. 1994. "*Guanxi* and the Allocation of Urban Jobs in China." *China Quarterly* 140 (Dec.): 971–99.

Biggart, Nicole W. 1989. *Charismatic Capitalism: Direct Selling Organizations in America*. Chicago: University of Chicago Press.

1990. "Institutionalized Patrimonialism in Korean Business." *Comparative Social Research* 12: 113–33.

Blanchard, Oliver Jean, Kenneth A. Froot, and Jeffrey D. Sachs. 1994. "Introduction." In *The Transition in Eastern Europe*, vol. 2., ed. Oliver Jean Blanchard, Kenneth A. Froot, and Jeffrey D. Sachs. Chicago: University of Chicago Press.

Blau, Peter M. 1964. *Exchange and Power in Social Life*. New York: Wiley.

Block, Fred. 1989. "Political Choice and the Multiple 'Logics' of Capital." In *Structures of Capital: The Social Organization of the Economy*, ed. Sharon Zukin and Paul DiMaggio, 263–91. Cambridge University Press.

1990. *Postindustrial Possibilities: A Critique of Economic Discourse*. Berkeley: University of California Press.

1994. "The Roles of the State in the Economy." In *The Handbook of Economic Sociology*, ed. Neil J. Smelser and Richard Swedborg, 691–710. Princeton: Princeton University Press.

Blok, Anton. 1974. *Violent Peasant Entrepreneurs: The Mafia of a Sicilian Village*. Oxford: Basil Blackwell.

Blustein, Paul, and R. Jeffrey Smith. 1996. "Economic, Political Concerns Put Clinton on the Spot in China Policy." *Washington Post* (February 11): A26.

Bohannan, Paul. 1959. "The Impact of Money on an African Subsistence Economy." *Journal of Economic History* 19: 491–503.

Boissevain, Jeremy. 1966. "Patronage in Sicily." *Man* 1: 18–33.

Bonacich, Edna. 1973. "A Theory of Middleman Minorities." *American Sociological Review* 38: 583–94.

Bourdieu, Pierre. 1979. *Outline of a Theory of Practice*. Cambridge University Press.

———. 1986. "The Forms of Capital." In *The Handbook of Theory and Research for the Sociology of Education*, ed. John Richardson, 241–58. New York: Greenwood.

Boycko, Maxim, Andrei Shleifer, and Robert Vishny. 1995. *Privatizing Russia*. Cambridge, Mass.: MIT Press.

Bradach, Jeffrey, and Robert G. Eccles. 1989. "Price, Authority, and Trust: From Ideal Types to Plural Forms." *Annual Review of Sociology* 15: 97–118.

Brook, Timothy. 1993. *Praying for Power: Buddhism and the Formation of Gentry Society in Late-Ming China*. Cambridge, Mass.: Council on East Asian Studies, Harvard University.

Bruun, Ole. 1993. *Business and Bureaucracy in a Chinese City: An Ethnography of Private Business Households in Contemporary China*, China Research Monograph 43. Berkeley: Institute of East Asian Studies, University of California.

———. 1995. "Political Hierarchy and Private Entrepreneurship in a Chinese Neighborhood." In *The Waning of the Communist State: Economic Origins of Political Decline in China and Hungary*, ed. Andrew G. Walder, 184–212. Berkeley: University of California Press.

Bunce, Valerie, and Maria Csanadi. 1993. "Uncertainty in the Transition: Post-Communism in Hungary." *East European Politics and Society* 7 (2): 240–75.

Burns, John P. 1981. "Rural Guangdong's 'Second Economy.' 1962–74." *China Quarterly* 88: 629–44.

Burt, Ronald S. 1992. *Structural Holes: The Social Structure of Competition*. Cambridge, Mass.: Harvard University Press.

Byrant, Christopher G. A., and Edmund Mokrzycki. 1994. "Introduction: Theorizing the Changes in East-Central Europe." In *The New Great Transformation? Change and Continuity in East-Central Europe*, ed. Christopher G. A. Byrant and Edmund Mokrzycki, 1–13. London: Routledge.

Campbell, John L., and Leon N. Lindberg. 1990. "The Evolution of Governance Regimes." In *Governance of the American Economy*, ed. John L. Campbell, J. Rogers Hollingsworth, and Leon N. Lindberg, 319–55. Cambridge University Press.

Campbell, John L., and Ove K. Pederson. 1996. *Legacies of Change: Transformations of Postcommunist European Economies*. New York: Aldine de Gruyter.

Carlo, Antonio. 1974. "The Socio-Economic Nature of the USSR." *Telos* 21: 2–86.

Castoriadis, Cornelius. 1978–9. "The Social Regime in Russia." *Telos* 38: 212–48.

Chan, Anita, Richard Madsen, and Jonathan Unger. (1984) 1992. *Chen Village Under Mao and Deng.* Berkeley: University of California Press.

Chan, Anita, and Jonathan Unger. 1982. "Grey and Black: The Hidden Economy of Rural China." *Pacific Affairs* 55 (3): 452–71.

Chan, Kwok Bun, and Claire Chiang. 1994. *Stepping Out: The Making of Chinese Entrepreneurs.* Singapore: Centre for Advanced Studies, National University of Singapore and Prentice-Hall.

Chang, Maria Hsia. 1989. "The Meaning of the Tiananmen Incident." *Global Affairs* 4 (4): 12–35. Cited in Chalmers Johnson, "Forward." In *The Broken Mirror: China after Tiananmen,* ed. George Hicks, x. Essex, U.K.: Longman.

Chaudry, Kiren Aziz. 1994. "Economic Liberalization and the Lineages of the Rentier State." *Comparative Politics* 27 (1): 1–25.

China Daily. 1989. "Business Lures Party Members." March 11: 3.

1994. Quoted in *International Herald Tribune* article, "Beijing Banker Asks Public to Aid Fight on Inflation." November 30: 16.

1995a. "Sugar not a Private Sweetie." March 21: 2.

1995b. "Probe Targets Illegal Firms." March 24: 1.

China Statistical Publishers. 1993. *Xiamen Tongji Nianjian* (Almanac of Xiamen Statistics). Beijing.

1995. *Xiamen Tongji Nianjian* (Almanac of Xiamen Statistics). Beijing.

Clague, Christopher. 1992. "Introduction: The Journey to a Market Economy." In *The Emergence of Market Economies in Eastern Europe,* ed. Christopher Clague and Gordon C. Rausser, 1–22. Cambridge, Mass.: Basil Blackwell.

Clark, Hugh R. 1991. *Community, Trade, and Networks: Southern Fujian Province from the Third to the Thirteenth Century.* Cambridge University Press.

Coble, Parks M., Jr. 1980. *The Shanghai Capitalists and the Nationalist Government 1927–1937.* Cambridge, Mass.: Harvard University Press.

Cohen, Abner. 1969. *Custom and Politics in Urban Africa.* Berkeley: University of California Press.

1971. "Cultural Strategies in the Organization of Trading Diasporas." In *The Development of Indigenous Trade and Markets in West Africa,* ed. Claude Meillassoux, 266–84. London: Oxford University Press.

Coleman, James S. 1988. "Social Capital in the Creation of Human Capital." *American Journal of Sociology* 94 (Supplement): 95–120.

Dahrendorf, Ralph. 1968. "Market and Plan: Two Types of Rationality." In *Essays in the Theory of Society,* 215–31. Stanford, Calif.: Stanford University Press.

Dasgupta, Partha. 1988. "Trust as a Commodity." In *Trust: Making and Breaking Cooperative Relations,* ed. Partha Dasgupta, 49–71. Oxford: Basil Blackwell.

DeGlopper, Donald R. 1972. "Doing Business in Lukang." In *Economic Organization in Chinese Society,* ed. W. E. Willmott, 297–326. Stanford, Calif.: Stanford University Press.

1995. *Lukang: Commerce and Community in a Chinese City.* Albany: State University of New York Press.

Demsetz, Harold. 1969. "Information and Efficiency: Another Viewpoint." *Journal of Law and Economics* 12 (1): 1–22.

DiMaggio, Paul. 1990. "Cultural Aspects of Economic Action and Organization." In *Between the Marketplace: Rethinking Economy and Society,* ed. Roger Friedland and A. F. Robertson, 113–36. New York: Aldine de Gruyter.

DiMaggio, Paul J., and Walter W. Powell. 1983. "The Iron Cage Revisited: Institutional Isomorphism and Collective Rationality in Organizational Fields." In *The New Institutionalism in Organizational Analysis,* ed. Walter W. Powell and Paul J. DiMaggio, 63–82. Chicago: University of Chicago Press.

1991. "Introduction." In *The New Institutionalism in Organizational Analysis,* ed. Walter W. Powell and Paul J. DiMaggio, 1–38. Chicago: University of Chicago Press.

Ding, X. L. 1994a. *The Decline of Communism in China: Legitimacy Crises, 1977–1989.* Cambridge University Press.

1994b. "Institutional Amphibiousness and the Transition from Communism: The Case of China." *British Journal of Political Science* 24: 293–318.

Dirlik, Arif, and Maurice Meisner. 1989. "Politics, Scholarship, and Chinese Socialism." In *Marxism and the Chinese Experience,* ed. Arif Dirlik and Maurice Meisner, 3–26. Armonk, N.Y.: M. E. Sharpe.

Dissanayake, Wimal. 1996. *Narratives of Agency: Self-Making in China, India, and Japan.* Minneapolis: University of Minnesota Press.

Djilas, Milovan. 1957. *The New Class: An Analysis of the Communist System of Power.* New York: Praeger.

Dore, Ronald. 1983. "Goodwill and the Spirit of Market Capitalism." *British Journal of Sociology* 34 (4): 459–82.

1986. *Flexible Rigidities: Industrial Policy and Structural Adjustment in the Japanese Economy.* London: Athlone.

Durkheim, Emile. (1915) 1965. *The Elementary Forms of the Religious Life.* New York: Free Press.

1933. *The Division of Labor in Society.* New York: Free Press.

East Asia Analytical Unit. 1995. *Overseas Chinese Business Networks in Asia.* Canberra, Australia: Department of Foreign Affairs and Trade.

*Economist.* 1998. "Emerging Market Indicators." *The Economist* 346 (March 14–20): 122.

Eggertsson, Thráinn. 1990. *Economic Behavior and Institutions.* Cambridge University Press.

1993. "The Economics of Institutions: Avoiding the Open-Field Syndrome and the Perils of Path Dependence." *Acta Sociologica* 36 (3): 223–37.

Eisenstadt, S. N., and L. Roniger. 1984. *Patrons, Clients and Friends: Interpersonal Relations and the Structure of Trust in Society.* Cambridge University Press.

Emirbayer, Mustafa, and Jeff Goodwin. 1994. "Network Analysis, Culture, and the Problem of Agency." *American Journal of Sociology* 99 (6): 1411–54.

Ensminger, Jean. 1992. *Making a Market: The Institutional Transformation of an African Society*. Cambridge University Press.

Entwisle, Barbara, Gail E. Henderson, Susan E. Short, Jill Bouma, and Zhai Fengying. 1995. "Gender and Family Businesses in Rural China." *American Sociological Review* 60 (February): 36–57.

Erbaugh, Mary S., and Richard Curt Kraus. 1990. "The 1989 Democracy Movement in Fujian and Its Aftermath." *Australian Journal of Chinese Affairs* 23 (January): 145–60.

Etzioni, Amitai. 1988. *The Moral Dimension: Towards a New Economics*. New York: Free Press.

Evans, Peter. 1995. *Embedded Autonomy: States and Industrial Transformation*. Princeton: Princeton University Press.

Falkenheim, Victor. 1988. "The Political Economy of Regional Reform: An Overview." In *Chinese Economic Policy: Economic Reform at Midstream*, ed. Bruce Reynolds, 285–309. New York: Paragon House.

Fang, Xin, and Li Meiqing. 1989. "Shousuo Hu, Fazhan Hu, Dui Geti, Siying, Jingji De Zai Renshi" (Contraction or Expansion? Some Second Thoughts Regarding the Individual and Private Economy). *Ban Yue Tan* (Fortnightly Discussions) 20: 12–15.

Feher, Ferenc, Agnes Heller, and Gyorgy Markus. 1983. *Dictatorship Over Needs: An Analysis of Soviet Societies*. Oxford: Basil Blackwell.

Fei, Xiaotong. (1948) 1992. *From the Soil: The Foundations of Chinese Society*, trans. Gary G. Hamilton and Wang Zheng. Berkeley: University of California Press.

Firth, Raymond. (1951) 1964. *Elements of Social Organization*. Boston: Beacon Press.

Fischer, Stanley. 1992. "Privatization in East European Transformation." In *The Emergence of Market Economies in Eastern Europe*, ed. Christopher Clague and Gordon C. Rausser, 227–43. Cambridge, Mass.: Basil Blackwell.

Fitzgerald, C. P. 1972. *The Southern Expansion of the Chinese People*. Bangkok: White Lotus.

Flap, H. D. 1990. "Patronage: An Institution in Its Own Right." In *Social Institutions: Their Emergence, Maintenance, and Effects*, ed. Michael Hechter, Karl-Dietrich Opp, and Reinhard Wippler, 225–43. New York: Aldine de Gruyter.

Fligstein, Neil. 1990. *The Transformation of Corporate Control*. Cambridge, Mass.: Harvard University Press.

———. 1996. "The Economic Sociology of the Transitions from Socialism." *American Journal of Sociology* 101 (4): 1074–81.

Foster, George M. 1963. "The Dyadic Contract in Tzintzuntzan, II: Patron-client Relationships." *American Anthropologist* 65 (6): 1280–94.

Francis, Corinna-Barbara. 1996. "Reproduction of *Danwei* Institutional Features in the Context of China's Market Economy: The Case of Haidian District's High-Tech Sector." *China Quarterly* 147 (September): 639–59.

Fraser, David. 2000. "Inventing Oasis: Luxury Housing Advertisements and Reconfiguring Domestic Space in Shanghai." In *The Consumer Revolu-*

*tion in Urban China,* ed. Deborah Davis, 25–53. Berkeley: University of California Press.

Freedman, Maurice. 1959. "The Handling of Money: A Note on the Background to the Economic Sophistication of the Overseas Chinese." *Man* 59: 64–5.

Fried, Morton. 1953. *The Fabric of Chinese Society: A Study of the Social Life of a Chinese County Seat.* New York: Praeger.

Friedman, Milton, 1962. *Capitalism and Freedom.* Chicago: Chicago University Press.

Friedland, Roger, and A. F. Robertson. 1990. "Beyond the Marketplace." In *Beyond the Marketplace: Rethinking Economy and Society,* ed. Roger Friedland and A. F. Robertson, 3–49. New York: Aldine de Gruyter.

Fujian Province Statistical Bureau. 1989. *Fujian Fenjin de Sishinian, 1949–1989* (Forty Years of Vigorous Advance in Fujian, 1949–1989). Fujian: China Statistical Publishers.

1992. *Fujian Tongji Nianjian, 1992* [Fujian Statistical Yearbook, 1992]. Fujian: China Statistical Publishers.

Gábor, István R. 1989. "Second Economy and Socialism: The Hungarian Experience." In *The Underground Economies: Tax Evasion and Information Distortion,* ed. Edgar L. Feige, 339–60. Cambridge University Press.

1990. "On the Immediate Prospects for Private Entrepreneurship and Re-Embourgeoisement in Hungary." Working paper of Cornell Project on Comparative Institutional Analysis. Ithaca, N.Y.: Cornell University.

Gambetta, Diego. 1993. *The Sicilian Mafia: The Business of Private Protection.* Cambridge, Mass.: Harvard University Press.

Gates, Hill. 1991. "'Narrow Hearts' and Petty Capitalism: Small Business Women in Chengdu, China." In *Marxist Approaches in Economic Anthropology,* ed. Alice Littlefield and Hill Gates, 13–36. Society for Economic Anthropology Monograph 9.

1993. "Cultural Support for Birth Limitation among Urban Capital-Owning Women." In *Chinese Families in the Post-Mao Era,* ed. Deborah Davis and Stevan Harrell, 251–74. Berkeley: University of California Press.

1996. *China's Motor: A Thousand Years of Petty Capitalism.* Ithaca, N.Y.: Cornell University Press.

Geertz, Clifford. 1963. *Peddlers and Princes: Social Change and Modernization in Two Indonesian Towns.* Chicago: University of Chicago Press.

1964. "Ideology as a Cultural System." In *Ideology and Discontent,* ed. David Apter, 47–56. Glencoe, Ill.: Free Press.

1978. "The Bazaar Economy: Information and Search in Peasant Marketing." *Supplement to the American Economic Review* 68 (May): 28–32.

1983. "Culture and Social Change: The Indonesian Case." *Man* (n.s.) 19: 511–32.

Geng, Yuxin. (1986) 1989. "Profit and Morality." In *China Tackles Reform. China in Focus,* no. 33, ed. Su Wenming, 31–3. Beijing: Beijing Review.

Gerschenkron, Alexander. 1962. *Economic Backwardness in Historical Perspective.* Cambridge, Mass.: Harvard University Press.

Giddens, Anthony. 1984. *The Constitution of Society: Outline of the Theory of Structuration.* Berkeley: University of California Press.

(1976) 1993. *New Rules of Sociological Methods.* Cambridge: Polity Press.

Glassman, Ronald. 1991. *China in Transition: Communism, Capitalism and Democracy.* Westport, Conn.: Praeger.

Glinski, Piotr. 1992. "Acapulco Near Konstancin." In *The Unplanned Society: Poland During and After Communism,* ed. Janine Wedel, 144–52. New York: Columbia University Press.

Gold, Thomas B. 1985. "After Comradeship: Personal Relations in China Since the Cultural Revolution." *China Quarterly* 104 (December): 657–75.

1986. *State and Society in the Taiwan Miracle.* Armonk, N.Y.: M. E. Sharpe.

1989a. "Guerrilla Interviewing among the *Getihu.*" In *Unofficial China: Popular Culture and Thought in the People's Republic,* ed. Perry Link, Richard Madsen, and Paul G. Pickowicz, 175–92. Boulder, Colo.: Westview.

1989b. "Urban Private Business in China." *Studies in Comparative Communism* 22 (2–3): 187–201.

1990a. "Urban Private Business and Social Change." In *Chinese Society on the Eve of Tiananmen: The Impact of Reform,* ed. Deborah Davis and Ezra F. Vogel, 157–78. Cambridge, Mass.: Council on East Asian Studies, Harvard University Press.

1990b. "The Party-State versus Society in China." In *Building a Nation-State: China after Forty Years,* China Research Monograph 37, ed. Joyce K. Kallgren, 125–51. Berkeley: Institute for East Asian Studies, University of California.

1991. "Urban Private Business and China's Reforms." In *Reform and Reaction in Post-Mao China: The Road to Tiananmen,* ed. Richard Baum, 84–103. New York: Routledge.

Goldstein, Avery. 1991. *From Bandwagon to Balance-of-Power Politics: Structural Constraints and Politics in China, 1949–1978.* Stanford, Calif.: Stanford University Press.

Goldstein, Steven M. 1995. "China in Transition: The Political Foundations of Incremental Reform." *China Quarterly* 144 (December): 1105–31.

Granovetter, Mark. 1973. "The Strength of Weak Ties." *American Journal of Sociology* 78: 1360–80.

1985. "Economic Action and Social Structure: The Problem of Embeddedness." *American Journal of Sociology* 91: 481–510.

1993. "The Nature of Economic Relationships." In *Explorations in Economic Sociology,* ed. Richard Swedberg, 3–41. New York: Russell Sage Foundation.

Greenhalgh, Susan. 1988. "Families and Networks in Taiwan's Economic Development." In *Contending Approaches to the Political Economy of Taiwan,* eds. Edwin Winckler and Susan Greenhalgh, 224–45. Armonk, N.Y.: M. E. Sharpe.

Grossman, Gregory. 1977. "The 'Second Economy' of the USSR." *Problems of Communism* 26 (5): 25–40.

1983. "The 'Shadow Economy' in the Socialist Sector of the USSR." In *The CMEA Five-Year Plans (1981–1985) in a New Perspective.* Brussels: NATO.

(ed.) 1987. *Studies in the Second Economy of Communist Countries.* Berkeley: University of California Press.

Hall, Peter A. 1992. "The Movement from Keynesianism to Monetarism: Institutional Analysis and British Economic Policy in the 1970s." In *Structuring Politics: Historical Institutionalism in Comparative Perspective*, ed. Sven Steinmo, Kathleen Thelen, and Frank Longstreth, 90–113. Cambridge University Press.

Hamilton, Gary G. (ed.) 1991. *Business Networks and Economic Development in East and Southeast Asia*. Hong Kong: University of Hong Kong, Centre of Asian Studies.

1992. "Introduction: Fei Xiaotong and the Beginnings of a Chinese Sociology." In *From the Soil: The Foundations of Chinese Society*, trans. Gary G. Hamilton and Wang Zheng, 1–34. Berkeley: University of California Press.

1994. "Civilization and the Organization of Economies." In *The Handbook of Economic Sociology*, ed. Neil J. Smelser and Richard Swedborg, 183–205. Princeton: Princeton University Press and Russell Sage Foundation.

Hamilton, Gary G., and Nicole W. Biggart. 1988. "Market, Culture, and Authority: A Comparative Analysis of Management and Organization in the Far East. *American Journal of Sociology* (Special Issue, July): S52–S94.

Hamilton, Gary G., and Kao Cheng-shu. 1990. "The Institutional Foundations of Chinese Business: The Family Firm in Taiwan." *Comparative Social Research* 12: 95–112.

Handelman, Stephen. 1995. *Comrade Criminal: Russia's New Mafiya*. New Haven: Yale University Press.

Hankiss, Elemér. 1988. "The 'Second Society': Is There an Alternative Model Emerging in Hungary?" *Social Research* 55 (Spring–Summer): 13–42.

Hechter, Michael. 1987. *Principles of Group Solidarity*. Berkeley: University of California Press.

Henderson, Gail, and Myron Cohen. 1984. *The Chinese Hospital*. New Haven: Yale University Press.

Hershkovitz, Linda. 1985. "The Fruits of Ambivalence: China's Urban Individual Economy." *Pacific Affairs* 58 (3): 427–50.

Hirsch, Paul, Stuart Michaels, and Ray Friedman. 1990. "Clean Models vs. Dirty Hands: Why Economics Is Different from Sociology." In *Structures of Capital: The Social Organization of the Economy*, ed. Sharon Zukin and Paul DiMaggio, 39–56. Cambridge University Press.

Hou, Jie. 1988. "Shilun Laodong Fuwu Gongsi Jiti Jingji" (Examining the Labor Service Companies' Collective Economy). *Zhongguo Laodong Kexue* (China Labor Science) 2: 3–7.

Howell, Jude. 1993. *China Opens Its Doors: The Politics of Economic Transition*. Boulder, Colo.: Lynne Rienner.

Hsu, Francis L. K. (1953) 1981. *Americans and Chinese: Passages to Difference*. Honolulu: University of Hawaii Press.

Hu, Hsien-chin. 1944. "The Chinese Concept of Face." *American Anthropologist* 1(1): 45–64.

Hu, Mengzhou. 1988. "Dui Laodong Fuwu Gongsi Ji Qi Suo Ban Jiti Qiye Jige Wenti De Kanfa" (An Opinion on the Problems of the Labor Service

Company and Its Collective Enterprises). *Zhongguo Laodong Kexue* (China Labor Science) 3: 12–15.

Huang, Shu-ming. 1989. *The Spiral Road: Change in a Chinese Village Through the Eyes of a Communist Party Leader.* Boulder, Col.: Westview.

Huang, Yasheng. 1996. *Inflation and Investment Controls in China: The Political Economy of Central–Local Relations During the Reform Era.* Cambridge University Press.

Humphrey, Caroline. 1991. "'Icebergs,' Barter, and the Mafia in Provincial Russia." *Anthropology Today* 7 (2): 8–13.

Hwang, Kwang-kuo. 1987. "Face and Favor: The Chinese Power Game." *American Journal of Sociology* 92 (4): 944–74.

Ionescu, Ghita. 1977. "Patronage under Communism." In *Patrons and Clients,* ed. E. Gellner and J. Waterbury, 97–102. London: Duckworth.

Jacobs, J. Bruce. 1979. "A Preliminary Model of Particularistic Ties in Chinese Political Alliances: *Kan-ch'ing* and *Kuan-hsi* in a Rural Taiwanese Township." *China Quarterly* 78: 237–73.

Jepperson, Ronald L. 1991. "Institutions, Institutional Effects, and Institutionalism." In *The New Institutionalism in Organizational Analysis,* ed. Walter W. Powell and Paul J. DiMaggio, 143–63. Chicago: University of Chicago Press.

Jia, Ting, and Wang Kaicheng. 1989. "Siying Qiyezhu Jieceng Zai Zhongguo De Jueqi He Fazhan" (The Rise and Development of the Private Enterprise Owner Strata in China). *Zhongguo Shehui Kexue* (Chinese Sociology) 2: 89–100.

Jiang, Yang. 1989. "Gongsi Bing" (Company Sickness). *Shidai* (Era) 12: 16–21.

Johnson, Chalmers. 1982. *MITI and the Japanese Miracle.* Stanford, Calif.: Stanford University Press.

Johnson, Hazel. 1993. *The Banking Keiretsu.* Chicago: Probus.

Johnson, Simon, and Gary W. Loveman. 1995. *Starting Over in Eastern Europe: Entrepreneurship and Economic Renewal.* Boston: Harvard Business School Press.

Jones, Anthony, and William Moskoff. 1991. *Ko-ops: The Rebirth of Entrepreneurship in the Soviet Union.* Bloomington: Indiana University Press.

Jones, Leroy P., and I. Sakong. 1980. *Government, Business, and Entrepreneurship in Economic Development: The Korean Case.* Cambridge, Mass.: Harvard University Press.

Kao, Cheng-shu. 1991. "'Personal Trust' in the Large Businesses in Taiwan." In *Business Networks and Economic Development in East and Southeast Asia,* ed. Gary Hamilton, 66–93. Hong Kong: Centre of Asian Studies, University of Hong Kong.

Karl, Terry Lynn. 1990. "Dilemmas of Democratization in Latin America." *Comparative Politics* 23: 1–21.

Kawalec, Stefan. 1992. "The Dictatorial Supplier." In *The Unplanned Society: Poland During and After Communism,* ed. Janine R. Wedel, 129–43. New York: Columbia University Press.

Kaye, Lincoln. 1995. "Southern Cooking: Coast's Hot Economies Find Centre Distasteful." *Far Eastern Economic Review* (May 25): 22–4.

Keane, John. 1988. "Introduction." In *Civil Society and the State: New European Perspectives*, ed. John Keane, 1–31. London: Verso.

Kelliher, Daniel. 1992. *Peasant Power in China: The Era of Rural Reform, 1979–1989*. New Haven: Yale University Press.

Kemény, István. 1982. "The Unregistered Economy in Hungary." *Soviet Studies* 34 (3): 349–66.

King, Ambrose Yeo-chi. 1985. "The Individual and the Group in Confucianism: A Relational Perspective." In *Individualism and Holism: Studies in Confucian and Taoist Values*, ed. Donald Munro, 57–70. Ann Arbor: Center for Chinese Studies, University of Michigan.

——— 1991. "*Kuan-hsi* and Network Building: A Sociological Interpretation." *Daedalus* (Spring): 63–84.

Kipnis, Andrew. 1997. *Producing Guanxi: Sentiment, Self, and Subculture in a North China Village*. Durham: Duke University Press.

Knight, Jack. 1992. *Institutions and Social Conflict*. Cambridge University Press.

Kornai, Janos. 1990. *The Road to a Free Economy: Shifting from a Socialist System: The Example of Hungary*. New York: Norton.

——— 1992. *The Socialist System: The Political Economy of Communism*. Princeton: Princeton University Press.

Kraus, Willy. 1991. *Private Business in China: Revival Between Ideology and Pragmatism*. Honolulu: University of Hawaii Press.

Krueger, Anne O. 1974. "The Political Economy of the Rent-seeking Society." *American Economic Review* 64 (3): 291–303.

Kuan, Ta-t'ung. 1960. *The Socialist Transformation of Capitalist Industry and Commerce in China*. Beijing: Foreign Languages Press.

Kuhn, Anthony. 1994. "Private Guardians." In *China in Transition*, ed. Frank Ching, 196–99. Hong Kong: Review Publishing.

Kumar, Anjali. 1994. "China's Reform, Internal Trade and Marketing." *Pacific Review* 7 (3): 323–39.

Lardy, Nicholas R. 1992. *Foreign Trade and Economic Reform in China, 1978–1990*. Cambridge University Press.

Lazerson, Mark. 1988. "Organizational Growth of Small Firms: An Outcome of Markets and Hierarchies?" *American Sociological Review* 53: 330–42.

——— 1993. "Future Alternatives of Work Reflected in the Past: Putting-Out Production in Modena." In *Explorations in Economic Sociology*, ed. Richard Swedberg, 403–27. New York: Russell Sage Foundation.

Lazonick, William. 1991. *Business Organization and the Myth of the Market Economy*. Cambridge University Press.

——— 1993. "Future Alternatives of Work Reflected in the Past: Putting-Out Production in Modena." In *Explorations in Economic Sociology*, ed. Richard Swedberg, 403–27. New York: Russell Sage Foundation.

Leff, Nathaniel H. 1964. "Economic Development through Bureaucratic Corruption." *American Behavioral Scientist* 8 (November ): 8–14.

*Legal System Daily* (*Fazhi Bao*). 1990. "Wo Guo Siying Qiye Dengji Zhuce Yu Jin 90,000 Hu" (Licensed Private Enterprise Exceeds 90,000). June 16: 6.

Levi, Margaret. 1988. *Of Rule and Revenue*. Berkeley: University of California Press.

Levi, Margaret. 1988. *Of Rule and Revenue*. Berkeley: University of California Press.

Levine, Victor T. 1989. "Supportive Values of the Culture of Corruption in Ghana." In *Political Corruption: A Handbook*, ed. Arnold J. Heidenheimer, Michael Johnston, and Victor T. Levine, 363–73. New Brunswick, N.J.: Transaction Publishers.

Li, Hui, Chaozheng Ma, and Lei Ma. 1993. "Farming for Firepower: China's Soldiers Reshape the Iron Rice Bowl." In *Military Capitalism*, special section of *World Paper* prepared for *Mainichi Daily News*. December 12: 6–7

Li, Siming, and Lingxun Zhao. 1992. "Xiamen: Regional Center and Hometown of Overseas Chinese." In *China's Coastal Cities: Catalysts for Modernization*, ed. Y. Yeung and X. Hu, 221–39. Honolulu: University of Hawaii Press.

Li, Wei. 1994. *The Chinese Staff System: A Mechanism for Bureaucratic Control and Integration*, China Research Monograph 44. Berkeley: Institute of East Asian Studies, University of California.

Lie, John. 1992. "The Concept of Mode of Exchange." *American Sociological Review* 57(August): 508–23.

——— 1993. "Visualizing the Invisible Hand: The Social Origins of 'Market Society' in England, 1550–1750." *Politics and Society* 21 (3): 275–305.

Lieberthal, Kenneth G. 1980. *Revolution and Tradition in Tientsin, 1949–1952*. Stanford, Calif.: Standford University Press.

Lim, Linda Y. C., and L. A. Peter Gosling (eds.). 1983. *The Chinese in Southeast Asia*: vol. 1, *Ethnicity and Economic Activity*. Singapore: Maruzen Asia.

Lin, Jincheng. 1989. "Jiantan 'Jia Jiti' Di Ruogan Wenti" (A Discussion of Some Problems of the "False Collectives"). *Jingji Fazhi* (Economic Legal System) 8: 34–6.

Lin, Nan. 1988. "Chinese Family Structure and Chinese Society." *Bulletin of the Institute of Ethnology* 65 (Spring): 58–129.

——— 1995. "Local Market Socialism: Local Corporatism in Action in Rural China." *Theory and Society* 24: 301–54.

Lin, Qingsong. 1990. "Private Enterprises: Their Emergence, Rapid Growth, and Problems." In *China's Rural Industry: Structure, Development, and Reform*, ed. William A. Byrd and Lin Qingsong, 172–88. Oxford: World Bank, Oxford University Press.

Lin, Yueh Hua. 1947. *The Golden Wing*. New York: Oxford University Press.

Ling, Ken. 1972. *Red Guard: From Schoolboy to "Little General" in Mao's China*, trans. Miriam London and Ta-ling Lee. London: Macdonald.

Lipset, Seymour Martin. 1992. "Conditions of the Democratic Order and Social Change: A Comparative Discussion." In *Studies in Human Society: Democracy and Modernity*, ed. S. N. Eisenstadt, 1–14. New York: E. J. Brill.

——— 1993. "The Social Requisites of Democracy Revisited." *American Sociological Review* 59 (February): 1–22.

Liu, Qing, et al. 1995. "Zhonguo Minying Qiyejia Toushen Guangcai Shiye" (China's Nonstate Entrepreneurs Plunge into Glorious Enterprise). *Gong Shang Shi Bao* (Industrial and Commercial Times). February 10: 2.

Liu, Yia-ling. 1992. "The Reform from Below: The Private Economy and the Local Politics in the Rural Industrialization of Wenzhou." *China Quarterly* 130 (June): 293–316.

Lockett, Martin. 1988. "The Urban Collective Economy." In *Transforming China's Economy in the Eighties*, vol. 2, *Management, Industry, and the Urban Economy*, ed. Stephan Feuchtwang, Athar Hussain, and Thierry Pairault, 118–37. Boulder, Colo.: Westview.

Lofland, John, and Lyn H. Lofland. 1995 (3d. ed.). *Analyzing Social Settings: A Guide to Qualitative Observation and Analysis*. Belmont, Calif.: Wadsworth.

Los, Maria (ed.). 1990. *The Second Economy in Marxist States*. London: Macmillan.

Lu, Shanqing, et al. (eds.). 1989. *Zhongguo Yanhai Chengshi Touzi Huanjing Zhonglan, Xiamen Juan* (A Comprehensive Review of Investment Environments in China's Coastal Cities, Xiamen Volume). Shanghai: East China Normal Teachers' University Publishing House.

Lukes, Steven. 1974. *Power: A Radical View*. London: Macmillan.

Luo, Qi, and Christopher Howe. 1995. "Direct Investment and Economic Integration in the Asia Pacific: The Case of Taiwanese Investment in Xiamen." In *Greater China: The Next Superpower?* ed. David Shambaugh, 94–117. Oxford: Oxford University Press.

Macaulay, Stewart. 1963. "Non-contractual Relations in Business: A Preliminary Study." *American Sociological Review* 28 (February): 55–66.

MacGaffey, Janet. 1987. *Entrepreneurs and Parasites: The Struggle for Indigenous Capitalism in Zaire*. Cambridge University Press.

——— 1991. "Historical, Cultural and Structural Dimensions of Zaire's Unrecorded Trade." In *The Real Economy of Zaire: The Contribution of Smuggling & Other Unofficial Activities to National Wealth*, ed. Janet MacGaffey et al., 26–40. Philadelphia: University of Pennsylvania Press.

Manchin, Robert. 1988. "Individual Economic Strategies and Social Consciousness." *Social Research* 55 (1–2): 77–95.

Mann, Michael. 1986. *The Sources of Social Power*, vol. 1, *A History of Power from the Beginning to 1760*. Cambridge University Press.

Marx, Karl. (1867) 1976. *Capital: A Critique of Political Economy*, vol. 1, trans. Ben Fowkes. London: Penguin Books.

Marx, Karl, and Friedrich Engels. 1970. *The German Ideology*, ed. C. J. Arthur. London: Lawrence & Wishart.

Mauss, Marcel. (1925) 1969. *The Gift: Forms and Functions of Exchange in Archaic Societies*. London: Cohen and West.

Meany, Connie Squires. 1991. "Market Reform and Disintegrative Corruption in Urban China." In *Reform and Reaction in Post-Mao China: The Road to Tiananmen*, ed. Richard Baum, 124–42. New York: Routledge.

Meyer, John W., John Boli, and George M. Thomas. 1987. "Ontology and Rationalization in the Western Cultural Account." In *Institutional Structure: Constituting State, Society, and the Individual*, ed. George M. Thomas et al. 12–37. Newbury Park, Calif.: Sage.

Meyer, John W., and Brian Rowan. 1977. "Institutionalized Organizations:

Formal Structure as Myth and Ceremony." *American Journal of Sociology* 83: 340–63.

Meyers, James T. 1987. "Another Look at the Corruption Lessons of the Career of the 'God of Fortune.'" *Issues and Studies* 23 (11): 28–49.

Meyers, Ramon H. 1994. "The Socialist Market Economy in the People's Republic of China: Fact or Fiction?" Morrison Lecture, Australian National University, November 8.

Misztal, Bronislaw. 1981. "The Petite Bourgeoisie in Socialist Society." In *The Petite Bourgeoisie: Comparative Studies of the Uneasy Stratum*, ed. Frank Bechhofer and Brian Elliot, 90–104. London: Macmillan.

Mizruchi, Mark S. 1992. *The Structure of Corporate Political Action: Interfirm Relations and Their Consequences.* Cambridge, Mass.: Harvard University Press.

Mokrzycki, Edmund. 1993. "Socialism after Socialism: Continuity in the East European Transition." *European Journal of Sociology* 34: 108–15.

Montinola, Gabriella, Yingyi Qian, and Barry R. Weingast. 1995. "Federalism, Chinese Style: The Political Basis for Economic Success in China." *World Politics* 48 (October): 50–81.

Moore, Barrington, Jr. 1966. *Social Origins of Dictatorship and Democracy: Lord and Peasant in the Making of the Modern World.* Boston: Beacon.

Naughton, Barry. 1988. "The Third Front: Defense Industrialization in China's Interior." *China Quarterly* 115: 351–86.

    1995. *Growing Out of the Plan: Chinese Economic Reform, 1978–1993.* Cambridge University Press.

Nee, Victor. 1985. "Peasant Household Individualism." In *Chinese Rural Development: The Great Transformation*, ed. W. L. Parish, 164–90. Armonk, N.Y.: M. E. Sharpe.

    1989a. "Theory of Market Transition: From Redistribution to Market in State Socialism." *American Sociological Review* 54 (5): 663–81.

    1989b. "Peasant Entrepreneurship and the Politics of Regulation." In *Remaking the Economic Institutions of Socialism: China and Eastern Europe*, ed. Victor Nee and David Stark, 169–207. Stanford, Calif.: Stanford University Press.

    1990. "Institutional Change and Economic Growth in China: The View from the Villages." *Journal of Asian Studies* 49 (1): 3–25.

    1991. "Social Inequalities in Reforming State Socialism: Between Redistribution and Markets in China." *American Sociological Review* 56 (June): 267–82.

    1992. "Organizational Dynamics of Market Transition: Hybrid Forms, Property Rights, and Mixed Economy in China." *Administrative Science Quarterly* 37: 1–27.

    1996. "The Emergence of Market Society: Changing Mechanisms of Stratification in China." *American Journal of Sociology* 101 (4): 908–49.

Nee, Victor, and David Stark. 1989. "Toward an Institutional Analysis of State Socialism." In *Remaking the Economic Institutions of Socialism: China and Eastern Europe*, ed. Victor Nee and David Stark, 1–31. Stanford, Calif.: Stanford University Press, 1989.

Nelson, Richard, and Sidney G. Winter. 1982. *An Evolutionary Theory of Economic Change.* Cambridge University Press.

Nevitt, Christopher Earle. 1996. "Private Business Associations in China: Evidence of Civil Society or Local State Power?" *China Journal* 36 (July): 25–43.

Ng, Chin-Keong. 1973–4. "Gentry-Merchants and Peasant-Peddlers – The Response of Southern Fukienese to Offshore Trading Opportunities, 1522–66. *Journal of Nanyang University* 7: 161–75.

1983. *Trade and Society: The Amoy Network on the China Coast, 1683–1735.* Singapore: Singapore University Press.

Nohria, Nitin, and Ranjay Gulati. 1994. "Firms and Their Environments." In *The Handbook of Economic Sociology*, ed. Neil Smelser and Richard Swedborg, 529–51. Princeton: Princeton University Press.

North, Douglass C. 1981. *Structure and Change in Economic History.* New York: Norton.

1990a. *Institutions, Institutional Change and Economic Performance.* Cambridge University Press.

1990b. "Institutions and a Transaction Cost Theory of Exchange." In *Perspectives on Positive Political Economy*, ed. James E. Alt and Kenneth A. Shepsle, 182–94. Cambridge University Press.

Numazaki, Ichiro. 1991. "The Role of Personal Networks in the Making of Taiwan's *Guanxiqiye* (Related Enterprises)." In *Business Networks and Economic Development in East and Southeast Asia*, ed. Gary Hamilton, 77–93. Hong Kong: University of Hong Kong, Centre of Asian Studies.

Odgaard, Ole. 1992. *Private Enterprises in Rural China: Impact on Agriculture and Social Stratification.* Aldershot, England: Avebury.

Oi, Jean. 1985. "Communism and Clientelism: Rural Politics in China." *World Politics* 37 (2): 238–66.

1989. *State and Peasant in Contemporary China: The Political Economy of Village Government.* Berkeley: University of California Press.

1990. "The Fate of the Collective After the Commune." In *Chinese Society on the Eve of Tiananmen: The Impact of Reform*, ed. Deborah Davis and Ezra Vogel, 15–36. Cambridge, Mass.: Council on East Asian Studies, Harvard University Press.

1991. "Partial Market Reform and Corruption in Rural China." In *Reform and Reaction in Post-Mao China: The Road to Tiananmen*, ed. Richard Baum, 143–61. New York: Routledge.

1992. "Fiscal Reform and the Economic Foundations of Local State Corporatism in China." *World Politics* 45 (October): 99–126.

1994. "Rational Choices and Attainment of Wealth and Power in the Countryside." In *China's Quiet Revolution: New Interactions Between State and Society*, ed. David S. G. Goodman and Beverley Hooper, 64–79. New York: St. Martin's.

1995. "The Role of the Local State in China's Transitional Economy." *China Quarterly* 144 (December): 1132–49.

Olson, Mancur. 1982. *The Rise and Decline of Nations: Economic Growth, Stagflation, and Social Rigidities.* New Haven: Yale University Press.

Omohundro, John. 1981. *Chinese Merchant Families in Iloilo*. Athens: Ohio University Press.

Orrù, Marco, Nicole W. Biggart, and Gary G. Hamilton. 1990. "Organizational Isomorphism in East Asia." In *The New Institutionalism in Organizational Analysis*, ed. Walter W. Powell and Paul J. DiMaggio, 361–89. Chicago: University of Chicago Press.

Paltiel, Jeremy T. 1989. "China: Mexicanization or Market Reform?" In *The Elusive State: International and Comparative Perspectives*, ed. James A. Caporaso, 355–78. Newbury Park, Calif.: Sage.

Pan, Lynn. 1990. *Sons of the Yellow Emperor: The Study of the Overseas Chinese*. London: Mandarin Paperbacks.

Parish, William L., and Ethan Michelson. 1996. "Politics and Markets: Dual Transformations." *American Journal of Sociology* 101 (4): 1042–59.

Parris, Kristen. 1993. "Local Initiative and National Reform: The Wenzhou Model of Development." *China Quarterly* 134 (June): 242–63.

Parry, Jonathan, and Maurice Bloch. 1989. 'Introduction: Money and the Morality of Exchange." In *Money and the Morality of Exchange*, ed. J. Parry and M. Bloch, 1–32. Cambridge University Press.

Parsons, Talcott. 1937. *The Structure of Social Action*. New York: McGraw-Hill.

Pawlik, Wojciech. 1992. "Intimate Commerce." In *The Unplanned Society: Poland During and After Communism*, ed. Janine R. Wedel, 78–94. New York: Columbia University Press.

Pearson, Margaret M. 1997. *China's New Business Elite: The Political Consequences of Economic Reform*. Berkeley: University of California Press.

Pei, Minxin. 1994. *From Reform to Revolution: The Demise of Communism in China and the Soviet Union*. Cambridge, Mass.: Harvard University Press.

Pelczynski, Z. A. 1988. "Solidarity and the 'Rebirth of Civil Society.'" In *Civil Society and the State: New European Perspectives*, ed. John Keane, 361–80. London: Verso.

Perrow, Charles. 1993. "Small Firm Networks." In *Explorations in Economic Sociology*, ed. Richard Swedberg, 377–402. New York: Russell Sage Foundation.

Pin, Ho, and Gao Xin. 1992. *The Gang of Princelings of the Chinese Communist Party*. Taipei: China Times Press.

Piore, Michael J., and Charles F. Sabel. 1984. *The Second Industrial Divide: Possibilities for Prosperity*. New York: Basic Books.

Polanyi, Karl. (1944) 1957. *The Great Transformation*. Boston: Beacon.

——— 1957. "The Economy as Instituted Process." In *Trade and Market in Early Empires*, ed. Karl Polanyi, Conrad M. Arensberg, and Harry W. Pearson, 243–70. Glencoe, Ill.: Free Press.

Powell, J. D. 1970. "Peasant Society and Clientelistic Politics." *American Political Science Review* 64 (2): 411–25.

Powell, Walter W. 1987. "Hybrid Organizational Arrangements: New Form or Transitional Development?" *California Management Review* (Fall): 67–87.

——— 1990. "The Transformation of Organizational Forms: How Useful Is Organizational Theory in Accounting for Social Change?" In *Beyond the Market-*

place: *Rethinking Economy and Society*, ed. Robert Friedland and A. F. Robertson, 301–29. New York: Aldine de Gruyter.

Powell, Walter W., and Laurel Smith-Doerr. 1994. "Networks and Economic Life." In *The Handbook of Economic Sociology*, ed. Neil J. Smelser and Richard Swedborg, 368–402. Princeton: Princeton University Press.

Prybyla, Jan S. 1990. *Reform in China and Other Socialist Economies*. Washington, D.C.: AEI Press.

Przeworski, Adam, and Fernando Limongo. 1993. "Political Regimes and Economic Growth." *Journal of Economic Perspectives* 7 (3): 51–69.

Rizzi, Bruno. (1939) 1967. *The Bureaucratization of the World*, trans. Adam Westoby. London: Tavistock.

Rofel, Lisa. 1989. "Hegemony and Productivity." In *Marxism and the Chinese Experience*, ed. Arif Dirlik and Maurice Meisner, 235–52. Armonk, N.Y.: M. E. Sharpe.

Róna-tas, Ákos. 1990. "The Second Economy in Hungary: The Social Origins of the End of State Socialism." Ph.D. dissertation, University of Michigan.

——— 1994. "The First Shall Be Last?: Entrepreneurship and Communist Cadres in the Transition from Socialism." *American Journal of Sociology* 100 (1): 40–69.

Roniger, Luis, and Ayse Günes-Ayata (eds.). 1994. *Democracy, Clientelism, and Civil Society*. Boulder, Colo.: Lynne Rienner.

Rosen, Stanley, ed. 1987–8. "The Private Economy," Parts 1 and 2. *Chinese Economic Studies* 21 (1–2).

Rowe, William T. 1984. *Hankow: Commerce and Society in a Chinese City, 1796–1889*. Stanford, Calif.: Stanford University Press.

Rueschemeyer, Dietrich, and Peter B. Evans. 1985. "The State and Economic Transformation: Toward an Analysis of the Conditions Underlying Effective Intervention." In *Bringing the State Back In*, ed. Peter B. Evans, Dietrich Rueschemeyer, and Theda Skocpol, 44–77. Cambridge University Press.

Rueschemeyer, Dietrich, Evelyne H. Stephens, and John D. Stephens. 1992. *Capitalist Development and Democracy*. Chicago: University of Chicago Press.

Rupp, Kalman. 1983. *Entrepreneurs in Red: Structure and Organizational Innovation in the Centrally Planned Economy*. Albany: State University of New York Press.

Sabel, Charles F. 1993. "Studied Trust: Building New Forms of Cooperation in a Volatile Economy." In *Explorations in Economic Sociology*, ed. Richard Swedberg, 104–44. New York: Russell Sage Foundation.

Sabin, Lora. 1994. "New Bosses in the Workers' State: The Growth of Non-State Sector Employment in China." *China Quarterly* 140 (December): 944–70.

Sahlins, Marshall. 1972. *Stone Age Economics*. New York: Aldine.

Sajo, Andras. 1994. "Has State Ownership Truly Abandoned Socialism? The Survival of Socialist Economy and Law in Postcommunist Hungary." In *A Fourth Way? Privatization, Property, and the Emergence of New Market Economies*, ed. Gregory. S. Alexander and Grazyna Skapska, 198–214. New York: Routledge.

Silin, Robert H. 1972. "Marketing and Credit in a Hong Kong Wholesale Market." In *Economic Organization in Chinese Society*, ed. W. E. Willmott, 327–52. Stanford, Calif.: Stanford University Press.

Sampson, Steven L. 1987. "The Second Economy of the Soviet Union and Eastern Europe." *Annals of the American Academy of Political and Social Science* (September): 120–36.

Schatzman, Leonard, and Anselm L. Strauss. 1973. *Field Research: Strategies for a Natural Sociology*. Englewood Cliffs, N.J.: Prentice-Hall.

Schmidt, Steffem W. 1977. *Friends, Followers and Factions*. Berkeley: University of California Press.

Schoppa, R. Keith. 1982. *Chinese Elites and Political Change: Zhejiang Province in the Early 20th Century*. Cambridge, Mass.: Harvard University Press.

Schumpeter, Joseph A. (1943) 1987. *Capitalism, Socialism and Democracy*. London: Unwin Paperbacks.

Schurmann, Franz. (1966) 1968. *Ideology and Organization in Communist China*. Berkeley: University of California Press.

Scott, James C. 1972a. "Patron–client Politics and Political Change in Southeast Asia" *American Political Science Review* 66: 103–27.

——— 1972b. *Comparative Political Corruption*. Englewood Cliffs, N.J.: Prentice-Hall.

Shefter, Martin. 1994. "Patronage and Its Opponents: A Theory and Some European Cases." In *Political Parties and the State: The American Historical Experience*, 21–60. Princeton: Princeton University Press.

Shi, Xianmin. 1993. "Beijing's Privately Owned Small Businesses: A Decade's Development." *Social Sciences in China* 114 (Spring): 153–64.

Shirk, Susan. 1989. "The Political Economy of Chinese Industrial Reform. In *Remaking the Economic Institutions of Socialism: China and Eastern Europe*, ed. Victor Nee and David Stark, 328–62. Stanford, Calif.: Stanford University Press.

——— 1993. *The Political Logic of Economic Reform in China*. Berkeley: University of California Press.

Silin, Robert H. 1976. *Leadership and Values: The Organization of Large-Scale Taiwanese Enterprises*. Cambridge, Mass.: Harvard University Press.

Silverman, S. T. 1970. "Exploitation in Rural Central Italy: Structure and Ideology in Stratification Study." *Comparative Studies in Society and History* 12: 327–39.

Siu, Helen. 1989. "Socialist Peddlers and Princes in a Chinese Market Town." *American Ethnologist* 16 (2): 196–212.

Skinner, G. William. 1977. "Regional Urbanization in Nineteenth-Century China." In *The City in Late Imperial China*, ed. G. William Skinner, 211–49. Stanford, Calif.: Stanford University Press.

Skocpol, Theda. 1979. *States and Social Revolutions: A Comparative Analysis of France, Russia, & China*. Cambridge: Cambridge University Press.

——— 1985a. "Bringing the State Back In: Strategies of Analysis in Current Research." In *Bringing the State Back In*, ed. Peter. B. Evans, Dietrich Rueschemeyer, and Theda Skocpol, 3–37. Cambridge University Press.

1985b. "Cultural Idioms and Political Ideologies in the Revolutionary Reconstruction of State Power: A Rejoinder to Sewell." *Journal of Modern History* 57: 86–96.

Smart, Alan. 1993. "Gifts, Bribes, and *Guanxi*: A Reconsideration of Bourdieu's Social Capital." *Cultural Anthropology* 8 (2): 388–403.

Smelser, Neil J., and Richard Swedborg. 1994. "The Sociological Perspective on the Economy." In *The Handbook of Economic Sociology*, ed. Neil J. Smelser and Richard Swedborg, 3–26. Princeton: Princeton University Press.

Smith, Charles W. 1989. *Auctions: The Social Construction of Value*. Berkeley: University of California Press.

Solinger, Dorothy J. 1984. *Chinese Business Under Socialism: The Politics of Domestic Commerce, 1949–1980*. Berkeley: University of California Press.

1991. "Urban Reform and Relational Contracting in Post-Mao China: An Interpretation of the Transition from Plan to Market." In *Reform and Reaction in Post-Mao China: The Road to Tiananmen*, ed. Richard Baum, 104–23. New York: Routledge.

1992. "Urban Entrepreneurs and the State: The Merger of State and Society." In *State and Society in China: The Consequences of Reform*, ed. Arthur L. Rosenbaum, 121–41. Boulder, Colo.: Westview.

Staniszkis, Jadwiga. 1991. "'Political Capitalism' in Poland." *East European Politics and Society* 5 (1): 127–41.

Stark, David. 1989. "Coexisting Organizational Forms in Hungary's Mixed Economy." In *Remaking the Economic Institutions of Socialism: China and Eastern Europe*, ed. Victor Nee and David Stark, 137–68. Stanford, Calif.: Stanford University Press.

1996. "Recombinant Property in East European Capitalism." *American Journal of Sociology* 101 (4): 993–1027.

Stark, David, and Victor Nee. 1989. "Towards an Institutional Analysis of State Socialism." In *Remaking the Economic Institutions of Socialism: China and Eastern Europe*, ed. Victor Nee and David Stark, 1–31. Stanford, Calif.: Stanford University Press.

State Council. 1986. "Interim Regulations on Income Tax for Urban and Rural Individual Businesses in the People's Republic of China." In *Geti Gongshangye Jingying Guanli Shouce* (Handbook of Individual Industrial and Commercial Enterprise Management and Administration), ed. Jia Zhenxing and Lao Shengzeng, 444–7. Beijing: Beijing University Press.

1988. "Zhonghua Renmin Gongheguo Siying Qiye Zhanxing Tiaoli" (Interim Regulations on Private Enterprises of the People's Republic of China). In *Geti Jingji, Siying Jingji* (Individual Economy, Private Economy), 14–24. Beijing: People's Daily Publishing House.

State Statistical Bureau. 1989. *Changes and Development in China (1949–1989)*. Beijing: Beijing Review Press.

1994. *Zhongguo Tongji Gaiyao* (A Statistical Survey of China). Beijing: National Statistical Bureau.

State Statistical Bureau, Xiamen branch. 1989. *Doujinde Xiamen*. (Fighting Xiamen). Xiamen: Xiamen Municipal Statistical Bureau.

Stinchcombe, Arthur L. 1990. *Information and Organizations*. Berkeley: University of California Press.

Sun, Shouwen, et al. 1994. "Changyi Shu" (A Written Proposal). Xiamen: Xiamen Zong Shanghui (Xiamen General Chamber of Commerce), December 10.

Swain, Nigel. 1990. "Small Cooperatives and Economic Work Partnerships in the Computing Industries: Exceptions that Prove the Rule." In *Market Economy and Civil Society in Hungary*, ed. C. M. Hann, 85–109. London: Frank Cass.

Swedberg, Richard, and Mark Granovetter. 1992. "Introduction." In *The Sociology of Economic Life*, ed. Mark Granovetter and Richard Swedborg, 1–28. Boulder, Col.: Westview.

Swedberg, Richard, Ulf Himmelstrand, and Goran Brulin. 1990. "The Paradigm of Economic Sociology." In *Structures of Capital: The Social Organization of the Economy*, ed. Paul DiMaggio and Sharon Zukin, 57–86. Cambridge University Press.

Szelenyi, Ivan. 1978. "Social Inequalities in State Socialist Redistributive Economies." *International Journal of Comparative Sociology* (1–2): 63–87.

1988. *Socialist Entrepreneurs: Embourgeoisement in Rural Hungary*. Madison: University of Wisconsin Press.

1989. "Eastern Europe in an Epoch of Transition: Towards a Socialist Mixed Economy?" In *Remaking the Economic Institutions of Socialism: China and Eastern Europe*, ed. Victor Nee and David Stark, 208–32. Stanford, Calif.: Stanford University Press.

Tang, Jianzhang, and Laurence J. C. Ma. 1985. "Evolution of Urban Collective Enterprises in China." *China Quarterly* 104 (December): 614–40.

Tao, Julia, and Wai-nang Ho. 1997. "Chinese Entrepreneurship: Culture, Structure and Economic Actors." In *The Limits of Globalization: Cases and Arguments*, ed. Alan Scott, 143–77. London: Routledge.

Tarkowski, Jacek. 1983. "Patronage in a Centralized Socialist System: The Case of Poland." *International Political Science Review* 4 (4): 495–518.

Taussig, Michael. 1980. *The Devil and Commodity Fetishism in South America*. Durham: University of North Carolina Press.

Tempest, Rone. 1996. "The Princelings Thrive: Inherited Privilege in the Land of Mao." *Los Angeles Times*, reprinted in the *International Herald Tribune*, February 16: 1.

Thelen, Kathleen, and Sven Steinmo. 1992. "Historical Institutionalism in Comparative Politics." In *Structuring Politics: Historical Institutionalism in Comparative Analysis*, ed. Sven Steinmo, Kathleen Thelen, and Frank Longstreth, 1–32. Cambridge University Press.

Thomas, William I., and Florian Znaniecki. 1984. *The Polish Peasant in Europe and America*, abridged by Eli Zaretsky. Urbana: University of Illinois Press.

T'ien Ju-K'ang. 1953. *The Chinese of Sarawak: A Study of Social Structure*. London: London School of Economics and Political Science.

Tilly, Charles. 1978. *From Mobilization to Revolution*. Reading, Mass.: Addison-Wesley.

1984. *Big Structures, Large Processes, Huge Comparisons.* New York: Russell Sage Foundation.

Tong, Yanqi. 1994. "State, Society, and Political Change in China and Hungary." *Comparative Politics* 26 (3): 333–53.

Trigilia, Carlo. 1995. "A Tale of Two Districts: Work and Politics in the Third Italy." In *Small and Medium-Size Enterprises,* ed. Arnaldo Bagnasco and Charles Sabel, 31–50. London: Pinter.

Trotsky, Leon. (1937) 1972. *The Revolution Betrayed: What Is the Soviet Union and Where Is It Going?,* trans. M. Eastman. New York: Pathfinder Press.

Tu, I-Ching. 1991. "Family Enterprises in Taiwan." In *Business Networks and Economic Development in Southeast Asia,* ed. Gary Hamilton, 114–25. Hong Kong: University of Hong Kong, Centre of Asian Studies.

Tyson, James, and Ann Tyson. 1995. *Chinese Awakenings: Life Stories from the Unofficial China.* Boulder, Colo.: Westview.

Unger, Jonathan. 1996. "'Bridges': Private Business, the Chinese Government and the Rise of New Associations." *China Quarterly* 147 (September): 795–819.

Unger, Jonathan, and Anita Chan. 1995. "China, Corporatism, and the East Asian Model. *Australian Journal of Chinese Affairs* 33 (January): 29–53.

Unger, Roberto M. 1987. *False Necessity: Anti-Necessitarian Social Theory in the Service of Radical Democracy.* Cambridge University Press.

Vadja, Mihály. 1988. "East-Central European Perspective." In *Civil Society and the State: New European Perspective,* ed. John Keane, 333–60. London: Verso.

Verdery, Katherine. 1996. "A Transition from Socialism to Feudalism?: Thoughts on the PostSocialist State." In *What Was Socialism and What Comes Next?,* 204–28. Princeton: Princeton University Press.

Vogel, Ezra F. 1967. "From Revolutionary to Semi-Bureaucrat: The 'Regularization' of Cadres." *China Quarterly* 29 (January–March): 36–60.

1969. *Canton Under Communism: Programs and Politics in a Provincial Capital, 1949–1968.* Cambridge, Mass.: Harvard University Press.

1989. *One Step Ahead in China: Guangdong Under Reform.* Cambridge, Mass.: Harvard University Press.

Voslensky, Michael. 1983. *Nomenklatura: The Soviet Ruling Class, An Insider's Report,* trans. E. Mosbacher. Garden City, N.Y.: Doubleday.

Wade, Robert. 1990. *Governing the Market: Economic Theory and the Role of Government in East Asian Industrialization.* Princeton: Princeton University Press.

Walder, Andrew G. 1986. *Communist Neo-Traditionalism: Work and Authority in Chinese Industry.* Berkeley: University of California Press.

1992. "Local Bargaining Relationships and Urban Industrial Finance." In *Bureaucracy, Politics, and Decision-making in Post-Mao China,* eds. Kenneth G. Lieberthal and David M. Lampton, 308–33. Berkeley: University of California Press.

1994a. "The Decline of Communist Power: Elements of a Theory of Institutional Change." *Theory and Society* 23: 297–323.

    *and Reforming Communist States*, ed. Vedat Milor, 53–66. Boulder, Col.: Lynne Rienner.

1995. China's Transitional Economy: Interpreting Its Significance." *China Quarterly* 144 (December): 963–79.

1996. "Markets and Inequality in Transitional Economies: Towards Testable Theories." *American Journal of Sociology* 101 (4): 1060–73.

Wallerstein, Immanuel. 1974. *The Modern World-System: Capitalist Agriculture and the Origins of the European World-Economy in the Sixteenth Century.* New York: Academic Press.

Wang, Fang. 1994. "The Political Economy of Authoritarian Clientelism in Taiwan." In *Democracy, Clientelism and Civil Society*, ed. Luis Roniger and Ayse Günes-Ayata, 181–206. Boulder, Colo.: Lynne Rienner.

Wang, Gungwu. 1991. *China and the Overseas Chinese.* Singapore: Times Academic Press.

Wank, David L. 1990. "Private Commerce as a Vocation: Social Mobility and the Wholesale Trade in Urban China." *China News Analysis* 1424 (December 15): 1–9.

1993. "From State Socialism to Community Capitalism: State Power, Social Structure, and Private Enterprise in a Chinese City." Ph.D. dissertation, Harvard University.

1994. "Exchange and Power in Late Communist Market Reform: Towards a Theory of Bureaucratic Commodification." Tokyo: Department of Comparative Culture, Sophia University.

1995a. "Civil Society in Communist China?: Private Business and Political Alliance, 1989." In *Civil Society: Theory, History, Comparison*, ed. John A. Hall, 56–73. Cambridge: Polity Press.

1995b. "Bureaucratic Patronage and Private Business: Changing Networks of Power in Urban China." In *The Waning of the Communist State: Economic Origins of Political Decline in China and Hungary*, ed. Andrew G. Walder, 153–83. Berkeley: University of California Press.

1996. "The Institutional Process of Market Clientelism: *Guanxi* and Private Business in a South China City." *China Quarterly* 29 (September): 820–38.

1999. "Producing Property Rights: Strategies, Networks, and Efficiency in Urban China's Nonstate Firms." In *Property Rights and Economic Reform in China*, ed. Jean C. Oi and Andrew G. Walder. Stanford, Calif.: Stanford University Press.

2000. "Cigarettes and Domination in Chinese Business Networks: Institutional Change During Market Transition." In *The Consumer Revolution in Urban China,* ed. Deborah Davis 268–86. Berkeley: University of California Press.

Watson, James L. 1982. "Chinese Kinship Reconsidered: Anthropological Perspectives on Historical Research." *China Quarterly* 92: 589–627.

Weber, Max. (1904–5) 1958. *The Protestant Ethic and the Spirit of Capitalism*, trans. Talcott Parsons. New York: Scribner.

(1922) 1978. *Economy and Society: An Outline of Interpretive Sociology*, ed. and trans. Guenther Roth and Claus Wittich. Berkeley: University of California Press.

ed. and trans. Guenther Roth and Claus Wittich. Berkeley: University of California Press.

(1922) 1961. *General Economic History*, trans. Frank Knight. New York: Collier.

Wedel, Janine. 1986. *The Private Poland*. New York: Facts on File.

1992. "Introduction." In *The Unplanned Society: Poland During and After Communism*, ed. Janine Wedel, 2–20. New York: Columbia University Press.

Weingrod, A. 1968. "Patrons, Patronage and Political Parties." *Comparative Studies in Society and History* 19: 377–400.

1977. "Patronage and Power." In *Patrons and Clients in Mediterranean Societies*, ed. E. Gellner and J. Waterbury, 41–52. London: Duckworth.

Weitzman, Martin L., and Chenggang Xu. 1994. "Chinese Township-Village Enterprises as Vaguely Defined Cooperatives." *Journal of Comparative Economics* 18: 121–45.

Welch, Holmes. 1968. *The Buddhist Revival in China*. Cambridge, Mass.: Harvard University Press.

Weller, Robert P. 1987. *Unities and Diversities in Chinese Religion*. Seattle: University of Washington Press.

White, Harrison C. 1981. "Where Do Markets Come From?" *American Journal of Sociology* 87: 517–47.

1985. "Agency as Control." In *Principles and Agents: The Structure of Business*, ed. J. W. Pratt and R. Zeckhauser, ch. 8. Boston: Harvard University Press.

1992. *Identity and Control: A Structural Theory of Action*. Princeton: Princeton University Press.

1993a. "Values Come in Styles: Which Mate to Change." In *The Origin of Values*, ed. Michael Hechter, Lynn Nadel, and Richard E. Michod, 63–91. New York: Aldine de Gruyter.

1993b. "Markets in Production Networks." In *Explorations in Economic Sociology*, ed. Richard Swedberg, 161–75. New York: Russell Sage Foundation.

Whyte, Martin K. 1974. *Small Groups and Political Rituals in Communist China*. Berkeley: University of California Press.

Whyte, Martin K., and William Parrish. 1984. *Urban Life in Contemporary China*. Chicago: University of Chicago Press.

Willerton, J. P. 1979. "Clientelism in the Soviet Union: An Initial Examination." *Studies in Comparative Communism* 12: 159–211.

Wilson, Scott, 1994. "Banquet Buddies (*Jiurou Pengyou*): Rural Industrialization as Instituted Process." Paper presented at Association of Asian Studies Annual Meeting, Boston.

1997. "The Cash Nexus and Social Networks: Mutual Aid and Gifts in Contemporary Shanghai Villages." *China Journal* 37 (January): 91–112.

Winiecki, Jan. (1990) 1996. "Why Economic Reforms Fail in the Soviet System: A Property Rights-Based Approach." In *Empirical Studies in Institutional Change*, ed. Lee J. Alston, Thráinn Eggertsson, and Douglass C. North, 63–91. Cambridge University Press.

Wittman, Donald. 1989. "Why Democracies Produce Efficient Results." *Journal of Political Economy* 97 (6): 1395–424.

Wolf, Eric. 1966. "Kinship, Friendship and Patron–Client Relationship in Complex Societies." In *The Social Anthropology of Complex Societies*, ed. M. Banton, 1–22. A. S. A. Monographs. London: Tavistock Press.

Wong, Gilbert. 1991. "Business Groups in a Dynamic Environment: Interlocking Directorates: Hong Kong, 1976–1986. In *Business Networks and Economic Development in East and Southeast Asia*, ed. Gary Hamilton, 126–54. Hong Kong: Centre of Asian Studies, University of Hong Kong.

Wong, Siu-lun. 1985. "The Chinese Family Firm: A Model." *British Journal of Sociology* 36 (1): 58–72.

1988. *Emigrant Entrepreneurs: Shanghai Industrialists in Hong Kong*. Oxford: Oxford University Press.

1991. "Chinese Entrepreneurs and Business Trust." In *Business Networks and Economic Development in East and Southeast Asia*, ed. Gary Hamilton, 13–29. Hong Kong: Centre of Asian Studies, University of Hong Kong.

Wu, Nai-teh. 1987. "The Politics of a Regime Patronage System: Mobilization and Control within an Authoritarian Regime." Ph.D. dissertation, University of Chicago.

Wuthnow, Robert. 1987. *Meaning and Moral Order: Explorations in Cultural Analysis*. Berkeley: University of California Press.

Xiamen Chamber of Commerce (Xiamen Shi Shanghui). 1988. "Forming Same Business Line Committees Will Lead to Order" (*Zujian Tongye Gonghui Jiang Youzhang Kexun*). *Xiamen Industry and Commerce* (*Xiamen Gong Shang*) 17 (January 20): 4.

Xiamen City Glorious Enterprise Promotion Office (Xiamen Shi Tuidong "Guangcai Shiye" Bangongshi). 1995. *Guangcai Shiye Jianxun* (Glorious Enterprise News Brief) 2 (January 3), 3 (January 6), 4 (January 9), 5 (January 12), 6 (January 16), 7 (February 9). Xiamen: Xiamen Zong Shanghui (Xiamen General Chamber of Commerce).

*Xiamen Daily* (*Xiamen Ribao*). 1987a. "Simingqu Getihu Ye Yonghui Guangrong Rudang" (Siming District *Getihu Ye Yonghui* Gloriously Enters the Party). March 3: 1.

1987b. "Zuori Buzuo Pudu Zhaochang Jingying" (No *Pudu* Yesterday Business as Usual). August 27: 1.

1988a. 'Zhe Ci Qingli Zhengdun Gongsi shi Dongzhengede" (This Time the Cleanup and Rectification of Companies Is for Real). November 11: 1.

1988b "Wo Shi Jiang Dui Gelie Gongsi Jinxing Quanmian Zhengdun" (Our City Will Commence a Thorough Rectification of All Types of Companies). November 4: 1.

1988c. "Shi Jianchayuan Tanwu Huilu Zuian Jubao Zhongxin Chengli" (City Procuratorate Graft and Bribery Reporting Center Established). September 1: 1.

1988d. "Kaiyuanqu Getihu Yongyue Rengou Guokujuan" (Kaiyuan District *Getihu* Enthusiastically Subscribe to National Treasury Bonds). July 23: 1.

1988e. "Shi Getigongshanghu Siying Qiye Congye Renyuan Peixunban

Kaixue" (Cultivation Class Starts for Personnel Involved in the City's Individual and Private Enterprises). June 22: 1.

1989a. "Quanguo Getigongshanghu Toushuiloushui Yanzhong" (The Tax Evasion of *Getigongshanghu* Nationwide Is Serious). August 2: 1.

1989b. "Jiaqiang Shuishou Zhengshou Guanli Daji Baoli Kangshui Fanzui" (Strengthen the Administration of Tax Collecting, Crack Down on the Crime of Violent Tax Resistance). September 4: 1.

1989c. "Guanyu Zhengdun Chengxiang 'Sanhu Yishui' Shuishou Chixu de Tonggao" (Announcement Regarding the Rectification of the Urban and Rural and "Three Family, One Tax" Tax Revenue Order). August 6: 1.

1989d. "Peiyang Nashui Yishi Qianghua Shuifa Gangxing" (Cultivate a Tax-paying Consciousness, Strengthen the Tax Laws). January 6: 1.

1989e. "Gongwu Gongkai, Guifan Gongkai, Shenfen Gongkai" (Open Up Public Affairs, Make Public the Standards, Make Public the Status). November 11: 1.

1989f. "Nashui Yishi Danbo, Tiaolou Shuishou Yanzhong" (Taxpaying Consciousness Weak, Tax Evasion Serious). April 12: 2.

1989g. "Shemma shi Shouhuixinghui Xingwei ji Biaoxian" (What Is the Behavior and Expression of Bribery?). September 26: 2.

1989h. "Dui Gongchandangyuan Canyu Pudu Bixu Yanxu Chajiu" (Thoroughly Root Out Communist Party Members Participating in *Pudu*). August 3: 1.

1989i. "Gongyuan Jiedao he Geti Shanghu Guanxin Gulao Zhuankuan Qianyuan Zeng Xiaqu 24 Ming Gulao Guonian" (The Gongyuan Street Committee and *Getihu* Care for Orphans and Elderly; Donations of 1,000 Yuan Presented to 24 Orphans and Elderly in Jurisdiction to Celebrate New Year). January 27: 1.

1989j. "Gongsi Yiwai de Qiye ye Ying Qingli Zhengdun" (Enterprises Other Than Companies Should Also Be Sorted Out and Rectified). November 9: 1.

1989k. "Xinglin Jimei Qu Fenbie Zhaokao Toushui Anjian Kuanyuan Da Hui" (Xinglin and Jimei Districts Separately Convene Mass-Sentencing Rallies for Tax Evasion Cases). November 11: 1.

1989l. "Yansu Shuishou Fagui; Duse Toushuiloushui" (Enforce Tax Laws and Regulations; Stop Tax Evasion and Cheating). August 6: 1.

1990. "Kaiyuanqu Getigongshanghu Canjia Shuifa Zhishi Jingsai" (Kaiyuan District Individual Business Families Participate in Competition on Tax Law Knowledge). April 25: 1.

Xie, Yu, and Emily Hannum. 1996. "Regional Variation in Earnings Inequality in Reform-Era Urban China." *American Journal of Sociology* 101 (4): 950–92.

Xinhua News Agency. 1987. "*Renmin Ribao* Reports on Small-Scale Leasing." May 24.

Yan, Yunxiang. 1995. "Everyday Power Relations: Changes in a North China Village." In *The Waning of the Communist State: Economic Origins of Political Decline in China and Hungary*, ed. Andrew G. Walder, 215–41. Berkeley: University of California Press.

Yang, C. K. 1961. *Religion in Chinese Society: A Study of Contemporary Social Functions of Religion and Some of Their Historical Factors.* Berkeley: University of California Press.

Yang, Lien-sheng. 1957. "The Concept of 'Pao' as a Basis for Social Relations in China." In *Chinese Thought and Institutions,* ed. John K. Fairbank, 291–309. Chicago: University of Chicago Press.

Yang, Mayfair Mei-hui. 1989a. "Between State and Society: The Construction of Corporateness in a Chinese Socialist Factory." *Australian Journal of Chinese Affairs* 22 (July): 31–60.

1989b. "The Gift Economy and State Power in China." *Comparative Studies in Society and History* 1(1): 25–54.

1994. *Gifts, Favors, and Banquets: The Art of Social Relationships in China.* Ithaca, N.Y.: Cornell University Press.

Yong, C. F. 1989. *Tan Kah-kee: The Making of an Overseas Chinese Legend.* Singapore: Oxford University Press.

Yoshihara, Kunio. 1988. *The Rise of Ersatz Capitalism in South-East Asia.* Singapore: Oxford University Press.

Young, Susan. 1989. "Policy, Practice and the Private Sector in China." *Australian Journal of Chinese Affairs* 21: 57–80.

1992. "Wealth but Not Security: Attitudes Towards Private Business in the 1980s." In *Economic Reform and Social Change in China,* ed. Andrew Watson, 63–87. London: Routledge.

1995. *Private Business and Economic Reform in China.* Armonk, N.Y.: M. E. Sharpe.

Yudkin, Marcia. 1986. *Making Good – Private Business in Socialist China.* Beijing: Foreign Languages Press.

Yue, Haitao. (1986) 1989. "On Leasing Businesses." In *China Tackles Reform,* no. 33, ed. Su Wenming, 187–9. Beijing: Beijing Review.

Zhang, Houyi. 1994. "Siying Qiyezhu Jieceng Zai Wo Guo Shehui Jiegou Zhong de Diewei" (The Status of the Private Entrepreneurial Strata in the National Social Structure). *Zhongguo Shehui Kexue* (China Social Science) 6: 100–16.

Zhao, Suisheng. 1993. "Deng Xiaoping's Southern Tour: Elite Politics in Post-Tiananmen China." *Asian Survey* 33 (8): 739–56.

Zhou, Xueguang. 1993. "Unorganized Interests and Collective Action in Communist China." *American Sociological Review* 58 (1): 54–73.

Znaniecki, Florian. 1986. *The Social Role of the Man of Knowledge.* Oxford: Transactions Books.

Zukin, Sharon, and Paul DiMaggio. 1990. "Introduction." In *Structures of Capital: The Social Organization of the Economy,* ed. Paul DiMaggio and Sharon Zukin, 1–36. Cambridge University Press.

# Name Index

# Subject Index

actively (*zhudong*) intercede, 72. *See also* patron-client ties
activists (*jiji fenzi*), 112, 178. *See also* taxpaying activists
administrative agencies, 34, 189; and employment contracts, 112; goods and services provided by, 87; harassment by, 110; private companies' relations with, 72–5
administrative controls, 34
administrative officials, 15; moonlighting for private companies, 100
administrative pricing, 87, 226
advisors (*guwen*), 100
affect (*ganqing*), 142, 168, 221; as emotive *guanxi*, 226. *See also* gift-giving
affect management (*ganqing guanli*), 38
affective/emotive (*ganqing*) *guanxi*, 96, 102
affiliated firms: types of, 79–81. *See also* business affiliations
affinal ties, 30n16
affixing an official seal (*gaizhang*), 70. *See also* patron-client ties
agnatic kin/ties, 30n16, 111
All-China Federation of Industry and Commerce (*Gong Shang Lian*), 138, 184n5, 185
allocation, 157; administrative, 77; particularistic, 155, 174, 227, 228. *See also* resource allocation
anarchy (*wuzhengfu zhuangtai*), 182
ancestor cult, 165
Anti-Rightist Campaign, 118
art of social relations (*guanxixue*), 4–5, 54, 122
Artists and Entrepreneurs Association, 15
assets: bureaucratically mediated, 46; control of, 30
authoritarianism, 229; enlightened, 182
authority, 162, 175; dependence and, 178; institutional, 163, 164–5;

projection of, 128–9; traditional culture of, 179–80
authority relations: eroded, 200–2
automotive trade, 63–4, 210–11
autonomy, 3, 6, 202; of locales, 218

backers (*kaoshan*), 70, 72
backstage bosses (*houtai laoban*), 70
Baden-Württemberg (Germany), 155
Balcerowicz plan, 159n7
bank lending/loans, 145, 146, 204, 211, 214, 228; access to, 212; campaign against, 206, 208
bank transfers, 76, 77
banks/banking, 55, 75, 190. *See also* state banks; savings and loan cooperative
banqueting, 97–8, 99, 113, 194, 195
bargaining, in markets, 13, 33
bargaining relations, between entrepreneurs and officials, 226–7
barter exchanges/relations, 76–7, 209, 227
be the boss (*dang laoban*), 61
behavior, expectations of, 93, 94–5
Beijing, 47, 82
black factories (*dixia hei gongchang*), 135. *See also* speculator path
black market activities, 135–6
*blat*, 6
brain trusts, 100
branch/representative enterprise (*neilian qiye*), 53–4
breach of contract, 110–11
bribes/bribery, 36, 77, 99, 148, 190, 192, 196
bricoleurs, 31n19
broad bosom (*xionghuai kuankuo*), 142. *See also* impression
Buddhism, 141, 165
bureaucracy, 4, 28, 130; administrative procedures of, 65–6; clientelist networks in, 6; dependence and authority in, 178;

283